ACID RAIN IN THE ADIRONDACKS

AN ENVIRONMENTAL HISTORY

ACID RAIN IN THE ADIRONDACKS

AN ENVIRONMENTAL HISTORY

JERRY JENKINS, KAREN ROY, CHARLES DRISCOLL, AND CHRISTOPHER BUERKETT

Published in association with the Adirondack Lakes Survey Corporation with the support of the Wildlife Conservation Society, United States Environmental Protection Agency, New York State Department of Environmental Conservation, and New York State Energy Research and Development Authority

NYSERDA New York State Energy Research and Development Authority

COMSTOCK PUBLISHING ASSOCIATES
a division of
CORNELL UNIVERSITY PRESS
Ithaca and London

An earlier version of this work was previously published as *Acid Rain and the Adirondacks: A Research Summary* by the Acid Lakes Survey Corporation, 2005.

Current edition first published by Cornell, 2007
First printing, Cornell Paperbacks, 2007

Library of Congress Cataloging-in-Publication Data

Acid rain in the Adirondacks : an environmental history / Jerry Jenkins ... [et al.].
    p. cm.
 Includes bibliographical references and index.
 ISBN 978-0-8014-4651-1 (cloth : alk. paper) -- ISBN 978-0-8014-7424-8 (pbk. : alk. paper)
 1. Acid rain--New York (State)--Adirondack Mountains Region. 2. Lakes--New York (State)--Adirondack Mountains Region. 3. Adirondack Mountains Region (N.Y.)--Environmental conditions. I. Jenkins, Jerry (Jerry C.) II. Title.

TD195.52.N72A3523 2007
363.738'6097475--dc22

                    2007022215

Cornell University Press strives to use environmentally responsible suppliers and materials to the fullest extent possible in the publishing of its books. Such materials include vegetable-based, low-VOC inks and acid-free papers that are recycled, totally chlorine-free, or partly composed of nonwood fibers. For further information, visit our website at www.cornellpress.cornell.edu.

General funding for the Adirondack Lakes Survey Corporation and the Adirondack Long-Term Monitoring Program comes from the New York State Energy Research and Development Authority, the U.S. Environmental Protection Agency's Office of Research and Development, and the New York State Department of Environmental Conservation. This book has not been subject to peer or administrative review by any of the support agencies and does not necessarily reflect their views. No official endorsement by any of them should be inferred.

Printed in China

Paperback printing   10 9 8 7 6 5 4 3 2 1
Cloth printing   10 9 8 7 6 5 4 3 2 1

CONTENTS

PREFACE

This book attempts to tell two stories. The first is how, starting more than a century ago, the deposition of acids and mercury from the combustion of fossil fuels has changed the Adirondacks. The second is how researchers, working in the Adirondacks and elsewhere, rediscovered acid rain, measured it and characterized it, and traced its ecological effects.

The book is a product of the Adirondack Lakes Survey Corporation (ALSC), a nonprofit scientific organization with its headquarters in Ray Brook, New York.* The ALSC is itself a part of the acid rain story, and its history provides a useful context for much of what follows.

In the early 1980s, Adirondack acid rain research was limited to a relatively few lakes and ponds. The first chemical surveys of Adirondack lakes had been done by the New York State Department of Environmental Conservation (DEC) in the early 1970s. They were followed by two watershed surveys in the late 1970s and early 1980s. These led to the creation of the Adirondack Long-Term Monitoring program in 1982. Its primary purpose was to make monthly measurements of the chemistry of 17 lakes in the southwestern Adirondacks and to track their responses to changes in atmospheric deposition.*

By 1983, these surveys had shown that lake acidification was occurring in the Adirondacks. No one knew, however, how extensive it was and what biological consequences it was having. To answer this question, researchers from the DEC and the Empire State Electric Energy Research Corporation proposed a large-scale survey of the chemistry and biology of Adirondack lakes, and created the Adirondack Lakes Survey Corporation to carry it out. In the next three years, the Adirondack Lakes Survey sampled 1,469 lakes, and in 1990 published its finding as the *Interpretive Analysis of Fish Communities and Water Chemistry, 1984-1987.**

The *Interpretive Analysis* was the first book-length report on lake acidification in the United States. Its major findings — that lake acidification from atmospheric deposition was widespread in the Adirondacks, that some types of lakes were more sensitive to acidification than others, and that fish population losses had occurred as a result of acidification — provided the conceptual underpinings for much subsequent research, as well as a core data set that is still in use.

After 1990, the ALSC's principal mission became surface-water monitoring. It had taken over the original Adirondack Long-Term Monitoring program in 1985; they expanded it to 52 lakes and 3 streams in 1992 and then added annual samples from another 43 lakes in 1997. The resulting databases, which include 25 years of monthly data from the original 17 lakes and 15 years of data on an additional 35 lakes, are widely known in the acid rain community and have been used in many American, Canadian, and European studies.

The idea for a history of Adirondack acid rain research originated in 1998, when the ALSC received a grant from the EPA to summarize the findings from the Adirondack Long-Term Monitoring program and make the results available for environmental decision-making and policy

*Formally, the Adirondack Lakes Survey Corporation is a New York State not-for-profit corporation supported by the New York State Energy Research and Development Authority, the New York State Department of Environmental Conservation, and the U.S. Environmental Protection Agency and charged with the scientific investigation and monitoring of Adirondack lakes and streams.

*For a summary of these and other major Adirondack studies, see Appendix I, p. 226.

*Baker, J.P. et al., *Adirondack Lakes Survey: An Interpretive Analysis of Fish Communities and Water Chemistry, 1984-1987,* 1990.

development. The first result of the grant was the ALSC website, www.adirondacklakessurvey.org (p. 227), which went on-line in March 2001. The second was this book, which was begun in summer 2002, published as a report to the EPA in September 2005, and has now been revised and published as a book in the fall of 2007.

Like all historians we have had to be selective, sometimes arbitrarily so, about what we included. Our goal was to present the story of acid rain from an Adirondack viewpoint and in an Adirondack context (p. 3). To this end we have omitted much fine work from elsewhere, and we apologize in advance to the authors and the projects we have slighted.

The book is a collaborative effort of the four authors. Jerry Jenkins, a researcher with the North America Program of the Wildlife Conservation Society, wrote the text, prepared the illustrations, and designed and typeset the book.* Charles Driscoll of Syracuse University, a leader in acid rain research since the 1970s and with the ALTM program since its beginning, served as a technical editor. Karen Roy of the DEC, the scientific manager of the ALSC research program, organized and directed the project and was responsible for its overall shape and many details of the presentation. Christopher Buerkett of the technical staff of the ALSC assembled the scientific information, prepared the bibliography, was responsible for technical editing, and obtained the many permissions we required to reuse copyrighted material.

A scientific summary of this type could not have been possible without the depth and richness of the research base that is available in the Adirondacks. We have it because of the extraordinary, sustained interest and commitment of individuals who have devoted years of effort to understanding the acidification problem and, we hope, its solution. To those researchers, their students, and the various institutions that support them, we are greatly indebted.

A special acknowledgment goes to the Adirondack Lakes Survey Corporation staff for their continual commitment to making the Adirondack long-term monitoring effort a success. Members of the ALTM program team during the preparation of this book included Dale Bath, Linda Branch, Jeff Brown, Sara Burke, Mike Cantwell, Sue Capone, Paul Casson, Craig Cheeseman, Theresa Cleary, Rick Costanza, Tom Dudones, Jed Dukett, Nathan Houck, Pam Hyde, Monica Schmidt, and Phil Snyder.

We are also grateful to Walt Kretser, who along with John Holsapple, Sandra Meier, and Charley Driscoll, initiated this proposal with the EPA; to Howard Simonin, who provided substantial direction and review comments throughout many drafts; to Rona Birnbaum, Jennifer Kramer, and Tamara Saltman at the EPA for their comments and patient support; to our copy editor, Sally Atwater; to Heidi Lovette, science editor at Cornell University Press; to a number of reviewers who provided comments and suggestions for various portions of the book along the way; and to Margot and John Ernst and the Wildlife Conservation Society for providing support for publication.

*All the illustrations were drawn for this book. About two-thirds of them (labeled "redrawn from") are based directly on published illustrations, covered by the original copyrights, and used here by permission. The remainder are either new illustrations or substantial modifications of published illustrations and are copyrighted by the Adirondack Lakes Survey, 2007.

1845 Ducros, a French pharmacist, identifies nitric acid formed by electrical discharges in hail from a thunderstorm and describes his observation as *pluie acide.*

1852 Angus Smith identifies sulfuric acid, produced by burning coal, in the rain of Manchester, England. In 1872 he publishes *Air and Rain: The Beginnings of a Chemical Climatology.*

1911–1913 Crowther and his colleagues show that the acidity of the rain of Manchester, England, decreases with distance from the city and that the acids in the rain can affect tree growth, soil microbes, and seedling germination.

1919 Rusnov, working in Austria, shows that acid rain has acidified forest soils.

1950–1960 Studies in Scandinavia, England, and North America show a general correlation between the acidity of precipitation and the concentration of sulfate in rural lakes.

1963 The Hubbard Brook Experimental Forest in northern New Hampshire begins monitoring precipitation and runoff chemistry.

1970 Congress passes the Clean Air Act Amendments, regulating emissions of sulfur oxides and volatile organic compounds.

1972 Likens, Bormann, and Johnson publish an article titled "Acid Rain," based on records from Hubbard Brook. They point out that 40% of the acidity at Hubbard Brook was associated with nitric rather than sulfuric acid.

1973 U.S. emissions of sulfur dioxide peak at 28.8 million metric tons and then fall by about 25% in the next 22 years as the Clean Air Act Amendments take effect. Nitrogen oxide emissions, which have not been regulated, increase in the same period.

1974 Cogbill and Likens, by reviewing earlier surveys, show that acid precipitation is occurring over much of the eastern United States.

1972–1979 Researchers in Scandinavia, England, Germany, Canada, and the United States document reproductive failure and increased mortality in fish in acidified lakes.

1975 The first international conference on acid rain is held in Dayton, Ohio.

1976 Schofield surveys 214 Adirondack lakes for the New York State Department of Environmental Conservation and reports that half of the lakes over 2,000 feet in elevation are acidified, and many of these have no fish.

1978 A consortium of state and federal agencies and private research organizations opens the first 22 precipitation monitoring stations in the National Trends Network of the National Atmospheric Deposition Program.

1980 The U.S. Acid Precipitation Act of 1980 creates the National Acid Precipitation Assessment Program (NAPAP). In the next ten years NAPAP, at that time the largest environmental research program ever conducted, funds more than $500 million of acid rain research, including many major Adirondack studies.

1982 The Regionalized Integrated Lake-Watershed Acidification Study (RILWAS) begins the monthly monitoring of 20 Adirondack lakes.

1984 New York State initiates a sulfur dioxide control policy, identifying the Adirondacks and Catskills as sensitive receptor areas, and issues its first mercury advisory, warning against consumption of fish from Stillwater Reservoir in the western Adirondacks.

1990 Congress passes Title IV of the Clean Air Act Amendments. This creates a "cap and trade" program that requires utilities to reduce sulfur emissions 40% below their 1980 levels and creates a market that allows utilities to buy, sell, and bank allowances. Title IV requires only a 10% reduction in nitrogen oxide emissions and imposes no cap on them.

1995 Phase I of the 1990 Clean Air Act Amendments takes effect, and sulfur dioxide emissions decline 14% in the next three years. Nitrogen oxide emissions, which have not been capped, decline by only 2%.

2003 A review of the effects of the Clean Air Act Amendments finds, for the first time, small but significant increases in the acid-neutralizing capacities of surface water in the Adirondacks.

INTRODUCTION AND SYNOPSIS

WHAT THIS BOOK CONTAINS AND HOW TO USE IT

This is a book about acid rain in the Adirondacks: where it comes from, what it does, how it has been studied, and what has been learned from those studies. It is, by necessity, a scientific story. And because acid rain is invisible and subtle, it is something of a detective story as well. But even more it is an Adirondack story. The Adirondacks have more protected lakes, streams, and forests than any place in the lower forty-eight states. Acid rain threatens these waters and forests and, by so doing, threatens the beauty and uniqueness of the Adirondacks themselves.

The central story in this book is not so much the threat of acid rain but rather how that threat has been confronted. Our focus is on 30 years of hard and creative work by scientists and policy makers. At the beginning of this period a major environmental threat had just been discovered. Now that threat has been identified, explained, measured, and at least partly regulated. The way that the threat was identified and measured is a fascinating scientific story; the way it has been regulated is a major public achievement. One of our purposes in writing this book is to tell the story and honor the achievement.

Another reason for writing is to counter perceptions, which we fear may be widely held, that acid rain is no longer a problem. Within the last year we have been asked (by an atmospheric physicist in California) whether acid rain really existed or was simply an environmental myth. And we have spoken with several students, closer to home, who believed that acid rain was an old problem that now had been solved.

Neither, sadly, is true. Despite many denials, acid rain did and does exist and was and is a significant ecological threat. It has been significantly but only partially abated, and the Adirondacks are still threatened. More abatement is needed, and even then recovery will be slow. Acid rain – and this is another message of this book – is cumulative and persistent. Its effects on the Adirondacks began more than a century ago, and even our most optimistic calculations suggest that they will continue through our lifetimes and beyond.

Audience and Design

In writing this book we have had two sorts of readers in mind. The first is a serious but nontechnical reader – a student, teacher, citizen, environmental advocate, or government administra-

ADIRONDACK WET SULFATE DEPOSITION

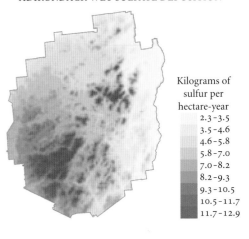

Kilograms of
sulfur per
hectare-year
2.3 - 3.5
3.5 - 4.6
4.6 - 5.8
5.8 - 7.0
7.0 - 8.2
8.2 - 9.3
9.3 - 10.5
10.5 - 11.7
11.7 - 12.9

ADIRONDACK WET NITRATE DEPOSITION

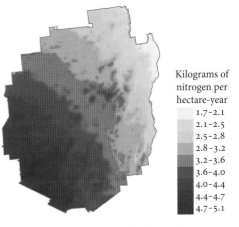

Kilograms of
nitrogen per
hectare-year
1.7 - 2.1
2.1 - 2.5
2.5 - 2.8
2.8 - 3.2
3.2 - 3.6
3.6 - 4.0
4.0 - 4.4
4.4 - 4.7
4.7 - 5.1

Estimated wet deposition of sulfate and nitrate, from spatial models that predict deposition as a function of latitude, longitude, and elevation. Note that the models do not include dry deposition or the wet deposition of ammonium. Reproduced with permission from Ito, Mitchell, and Driscoll, "Spatial patterns of precipitation quantity and chemistry and air temperature in the Adirondack region of New York." Copyright 2002 Elsevier. The model used 1988-1999 data from 24 stations measuring precipitation and 4 stations measuring acid deposition. The deposition is highest at high elevations and in the southwestern Adirondacks, where precipitation is high; the maximum rates of sulfate and nitrate deposition correspond to about 750 equivalents of sulfate and 350 equivalents of nitrate per hectare-year.

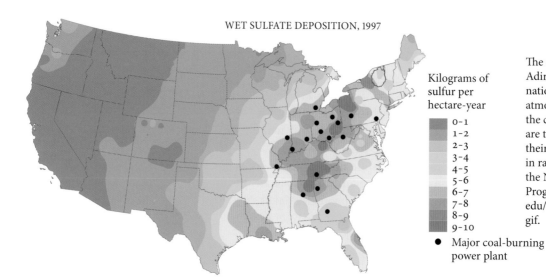

WET SULFATE DEPOSITION, 1997

Kilograms of
sulfur per
hectare-year

0–1
1–2
2–3
3–4
4–5
5–6
6–7
7–8
8–9
9–10

● Major coal-burning
power plant

The deposition in the Adirondacks is part of a larger national pattern in which atmospheric acids generated by the combustion of fossil fuels are transported eastward from their sources and deposited in rain and snow. Map from the National Acid Deposition Program, http://nadp.sws.uiuc.edu/isopleths/maps1997/so4dep.gif.

tor – who is interested in acid rain and wants to understand how it works and what we know about it and where we are in our attempts to control it. The second is a technical reader – a scientist or engineer or manager, perhaps professionally concerned with acid rain, perhaps even involved in acid-related research – who wants a coherent account of what has been learned in the past 30 years, and who is interested not only in the conclusions researchers have reached but in the facts from which they drew those conclusions.

To accommodate both sorts of readers, we have prepared a dual narrative. The main text of the book is a historical account of Adirondack acid rain research, organized around the principal scientific results. It is technically simple and, in so far as was practical, unencumbered by symbols and citations. Its job is to tell the story as continuously and straightforwardly as we could manage.

The graphs and diagrams and their accompanying notes and citations are a second and more technical narrative. There are about 400 of them, and they illustrate, we think for the first time in any book on acid rain, one or more of the major results of almost every paper we discuss in the text.

The job of the graphics is to present the data from which the researchers drew their conclusions. We think this very important. Acid rain research is a deeply empirical business with many numbers and much bookkeeping. Its practitioners study element budgets, balance anions against cations, count lakes, and look for trends. In their world, small quantitative details are very important: a few tenths of a pH unit may mean the difference between recovery and degradation; a small curve in a plot may mean a missing ion that needs to be accounted for. We have included the graphs so that you can, in effect, look over their shoulders while they work and understand both the story and the numbers on which it is based.

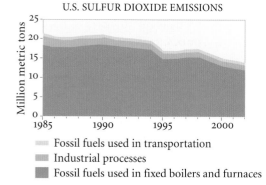

U.S. SULFUR DIOXIDE EMISSIONS

Million metric tons

▪ Fossil fuels used in transportation
▪ Industrial processes
▪ Fossil fuels used in fixed boilers and furnaces

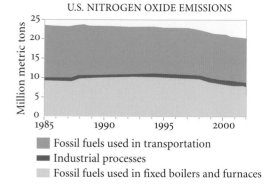

U.S. NITROGEN OXIDE EMISSIONS

Million metric tons

▪ Fossil fuels used in transportation
▪ Industrial processes
▪ Fossil fuels used in fixed boilers and furnaces

Sulfur dioxide emissions come principally from the sulfur in the coal burned in furnaces and boilers; they have been greatly reduced by the Clean Air Act of 1970 and its amendments of 1990. Nitrogen oxide emissions, which are less accurately known, come from the nitrogen in the air and are generated by any combustion process, stationary or mobile. The most recent EPA estimate is that they have decreased by 15% since 1983. Graphs from the EPA's *National Air Quality and Trends Report* for 2003, www.epa.gov/air/airtrends/aqtrnd03/toc.html.

With the ability to see the data comes the ability to judge the conclusions reached. Graphs and data are, of course, evidence rather than verdicts. Some are clear and persuasive, some suggestive, some deceptive or meaningless. Like all researchers, we spend a good deal of time thinking about data and asking ourselves which numbers we really believe and what we can conclude from them. To be faithful to our own thinking, which involves both confidence and doubt, and to give you a chance to believe and doubt for yourselves, we have included as much of the original data as we could.

We hope that you will be interested in both narratives. The text has more coherence and historical shape than the graphs. The graphs have more exactness and, we also hope, some of the empirical stubbornness and puzzlement of actual scientific work. Either can stand by itself but also has, we think, something to add to the other.

Boundaries

To keep the book organized and manageable, we gave it the following restrictions:

It deals with the effects of atmospheric acids on watersheds and surface waters. The cycling of nutrients through forests is discussed; the direct and very important effects of acid deposition on forest trees are not.*

It begins, arbitrarily, in 1976 and, except for a few important recent results, concludes about 2002.

It is principally concerned with Adirondack waters and Adirondack research. Results from other regions are mentioned when they are of particular importance or afford interesting comparisons, but it is not and could not be a full history of acid rain research.

It contains data and conclusions but little about chemical theory or experimental methods. If you wish to know, say, how ion exchange works or how pH is inferred from fossil diatoms, you will have to go to the original papers.

It avoids, for the most part, the computer modeling of deposition and acidification. But we have included a few historical models to give the flavor of the times and a few more recent ones because they seem to be yielding results that cannot be obtained in any other way.

It focuses on scientific results and does not contain institutional, biographical, or political detail. The ways that politics

MAIN STATIONARY SOURCES CONTROLLED BY THE 1990 CLEAN AIR ACT AMENDMENTS

ATMOSPHERIC SULFUR DIOXIDE CONCENTRATIONS, 2002

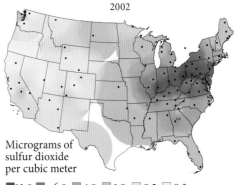

Micrograms of sulfur dioxide per cubic meter

■ 12.0 ■ 6.0 ■ 4.0 ■ 1.0 □ 0.5 □ 0.2
• Clean Air Status and Trends Network station

The main source of atmospheric sulfur is the sulfur dioxide emitted by the power plants and industrial facilities regulated by Phases I and II of the Clean Air Act Amendments. They are found throughout the country but are most concentrated and generate the largest amounts of sulfur dioxide in the Mississippi and Ohio river valleys and the upper Midwest. Locations of sources from http://www.epa.gov/airmarkets/cmap/mapgallery/mg_affected_sources.html; sulfur dioxide concentrations from the *Clean Air Status and Trends Network (CASTNET) 2002 Annual Report*, available on-line at http://www.epa.gov/castnet/library.html.

*For reviews of the terrestrial effects of acid deposition, see Irving, *Acidic Deposition, the State of the Science, Volume III: Terrestrial, Materials, Health, and Visibility Effects,* 1990; Eagar and Adams, *The Ecology and Decline of Red Spruce in the Eastern United States,* 1992; Lawrence and Huntington, "Soil-calcium depletion linked to acid rain and forest growth in the eastern United States," 1999; and National Acid Precipitation Assessment Program, *NAPAP Biennial Report to Congress: An Integrated Assessment,* 1998.

and research interacted to produce our current regulatory programs were complex and contentious. Their history is fascinating and instructive but beyond what we have space for or are qualified to undertake.*

Outlines and References

To make the book manageable for the reader, we have supplied several aids and summaries and interspersed some reference material with the text. In particular:

Most chapters open with a chronology of the events pertinent to the chapter and close with a summary of the main scientific results.

The notes that accompany the illustrations are the major references for the text as well. Additional references, where necessary, will be found in the notes at the ends of the chapters.

In addition, the Bibliography at (p. 228) gives the pages in the text where each paper is discussed or where its results are illustrated..

The Primer

The second chapter of the book, the Primer and Glossary, defines the technical terms used in this book and contains some longer entries on important processes and concepts – acidity, assimilation, cation exchange, deposition, emissions, *etc.* — that are used throughout the book. It is principally intended for the nontechnical reader, but we have also used it to note a few technical details that seemed out of place in the main text.

A Preprimer

For readers who don't want to bother with the primer, we offer here a lightning guide to the technical elements of the acid rain story. To understand the material presented in this book you will need, at a minimum, some familiarity with:

Five elements: *aluminum, calcium, mercury, nitrogen,* and *sulfur.*

Three gases: *sulfur dioxide, gaseous mercury,* and the *nitrogen oxides.*

Two generic groups of ions: *acid anions* and *base cations.*

Six specific ions: *aluminum, ammonium, calcium, hydrogen, nitrate,* and *sulfate.*

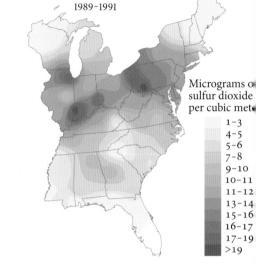

SULFUR DIOXIDE CONCENTRATIONS, 1989-1991

Micrograms of sulfur dioxide per cubic meter

1-3
4-5
5-6
7-8
9-10
10-11
11-12
13-14
15-16
16-17
17-19
>19

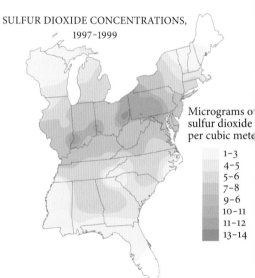

SULFUR DIOXIDE CONCENTRATIONS, 1997-1999

Micrograms of sulfur dioxide per cubic meter

1-3
4-5
5-6
7-8
9-6
10-11
11-12
13-14

As a result of the Clean Air Act regulations, atmospheric sulfur dioxide concentrations fell significantly in both the 1980s and the 1990s. The decreases were greatest near the source areas and lower farther away. From the *Clean Air Status and Trends Network (CASTNET) 2002 Annual Report*, available on-line at http://www.epa.gov/airmarkets/cmap/mapgallery/mg_so2.html.

*Major documents in the development of acid rain policy include Irving, 1990, *Acidic Deposition: State of Science and Technology, Volume I–IV*; the 1995 EPA *Acid Deposition Standard Feasibility Study*; the 1998 NAPAP *Biennial Report to Congress*; and Stoddard et al., 2003, *Response of Surface Water to the Clean Air Act Amendments of 1990.*

Two complex mixtures: *dissolved organic carbon* and *dissolved ("monomeric") aluminum.*

Five common chemical or biochemical transformations: *assimilation, mineralization, ion exchange, oxidation,* and *reduction.*

Two measures of acidification: *acid-neutralizing capacity* (*ANC*) and *pH.*

And four measures of deposition, flux, and change: *eq/ha, eq/ha-yr, μeq/l,* and *μeq/l-yr.*

All of these are defined in Chapter 2.

SYNOPSIS

In outline, the argument of this book is that:

1 *Acid deposition*, the broader and more formal term for what we informally call acid rain, is any deposition of acids from the atmosphere. The most important of these acids are nitric acid and sulfuric acid. These are produced from the oxidation of sulfur dioxide and various nitrogen oxides, which in turn are produced by combustion. The ultimate source of sulfur dioxide is the sulfur in fossil fuels, particularly coal. The ultimate source of the nitrogen oxides is the nitrogen in the atmosphere and in fossil fuels. (Chapter 2.)

2 Acid deposition is thus caused by *sulfur dioxide* and *nitrogen oxide emissions* from the combustion of fossil fuels. These are then converted into the atmospheric acids sulfuric acid and nitric acid and deposited by wet and dry deposition.

The acid emissions that cause acid deposition began in the 19th century andincreased for much of the 20th century. Sulfur dioxide emissions peaked at 28.8 million metric tons in 1973 and have, as a result of the 1970 and 1990 Clean Air Act Amendments, decreased 50%, to 14.3 million tons in 2003. Nitrogen oxide emissions peaked at about 25 million tons sometime around 1980 and then declined 26%, to 19 million tons in 2003. (Graphs, pp. 2–5.)

3 Within the atmosphere, the *atmospheric acids* occur as gases, droplets, and surface films on particles. They are transported by wind and may travel hundreds of kilometers from their sources. They are deposited in at least four ways: in precipitation, in cloudwater, by the settling of particulates, and by the adsorption of gases by soils and vegetation. The first two ways are collectively called wet deposition and the remaining two, dry deposition. (Chapter 2.)

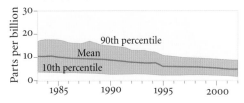

U.S. SULFUR DIOXIDE CONCENTRATIONS

The overall result of the Clean Air Act regulations has been a 54% decrease in average U.S. atmospheric sulfur dioxide concentrations since 1983. Note that this is an arithmetic average; it has not been weighted by area and reflects the greater density of monitoring stations in the areas of highest emissions, where the greatest decreases have occurred. Nonetheless it represents a very significant decrease. From the EPA website, at http://www.epa.gov/airtrends/sulfur.html.

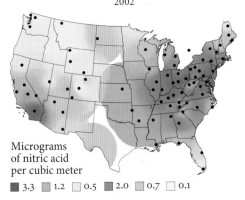

ATMOSPHERIC NITRIC ACID CONCENTRATIONS, 2002

Micrograms of nitric acid per cubic meter

■ 3.3 ▨ 1.2 ☐ 0.5 ◩ 2.0 ◨ 0.7 ☐ 0.1

• Clean Air Status and Trends Network station

Because nitrogen oxides are rapidly oxidized to nitric acid, the atmospheric nitric acid concentration is a commonly used measure of atmospheric nitrogen pollution. U.S. nitric acid levels are lower than sulfur dioxide levels (p. 3) but, because more than half the nitrogen emissions are from cars and trucks, more widespread, especially in the South and Southwest. From the *Clean Air Status and Trends Network (CASTNET) 2002 Annual Report,* available on-line at www.epa.gov/castnet/library.html.

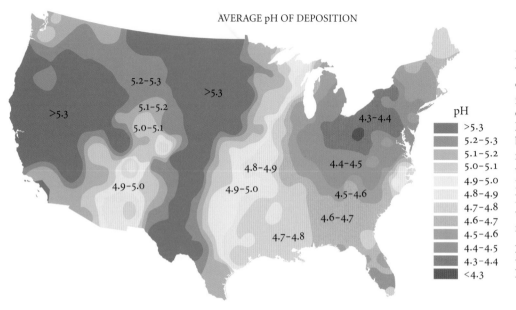

5.2–5.3

>5.3

>5.3

5.1–5.2

5.0–5.1

4.3–4.4

4.8–4.9

4.4–4.5

4.9–5.0

4.9–5.0

4.5–4.6

4.6–4.7

4.7–4.8

pH

>5.3
5.2–5.3
5.1–5.2
5.0–5.1
4.9–5.0
4.8–4.9
4.7–4.8
4.6–4.7
4.5–4.6
4.4–4.5
4.3–4.4
<4.3

Pure rainwater, in equilibrium with atmospheric carbon dioxide, would have a pH of 5.7. Sulfur and nitrogen oxide emissions generate acids that lower the pH up to 1.5 units below that of pure rain. In most parts of the United States the rain is at least slightly acid. In the most acid parts of the Northeast it has about 25–30 times more acid than pure rain. Map from the National Acid Deposition Program, http://nadp.sws.uiuc.edu/iso-pleths/maps1999/phlab.gif.

4 Almost the entire eastern half of the United States is affected to some degree by acid deposition. The most concentrated emissions are in the Ohio and Mississippi river valleys. The acids from these sources move generally north and east and reach their highest concentrations in the northern Appalachians, Pennsylvania, and New York. (Graphs, pp. 2, 6, 9, 10.)

5 *Wet deposition* has been extensively studied. Regional deposition rates are monitored regularly at the 245 stations of the National Trends Network and, in New York, by an additional 20 stations belonging to the New York State Acid Rain Monitoring Network. Wet deposition rates depend mostly on air chemistry, precipitation, and elevation, and both regional and local rates may be predicted reasonably accurately with computer models. (Chapter 9.)

6 The *direct deposition of cloudwater*, a specialized form of wet deposition that is extremely important in the mountains, has been studied at only a few sites; currently, Whiteface Mountain in the Adirondacks has the only active cloudwater monitoring program in the country. (Chapter 9.)

7 *Mercury deposition* is less well studied. The monitoring of mercury, which is technically demanding, began in 1994; currently, the wet deposition of mercury in the United States is monitored at the 84 sites of the Mercury Deposition Network.

8 *Dry deposition* is much harder to study than wet deposition and much less studied. Dry deposition measurements exist for the stations in the Clean Air Status and Trends Network, including

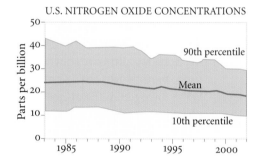

U.S. NITROGEN OXIDE CONCENTRATIONS

90th percentile

Mean

10th percentile

Parts per billion

1985   1990   1995   2000

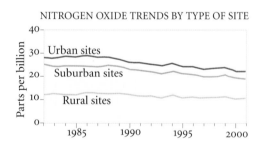

NITROGEN OXIDE TRENDS BY TYPE OF SITE

Urban sites

Suburban sites

Rural sites

Parts per billion

1985   1990   1995   2000

Average U.S. nitrogen oxide levels have declined 21% since 1982. As with the sulfur dioxide levels (p. 5), these are arithmetic averages and strongly reflect the concentration of monitoring sites in high-emission areas. Most of the decrease is urban and suburban; rural areas like the Adirondacks have seen very little change. From http://www.epa.gov/airtrends/nitrogen2.html.

Huntington Forest in the central Adirondacks. The dry deposition of mercury is not routinely monitored but is measured at a few intensive research sites like Huntington Forest, where it makes up about 70% of total mercury deposition.

Dry deposition is a complex process that is much influenced by vegetation and topography. No computer models of regional dry deposition exist, and there are no accepted ways of computing dry deposition for places where it has not been measured. (Chapter 9.)

9 The *main conclusions* of the research of the 1970s and early 1980s were that the acids deposited on the Adirondacks

migrate through soils, releasing toxic forms of aluminum;

enter surface waters, reducing pH and acid-neutralizing capacity (ANC); and

are responsible, in connection with inorganic aluminum, for killing fish in acidic streams and lakes.

If the effects of acid rain had been uniform – if all waters had been equally acidified and all fisheries equally harmed – little more research would have been required. But the effects of acid rain are anything but uniform. Similar amounts of deposition acidified some lakes and left others unchanged and damaged some fisheries and left others unharmed. Further, the effects of acids were highly seasonal, and deposition rates that were innocuous in the summer could be very damaging in the winter and spring. And further again, it was discovered that lake acidity had two sources: some lakes were naturally acidic from organic acids and some artificially acidic with mineral acids from atmospheric deposition. (Chapter 3.)

10 This *variability of response* posed three major scientific problems, one explanatory, one diagnostic, and one quantitative. The explanatory problem was why acid deposition acidified some lakes and not others. The diagnostic problem was to determine which lakes were naturally acid and which acidified by acid deposition. The quantitative problem was to relate the amount of acid that a lake received to the amount of acidification that resulted.

All three problems were critical. The explanatory problem had to be solved to prove that acid deposition was in fact causing lake acidification. The diagnostic problem had to be solved to assess the geography of atmospheric acidification. And the quantitative problem had to be solved to design a successful regulatory program. (Chapter 3.)

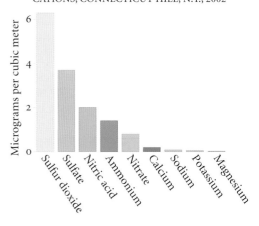

ATMOSPHERIC SULFUR, NITROGEN, AND BASE CATIONS, CONNECTICUT HILL, N.Y., 2002

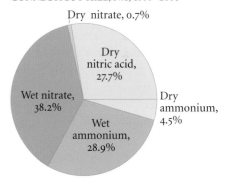

NITROGEN DEPOSITION AT CONNECTICUT HILL, N.Y., 1999–2001

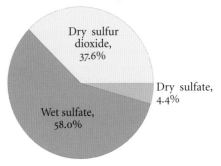

SULFUR DEPOSITION AT CONNECTICUT HILL, N.Y., 1999–2001

By the time air reaches the Adirondacks, most of the nitrogen oxides have been oxidized to nitric acid and nitrates. Both sulfur dioxide and its oxidation product sulfate are present. In addition there is ammonia, derived from both agricultural and industrial sources, and small amounts of base cations, derived from dust and industry. From the *Clean Air Status and Trends Network (CASTNET) 2002 Annual Report*, available on-line at http://www.epa.gov/castnet/library/annual02.html. The Connecticut Hill station is located near Ithaca, New York, and is the nearest CASTNET station for which summarized data exist.

11 Solving these problems required a very large research effort – the National Acid Precipitation Assessment Program spent approximately $500 million on research in the 1980s – and took almost a decade. The solutions, which involved new models of lake and watershed hydrology, new chemical diagnostics, and new methods for reconstructing the chemical histories of lakes, made fundamental changes in how we looked at watersheds and lakes and what we were able to learn by studying them. (Chapter 3.)

12 All acid precipitation research is ultimately dependent on the measurements of air and water chemistry conducted by *monitoring networks*. Many of these networks are research cooperatives, with many participating organizations and multiple sources of funding. Thus the National Trends Network includes the deposition monitoring station at Newcomb, New York, which began as a research project of the State University of New York College of Environmental Science and Forestry and the Huntington Wildlife Forest. Likewise, the national Long-Term Monitoring Project includes 17 lakes that were first studied by the Regionalized Integrated Lake-Watershed Acidification Study and are now part of the 52 lakes currently monitored by the Adirondack Lakes Survey Corporation, which is funded in part by New York State and in part by the New York State Energy Research and Development Authority (NYSERDA). (Chapter 9.)

13 By the late 1980s, six major *national networks* were involved in acid deposition monitoring. The Clean Air Status and Trends Network and the Interagency Monitoring of Protected Visual Environments Network monitored ambient air quality, visibility, and dry deposition; the National Trends Network monitored wet deposition; the Long-Term Monitoring and Temporally Integrated Monitoring of Ecosystems networks monitored surface waters, and the Atmospheric Integrated Research and Monitoring Network did research in monitoring, in effect monitoring the monitoring process. (Chapter 9.)

14 The new models and diagnostics developed in the 1980s were quickly employed by *large synoptic surveys* that examined thousands of lakes in the eastern United States. These surveys showed that acidification by atmospheric acids was common and recent, that it was differentiated chemically and geographically from natural acidity, that it was particularly severe in the Adirondacks, and that it was always associated with the historical markers of fossil fuel use. The Adirondack Lakes Survey, the largest Adirondack survey and the only one with a major biological component, was able to establish a clear association between acidification and fish

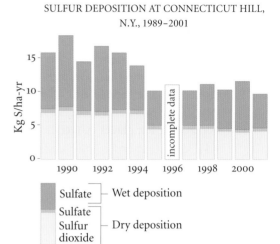

SULFUR DEPOSITION AT CONNECTICUT HILL, N.Y., 1989–2001

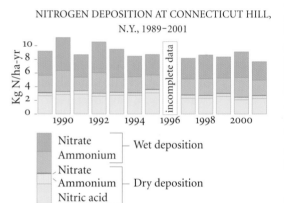

NITROGEN DEPOSITION AT CONNECTICUT HILL, N.Y., 1989–2001

The atmospheric sulfur and nitrogen compounds are deposited by different routes. Ionic compounds like nitrate, sulfate, and ammonium are dissolved in cloudwater and deposited principally in wet deposition. Gases, particulates, and aerosols, including ammonia, sulfur dioxide, and nitric acid, are deposited principally in dry deposition. Wet deposition, which includes rain, snow, and fog, is the more important route: at Connecticut Hill it accounts for 68% of the deposition of nitrogen and 58% of the deposition of sulfur. Dry deposition, a complex process involving settling, filtering and adsorption, is the less important of the two routes but still accounts for 32% of the nitrogen deposition and 42% of the sulfur deposition.

Both dry and wet sulfur deposition decreased abruptly in 1995 when the 1990 Clean Air Act Amendments took affect. Nitrogen deposition, on the other hand, was largely unchanged. From the *Clean Air Status and Trends Network (CASTNET) 2002 Annual Report*, available on-line at http://www.epa.gov/castnet/charts/cth11otn.gif.

population losses and show that the more acidic a lake, the lower its fish diversity.

The publication of these studies concluded a period in which acid deposition was discovered, characterized, and measured. At the start of the 1980s atmospheric acids had a relatively simple role: they arrived, migrated, killed fish, and then left. By 1990s the story was much more complex: after arrival, some of the acids were accumulated, assimilated, neutralized, or transformed; the remainder migrated by specific flowpaths, in specific seasons, and with specific chemical companions. Acidification had, in short, acquired chemical and spatial detail, and with that detail our picture of it became both quantitative and more realistic. (Chapter 4.)

15 Within the details of the large synoptic studies, however, were additional complexities that have become major topics of research. The *summer acidities* that had been measured in most of the large synoptic surveys were found to underrepresent the true extent of acidification. Many lakes that were near neutral in the summer were found to be highly acidic in the spring. *Nitrogen inputs,* which were supposed to be assimilated by forests and not contribute to acidification, were instead found to accumulate in the winter and generate springtime acidity. *Watershed budgets,* a new area of study, showed telltale imbalances: many watersheds were losing calcium and sulfur and failing to retain the nitrogen that they were supposed to be storing. (Chapters 4, 5.)

16 All of these complexities had a common theme. They were indications that the *natural element cycle,* which in undisturbed forests was tight and conservative, became leaky when forests were loaded with nitrogen and sulfur from acid deposition.

The changes in the sulfur, nitrogen, and calcium cycles were particularly striking. All three are essential nutrients. In undisturbed forests they cycle rapidly but conservatively between living and dead biomass and only enter or leave the forest in small quantities. In acidified forests the rate of cycling often increases and the imports and exports are much altered: unnaturally large quantities of sulfur and nitrogen are entering and leaving forests and unnaturally large quantities of calcium and other bases are being leached out. (Chapters 5, 6.)

17 These results have inspired much recent work on the ways that atmospheric acids are *cycled within watersheds.* The subject is complex and far from understood but still clearer than it was in 1990. The central results are that:

Much sulfur has been stored in northern forest soils. As sulfur inputs from deposition have decreased, the stored sulfur has

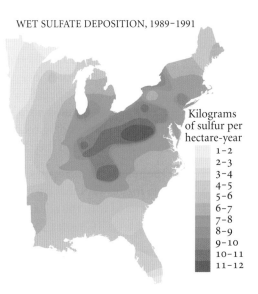

WET SULFATE DEPOSITION, 1989–1991

Kilograms of sulfur per hectare-year

1–2
2–3
3–4
4–5
5–6
6–7
7–8
8–9
9–10
10–11
11–12

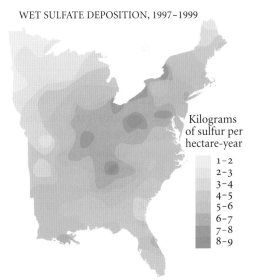

WET SULFATE DEPOSITION, 1997–1999

Kilograms of sulfur per hectare-year

1–2
2–3
3–4
4–5
5–6
6–7
7–8
8–9

The decreases in sulfur emissions in the 1990s resulted in significant reductions in sulfur deposition in most parts of the eastern United States. In the Adirondacks the reduction in wet sulfate deposition was about a third. Maps use data from the Clean Air Status and Trends Network and the National Trends Network, and are redrawn from the EPA Clean Air Markets website, http://www.epa.gov/airmarkets/cmap/mapgallery/mg_wetsulfate phase1.html.

been mobilized, and many watersheds are now exporting more sulfur than they receive. (Chapter 5.)

The nitrogen storage capacity of forests is more limited than had been assumed. Above certain threshold rates of nitrogen deposition forests begin to leak nitrogen and nitrogen-cycle acids, a process called *nitrogen saturation*. At very high rates of deposition their storage capacity breaks down and they release more nitrogen than they receive. (Chapter 5.)

The release of nitrogen-cycle acids from forests is one of the two major ways that spring acidity pulses are generated and is associated with the release of inorganic aluminum and the loss of fisheries. (Chapter 5.)

In watersheds with thin soils and bedrock with a low capacity to neutralize acids, acid deposition can cause progressive losses of biologically available calcium and magnesium, collectively called *base cation depletion*. At least some eastern watersheds seem to have lost a significant fraction of their original base cation supply in the past 100 years, reducing their ability to neutralize acid rain and support forest growth. (Chapter 6.)

18 All of these results involve *cumulative changes* in the amounts of acids and bases stored in watersheds. The storage of sulfur and nitrogen in soils prevents the immediate acidification of surface waters but creates, in effect, a chemical debt that will be paid when they are eventually released. The loss of calcium and base cations from soils increases the acid-neutralizing capacity of surface waters in the short term but in the long term reduces forest growth and makes surface waters more sensitive to acidification. (Chapters 5, 6.)

19 The documentation of the cumulative effects of acid rain in the 1990s resulted in *enlarged concepts of acidification and watershed processes*. In the 1980s acidification was principally measured below the waterline and thought of mainly as a process that decreased pH and made lakes inhospitable to fish. By 2000 it was being measured above the waterline as well and thought of as a process involving sulfur and nitrogen storage, base cation loss, and nitrogen-cycle acidity.

Likewise, in the 1980s watershed processes were thought of principally as processes that changed the chemistry of groundwater. Now they are thought of as changing soils and nutrient cycles as well. When a watershed deacidifies precipitation, it also becomes acidified itself. As a result, its ability to neutralize acids decreases, its ability to generate acids increases, and its response to decreases in deposition slows. (Chapters 5, 6, 9.)

WET NITRATE DEPOSITION, 1989–1991

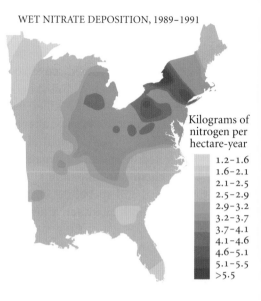

Kilograms of nitrogen per hectare-year

1.2–1.6
1.6–2.1
2.1–2.5
2.5–2.9
2.9–3.2
3.2–3.7
3.7–4.1
4.1–4.6
4.6–5.1
5.1–5.5
>5.5

WET NITRATE DEPOSITION, 1997–1999

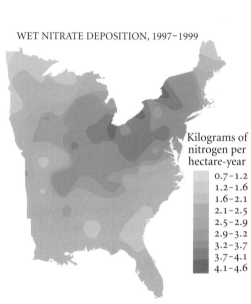

Kilograms of nitrogen per hectare-year

0.7–1.2
1.2–1.6
1.6–2.1
2.1–2.5
2.5–2.9
2.9–3.2
3.2–3.7
3.7–4.1
4.1–4.6

In contrast to sulfate deposition, U.S. nitrate deposition showed little change in the 1990s. There were significant reductions in local pollution near some of the urban source areas but almost none in rural areas away from the sources. Neither the Connecticut Hill station (p. 8) nor the Adirondack region had significant reductions. Maps redrawn from the EPA Clean Air Markets website, http://www.epa.gov/airmarkets/ cmap/mapgallery/mg_wetnitrate-phase1.html

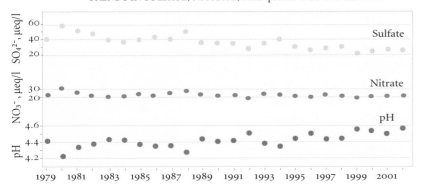

TRENDS IN SULFATE, NITRATE, AND pH IN WET DEPOSITION

A 23-year record of deposition chemistry from the Huntington Forest in the central Adirondacks, showing long-term changes in acid deposition. Since 1980 volume-weighted sulfate concentrations have decreased by about 50% and pHs have increased by about 0.3 unit, but nitrates have shown at most a slight very decrease. Data from the National Trends Network station at Huntington Forest, http://nadp.sws.uiuc.edu//sites/siteinfo.asp?id=NY20&net=NTN. For more data from this station, see page 196.

20 *Mercury* is another pollutant with complex links to watershed processes and biological cycling. It is not an atmospheric acid but is in many ways similar to one. It originates from many of the same sources as atmospheric acids, travels with them and is deposited in the same way, and like them accumulates in soil and biomass. It is frequently studied by acid rain researchers and has come to be thought of as a component of acid deposition.

Although the toxicity of mercury has been known for a long time, until the 1980s mercury pollution was thought to be local, waterborne, and urban. The discovery that it was, instead, airborne, widespread, and significant in remote areas has generated much research interest, and results have been coming quickly. (Chapter 7.)*

* Mercury has three peculiarities not shared by the atmospheric acids. First, because it can remain in the atmosphere for several months, it can travel long distances and is to some extent a global problem. Second, it is extremely toxic to animals, even in quantities of a few millionths of a gram. And third, because it is not readily metabolized or excreted, it accumulates ecologically as it passes up the food chain and may be 1 million to 10 million times more concentrated in animal tissue than in the water or soil .

21 New York State did its first *mercury surveys* in 1976, issued its first advisory about mercury in sport fish in 1984, and began widespread surveys of mercury deposition and transport in the early 1990s. The complex relationship between Adirondack wetlands, dissolved organic carbon, and methylmercury was first documented in 1994. The national Mercury Deposition Network was created in 1995. The monitoring of mercury in loons began in 1998, and the first reconstructions of mercury deposition from sediment cores were published in 1999. The first mercury budgets for Adirondack watersheds were reported in 2004.*

Because of the speed at which the mercury story has developed and the amount of research currently going on, we document the mercury problem but attempt no summary. The Adirondack work done thus far suggests that mercury pollution is widespread and ecologically consequential. It seems to arrive in deposition, be stored in watersheds, and be converted to its toxic derivative methylmercury in wetlands where sulfate reduction is occurring. Mercury deposition rates are currently near the highest they have ever been, and since mercury emissions from coal-burning elec-

* Because of the extremely small quantities of mercury involved, until about 1985 most mercury studies focused on mercury in tissue and did not determine mercury levels in soil, water, and air. Even so, some very significant work was done: see Bloomfield et al., "Atmospheric and watershed inputs of mercury to Cranberry Lake, St. Lawrence County, New York," 1980, for an early attempt to construct a mercury budget; Sloan and Schofield, "Mercury levels in brook trout (*Salvelinus fontinalis*) from selected acid and limed Adirondack lakes," 1983, for fish studies; and McIntyre, 1992, for early loon studies.

tric utilities are not controlled by the Clean Air Act, mercury deposition and mercury pollution may well be with us for some time. (Chapter 7.)

22 In contrast to mercury, *wetlands and the organic carbon and natural acids they generate* have only gradually emerged as an important topic. At first they were seen mostly as a complication: they were the sources of the organic acids that interfered with ANC calculations and had to be distinguished from the mineral acids that were the markers of acid deposition (7).

Only in the 1990s did wetlands start to become interesting in their own right. They were discovered to be both highly active and highly variable. In the case studies we examine they are complex and versatile. They both store and release acids and generate and consume ANC. They reduce sulfur and generate ferrous iron and ammonium. As a vicious by-product, they generate methylmercury, the highly toxic mercury derivative that accumulates in animal tissue. They produce large quantities of dissolved organic carbon, a keystone organic material that is important physically, chemically, and biologically. And they vary their behavior in response to small changes in climate and hydrology, making them wildcards in the recovery story and as much a challenge to the watershed modelers in this decade as they were to the water chemists two decades ago. (Chapter 7.)

23 Compared with the many advances in aquatic chemistry in the 1990s, research in *aquatic biology* was limited in scope and to some extent retrospective. The large-scale biological investigations that had been part of the synoptic surveys of the 1980s had ended, and few new data were coming in. The relation of historical acidification to fish population losses was revisited and conclusively established. Two ambitious biological monitoring programs were established, the Environmental Monitoring and Assessment Program's Surface Waters Program and the Adirondack Effects Assessment Program. The first yielded several interesting studies but was discontinued in 1994. The second is still active. (Chapter 8.)

24 A considerable amount of acid-related *forest biology* was done in the 1990s, particularly on the effects of acid deposition and cation depletion on red spruce and sugar maple, and many important results obtained. These, however, lie outside the scope of this book.*

25 Currently, Adirondack *lake chemistry* is monitored by three organizations. The Adirondack Lakes Survey Corporation samples 52 lakes each month as part of the Adirondack Long-Term Monitoring (ALTM) project and collects annual samples from another

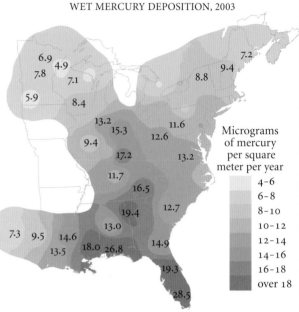

Micrograms of mercury per square meter per year

4–6
6–8
8–10
10–12
12–14
14–16
16–18
over 18

Wet mercury deposition from the National Acid Deposition Program's Mercury Deposition Network, http://nadp.sws.uiuc.edu/mdn/maps/map.asp?imgFile=2003/03MDNdepo.gif. Because of its high toxicity (p. 164), mercury deposition is significant at much lower levels than nitrogen or sulfur deposition. Ten micrograms of mercury per square meter per year, a rate that can have serious biological consequences, is only 0.1 gram per hectare per year, 50,000 times lower than typical rates of sulfur deposition.

Dry mercury deposition is believed to be significant as well. In the Sunday Lake watershed in the western Adirondacks (p. 169) it is believed to be more than two times wet deposition. It is not routinely monitored and has never been mapped on a large scale.

* For general discussions of the effects of acid rain on forests, see the references on the effects of acid rain on terrestrial ecology on page 3. The most detailed Adirondack study of acid rain and forests was the Ecosystem Research Program on Whiteface Mountain, which began in 1984 and was discontinued after it lost its funding in 1998. See Battles et al., "Red spruce death: Effects on forest composition and structure on Whiteface Mountain, New York," 1992, and other papers by the same authors.

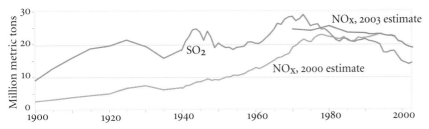

U.S. SULFUR AND NITROGEN OXIDE EMISSIONS

43 lakes for analysis by the EPA Temporally Integrated Monitoring of Ecosystems (TIME) project. The Darrin Freshwater Institute of Rensselaer Polytechnic Institute samples 30 southwestern Adirondack lakes annually for the EPA Adirondack Effects Assessment Program.

Only four Adirondack streams are sampled, three by the ALTM program and one by Huntington Forest. Only the watershed at Huntington Forest has precipitation and flow gauges and so can compute fluxes and capture transient events. (Chapter 9.)

26 U.S. *sulfur dioxide emissions,* which peaked in 1973 as the 1970 Clean Air Act Amendments took effect, fell 29% in the next 20 years and then another 21% between 1993 and 2003 as the 1990 Clean Air Act Amendments were phased in. It was widely hoped that the reductions would lead to a recovery in aquatic chemistry and in particular to increases in ANC, pH, and DOC and decreases in inorganic aluminum.

Expectations differed as to how large the increases would be and how quickly they would come. In the 1980s, when sulfate was thought to move fairly quickly through watersheds, the hope was that they would come quickly: turn down the acid inputs, the feeling was, and the surface waters would quickly recover. In the 1990s, after it had been discovered that watersheds were storing acids and losing the base cations needed for recovery, the predictions were less optimistic: turn off the inputs, researchers now said, and you will still have to deal with the accumulated acids in the watersheds and replace the base cations that have been lost. This will eventually happen but will take time. The watersheds have been exposed to more than a hundred years of acid, and they may take that much time or longer for a full recovery. (Chapter 9.)

27 Given both the hopes for the recovery and the uncertainties about when recovery might happen, scientific and political interest in the monitoring programs has been great. Thus far, the results support the 1990s view that *surface water recovery will be slow.* Recovery has been detected but only after a long delay and, at least by 2000, only to a small extent.

Although widespread acid deposition was first discovered in the 1960s, elevated U.S. sulfur emissions are believed to have begun almost a hundred years earlier, when coal became widespread as a heating and industrial fuel. As a result, Adirondack watersheds have been exposed to significant amounts of acid rain for more than a century. Chen and Driscoll (p. 215) estimate that Huntington Forest was receiving as much sulfate deposition in 1910 as it does today. This means that Adirondack forests and watersheds have by now had a long exposure to the cumulative effects of acid rain, and it suggests that recovery may be correspondingly slow.

The graph combines pre-1940 data from Irving et al., *Acidic Deposition, State of Science and Technology,* vol. 1, *Emissions, Atmospheric Processes, and Deposition,* 1990; estimates for 1940–1998 from Environmental Protection Agency, *National Air Pollutant Emission Trends, 1900–1998,* 2000; and current estimates through 2003 from the EPA website, http://www.epa.gov/airtrends.

CURRENT AND FORMER ESTIMATES
OF U.S. NO$_X$ EMISSIONS

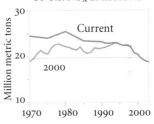

Current and former estimates of U.S. NO$_X$ emissions, enlarged from the graph above left. Emissions are calculated from fuel consumption, using assumptions about fuel efficiency and combustion chemistry. The methods used to make these calculations have changed over time, and this has changed the estimates of both contemporary and historical emissions. Former estimates showed little change in NO$_X$ emissions between 1980 and 1998; current estimates show a gradual decline between 1980 and 1995 and a more rapid decline between 1995 and 2003.

As sulfur emissions changed, sulfate deposition changed as well. Since 1980, sulfate deposition at Huntington Forest has fallen about 50%, clearly showing the link between sulfur emissions and sulfate deposition and in the process settling conclusively an old dispute about where the sulfur in acid deposition had come from .

Monitoring results from the 1980s and early 1990s showed parallel but smaller decreases in the amounts of sulfate in surface waters. Unfortunately, these reductions in sulfate were offset by decreases in base cations, and there was little if any increase in ANC or pH.

Only in the late 1990s, 25 years after sulfur emissions began to decline, were the first widespread increases in ANC and pH seen in Adirondack lakes. These increases were small but promising. They were associated with decreases in inorganic aluminum and increases in DOC, suggesting that they were part of an overall pattern of recovery. But they were considerably slower than the decreases in the deposition of sulfate and were matched by decreases in base cations, both suggesting that watershed soils have been acidified and raising doubts about how long the recovery will continue and how complete it will be. (Chapter 9.)

NOTES

p. viii For the early history of acid rain, see Gorham, "Acid deposition and its ecological effects: A brief history of research," 1998. Gene Likens's original acid rain papers include Likens, Bormann, and Johnson, "Acid rain," 1972; Cogbill and Likens, "Acid precipitation in the Northeast U.S.," 1974; Likens and Bormann, "Acid rain, a serious regional problem," 1974. For the first DEC acidification survey, see Schofield, "Acid precipitation, effects on fish," 1976. For the Regionalized Integrated Lake-Watershed Acidification Study, see p. 48. For the Clean Air Amendments, see Driscoll et al., "Acidic deposition in the northeastern United States: Sources and inputs, ecosystem effects, and management strategies," 2001. The EPA review is Stoddard et al., "Response of surface water chemistry to the Clean Air Act Amendments of 1990," 2003, discussed on pp. 207–210.

ABBREVIATIONS AND SYMBOLS

For readability, we have tried to limit the use of technical abbreviations and symbols in the text: even chemists, after all, say *sulfate* and *nitrate* rather than SO_4^{2-} and NO_3^{-}. But we have used freely the symbol pH and the abbreviations ANC, DOC, and DIC (acid-neutralizing capacity, dissolved organic carbon, dissolved inorganic carbon), which are commonly used in speech.

We have also, for the same reasons, tended to spell out the names of organizations, thus sparing you the work of decoding the informat that, for example, the EPA's NTN-MDN and AIRMON programs are

GRAPHICAL SYMBOLS

Several graphical conventions are used to represent chemical substances. Cations and anions are shown as boxes with points:

Na^+ sodium ion Cl^- chloride ion

Na^+ Cl^- sodium chloride, an ionic compound.

Cations and anions associated with acids are in reds and browns, except for nitrate, which because of its association with biological cycling is green:

H^+ hydrogen SO_4^{2-} sulfate

NO_3^- nitrate ion

Ions associated with bases are blue or green:

Ca^{2+} calcium HCO_3^- bicarbonate

NH_4^+ ammonium OH^- hydroxyl

And metals are grays:

Al_i^{3+} inorganic aluminum

Hg^{2+} ionic mercury

Gases are ellipses, colored similarly to the ions derived from them:

Hg mercury O_2 oxygen

NO_x nitrogen oxides N_2 nitrogen

SO_2 sulfur dioxide CO_2 carbon dioxide

And nonionic compounds are square or rounded boxes:

FeS ferrous sulfide DOC dissolved organic carbon

Ions that bind to solids and so are part of the ion exchange complex are shown abutting brown boxes:

OH^- OH^- anions on exchanger

Ca^{2+} ion exchange complex cation on exchanger

supplemented regionally by the NYSDEC's ADMN. We do, however, use EPA freely for the U.S. Environmental Protection Agency, DEC for the New York State Department of Environmental Conservation, and ALS for the Adirondack Lakes Survey. A few others are are defined as they occur.

In the graphs and notes we have needed to be more compact and so have abbreviated more. When a symbol or abbreviation is not defined in the caption, the following list may help.

Acronyms

AEAP	Adirondack Effects Assessment Program
ALS	Adirondack Lakes Survey
ALSC	Adirondack Lakes Survey Corporation
ALTM	Adirondack Long-Term Monitoring program
AMMP	Adirondack Manipulation and Monitoring Project
ANC	acid-neutralizing capacity
CASTNET	Clean Air Status and Trends Network
DDRP	Direct Delayed Response Project
DEC	Department of Environmental Conservation (New York)
DIC	dissolved inorganic carbon
DOC	dissolved organic carbon
ELS	Eastern Lake Survey
EMAP	Environmental Monitoring and Assessment Program
EPA	Environmental Protection Agency (U.S.)
ERP	Episodic Response Project
EWLS	Experimental Watershed Liming Study
ILWAS	Integrated Lake-Watershed Acidification Study
LTM	Long-Term Monitoring project (EPA)
MDN	Mercury Deposition Network
NADP	National Atmospheric Deposition Program
NAPAP	National Acid Precipitation Assessment Program
NTN	National Trends Network
NYSERDA	New York State Energy Research and Development Authority
PIRLA	Paleoecological Investigation of Recent Lake Acidification studies
RILWAS	Regionalized Integrated Lake-Watershed Acidification Study
TIME	Temporally Integrated Monitoring of Ecosystems

Chemical Symbols

Al_i	inorganically complexed aluminum
Al_o	organically complexed aluminum
Ca^{2+}	calcium ion
C_A	summed concentration of acid anions
C_B	summed concentration of base cations
Cl^-	chloride ion
CO_3^{2-}	carbonate ion
eq	equivalents
eq/ha-yr	equivalents per hectare per year
eq/l	equivalents per liter
F^-	fluoride ion
H^+	hydrogen ion
H_2CO_3	carbonic acid
H_2SO_4	sulfuric acid
HCO_3^-	bicarbonate ion
HNO_3	nitric acid
Hg	elemental mercury
Hg^{2+}	mercuric ion
$MeHg^+$	methylmercury
Mg^{2+}	magnesium ion
μeq/l	microequivalents per liter
μg/kg	micrograms per kilogram
μg/m^2	micrograms per square meter
μmol/l	micromoles per liter
Na^+	sodium ion
ng	nanogram
NH^{4+}	ammonium ion
NO_3^-	nitrate ion
NO_X	nitrogen dioxide plus nitrogen oxide
pH	negative logarithm of concentration of hydrogen ion
OA^-	unspecified natural organic anions
OH^-	hydroxyl ion
SO_2	sulfur dioxide
SO_4^{2-}	sulfate ion

An Acid Deposition Lexicon

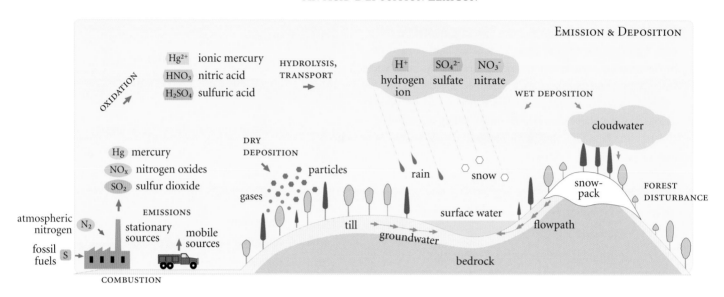

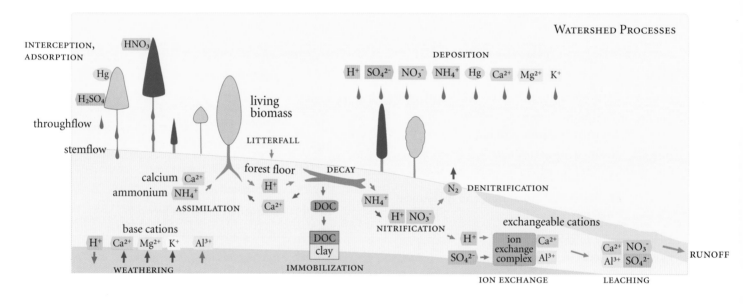

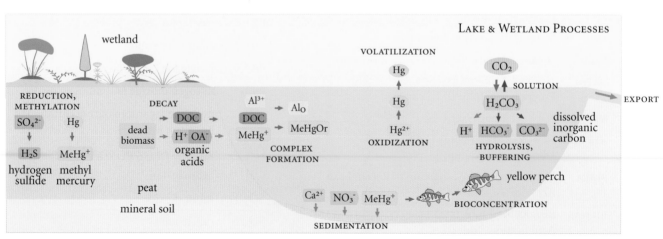

PRIMER AND GLOSSARY

DEFINITIONS, CHEMICAL FUNDAMENTALS, AND SOME NOTES ON
SCIENTIFIC STRATEGY

2

This chapter defines the main technical terms used in this book and indicates, very briefly, their importance for understanding the effects of acid rain. It is intended to be used in two ways: as a primer that can be read sequentially by readers who want a compact introduction to the concepts of acid rain chemistry, and as a glossary that can be consulted when needed.

accumulation The storage of a substance in water, soil, sediments, or biomass. Nitrogen, sulfur, and mercury, the main components of acid rain, all accumulate in ecosystems. As a result, the effects of acid rain can persist for a long time after deposition has been reduced.

acid Either a molecule like nitric acid (HNO_3) that ionizes in water to produce hydrogen ions (H^+) or an ion like aluminum that can bond to the hydroxyl ions (OH^-) in water. In either case, adding the acid to water increases the concentration of hydrogen ions and decreases the *pH* of a solution.

Acids are divided into *strong acids* and *weak acids*. In water, strong acids like nitric acid or sulfuric acid dissociate fully into hydrogen ions and acid anions. They thus have a strong influence on the pH of the solution and on the solubility of other substances. Weak acids like carbonic acid and many organic acids dissociate partly. They thus produce fewer hydrogen ions than strong acids, have less effect on pH, and are less able to dissolve minerals or free base cations from the ion exchange complex in soil.

acid anion An anion from an acid. In Adirondack waters, the commonest acid anions are nitrate (NO_3^-) from nitric acid and sulfate (SO_4^{2-}) from sulfuric acid.

acid-base ratio The ratio C_A/C_B of the sum of the acid anions to the sum of the base cations in stream or lake water. This ratio is a ion diagnostic; when it is high, it indicates that most of the mineral acid is passing through the watershed without being neutralized.

acid deposition The deposition of atmospheric acids to watersheds. It is divided into wet deposition (precipitation and cloudwater) and dry deposition (gases and particulates). Dry deposition and cloudwater are difficult to monitor, and many of the routine estimates of acid deposition include only wet deposition from precipitation.

SYMBOLS USED IN THIS CHAPTER

H^+	Cation (positive ion)
NO_3^-	Anion (negative ion)
HNO_3	Ionic compound
H_2O	Covalent compound
DOC	Mixture of compounds
SO_2	Gas
S	Solid
DOC clay	Solid with adsorbed compounds

ACIDS

$$HNO_3 \rightarrow H^+ + NO_3^-$$

Nitric acid, a strong acid, ionizes completely to hydrogen and nitrate ions in water.

$$HAc \rightarrow H^+ + Ac^- + HAc$$

Acetic acid, a weak acid, ionizes partially to hydrogen and acetate ions in water.

DEPOSITION RATES

H^+ 1 kg H^+ / ha-yr
     = 1000 eq H^+ / ha-yr

NO_3^- 1 kg NO_3^- / ha-yr
     = 16.1 mol NO_3^- / ha-yr
     = 16.1 eq NO_3^- / ha-yr
     = 0.226 kg N / ha-yr

SO_4^{2-} 1 kg SO_4^{2-} / ha-yr
     = 10.4 mol SO_4^{2-}/ ha-yr
     = 20.8 eq SO_4^{2-}/ ha-yr
     = 0.334 kg S / ha-yr

An equivalent of an ion is the molecular weight in grams divided by the charge of the ion. Thus an equivalent of hydrogen ion is 1 gram; an equivalent of nitrate, 62 grams; and an equivalent of sulfate, 96/2 = 48 grams.

Acid deposition is characterized in two ways: either by the concentrations of the major ions, measured in microequivalents per liter (µeq/l), or by the deposition rates of these ions, measured variously as kilograms, moles, or equivalents per hectare per year (kg/ha-yr, m/ha-yr, eq/ha-yr). Note that a rate in kilograms may refer to either the ion or the element: thus, as shown in the figure, a kilogram of sulfate per hectare per year is 0.33 kilograms of sulfur per year.

The deposition rates of mercury, which are tiny but significant, are mostly given in micrograms per square meter per year (µg/m²-yr).

acid episode A period, usually associated with high streamflows, in which the pH or ANC of a stream or lake decreases to a value significantly below its baseline level.

acidic lake or stream Broadly, any lake or stream with natural or atmospheric acidity, including both chronically (continuously) and episodically acid waters.

acidify, acidified, acidification To acidify a soil or waterbody is to decrease its pH, ANC, or base saturation. The soil or waterbody has then acidified, and the process involved is acidification.

The acidification of soils and waters may occur either through the transport of acid into a system, the transport of bases out of it, the generation of acids within it, or the consumption of bases within it. All four processes can be important in natural systems. The net acidification is the sum of all the processes acidifying some compartment in an ecosystem minus all the processes deacidifying it.

Note that acidification and deacidification are often coupled. Thus, when a soil neutralizes the acids from acid rain, the groundwater whose acid is neutralized becomes less acid and the soil that is doing the neutralizing becomes more acid. And when those acids later leach out of the soil and enter a lake, the soil becomes less acid and the lake more acid.

acidity A general term for the amount of acid in a system. In surface waters it is measured by the pH or ANC of the water. Lower pHs and ANCs indicate greater acidity. In soils, where the hydrogen ions are bound to the ion exchange complex, it is measured by the base saturation; as the base saturation decreases, the acidity of the soil increases.

Because hydrogen ions can be generated or consumed in chemical reactions, acidity is not a conserved quantity. When the microbes in a wetland reduce sulfate to hydrogen sulfide, they consume hydrogen ions, and the acidity of the wetland decreases. When the microbes in a forest soil oxidize ammonium to nitrate, they generate hydrogen ions, and the acidity of the forest increases.

DEPOSITION RATES
1 kg / ha-yr = 0.1 g / m²-yr
1 g / ha-yr = 100 µg / m²-yr

A hectare is 10,000 square meters, so the deposition rate per square meter is 0.0001 times the deposition rate per hectare. The wet deposition rate of 10 µg/m²-yr of mercury measured in the Arbutus Lake watershed equals 0.1 g per ha-yr, or a hundred-thousandth of the average deposition rate of sulfur (about 10 kg/ha- yr) in the same watershed.

SOME PROCESSES ACIDIFYING WATERSHEDS

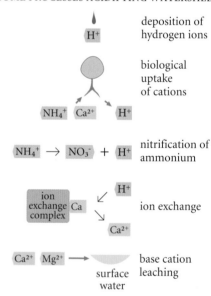

deposition of hydrogen ions

biological uptake of cations

nitrification of ammonium

ion exchange

base cation leaching

Acidifying processes include transport processes (deposition, leaching) which import acids to the watershed or export bases from it; transfers between compartments within the watershed (assimilation, ion exchange), which acidify one compartment and deacidify another; and oxidations (nitrification, assimilation of ammonium), which generate new hydrogen ions. (Also see the figure on p. 39.)

acid-neutralizing capacity (ANC) A widely used measure of the acidity of surface waters, particularly important in acid rain research. ANC measures the amount of strong base in a solution and so is a measure of the amount of strong acid that must be added to a sample to acidify it to a defined chemical endpoint. It thus describes the water's resistance to acidification with a strong acid. The higher the ANC, of a water the more acid is required to acidify it.

ANCs are commonly determined by a procedure called Gran titration and measured in microequivalents per liter (μeq/l). An ANC of 200 μeq/l or more indicates that the water contains a significant amount of strong base. The pH will be near 7.0 and the water very difficult to acidify. An ANC of 0-50 μeq/l indicates a much smaller amount of strong base. The pH will be somewhere between 4.5 and 6.5, the water will be relatively easy to acidify, and the ANC will often go below 0 in acid episodes. An ANC that is permanently less than 0 μeq/l indicates that strong bases are absent and strong acid is present. The water is both chronically acidified and very susceptible to further acidification.

In many waters, the measured ANC determined by a Gran titration is close to the base-acid difference, C_B-C_A, where C_B is the sum of the base cations and C_A the sum of the acid anions. This provides a very useful way of thinking about acidification and deacidification that has been extensively used in acid rain research (pp. 50-51, 74, 197). Any process that increases C_B without changing C_A will increase ANC. Any process that increases C_A without changing C_B will decrease ANC. And any process that changes C_A and C_B equally will leave the ANC unchanged. Thus forest fires (p. 141) release base cations and increase ANC; sulfur oxidation (pp. 39, 158) produces sulfate, an acid ion, and decreases ANC; and leaching of cations by strong acids (p. 132) produces both acid ions and base cations and leaves ANC unchanged.

acid-neutralizing capacity vs. pH Although ANC and pH both measure acidity, they measure different aspects of it. ANC tells how much base the water contains and how resistant the water will be to future acidification. It is extremely useful for assessing the cumulative effects of acid deposition and measuring the progress of acidification and recovery.

pH, on the other hand, tells how much free hydrogen ion there is in the water. Because the hydrogen ion concentration is a master variable that controls many physical and biological processes, pH is thus the quantity most used to characterize the current state of the water and the chemical conditions that the creatures living in it will encounter.

Which variable you use depends on what you are studying. If you are an acid rain chemist seeking to determine how much streams have acidified or how vulnerable they are to future acidification, you

COMPUTING ANC

1 Bases minus acids

$$OH^- + HCO_3^- + CO_3^{2-} + OB^- - H^+$$

2 Base cations minus acid anions

$$NH_4^+ + Ca^{2+} + Mg^{2+} + K^+ + Na^+ + Me^+$$
$$- (NO_3^- + SO_4^{2-} + Cl^- + F^-)$$

OB^- = organic bases

Me^+ = metal cations (iron, manganese, aluminum)

The ANC of a solution is defined as the total amount of strong base minus the total amount of strong acid in the solution, measured in equivalents. This is equivalent to, and often measured as, the difference between the cations from strong bases and the anions from strong acids. A strong base like NaOH contributes Na^+, a base cation; a strong acid like HCl contributes Cl^-, an acid ion. Thus the difference C_B - C_A between the sum of the cations associated with strong bases and the anions associated with strong acids measures the excess or strong bases of strong acid, which is the ANC.

ANC AND pH

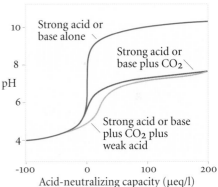

ANC and pH vary together but in a non-linear way. In a solution containing strong acids or bases but no weak ones, the pH changes rapidly when the ANC is near 0. Adding dissolved carbon dioxide or other weak acids doesn't change the ANC (since by definition ANC measures only strong acids and bases) but does change the pH, and hence the pH-ANC curve. The solution is said to be buffered, meaning its pH changes more gradually as acid or base is added. From Munson, Driscoll, and Gherini, "Phenomenological analysis of ALSC chemistry data," in Baker et al., *Adirondack Lakes Survey: An Interpretive Analysis of Fish Communities and Water Chemistry, 1984-1987,* 1990.

measure ANC. But if you are an aquatic ecologist trying to determine which insects can live in the streams, you measure pH.

Though different, pH and ANC are closely related. The red line on the graph on p. 19 shows the relationship in an unbuffered solution (one containing only strong acids and bases). When buffers are present – and in natural waters they always are – the pH-ANC relationship changes. Because buffers are weak acids or bases, a buffered solution has a different pH from an unbuffered one; and because buffers decrease the pH change as strong acids or bases are added, the slope of the pH-ANC curve is less in a buffered solution than in an unbuffered one. Graphically, this means that the pH-ANC curves of natural waters are usually lower and flatter than those for solutions of strong acids or bases. (Also see *buffers*, p. 24.)

acidophilic Of animals and plants, a species that reaches its maximum abundance in acid waters.

Adirondack Park A protected area of 2.4 million hectares in northern New York State, consisting of 1.0 million hectares of public land and 1.4 million acres of private land.

adsorption The binding of molecules and ions to charged surfaces through a mixture of electrostatic attraction and covalent bonds. Adsorption is commonly an ion exchange process in which hydrogen ions are released when cations are adsorbed and hydroxyl ions are released when anions are adsorbed.

aluminum (Al) The 13th element, abundant in silicate minerals and clays and so a normal component of almost all soils. Acid deposition releases aluminum ions from minerals, which then enter the groundwater as dissolved aluminum.

Dissolved aluminum occurs in three principal forms:

Polymeric aluminum, typically small particles of silica minerals and their dissolved or colloidal weathering products. This is relatively inert and usually not measured in acidification studies.

Organic monomeric aluminum, single aluminum ions complexed with organic compounds. This is also is relatively nontoxic.

Inorganic monomeric aluminum (labile monomeric aluminum), single aluminum ions, variously free or complexed with inorganic *anions.* This comes in a number of chemical species (pp. 25, 70), all toxic to aquatic animals.

The presence of elevated concentrations of inorganic aluminum in groundwater or surface water indicates that unneutralized mineral acids are moving through the mineral soil. This is possible only when a) mineral acids are being deposited on or generated in the forest

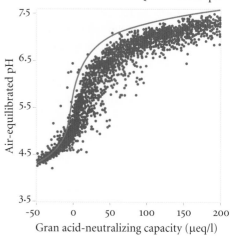

The measured ANC and the pH for the 1,469 lakes studied by the Adirondack Lakes Survey, from Munson, Driscoll, and Gherini, "Phenomenological analysis of ALSC chemistry data," in Baker et al., *Adirondack Lakes Survey: An Interpretive Analysis of Fish Communities and Water Chemistry, 1984-1987,* 1990. The red line is the ANC-pH curve expected for a solution that contained only strong acids and bases and dissolved carbon dioxide from the atmosphere. The measured values lie below the red curve, suggesting that buffers (weak acids) are present. They also suggest that for low ANCs the rate of change of pH with ANC is less than that suggested by the theoretical curve, indicating that lake water is at least weakly buffered near ANC = 0.

ADSORPTION AND DESORPTION

1 Adsorption & desorption of a negative ion

2 Adsorption & desorption of a positive ion

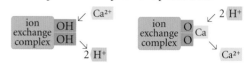

Adsorption often takes place at surface hydroxyl or carboxyl groups. When a cation is adsorbed, it replaces the hydrogen ion of the hydroxyl group; when an anion is adsorbed, it replaces the whole hydroxyl. Doubly charged ions, like those shown, replace two hydrogen ions or hydroxyls.

floor and b) there are not enough available bases (base cations) in the forest to neutralize them. The appearance of inorganic aluminum is thus an important ion diagnostic associated with both acid deposition and cation depletion.

aluminum speciation The relative proportions of the various forms of dissolved aluminum.

ammonium (NH_4^+) A nitrogen-containing ion, found in acid deposition and also produced by the decay of organic matter. The ammonium in precipitation comes from gaseous ammonia (NH_3), which in turn comes from fertilizers, animal wastes, and some natural sources.

Ammonium is readily assimilated by plants. The assimilation of ammonium releases hydrogen ions and so is acidifying; the release of ammonium during decay consumes hydrogen ions and so is deacidifying.

anion A negatively charged ion.

assimilation The process by which plants and microbes take up nutrients and incorporate them into organic compounds. Assimilation involves the movement of charges and must be balanced by the movement of opposite charges, most commonly hydrogen and hydroxyl ions. Thus when plants assimilate negative ions like nitrate or sulfate, they consume hydrogen ions or release hydroxyl ions, keeping the charges balanced both externally and internally. When plants assimilate positive ions like calcium or ammonium, they release hydrogen ions or consume hydroxyl ions, again keeping the charges balanced. If plants are assimilating equal numbers of cations and anions, there is no net effect. But if, as is often the case, plants are assimilating more cations than anions, then there is a net release of hydrogen ions, which results in the acidification of the soil and groundwater.

atmospheric acid Here, either nitric acid (HNO_3) or sulfuric acid (H_2SO_4), the two main mineral acids present in acid deposition.

available Of elements or ions, in a chemical form that is easily assimilated by plants and microbes. In forest soils, for example, the calcium dissolved in the groundwater and bound to the soil ion exchange complex is available for immediate use by plants. The calcium in soil organic matter and soil minerals is unavailable and must be freed by decay and weathering before it can be used.

base An atom or molecule that can accept hydrogen ions from other molecules. The simplest base is the hydroxyl ion (OH^-), which reacts with hydrogen ions to produce water. In natural waters the common-

AMMONIUM CYCLING

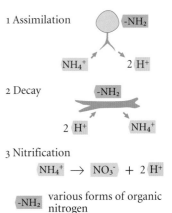

1 Assimilation

2 Decay

3 Nitrification
$$NH_4^+ \rightarrow NO_3^- + 2\ H^+$$

$-NH_2$ various forms of organic nitrogen

The ammonium ion is the most biologically active form of nitrogen. It is assimilated into organic compounds in living plant tissue, released from dead plants by microbial decay, and converted into nitrate (nitrified) by a microbial process involving assimilation and release. Assimilation and nitrification produce hydrogen ions; decay consumes them. If the assimilation and decay are balanced and no nitrate is produced, then the acidity produced by assimilation equals the acidity consumed in decay, and there is no net acidification. But if, as often happens during the winter, the ammonium produced by decay is converted to nitrate rather than reassimilated, there is a net production of hydrogen ions, and the forest is said to be generating *nitrogen-cycle acidity*.

ASSIMILATION

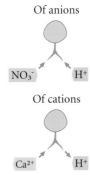

Of anions

Of cations

Charge balance requires that hydrogen ions be consumed when anions are assimilated, and released when cations are assimilated.

est bases are dissolved carbonates and bicarbonates (CO_3^{2-}, HCO_3^-) from carbonate rocks. Both are relatively plentiful in areas with sedimentary and metasedimentary rocks but quite scarce in areas like the western Adirondacks, where much of the bedrock is igneous.

Bases, like acids, may be strong or weak. Strong bases like the hydroxyl ion (OH^-) have a strong affinity for hydrogen ions and so a strong influence on pH. They are relatively rare in most natural waters. Weaker bases like the bicarbonate and hydrolyzed aluminum ions (HCO_3^-, $Al(H_2O)OH^{2+}$), which are more common in natural waters, have a lower affinity for hydrogen ions and correspondingly less influence on pH.

base cations The cations of the alkali earth metals, calcium (Ca^{2+}), magnesium (Mg^{2+}), sodium (Na^+), and potassium (K^+). All four are keystone elements that are essential nutrients for plants and animals and also regulate the ways that watersheds respond to acid rain.

In undisturbed watersheds the base cations are supplied by deposition and weathering, cycled through organic matter by assimilation and decay, and lost, usually in small amounts, in runoff and groundwater. Within the watershed they are stored in three forms: in unweathered mineral grains, in organic matter, and as exchangeable cations bound to the ion exchange complex in the soil. Only in the last form, as exchangeable cations in the soil, are they readily available for plant growth.

In watersheds receiving acid deposition the groundwater contains strong acids and free hydrogen ions. Some of these hydrogen ions displace (leach) base cations from the ion exchanger. The hydrogen ions remain in the soil, acidifying it; the base cations enter the groundwater and migrate out of the watershed.

base cation depletion A decrease in the quantity of base cations, especially exchangeable base cations, in soils. Base cation depletion is manifested by a decrease in base saturation and an increase in exchangeable hydrogen and aluminum ions. It can be caused by the assimilation of cations by woody plants, the leaching of cations by acid deposition, or the removal of cations by harvesting trees.

baseline (or baseflow) ANC The ANC of a lake or stream in summer and fall, when flows are low and the watershed is biologically active. In acidified watersheds, the baseline ANC is typically higher than the ANC measured during acid episodes, when vegetation is dormant and the soils are releasing nitrogen-cycle acids.

base-acid difference The difference between the sum of the base cations (C_B) and the sum of the inorganic acid anions (C_A). A positive base-acid difference indicates that the watershed is supplying more

ATMOSPHERIC ACIDS

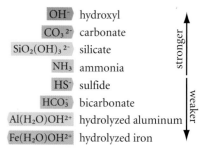

The two main atmospheric acids are nitric acids, generated by the oxidation of nitrogen oxides, and sulfuric acid, generated by the oxidation of sulfur dioxide.

COMMON BASES IN FRESH WATER

THE BASE CATIONS

Ca^{2+} Calcium Mg^{2+} Magnesium

K^+ Potassium Na^+ Sodium

BASE CATION CYCLING

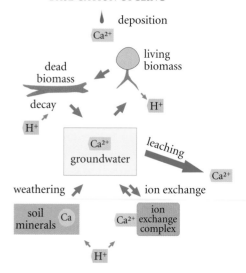

base cations than acid ions, and this in turn means that it is neutralizing most or all of the acid it receives from deposition.

If no organic acids are present, the base-acid difference $C_B - C_A$ equals the ANC (p. 19). When organic acids are present, the base-acid difference is greater than the ANC, but it is still a useful measure because any process that changes the base-acid difference will change the ANC by the same amount.

base-neutralizing capacity (BNC) A quantity, analogous to the acid-neutralizing capacity, that measures the amount of strong acid in solution.

base saturation In a soil, the percentage of the ion exchange sites that are occupied by base cations rather than hydrogen or aluminum ions. In unacidified soils and soils in which carbonate minerals are present, the base saturation may be 25% or more. In acidified soils without carbonates, it may be 5% or less. The base saturation is a commonly used index of the degree to which base cations, and particularly calcium, are available for forest growth. Good forest growth is believed to require a base saturation of 20% or more.

bioaccumulation (*bioconcentration*) The accumulation of substances, often toxic, in the tissues of animals and plants. Bioaccumulation occurs with substances like methylmercury that bind to tissue and are not readily excreted. Because predatory animals eat many times their own weight in prey, bioaccumulating substances tend to work their way up food chains and are most concentrated in the top predators.

bioconcentration factor In aquatic animals, the ratio of the concentration of a bioaccumulating substance in tissue to its concentration in the water. In yellow perch in Adirondack lakes, for example, the bioconcentration factors for mercury range from about 1 million to 10 million.

bioassay In aquatic biology, a test for toxicity using living animals, either in tanks or in cages in streams and lakes.

biomass The organic matter, both living and dead, in an ecosystem.

bog lake As used by the Adirondack Lakes Survey, a lake with bog vegetation (floating sedge-sphagnum-shrub mats) on 50% or more of its shores, which is often isolated from the regional groundwater flow by a layer of peat. Bog lakes with outlets are bog drainage lakes; bog lakes without outflows are bog seepage lakes.

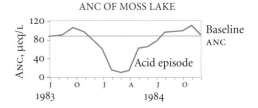

ANC OF MOSS LAKE

Redrawn with permission from Driscoll, Yatsko, and Unangst, "Longitudinal and temporal trends in the water chemistry of the North Branch of the Moose River." Copyright 1987 Springer Science and Business Media.

BASE-ACID DIFFERENCE

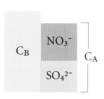

If the sum of base cations, C_B, exceeds the sum of the acid ions nitrate and sulfate, C_A, then the mineral acids from acid deposition are being fully neutralized in the watershed.

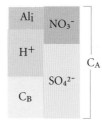

If the sum of acid anions, C_A, exceeds the concentration of base cations, C_B, then not all of the mineral acids from acid deposition have been neutralized, and some of the acidity in the water is mineral acidity.

BASE SATURATION

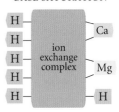

An ion exchanger with ten exchange sites (black lines) binding six hydrogen ions and two base cations. Because four of the ten exchange sites are occupied by base cations, the base saturation, on an equivalence basis, is 40%.

brook trout (*Salvelinus fontinalis*) Our common native trout of streams and small ponds. It tolerates mild acidity but is absent from strongly acid waters.

buffers Ions like bicarbonate and various aluminum complexes that can either donate or accept hydrogen ions and so can act as either weak acids or weak bases. Conceptually, what buffers do is change the relation between pH and ANC (diagram, p. 19). When no buffers are present, the pH-ANC curve is steep, showing that as strong acid or strong base is added to a solution the pH changes rapidly. When a buffer is present, the curve develops flatter spots in one or more places; these represent the pHs where the added acid or base is reacting with the buffer and so causing less change in pH.

Buffers are of considerable importance in natural waters because they tend to stabilize pH in certain ranges. In unacidified waters the most important bases are bicarbonate ions and carbonic acid (dissolved carbon dioxide), which tend to keep the pHs of unacidified lakes between 6 and 8.

calcium (Ca) The most abundant of the base cations, both in soils and in biomass. Calcium is an essential nutrient for plants and animals and is cycled rapidly between biomass and the forest floor. It is also the main base cation in the ion exchange complex, and thus a soil's ability to neutralize acid rain largely depends on the exchangeable calcium it contains. Soils in which the exchangeable calcium has been depleted by leaching by atmospheric acids cannot support normal forest growth and have only a limited ability to neutralize mineral acids.

calcium-aluminum ratio The ratio of the concentrations of calcium and aluminum in groundwater, which serves as an index of the availability of calcium for plant growth. Plants assimilate calcium, which they require, and aluminum, which is toxic to them, by similar pathways and apparently have trouble differentiating between them. When the calcium-aluminum ratio is high, calcium is readily available. When, as in many acidified soils where aluminum has replaced calcium on the ion exchange complex, the calcium-aluminum ratio is near 1, calcium is difficult to obtain and plant growth may be limited by aluminum toxicity.

carbonate minerals, carbonates Here, calcite ($CaCO_3$), dolomite ($CaMg(CO_3)_2$), and various sedimentary and metamorphic rocks containing them. Soils containing carbonate minerals have high base saturations and ANCs and are very resistant to acidification. Carbonate minerals are rare in the western Adirondacks but commoner in the eastern Adirondacks and the river valleys just outside the Adirondacks.

BOG LAKES

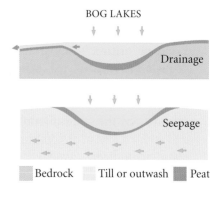

Bedrock   Till or outwash   Peat

BUFFERING

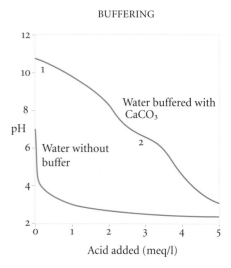

Two curves showing how pH changes when a strong acid is added to pure water and to water buffered by calcium carbonate (limestone), a common base in natural waters. For simplicity, dissolved carbon dioxide has been ignored. The pH of pure water begins at 7 and drops rapidly as acid is added. The pH of the buffered water, which is initially higher because calcium carbonate is a base, drops more gradually because some of the added hydrogen ions react with the carbonate, producing bicarbonate (HCO_3^-) ions and carbonic acid (H_2CO_3). The conversion of carbonate to bicarbonate is responsible for the rounded top of the curve (1); the conversion of bicarbonate to carbonic acid is responsible for the slightly lower slope in the middle (2). From Stumm and Morgan, *Aquatic Chemistry*, 1996. Also see *acid-neutralizing capacity vs. pH*, page 19.

carbon-nitrogen ratio The ratio of carbon to nitrogen in soils or plant tissue, often used as an index of the extent to which nitrogen from acid deposition is being retained in the watershed. When it is low, indicating much stored nitrogen, the watershed may be approaching nitrogen saturation and may begin to release stored nitrogen.

cation A positive ion. The commonest cations in Adirondack surface waters are hydrogen ions and the base cations calcium, magnesium, sodium, and potassium.

cation-anion difference The difference between the sum of the cations and the sum of the inorganic anions. A positive cation-anion difference indicates that anions from organic acids are present.

cation exchange An ion exchange process in which one positive ion is exchanged for another. Leaching, for example, is a cation exchange process in which hydrogen and aluminum ions replace base cations on the ion exchange sites and then the base cations are exported in groundwater.

cation depletion See *base cation depletion*.

cation exchange capacity, anion exchange capacity The total number of charged sites on the ion exchange complex available to bind cations or anions, usually measured in centimoles (hundredths of moles) of charge per kilogram of soil. The cation exchange capacity is related to the negative charges provided by clay particles and organic matter. When both are high, as in a fertile forest loam, the soil has a high exchange capacity. When both are low, as in a coarse sterile sand, it has almost none. The anion exchange capacity is related to the amount of oxidized iron and aluminum. It is high in the old, well-oxidized soils of the nonglaciated Southeast and relatively low in the younger and less oxidized ones of the glaciated Northeast.

chronic acidity Acidity in a lake or stream, indicated by negative ANC values, that is present throughout the year and thus distinct from the episodic acidity that occurs after storms and during snowmelt.

complex formation The bonding of a metal cation to one or more organic or inorganic anions (ligands) by relatively weak covalent bonds. The aluminum ion, for example, may be complexed with sulfate, silicate, hydroxide, and fluoride ions as well as many organic compounds.

Complexes are important in surface waters because they change the solubility, movement, and biological availability of metals and because many of them are buffers and so change the way the water responds to acidification. The organically complexed forms of mer-

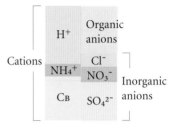

CATION-ANION DIFFERENCE

Most analyses of surface water measure only inorganic anions. When, as in this example, the sum of inorganic anions is less than the sum of the cations, organic anions are likely to be present and some of the hydrogen ions will be associated with organic anions and thus form organic acids.

SOME METAL COMPLEXES OCCURRING IN FRESH WATER

a Aluminum complexes

Al-F	Aluminum fluorides
Al-OH	Aluminum hydroxides
Al-OH-F	Aluminum hydroxy-fluorides
Al-org	Aluminum organic complexes
Al-Si	Aluminum silicates
Al-SO_4	Aluminum sulfates

b Iron complexes

| Fe-OH | Iron hydroxides |

c Silica complexes

| SiO_2-OH | Silica hydroxides |

d Mercury complexes

| Hg-org | Mercury organic complexes |
| MeHg-org | Methylmercury organic complexes |

The symbol for each of the above complexes represents a series of ions. The aluminum hydroxides, for example, include $Al(OH)^{2+}$, $Al(OH)_2^+$, and $Al(OH)_4^-$.

cury and aluminum, for example, are less biologically available and so less toxic than the free or inorganically complexed forms. The family of aluminum hydroxides is a buffer system and so tends to stabilize pH in acid waters.

cloudwater The droplets of water in clouds and fogs. Cloudwater is often highly acid and a significant – and poorly accounted for – source of acidity at high elevations.

compartment study Typically, a biogeochemical study in which relatively small plots in a biological community are divided into compartments – biomass, mineral soil, dead organic matter etc. – and the pools and fluxes of elements in and through these compartments are estimated. Compartment studies are more difficult and less accurate than mass-balance studies of whole lakes or watersheds but yield a much more detailed look at transformations and cycling.

concentration The amount of a chemical in a known volume of water. The concentrations of ions in deposition and surface water are usually measured in microequivalents per liter (µeq/l), except for mercury, which is usually measured in nanograms per liter (ng/l).

chrysophytes A relatively small group of microscopic algae, now usually placed in the phylum Xanthophyta, that produce characteristic silica scales and spines that can be identified in lake sediments. Like diatoms, chrysophytes are used in paleolimnological reconstructions of lake chemistry.

Clean Air Act, Clean Air Act Amendments The major federal legislation regulating acid emissions. The original Clean Air Act was passed in 1955; major sets of amendments, greatly restricting sulfur emissions, were passed in 1970 and 1990.

critical levels See *indices of acidification.*

cumulative effect Here, an effect of acid rain on an ecosystem that depends on the total amount of acid that has been deposited. One of the principal achievements of acid rain research in the 1990s was to document cumulative effects. The major cumulative effects thus far documented are the storage of sulfates and nitrates in soils, the nitrogen saturation of forests, and the depletion of base cations from soils.

decay The microbial decomposition of organic matter, which releases (mineralizes) the nutrients stored in it. Like assimilation, decay often involves oxidations and reductions and so generates and consumes acids. When it simply reverses assimilation – when, say, the calcium

COMPARTMENTS AND FLUXES IN A NUTRIENT-CYCLING STUDY

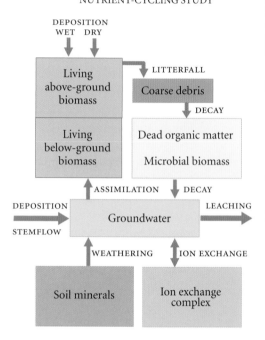

MILLEQUIVALENTS AND MICROEQUIVALENTS
1 equivalent/l = 1,000 millequivalents (meq/l) = 1,000,000 microequivalents (µeq/l).

CHRYSOPHYTE

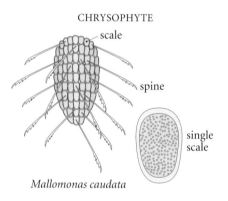

Mallomonas caudata

Mallomonas is a widespread genus of scaled chrysophytes in which the body is covered with small overlapping silica plates, some of which bear long spines. *M. caudata*, shown here, is a common species of clear-water lakes. It is about 0.05 mm long, fairly large for the group.

or sulfate that was assimilated is released in the same form – there is no net acidification or deacidification. But when, as in the nitrogen and carbon cycles, elements are assimilated in one form and released in another, there can be net acidification or deacidification.

denitrification In soils, the microbial reduction of nitrates to molecular nitrogen. Denitrification consumes hydrogen ions and is deacidifying.

deposition The atmospheric delivery of gases, particles, water, and solutes to a watershed. Deposition is divided into dry deposition, which includes the deposition of particles and the adsorption of gases, and wet deposition, which is the deposition of rain, snow, and cloudwater.

disturbance Here, processes like fire, blowdown, logging, and development that alter the amount of biomass and hence the way nutrients are cycled in a watershed.

dry deposition The deposition of acids, mercury, and salts by the settling or interception of small particles or the direct adsorption of gases. Much dry deposition is really a kind of filtering of the air by vegetation and so, because it depends on both the properties of the air and the vegetation, is quite difficult to quantify.

dissolved inorganic carbon (DIC) Carbonate ions and their relatives bicarbonate and carbonic acid (CO_3^{2-}, HCO_3^-, H_2CO_3), produced by the solution of atmospheric carbon dioxide and the weathering of carbonate rocks. Bicarbonate ion is a very effective buffer, and waters with substantial amounts of bicarbonate usually have pHs of 6 or above.

dissolved organic carbon (DOC) A mixture of organic compounds, particularly humic, fulvic, and tannic acids, produced by decay or excretion and typically staining the water brown. DOC includes the organic acids, which are the major source of natural acidity in Adirondack waters.

drainage lake A lake drained by an outlet stream, as opposed to a seepage lake, which has no outlet.

diatom A large group of microscopic algae, now usually placed in the phylum Bacillariophyta, with highly ornamented silica shells of characteristic shapes that can be identified in lake sediments. Like chrysophytes, diatoms are associated with characteristic pHs and are used in paleolimnological reconstructions of lake chemistry.

DECAY & MINERALIZATION

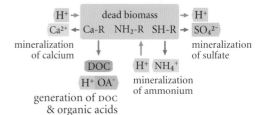

Ca-R, NH_2-R, and SH-R are organic calcium, nitrogen, and sulfur compounds, respectively.

DENITRIFICATION

NO_3^- + 1.25 CH_2O + H^+ →

0.5 N_2 + 1.75 H_2O + 1.25 CO_2

CH_2O organic carbon

N_2 nitrogen gas CO_2 carbon dioxide gas

Microbial denitrification is an anaerobic process, that uses organic matter as a reductant. It is believed to be commonest in wet soils with high nitrate concentrations.

REACTIONS OF DISSOLVED INORGANIC CARBON

1 Solution of carbon dioxide

CO_2 + H_2O ↔ CO_2 + H_2O ↔ H_2CO_3

2 Solution of carbonate minerals

$CaCO_3$ + CO_2 + H_2O ↔ Ca^{2+} + 2 HCO_3^-

$CaCO_3$ + H^+ ↔ Ca^{2+} + HCO_3^-

3 Interconversion of forms of DIC

H_2CO_3 ↔ HCO_3^- + H^+ ↔ CO_3^{2-} + 2 H^+

CO_2 gaseous carbon dioxide H_2CO_3 carbonic acid

CO_2 dissolved carbon dioxide HCO_3^- bicarbonate ion

$CaCO_3$ calcite (calcium carbonate) CO_3^{2-} carbonate ion

DIC is produced by the solution of atmospheric carbon dioxide and the dissolution of carbonate minerals like calcite and dolomite. Its three forms, carbonic acid, bicarbonate ion, and carbonate ion, are in equilibrium with each other and with hydrogen ion. In acid waters carbonic acid predominates; near neutrality bicarbonate predominates; in alkaline waters carbonate predominates.

dilute Of surface waters, having relatively small amounts of dissolved substances and so a total ionic strength of a few millimoles per liter or less.

emissions Here, releases of acids, mercury, and other combustion products into the atmosphere.

Environmental Monitoring and Assessment Program (EMAP) An umbrella program of the U.S. Environmental Protection Agency, created in the early 1990s. The EMAP surface water program includes the LTM and TIME long-term monitoring programs, both of which are ongoing in the Adirondacks.

equivalent See *moles and equivalents.*

exchange, exchanger See *ion exchange.*

exchangeable cations Cations held on the ion exchanger and thus available to neutralize acids or be assimilated by plants. The number of cations on the exchanger is usually measured in millimoles or centimoles of charge (mol_c) per kilogram of soil. In these units each atom of calcium counts twice because it has two charges. The percentage of sites on the exchanger occupied by base cations is the base saturation.

export Here, the loss of material from a watershed or lake. *Net export* is the excess of exports or imports.

f-factor A ratio of the changes in the concentrations of ions as a lake acidifies or deacidifies and thus one of several ion diagnostics used to characterize the state of or changes in surface waters. The f-factor for base cations, for example, is the ratio of the change in base cations to the change in sulfate, $\Delta C_B/\Delta SO_4^{2-}$.

F-factors characterize the response of a watershed to changes in acid inputs. An f-factor for base cations near 1 suggests that a watershed is storing or neutralizing most of the incoming acid; an f-factor for base cations of 0.5 suggests that half of the incoming acid is passing through the watershed unchanged.

flowpath The path that water takes within a watershed. Flowpaths through deep mineral soils, characteristic of deep-till watersheds, allow water to interact with soil minerals and the ion exchange complex, typically neutralizing acids and adsorbing DOC. Flowpaths near the surface, characteristic of thin-till watersheds, allow little neutralization and typically produce water richer in nitrogen-cycle acids and DOC.

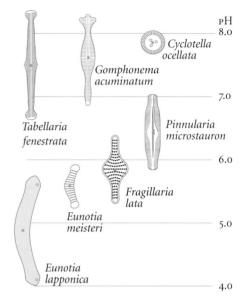

Seven diatoms of lake sediments, placed so that their centers (red dots) indicate the pH at which they are most abundant. The largest, *Eunotia lapponica,* is about 0.05 mm long. pH values from Dixit et al., "Assessing water quality changes in the lakes of the northeastern United States using sediment diatoms," 1999. Illustrations based on microphotographs in Camburn and Charles, *Diatoms of Low Alkalinity Lakes,* 2000.

THE F-FACTOR FOR BASE CATIONS

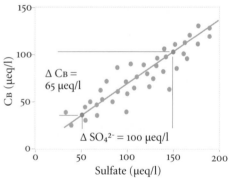

The graph shows a series of observations of base cation (C_B) and sulfate concentrations for a stream. The two are correlated and there is a clear trend, shown by the blue line; when sulfate is high, base cations are also high. The f-factor for base cations is the slope of the trend line, 0.65, and suggests that 65% of the hydrogen ions that are deposited with the sulfate are neutralized in the watershed and exchanged for base cations.

flow-through seepage lake A seepage lake hydrologically connected to the local water table, through which groundwater flows. Because flow-through seepage lakes receive mostly groundwater from deep flowpaths, they are relatively hard to acidify.

flux Any movement of water or materials in or out of a compartment in an ecosystem, generally measured in kilograms or equivalents per hectare per year. The *net flux* of an element is the difference between the inputs and outputs over some period of time; it is positive when the compartment is retaining the element and negative when the element is being depleted.

foliar chemistry The chemistry of leaves and needles, often used to diagnose the nutrient status of trees.

forest floor The uppermost organic layer of the soil, along with the litter (dead plant material) on top of it. Typically it is a zone of high biological activity in which much assimilation and decay occur and so a particular focus of nutrient-cycling studies.

fossil fuels The hydrocarbon fuels coal, oil, and natural gas. Of these, coal has the highest sulfur content and makes the largest contribution to sulfur emissions.

Gran ANC The ANC measured by a Gran titration. When organic acids are absent, the Gran ANC equals the base-acid difference, $C_B - C_A$.

hectare A metric unit of area, equal to 10,000 square meters or 2.47 acres.

Hubbard Brook Experimental Forest A group of experimental watersheds in the White Mountain National Forest, near West Thornton, New Hampshire, operated since the early 1960s by the U.S. Forest Service and a consortium of researchers who have focused on long-term monitoring and mass-balance studies.

Huntington Forest A research and teaching forest in Newcomb, New York, in the central Adirondacks, operated by the College of Environmental Science and Forestry of the State University of New York, at which deposition, long-term monitoring, and mass-balance studies have been carried out since the late 1970s.

hydraulic residence time The average time water remains in a lake before being flushed out by new water. It is normally approximated as the lake volume divided by the annual outflow of the lake. Lakes with short residence times are strongly influenced by their watersheds and

WATERSHED PROCESSES IN SOILS OF
DIFFERENT DEPTHS

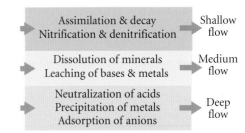

Groundwater moving at different depths in the soil is subject to different chemical processes. Shallow flows are influenced by assimilation and decay; here, nutrient pools turn over rapidly and organic and nitrogen-cycle acids are generated. Subsurface flows through leached layers acquire aluminum and other metals from the dissolution of soil minerals. Deep flows through unleached mineral soils neutralize acids and immobilize aluminum, anions, and DOC.

FLOW-THROUGH SEEPAGE LAKE

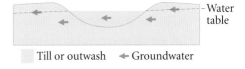

FLUXES IN A FOREST FLOOR

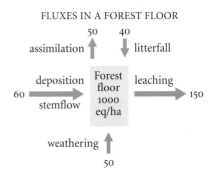

Fluxes of an element through a forest floor, in equivalents per hectare-year. The total input from litterfall, direct deposition, stemflow, and weathering is 150 eq/ha-yr. The total loss from assimilation and leaching is 200 eq/ha-yr. The *net flux* is -50 eq/ha-yr, indicating that the forest floor is losing 50/1000 = 5% of its pool of the element each year.

are often subject to acid episodes at high water. Lakes with longer residence times are more influenced by processes occurring within the lake and less by the chemistry of the water delivered by the watershed.

hydrogen ion (H⁺) A single proton, typically bound to one or more water molecules and whose concentration is one of the basic measures of acidity. Acids are substances that produce hydrogen ions in water, and pH is a measure of the concentration of hydrogen ions.

hydrology The movement of water through watersheds.

hydroxyl ion (OH⁻) A common anion found in many bases. Hydroxl ions react with hydrogen ions (H⁺) to produce water.

indices of acidification Chemical indicators thought to mark critical levels of acidification at which there are distinct shifts in ecology or nutrient cycling. For fresh water, these critical levels include pHs of less than 5.5, at which point aquatic diversity is much reduced; summer ANCS of less than 50 µeq/l, at which point the water is susceptible to episodic acidification; summer ANCS of less than 0 µeq/l, at which point the water is are considered chronically acidified; and inorganic aluminum concentrations above 2 µmol/l or 50 µg/l, at which point increased fish mortality is likely. For forest soils these include base saturation levels of less than 20% or calcium-aluminum ratios near 1, at which point forest growth may be limited by base cation availability; and carbon-nitrogen ratios of less than 20, at which point nitrification ratios increase and nitrogen retention decreases. For whole watersheds, the critical level is a deposition rate of more than about 10 kg N/ha-yr, at which point nitrogen retention decreases and the export of nitrogen-cycle acids increases.

inferred acidification In paleolimnological studies, the acidification calculated from the numbers and species of diatoms or chrysophytes in a sediment core.

inorganic aluminum (labile monomeric aluminum) See *aluminum.*

ion An atom or molecule that has gained or lost electrons and become electrically charged. Cations are positively charged, anions negatively charged. Except for gases and carbon compounds, most of the material that is dissolved in water is ionic.

ion diagnostics Various sums and ratios of the concentrations of ions that indicate the extent of acidification or distinguish between natural and human-caused acidification. Many diagnostics have been used by researchers; those of most importance here are:

HYDRAULIC RESIDENCE TIME

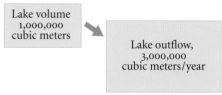

Estimated hydraulic residence time = (volume/outflow) years = 0.33 year = 4 months

If a lake discharges three times its volume of water every year, its hydraulic residence time is estimated to be one-third of a year, or four months.

PROCESSES GENERATING HYDROXYL IONS

1 Dissolution of carbonate minerals

$$CaCO_3 + H_2O \rightarrow Ca^{2+} + HCO_3^- + OH^-$$

2 Dissolution of strong bases

$$CaO + H_2O \rightarrow Ca^{2+} + 2\,OH^-$$

CRITICAL ACIDIFICATION LEVELS FOR SURFACE WATERS

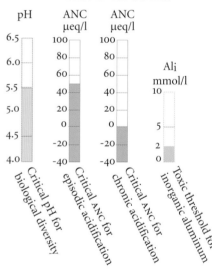

Threshold values from Cronan and Schofield, "Relationships between aqueous aluminum and acidic deposition in forested watersheds of North America and Northern Europe," 1990; Cronan and Grigal, "Use of calcium/aluminum ratios as indictors of stress in forest ecosystems," 1995; and Baker and Christensen, "Effects of acidification on biological communities in aquatic ecosystems," 1991.

The concentrations of *sulfate and nitrate ions*, which are typically low in undisturbed waters and elevated in waters that have received atmospheric acids.

The concentration of *monomeric aluminum*, also typically low in undisturbed waters, which when elevated suggests that a watershed is receiving atmospheric acids and that its base saturation is low.

The *cation-inorganic anion difference* (ion deficit), which when positive suggests that anions from organic acids are present.

The *base-acid difference*, $C_B - C_A$, used to explain fluctuations in the ANC.

The *acid-base ratio*, C_A/C_B, and the various *f-factors* like $\Delta C_B/\Delta SO_4^{2-}$, which indicate the fraction of mineral acid being neutralized in the watershed.

ion exchange The substitution of a free ion for an adsorbed (electrically bonded) one. Two common ion exchanger reactions of great importance in acid rain chemistry are the adsorption of sulfate (an anion exchange) and the leaching of base cations by hydrogen ions (a cation exchange).

ion exchange complex (the *exchanger*) The aggregate of charged surfaces in a soil on which ions are bound. The exchanger consists of a mixture of organic compounds and minerals; positive charges on it bind anions, and negative charges bind cations. The size of the exchanger is measured by the cation and anion exchange capacities, which are the number of charges per kilogram of soil.

isopleth diagram Any graph using contour lines to show values of a variable. In acid rain research, often a graph of the concentration of some ion in a lake or river, plotted with time on the x-axis and depth on the y-axis. (See page 146 for an example.)

isotope dating The dating of materials by the ratio of a radioactive isotope to its decay products. In acid deposition research the most useful isotope is lead-210, a decay product of uranium with a half-life of 23 years that gives accurate dates to about 200 years before present and is widely used to date the sediment cores used in paleolimnological reconstructions.

labile Changeable or reactive; often used for forms of elements that are easily assimilated or rapidly cycled.

lake classification A division of lakes into chemical and hydrological types. The original classification, developed by the Regionalized

ION DIAGNOSTICS IN AN
ACIDIFIED WATER

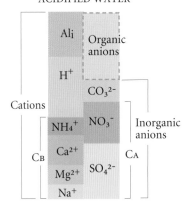

In this example, sulfate, nitrate, and inorganic aluminum are present in substantial quantities, indicating that the watershed is receiving significant amounts of atmospheric acids. The cation-inorganic anion difference is positive, indicating that organic acids are present. The base-acid difference $C_B - C_A$ is negative, indicating that the ANC is less than zero. And the acid-base ratio is fairly near 1, indicating that a significant portion of the atmospheric acid is being neutralized in the watershed.

CATION EXCHANGE REACTIONS

1 Adsorption of calcium

Ca^{2+} + H H → Ca + 2 H^+

2 Release (leaching) of calcium

2 H^+ + Ca → Ca^{2+} + H H

3 Release (leaching) of aluminum

3 H^+ + Al → Al^{3+} + H H H

ANION EXCHANGE REACTIONS

1 Adsorption of sulfate

SO_4^{2-} + OH OH → SO_4 + 2 OH^-

2 Desorption (leaching) of sulfate

2 OH^- + SO_4 → SO_4^{2-} + OH OH

▬ ion exchange complex

Integrated Lake-Watershed Acidification Study, required detailed information about watershed soils and hydrology. The revised classification used by the Adirondack Lakes Survey used lake chemistry as a proxy for soils and hydrology.

leaching The export of various ions in water draining from watershed soils, often driven by atmospheric acids. This is both the principal way that watersheds neutralize atmospheric acids and the principal cause of soil cation depletion. See the diagram of cation exchange on p. 31.

lead 210 See *isotope dating*.

maximum likelihood estimation In statistics, a means of fitting a mathematical model to a particular data set by calculating the probability of obtaining the observed data for a particular choice of the parameters of the model. The choice of parameters that gives the highest likelihood of obtaining the observed data is the maximum likelihood estimate of the parameters. Maximum likelihood estimation is widely used to fit complex models to large data sets.

litter Undecayed and partly decayed plant material on the surface of the ground.

long-term monitoring In acid rain research, the repeated sampling of air, precipitation, or water in order to detect trends.

Long-Term Monitoring Project (LTM) One of the two monitoring networks coordinated by the U.S. Environmental Protection Agency. The LTM consists of about 180 lakes and streams, monitored by several organizations, that are sampled yearly, monthly, or weekly. The Adirondack Long-Term Monitoring Program run by the Adirondack Lakes Survey Corporation is part of the LTM.

mass-balance study A study that measures the inputs to and outputs from a monitored watershed and, from these, determines which elements are being stored in the watershed and which released from it.

mercury (Hg) The 80th element, a trace metal that is toxic to animals in very small amounts. Mercury is rare in undisturbed watersheds but now widely distributed as a result of atmospheric deposition; it bioaccumulates in animal tissue and can reach tissue concentrations 1 million to 10 million times higher than the concentrations in the environment.

methylmercury (MeHg$^+$ or CH3Hg$^+$) A highly toxic organometallic compound produced by the microbial methylation of ionic mercury.

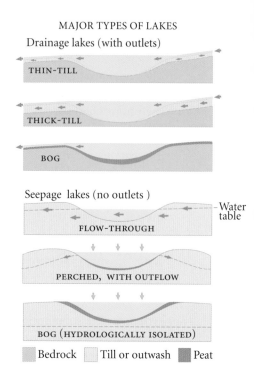

MAJOR TYPES OF LAKES

Drainage lakes (with outlets)

THIN-TILL

THICK-TILL

BOG

Seepage lakes (no outlets)

Water table

FLOW-THROUGH

PERCHED, WITH OUTFLOW

BOG (HYDROLOGICALLY ISOLATED)

Bedrock   Till or outwash   Peat

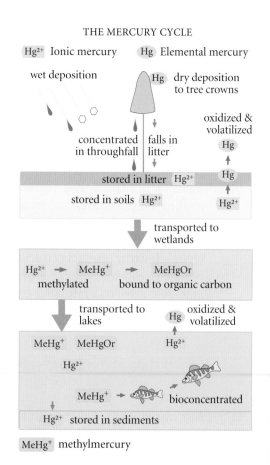

THE MERCURY CYCLE

Hg^{2+} Ionic mercury   Hg Elemental mercury

wet deposition   Hg dry deposition to tree crowns

oxidized & volatilized

concentrated in throughfall | falls in litter   Hg

stored in litter   Hg^{2+} Hg

stored in soils   Hg^{2+} Hg^{2+}

transported to wetlands

Hg^{2+} → MeHg$^+$ → MeHgOr
methylated   bound to organic carbon

transported to lakes   oxidized & volatilized Hg

MeHg$^+$ MeHgOr   Hg^{2+}

Hg^{2+}

MeHg$^+$ → bioconcentrated

Hg^{2+} stored in sediments

MeHg$^+$ methylmercury

It is easily assimilated by animals and is the principal form of mercury in animal tissue. It is produced most abundantly in wet, oxygen-poor, organic environments where sulfate reduction is occurring.

mineral acids Acids with inorganic anions. In the Adirondacks the only two mineral acids that occur in any abundance are nitric acid and sulfuric acid, both associated with acid rain.

mineralization The release of inorganic nutrients (N, S, Ca, etc.) during the microbial decay of organic matter.

mineral soil The middle and lower horizons of the soil, containing large amounts of sand, clay, and mineral grains and relatively small amounts of organic matter.

moles and equivalents Two standard chemical measures of quantity. A mole is the amount of a substance that contains the same number of atoms (6×10^{23}) as 1 gram of hydrogen. An equivalent is the amount of the substance that will react with 1 gram of hydrogen.

Because the atomic weight of hydrogen is 1, and because the amount of hydrogen that an ion will react to is proportional to its charge, for an ion of molecular weight M and charge c, 1 mole of ions equals M grams, and 1 equivalent of ions equals M/c grams.

monomeric aluminum See *aluminum*.

natural acid An acid generated from natural sources, as opposed to the man-made acids in acid rain. The most commonly occurring natural acids are organic acids. Small amounts of nitric acid are produced naturally by lightning and by decay that is not followed by regrowth.

neutralization The removal of hydrogen ions from a solution by ion exchange, assimilation, or reactions with bases.

nitrate (NO_3^-) The anion of nitric acid. Nitrates are relatively rare in undisturbed surface waters; elevated nitrate concentrations are one of the main diagnostic features that indicate nitrogen saturation and may result either from the deposition of more nitrogen than the vegetation can use or from the nitrification of excess ammonia during decay.

nitric acid (HNO_3) With sulfuric acid, one of the two major mineral acids supplied to ecosystems by acid deposition. Sulfuric and nitric acids are rare in undisturbed surface waters and are here called atmospheric acids or mineral acids to distinguish them from the natural organic acids.

THE MINERAL ACIDS

HNO_3 nitric acid

H_2SO_4 sulfuric acid

These are the main mineral acids in Adirondack waters. They come largely from acid deposition, and so are also called the atmospheric acids.

MOLES & EQUIVALENTS

	1 Mole (grams)	1 Eq. (grams)
H^+	1	1
S	32	16
SO_4^{2-}	96	48
N	14	14
NH_4^+	18	18
NO_3^-	62	62
Ca^{2+}	40	20

WATERSHED PROCESSES THAT NEUTRALIZE ACIDS

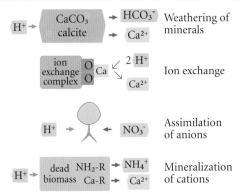

NH$_2$-R organic nitrogen compounds

Ca-R organic calcium compounds

nitrification, nitrification fraction The microbial oxidation of ammonium (NH_4^+) to nitrate (NO_3^-). Nitrification is an acidifying process that generates hydrogen ions. The nitrification fraction, a measure of the importance of nitrification, is the fraction of the ammonium produced by decay that is oxidized to nitrate rather than reassimilated by plants. It is generally low in undisturbed forests but rises when nitrate deposition is high and a forest is approaching nitrogen saturation.

nitrogen (N) The seventh element, abundant in the atmosphere in molecular form (N_2) and an essential component of all living cells in various reduced forms. Atmospheric nitrogen cannot be assimilated directly by plants or animals and must be converted to ammonium (NH_4^+) or nitrate (NO_3^-) ions before it is biologically available. This conversion is done naturally in small amounts by lightning and nitrogen-fixing bacteria and artificially in much larger amounts by boilers, internal combustion engines, and industrial processes.

nitrogen cycle The interconversion of various forms of nitrogen in ecosystems, involving deposition, fixation, assimilation, decay (mineralization), nitrification, denitrification, and export.

nitrogen-cycle acids Hydrogen ions produced during the nitrogen cycle when ammonium is either assimilated or oxidized (nitrified) to nitrate.

nitrogen fixation The conversion of atmospheric nitrogen (N_2) to ammonium (NH_4^+) by either free-living or symbiotic bacteria. Nitrogen fixation occurs in most habitats but is thought to be most important in wet soils and habitats where nitrogen-fixing plants (legumes, alders, sweet gale, etc.) occur.

nitrogen oxides Here, the gases nitric oxide (NO) and nitrogen dioxide (NO_2), collectively written NO_X, which are produced from atmospheric nitrogen during combustion and then converted to nitric acid (HNO_3) in the atmosphere.

nitrogen retention The percentage of the nitrogen deposited on a watershed that is retained in the forests and soils.

nitrogen saturation A decline in the ability of a forest or other ecosystem to retain nitrogen inputs from the atmosphere. Nitrogen saturation is marked by increased exports of nitrate, especially during the growing season; four saturation stages may be distinguished, based on the level and seasonal timing of nitrate exports (pp. 114–115).

nutrient cycle The cycling of a nutrient element between various compartments in an ecosystem, always involving inputs, assimila-

NITROGEN CYCLING

REACTIONS OF THE NITROGEN CYCLE

1 Fixation

$$N_2 + H_2O + 2\ R\text{-}OH \rightarrow 2\ R\text{-}NH_2 + 1.5\ O_2$$

2 Assimilation

$$NH_4^+ + R\text{-}OH \rightarrow R\text{-}NH_2 + H_2O + H^+$$

$$NO_3^- + R\text{-}OH + H^+ \rightarrow R\text{-}NH_2 + 2\ O_2$$

3 Mineralization

$$R\text{-}NH_2 + H_2O + H^+ \rightarrow NH_4^+ + R\text{-}OH$$

4 Nitrification

$$NH_4^+ + 2\ O_2 \rightarrow NO_3^- + 2\ H^+ + H_2O$$

5 Denitrification

$$NO_3^- + 1.25\ CH_2O + H^+ \rightarrow$$
$$0.5\ N_2 + 1.75\ H_2O + 1.25\ CO_2$$

N_2 Nitrogen gas NO_3^- Nitrate O_2 Oxygen gas

NH_4^+ Ammonium R-OH Biological hydroxyls

$R\text{-}NH_2$ Biological nitrogen compounds

CO_2 Carbon dioxide gas CH_2O Formaldehyde

tion, decay, and exports and often involving oxidations and reductions as well.

paleolimnology The reconstruction of the chemical and biological history of a lake by examination of sediment cores. A paleolimnological study usually involves some combination of isotope dating, chemical analysis, and counts of macrofossils like seeds and leaves or microfossils like diatoms and chrysophytes.

perched seepage lake A seepage lake surrounded by peat deposits that is raised above and largely isolated from the groundwater in its watershed.

pH The concentration of hydrogen ions, measured on a logarithmic scale: $pH = -\log(H^+)$. Note that because of the logarithmic scale, the further you are from neutrality, the more acid it takes to create the same pH change. It takes, for example, 0.9 μeq of strong acid to drop the pH of a liter of water from pH 7 to pH 6. But it takes 9 μeq of strong acid to drop the pH another unit from 6 to 5, and another 90 μeq to drop the pH another unit to pH 4.

As a result, the biological significance of a pH change depends greatly on where the change starts from. A change of, say, half a pH unit from pH 6.5 to pH 6.0 may be a relatively minor biological change. A change of half a pH unit from 5.5 to 5.0 may be a much larger change.

polycyclic aromatic hydrocarbons Combustion products containing two or more benzene rings that are emitted when fossil fuels are burned. They can be detected in lake cores and are useful paleolimnological markers for dating the onset of acid deposition.

polymeric aluminum See *aluminum*.

organic acids Any organic compound containing a carboxyl (-COOH) group and so able to ionize to produce a hydrogen ion (H^+) and an organic anion ($RCOO^-$, abbreviated OA^-).

Organic acids are the major source of natural acidity in northeastern watersheds. They are produced by the decay of organic matter in both forests and wetlands. They are chemically diverse and may be either strong or weak acids.

organic aluminum See *aluminum*.

oxidation and reduction Chemical reactions, collectively called redox reactions and often biologically mediated, which add (reduction) or remove (oxidation) electrons from atoms. Much biological

THE pH SCALE

pH	H+ μeq/l	
9.0	0.001	Highest pH measured in Woods Lake after liming
8.0	0.01	Highest natural lake pH recorded by ALS
7.0	0.1	Neutrality
	—	Zooplankton diversity begins to decline
	—	Mean pH of ALS drainage lakes
	—	Critical pH of blacknose dace
6.0	1.0	Critical pH for sensitive mayflies
	—	Pure water in equilibrium with CO_2
	—	Mean pH of ALS seepage lakes; critical pH of brook trout
5.0	10	Critical pH of yellow perch
	—	Average pH of deposition, Huntington Forest, 2002
	—	Average pH of deposition, Huntington Forest, 1980
4.0	100	
	—	Lowest pH recorded by ALS
3.0	1000	

Currently, Adirondack lakes have pHs between 3.5 and 8.0, with most of them between 4.0 and 7.0 (p. 81). Lakes with pHs above 6.0 are relatively diverse and contain all major groups of aquatic animals and plants. Lakes with pHs below 6.0 are less diverse, and those with pHs below 5.0 lack many groups altogether. Prior to acid deposition, the lowest pHs in drainage lakes were probably about 5.0, and the lowest pHs in seepage lakes about 4.5 (p. 86).

synthesis involves reduction, and much biological decay involves oxidation. Thus many element cycles involve redox reactions. Photosynthesis, nitrogen fixation, and sulfate assimilation involve reductions; respiration, nitrification, and the mineralization of organic sulfides involve oxidations.

All redox reactions involve an electron donor and an electron acceptor. Oxygen is the commonest electron acceptor, and oxidation takes place most easily in oxygen-rich environments like dry soils and aerated waters. Iron, sulfur, and decaying organic matter are common electron donors, and reduction occurs most easily in wet soils and anoxic waters where they are abundant and oxygen scarce.

Because many redox reactions transfer electrons to and from hydrogen, many generate or consume hydrogen ions. The assimilation of nitrate and sulfate, both reductions, consume hydrogen ions and so are deacidifying. The regeneration of sulfate and nitrate during decay, both oxidations, generate hydrogen ions and so are acidifying.

recovery Here, increases in the pHs and ANCs of surface waters that are associated with decreases in acid emissions and acid deposition.

reduction See *oxidation and reduction.*

release In mass-balance studies, a budget in which the output of an element from some compartment exceeds the inputs.

retention In mass-balance studies, a budget in which the input of an element to some compartment exceeds the output, indicating that the element is being stored in the compartment. The percentage retained is the fraction missing from the output, $100 \times (1 - output/input)$.

saturation stage See *nitrogen saturation.*

seepage lake A lake with no surface outlet. Seepage lakes typically have small watersheds and are often isolated from the local water table by peat deposits. They receive much of their water from precipitation and so are often susceptible to acidification. In the Adirondacks they are commonly small and acid and often associated with glacial outwash deposits.

snowmelt acidity Acidity in surface waters during spring thaws, including both atmospheric acids stored in the snowpack and nitrogen-cycle acids that have accumulated in the forest floor over the winter.

stemflow Precipitation that flows down the trunks of trees. Stemflow contains acids and mercury deposited in the tree crowns by dry depo-

BIOLOGICAL REDUCTIONS

1 Photosynthesis (reduction of organic carbon)

$$CO_2 + H_2O \rightarrow CH_2O + O_2$$

$$CO_2 + 2 H_2S \rightarrow CH_2O + 2 S + H_2O$$

2 Nitrogen fixation (reduction of nitrogen gas)

$$N_2 + H_2O + 2 R\text{-}OH \rightarrow 2 R\text{-}NH_2 + 1.5 O_2$$

3 Assimilation of nitrate & sulfate

$$NO_3^- + R\text{-}OH + H^+ \rightarrow R\text{-}NH_2 + 2 O_2$$

$$SO_4^{2-} + R\text{-}OH + 2 H^+ \rightarrow R\text{-}SH + 2 O_2 + H_2O$$

BIOLOGICAL OXIDATIONS

1 Aerobic respiration (oxidation of organic carbon)

$$CH_2O + O_2 \rightarrow CO_2 + H_2O$$

2 Anaerobic respiration by reduction of nitrate

$$NO_3^- + 1.25 CH_2O + H^+ \rightarrow$$
$$0.5 N_2 + 1.75 H_2O + 1.25 CO_2$$

3 Anaerobic respiration by reduction of sulfate

$$SO_4^{2-} + 2 H^+ + 2 CH_2O$$
$$\rightarrow 2 CO_2 + H_2S + 2 H_2O$$

4 Mineralization of organic sulfur

$$R\text{-}SH + 2 O_2 + H_2O \rightarrow SO_4^{2-} + R\text{-}OH + 2 H$$

5 Nitrification (oxidation of ammonium)

$$NH_4^+ + 2 O_2 \rightarrow NO_3^- + 2 H^+ + H_2O$$

6 Oxidation of inorganic sulfur

$$S + H_2O + 1.5 O_2 \rightarrow SO_4^{2-} + 2 H^+$$

$R\text{-}NH_2$ Organic nitrogen compounds

$R\text{-}OH$ CH_2O Organic carbon compounds

Three important biological reductions, all requiring energy and synthesizing organic compounds, and six biological oxidations, all yielding energy and all but the last two decomposing organic compounds. Note that because each reaction involves the oxidation of an electron donor and the reduction of an electron acceptor, the division into oxidations and reductions is arbitrary: photosynthesis is both the reduction of carbon and the oxidation of oxygen; nitrification is the oxidation of nitrogen and the reduction of oxygen.

sition and is typically more concentrated than precipitation that falls in the open.

storage (*retention*) In mass-balance studies, the accumulation of an element in a compartment, equal to the amount entering the compartment minus the amount released from it.

sulfate (SO_4^{2-}) The anion of sulfuric acid, usually found in low concentrations in undisturbed surface waters and so used to identify waters affected by atmospheric deposition.

sulfate adsorption A form of anion exchange in which sulfate ions are bound to the ion exchange complex and hydroxyl ions are released. Along with sulfate reduction, it is one of the two major ways that inorganic sulfur from acid deposition is stored in watersheds.

sulfate reduction The microbial reduction of sulfate to hydrogen sulfide (H_2S) and other sulfides by anaerobic bacteria that decompose organic matter and use sulfate instead of oxygen as an electron acceptor (see *oxidation and reduction*). Sulfate reduction consumes hydrogen ions and deacidifies waters. It is common in wetlands and lake sediments and, like sulfate adsorption, is one of the major ways that the sulfur from acid rain is stored in watersheds. Sulfate-reducing bacteria can also methylate mercury, and wetlands where sulfates are being reduced often generate methylmercury as well.

sulfide oxidation The microbial oxidation of hydrogen sulfide (H_2S) and other sulfides to sulfate (SO_4^{2-}), reversing the storage of sulfur accomplished by the sulfate-reducing bacteria and regenerating the hydrogen ions that were consumed when the sulfate was reduced. Sulfide oxidation is done by two ancient groups of bacteria: the purple sulfur bacteria that use H_2S as an electron donor in photosynthesis, and the chemoautotrophic sulfur bacteria that obtain the energy to fix carbon from chemical oxidations rather than from light.

sulfur (S) The 16th element, a relative scarce component of minerals and undisturbed waters and a major constituent of acid deposition. Sulfur is a necessary nutrient that is cycled biologically in small quantities and typically stored in organic forms. The inputs from acid deposition are much greater than the natural inputs and greatly alter the rates at which sulfur is stored and cycled.

sulfur cycle The interconversion of various forms of sulfur in ecosystems, involving deposition, assimilation, decay (mineralization), adsorption and desorption, oxidation and reduction, and export (diagram on page 38).

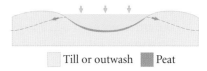

A PERCHED SEEPAGE LAKE

☐ Till or outwash ■ Peat

SULFATE ADSORPTION

1 Sulfate adsorption

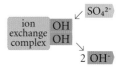

2 Sulfate desorption

REACTIONS IN THE SULFUR CYCLE

1 Microbial reduction of sulfate

$$SO_4^{2-} + 2\ H^+ + 2\ CH_2O$$
$$\rightarrow 2\ CO_2 + H_2S + 2\ H_2O$$

This is an anaerobic decay reaction in which organic matter (CH_2O) is oxidized and sulfur is reduced. Sulfate functions as an electron acceptor, much as oxygen does under aerobic conditions. Similar reactions produce elemental sulfur and dimethyl sulfide.

2 Microbial oxidation of sulfur

$$2\ H_2S + CO_2 \rightarrow CH_2O + 2\ S + H_2O$$

$$S + H_2O + 1.5\ O_2 \rightarrow SO_4^{2-} + 2\ H^+$$

The first reaction, carried out by purple sulfur bacteria, is an ancient form of photosynthesis in which hydrogen sulfide is used as an electron donor. The second is an energy-yielding reaction carried out by chemoautotrophic bacteria, which use the hydrogen ions to fix carbon.

sulfur dioxide (SO₂) A gaseous form of sulfur that is produced by the combustion of fossil fuels and converted to sulfuric acid (H_2SO_4) in the atmosphere. It can also be adsorbed directly by vegetation and so is an important component of dry deposition.

sulfuric acid (H_2SO_4) With nitric acid, one of the two major acids supplied to ecosystems by acid deposition. Elevated concentrations of sulfuric and nitric acids are characteristic of waters affected by atmospheric deposition and are here called atmospheric acids or mineral acids to distinguish them from the natural organic acids.

surface waters Natural fresh waters open to the air; lakes and streams, as distinguished from groundwater and seawater.

synoptic survey A regional survey that compares the chemistries of many lakes in a short period of time.

thick-till lake A drainage lake whose watershed has soils of glacial till that are several meters or more deep. Such soils tend to have large amounts of base cations in the lower mineral soil layers and so are able to neutralize acids moving through them. Deep-till lakes are typically fed, at least in part, by groundwater that moves through the lower parts of the soil profile and so are less acid than shallow-till lakes, where the flowpaths lie at or near the surface.

thin-till lake A lake whose watershed has shallow and often rocky soils averaging less than 3 meters deep. In such soils the *flowpaths* lie near the surface and there is little opportunity for acids to be neutralized by mineral soil. Thin-till lakes are easily acidified and often contain mineral acids.

throughfall Precipitation that falls through the crowns of trees. Like stemflow, it contains acids from dry deposition and is usually more concentrated than precipitation falling in the open.

Temporally Integrated Monitoring of Ecosystems (TIME) A long-term monitoring program, part of the Environmental Protection Agency's Ecological Monitoring and Assessment Program, that takes annual samples from statistically selected groups of lakes.

turnover time The average length of time an element remains in a compartment of an ecosystem. Elements that cycle quickly have short turnover times; those that cycle slowly have long ones.

yellow perch (*Perca flavescens*) A common northern fish, widely caught and eaten by fishermen and, because of its wide distribution, often used in studies of the bioconcentration of mercury.

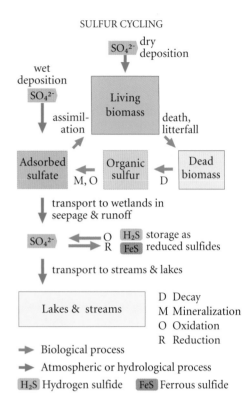

SULFUR CYCLING

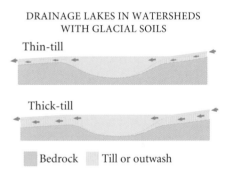

DRAINAGE LAKES IN WATERSHEDS WITH GLACIAL SOILS

WATER FLOWS THROUGH FOREST CANOPIES

variance In statistics, a measure of how much individual measurements differ, on average, from their mean value.

volatilization The conversion of a substance to a gas, often followed by its loss to the atmosphere. Nitrates, sulfates, and ionic mercury may all be reduced to volatile forms.

weak acid An acid like acetic acid (CH_2COOH) or carbonic acid (H_2CO_3) that dissociates partially in water and so generates fewer hydrogen ions and influences the pH less than a strong acid. Many of the weak acids are important buffers.

watershed processes The various biogeochemical processes that change the chemistry of water as it passes through the watershed.

weathering The chemical and physical decomposition of rocks, producing the clay minerals that are the commonest constituent of mineral soil and freeing base cations, sulfur, and phosphorus.

wet deposition The deposition of liquids and ice, as opposed to the dry deposition of gases and particles. Wet deposition includes rain, snow, sleet, and hail. It may also include the deposition of cloudwater, or this may be treated separately as occult deposition.

NOTES

The definitions in this chapter generally follow the Adirondack literature, but the reader should be aware that usage is not uniform. *Ion exchange* and *adsorption* are used almost interchangeably, as are *decay* and *mineralization*, *retention* and *storage*, and *labile* and *inorganic* aluminum. The acids in acid deposition are variously called *atmospheric, anthropogenic, artificial,* and *mineral;* the biologically generated acids in undisturbed waters are variously called *natural* or *organic.* And finally, the adjectives *acid* and *acidified* are used in many ways, different especially in regulatory contexts.

General references for this chapter and the sources of many of the equations in the diagrams are Stumm and Morgan, *Aquatic Chemistry,* 1966; and Schlesinger, *Biogeochemistry,* 1991.

p. 30 For further discussion of the indices of acidification, see Aber et al., "Is nitrogen deposition altering the nitrogen status of Northeastern forests?," 2003; Driscoll et al., "Effect of aluminum speciation on fish in dilute acidified waters," 1980; Driscoll, Yatsko, and Unangst, "Longitudinal and temporal trends in the water chemistry of the North Branch of the Moose River," 1987; Van Sikle et al., "Episodic acidification of small streams in the northeastern United States: Fish mortality in field bioassays," 1996.

WATERSHED PROCESSES THAT AFFECT ACIDITY

1 Processes that neutralize acids

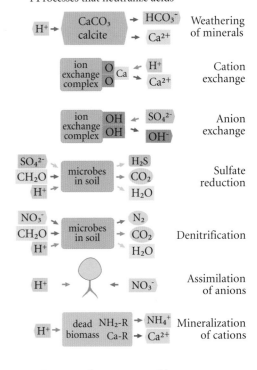

2 Processes that generate acids

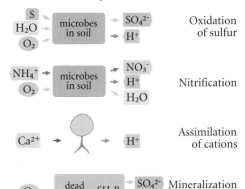

Ca-R   Organic calcium compounds
NH₂-R Organic nitrogen compounds
SH-R   Organic sulfur compounds

1926-1939 Biological surveys by the New York State Conservation Commission determine the pH and acid-neutralizing capacity of hundreds of lakes and rivers.

1976 Schofield surveys 214 Adirondack lakes for the New York State Department of Environmental Conservation (DEC), and reports that half of the lakes above 2,000 feet in elevation are acidic and many of these have no fish.

1978 The New York State Department of Health samples the chemistry of 57 remote lakes.

1978 Researchers at Huntington Forest begin the weekly monitoring of wet deposition.

1977-1981 The Electric Power Research Institute funds the Integrated Lake-Watershed Acidification Study (ILWAS), which examines the flowpaths of the water entering Panther, Sagamore, and Woods lakes to determine why lakes receiving the same amount of acid rain can have very different pHs.

1979 Cronan and Schofield review work from Norway, Sweden, Germany, England, Canada, and the United States and show that acid deposition leaches aluminum from forest soil.

1979 Colquhoun and his colleagues at the DEC discover that fishless Adirondack streams tend to have high levels of snowmelt acidity.

1980 Driscoll et al. show that Adirondack waters with elevated levels of inorganic aluminum are toxic to fish. Johannes, Galloway, and Troutman discover that snowmelt acidity is dominated by nitric acid rather than sulfuric acid.

1981 Whitehead and Charles begin to reconstruct the postglacial history of several high-elevation Adirondack ponds from sediment cores.

1982-1984 The Regionalized Integrated Lake-Watershed Acidification Study (RILWAS), designed to investigate the relations between geology, stream chemistry, and fish populations, takes monthly samples from 20 Adirondack lakes for two years, focusing on the North Branch of the Moose River and its tributaries. This is the first monthly sampling done in the Adirondacks.

1983-86 The Paleoecological Investigation of Recent Lake Acidification (PIRLA) project begins to reconstruct the chemical histories of 15 Adirondack lakes from microfossils and chemical indicators in sediment cores.

1984-1986 The first phase of the EPA's Eastern Lake Survey samples 1560 lakes in the eastern United States, including 185 in the Adirondacks. The Adirondack lakes are chosen statistically and are thought to be representative of a larger population of about 1,100 lakes.

1984 The Direct Delayed Response Project, a modeling study, attempts to predict the changes in chemistry of 37 low- or moderate-ANC Adirondack lakes selected from the ELS lakes. It is the first study to examine the sulfate balances of Adirondack watersheds.

1984-1987 The Adirondack Lakes Survey Corporation (ALSC), a cooperative project of the New York Electric Energy Research Corporation and the DEC, does chemical and biological surveys of 1,469 Adirondack lakes. The ALSC also takes over the monitoring of the RILWAS lakes, creating the Adirondack Long-Term Monitoring Program.

1985 Driscoll and Newton publish the first hydrological and chemical classification of Adirondack lakes.

1986 The second phase of the Eastern Lake Survey resamples 43 Adirondack lakes, taking samples in three seasons and doing more detailed studies of aluminum chemistry.

1987 Charles et al. publish a reconstruction of the chemical history of Big Moose Lake, showing that it had acidified about 0.9 pH units since 1950.

1989 Asbury et al. compare the contemporary and historical ANCs of 274 Adirondack lakes and find that most of the lakes have decreased in ANC.

1990 Davis et al. publish reconstructions of the chemical histories of Woods, Sagamore, and Panther Lakes showing that all three lakes have acidified by 0.5 pH unit or more in the previous 40 years.

ADIRONDACK RESEARCH BEGINS

THE ACID RAIN STORY EMERGES AND ACQUIRES CHEMICAL,
HYDROLOGICAL, AND HISTORICAL DETAIL

3

The Rediscovery of Acid Rain, 1950–1979

By 1970, scientists had known for a 120 years that the burning of coal produced sulfuric acid and for almost 70 that the sulfuric acid in acid rain could harm plants and acidify soils. But the monitoring of precipitation and stream chemistry had barely begun, and it had only been recently discovered that sulfuric and nitric acids were widespread in rural and wilderness lakes.

Thus, although in the early 1970s the general features of acid rain were more or less known to science, the existence of acid rain in America was known to few American scientists. Charles Cogbill, who wrote three papers on the history and geography of acid rain between 1974 and 1976, remembers that he first heard acid rain mentioned in a laboratory at Cornell University in 1970. The first edition of Stumm and Morgan's magisterial *Aquatic Chemistry*, which appeared in 1970 and became the technical bible of water chemistry researchers, contains detailed discussions of water pollution and eutrophication but no mention of lake acidification or acid rain.

In the next ten years this changed rapidly. Gene Likens and his collaborators at the Hubbard Brook Experimental Forest showed that atmospheric acids were ecologically significant and that acid deposition was at least a regional if not a national problem. Charles Cogbill reexamined synoptic data sets of precipitation chemistry from the 1950s and 1960s and found that acid deposition was already widespread. Researchers examining fishless lakes found that atmospheric acids were mobilizing aluminum ions; other researchers showed that dissolved aluminum was highly toxic to fish.

In the Adirondacks, which because of their high elevations, high rainfall, and igneous bedrock are very sensitive to acid deposition, research on the effects of acid deposition began early. In the middle 1970s Carl Schofield compared fish populations and water chemistry and found that many high-elevation lakes were acidic and that most of the highly acidic lakes were fishless. Martin Pfeiffer and Patrick Festa of the New York State DEC immediately extended Schofield's survey, finding acidic lakes at all elevations and in many parts of the state besides the Adirondacks. Another group of DEC researchers, led by Jim Colquhoun, found while doing a study on blackfly control that many streams can become highly acid during snowmelt or after rains and that the streams that were most acid in

FISHERIES IN HIGH-ELEVATION ADIRONDACK
LAKES, 1975

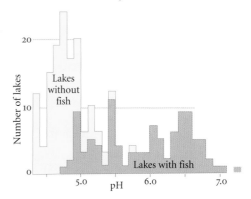

Redrawn with permission from Schofield, "Acid precipitation: Effects on fish." Copyright 1976 Royal Swedish Academy of Sciences. Schofield examined 217 lakes with elevations above 610 m. He found that 51% of the lakes had pHs below 5.0, and 90% of the lakes with pHs below 5.0 were fishless. In the next four years, fisheries scientists at the New York State Department of Environmental Conservation surveyed a total of 849 Adirondack lakes and found that 25% had pHs below 5.0.

DENSITY OF FISH IN ADIRONDACK STREAMS

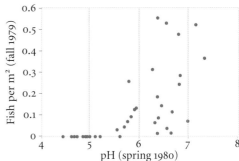

From Colquhoun et al., *Preliminary Report of Stream Sampling for Acidification Studies – 1980, 1981*. This was the first Adirondack research to associate fish densities with springtime pHs. The densities are for all species of fish. Streams with springtime pHs below 5.5, the level at which inorganic aluminum begins to increase, had no fish at all.

spring had the lowest fish populations in summer. Anticipating a connection that is still only partly explored, the authors noted that "Common sense would suggest that every acidified lake would drain into an acidified stream system and be affected by some acidified stream tributaries."

Also in the Adirondacks, Charles Driscoll and his collaborators looked more closely at the toxicology of the different forms of dissolved aluminum and found that what was variously called inorganic aluminum or labile monomeric aluminum (aluminum that is neither polymerized nor bound to organic radicals) was the most toxic form.

Those results and others like them demonstrated that acid rain was an international problem and a biological threat. The scientific and political reaction was surprisingly fast. The first international conference on acid rain was held in 1975; the first federal acid rain monitoring network was created in 1976; the Electric Power Research Institute began funding acid rain research in 1977; and the U.S. Acid Precipitation Act of 1980 created the National Acid Precipitation Assessment Program, which in the next ten years funded an extensive program of acid rain research.

By the end of the 1970s a picture of acid rain had emerged that, though simpler than our present picture, remains true in all its important details. Sulfuric acid and nitric acid are the important atmospheric acids. Sulfuric acid comes mostly from power plants that burn fossil fuels. Nitric acid is generated from both power plants and the engines and exhaust systems in vehicles. Both acids can travel long distances from their sources. When they are deposited, they acidify some but not all soils and lakes, mobilizing base cations and aluminum in the process. The acids and aluminum ions in acidified lakes kill fish and other aquatic animals and plants. Lakes acidified by acid deposition have a characteristic chemical signature, with relatively high amounts of nitrate, sulfate, and inorganic aluminum. Naturally acidic lakes have a different signature, with lower amounts of nitrate, sulfate, and inorganic aluminum and higher amounts of organic acids.

New Research Programs, 1978–1989

By 1980, it was widely believed by the scientific community that acid rain was damaging lakes and rivers and should be regulated. But there was no such consensus outside the scientific community and, even within the scientific community, no accurate way of assessing the damage from acid rain or predicting what sort of regulation would be effective. It would be another ten years before good damage assessments and predictive tools were available and five years more before new regulations requiring significant reductions of atmospheric acids took effect.

BASE CONTENT OF ADIRONDACK BEDROCK

	Zero to low		Low to medium
	Medium to high		Very high

Reprinted with permission from Jenkins, *The Adirondack Atlas,* copyright 2004 Wildlife Conservation Society. Based on a digital map of bedrock neutralizing capacity prepared by the Adirondack Lakes Survey. A watershed's ability to neutralize acid deposition depends on the chemistry of the bedrock and the depth of the soil above it. In the western Adirondacks, where acidification is worst, soils are typically very thin and the bedrock below them usually very low in bases. As a result, western Adirondack watersheds often have a very limited ability to neutralize atmospheric acids.

ACID IONS IN THE SNOWPACK AT SAGAMORE LAKE, 1979

Storage of atmospheric acids in the snowpack near Sagamore Lake. Redrawn with permission from Johannes, Galloway, and Troutman, "Snowpack storage and ion release." Copyright 1981 Electric Power Research Institute. This was the first Adirondack study to observe that snowmelt acidity is dominated by nitrate rather than sulfate. Subsequent studies (pp. 106–109) would establish that this was the result of nitrification (the conversion of ammonium to nitrate), which is an acidity-producing step in the nitrogen cycle and one of the diagnostic indicators of nitrogen saturation.

On the scientific side, much of the 1980s was spent in investigating lake acidification. The goals were to measure the amount of acidification, to determine how much of this acidification was caused by acid rain, and to estimate the reductions in acid emissions that would be required to correct it.

None of this was easy. Adirondack lakes vary enormously in size, hydrology, and chemistry. They can be very large or very small, strongly connected to their watersheds or almost unconnected, and naturally acid, basic, or neutral. As a result, there was no way to generalize about the effects of acid deposition. The same amount of deposition might acidify one lake strongly, acidify another weakly, and leave a third unchanged.

The variability in lakes complicated acid rain research greatly because it made it hard to show that the acidity observed in lakes was a direct result of acid deposition, and thus hard to argue that decreases in deposition would decrease the acidity of lakes.

To cope with the variability in lakes, it was necessary to treat them as a *population* of different types of lakes with different susceptibilities to acidification. This would require counting and classifying the lakes and developing a theory that explained why the different types responded differently to deposition.

To count the lakes and build the theory took both larger and more detailed studies than had yet been done. The larger studies – called synoptic studies – were intended to determine, either by direct counting or by extrapolation from a statistically selected set of sample lakes, how many lakes of a given type in a given region were acid. The detailed studies – many of which were lake-watershed studies – were intended to determine when the lakes had first acidified and how the chemistry and geology of their watersheds had influenced the rate of acidification.

The combination of the two types of studies proved scientifically powerful, and by 1990 a now classic series of synoptic studies, described in Chapter 4, was able to document, in convincing detail, both the mechanisms and the geography of acidification.

The first Adirondack watershed study, the Integrated Lake-Watershed Acidification Study (ILWAS), began in 1978 and examined the geology, hydrology and chemistry of Panther, Sagamore, and Woods lakes. Its goal was to determine why adjacent lakes receiving the same amount of acid rain could have very different pHs.

Other Adirondack studies came very rapidly. In 1981 a group of paleolimnologists, led by Whitehead and Charles, began to reconstruct the postglacial history of three small lakes in the High Peaks. By 1983 their work developed into the Paleoecological Investigation of Recent Lake Acidification(PIRLA) project which eventually examined 89 lakes in the Adirondacks and a similar number in other acidified areas.

ACID EPISODES IN CANACHAGALA
CREEK, 1977-1978

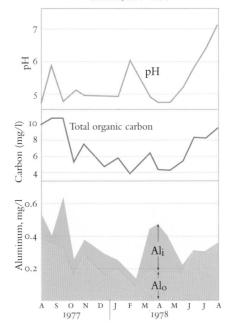

SURVIVAL OF FISH IN ACIDIFIED WATERS

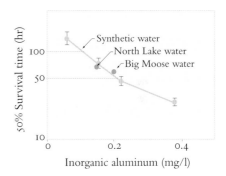

Both graphs from Driscoll et al., "Effect of aluminum speciation on fish in dilute acidified waters." Copyright 1980 Nature Publishing Group via the Copyright Clearance Center. Al_i is inorganic aluminum, Al_o organic aluminum. The researchers tested the survival of young fish in both natural lake water and synthetic lake water with different aluminum concentrations. This was the first Adirondack study to show that inorganic aluminum was elevated during acid episodes and that waters with elevated concentrations of inorganic aluminum were toxic to fish.

In 1982, the Integrated Lake-Watershed Acidification Study was expanded into a Regionalized Integrated Lake-Watershed Acidification Study (RILWAS). Like the ILWAS, the RILWAS examined the relation between watershed geology, stream and lake chemistry, and fish populations. It collected monthly samples from 20 Adirondack lakes, many of them in the watershed of the North Branch of the Moose River. It was the first Adirondack study to examine the seasonal pattern of acidity changes and the first to look for watershed-scale patterns in lake acidity.

In 1984 the Empire State Electric Energy Research Corporation and the New York State Department of Environmental Conservation created the Adirondack Lakes Survey Corporation (ALSC) to evaluate lake acidification in the Adirondack Park. In the next four years the ALSC examined 1,469 Adirondack lakes. The ALSC also took over the Adirondack Long-Term Monitoring (ALTM) program, which had continued the monthly sampling of 17 of the RILWAS lakes. The ALTM has since been enlarged to 52 lakes and three streams and is the major source of detailed trend data in the park today.

Also in 1984, the U.S. Environmental Protection Agency began the Eastern Lake Survey (ELS), which sampled about 185 lakes in the Adirondacks and a total of 1,560 lakes in New York and New England. In 1986 it was followed by a second study, the ELS-II, which resampled a subset of the lakes for a more detailed survey of aluminum chemistry and episodic acidification.

The ILWAS, RILWAS, and first phase of the PIRLA project were intensive and remarkably fruitful studies of small groups of lakes. They provided the lake classification that we now use, many of our basic concepts about watershed chemistry and hydrology, and our first estimates of how much lakes had acidified and how fast the acidification had happened.

The Adirondack Lakes Survey, Eastern Lake Survey, and the expanded PIRLA project were larger, synoptic programs that applied these concepts to large numbers of lakes to determine the extent of lake acidification. We discuss them in Chapter 4.

THE LAKE-WATERSHED STUDIES

The purpose of the lake-watershed studies was to find out why lakes had different sensitivities to acid. The answer, the researchers quickly found, lay not in the lakes themselves but in the soils around them.

This was not unexpected. The first DEC surveys of lake acidification had already shown that the most acidic lakes were in the southwestern Adirondacks, where acid deposition was the highest and the soils were least able to neutralize atmospheric acids. But even in areas where deposition was high and the soils generally

poor, there were some lakes with high ANCs and pHs near neutral. Clearly, the amount of deposition by itself was not enough to explain why some lakes acidified and some didn't.

The key to the differences between lakes turned out to be the relationship between the average soil depth and the flowpaths by which water moved through the soil. When the flowpaths were shallow, the lakes they led to were easily acidified. When they were deeper, the lakes were relatively insensitive to acidification.

The importance of flowpaths first emerged in a comparison of three lakes undertaken in the ILWAS. It was expanded and confirmed at the watershed scale in the RILWAS and then applied at the regional scale in the Eastern Lake Survey and Adirondack Lakes Survey.

The picture of lake-watershed hydrology that developed from these studies had three interrelated elements. The first was the connection between flowpaths and lake sensitivity just noted. The second was the realization that flowpaths could be used to group lakes into natural hydrological types, which differed in the extent to which the lake was influenced by groundwater. And the third was that each of the main hydrological types of lake had a fairly characteristic chemical signature, which could be used to determine which hydrological type it belonged to.

The ILWAS Model: Flowpaths Matter

Our current understanding of how acid deposition is modified within the soil was developed by the Integrated Lake-Watershed Acidification Study. The ILWAS was a multidisciplinary and multi-institutional study, involving at least 17 investigators from seven universities, two private companies, the U.S. Geological Survey, and Oak Ridge National Laboratory. It focused on three lakes, Panther, Woods, and Sagamore, in the southwestern Adirondacks.

The three ILWAS lakes were similar in size and elevation and received similar amounts of acid deposition. In spite of this they differed in chemistry: Woods Lake was very acid, Sagamore slightly acid, and Panther neutral to slightly alkaline.

To try to account for the differences, the investigators made a detailed hydrological analysis of the watersheds of Woods Lake and Panther Lake (p. 46). They mapped the depth, permeability, and composition of the soils and estimated how much of the flow received by each lake moved near the surface and how much through the lower soil.

The results showed clear differences. Woods, the most acidic lake, had shallow and relatively impermeable soils and received much of its water from the acid surface layers of the soil. Panther, the less acidic lake, had deeper soils and better conductivity. Its hydrology suggested that most of its flow, except during snowmelt,

THE ELS LAKES

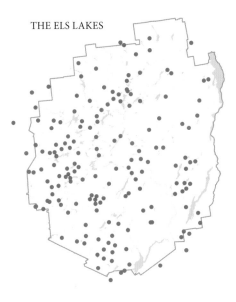

A FOREST SOIL

Litter: undecayed plant material

Organic layer: roots, organic matter, microbes, some inorganic material; acid but nutrient rich

Leached inorganic layer: weathered mineral soil from which the base cations have been removed by acids percolating down from the layer above; acid and nutrient-poor

Unleached inorganic layer: unweathered mineral soil, relatively rich in base cations; neutral or much less acid than the layers above

The forest soils studied in the lake-watershed studies had two to four layers, depending on the depth of the soil and whether mineral layers were present. There was always a litter layer a few centimeters deep, and below it an organic layer, derived from decayed litter, anywhere from 5 to 30 cm deep. If in addition there was mineral soil below the organic layer, the upper part of the mineral soil was usually a leached layer anywhere from 10 cm to a meter thick, and the layer below it an unleached layer extending down to bedrock.

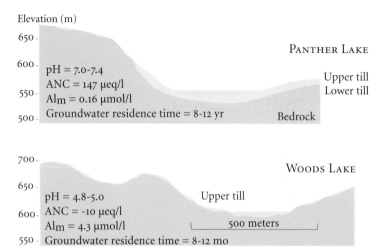

Elevation (m)

PANTHER LAKE

pH = 7.0-7.4
ANC = 147 μeq/l
Al$_m$ = 0.16 μmol/l
Groundwater residence time = 8-12 yr

Upper till
Lower till

Bedrock

WOODS LAKE

pH = 4.8-5.0
ANC = -10 μeq/l
Al$_m$ = 4.3 μmol/l
Groundwater residence time = 8-12 mo

Upper till

500 meters

Profiles of the watersheds of Panther and Woods lakes, two of the three lakes studied in the Integrated Lake-Watershed Study. From Chen et al., "Hydrologic analyses of acidic and alkaline lakes." Copyright 1984 American Geophysical Union. The vertical relief is exaggerated about two times. Panther Lake is in a basin with deep till and much of its base flow (the water entering it between rainstorms) is derived from deep, base-rich deposits of glacial till. Woods Lake has only shallow till interrupted by bedrock outcrops, and much of the water entering it moves through the acid soils near the surface. Chemistry from Davis et al., "Two-hundred-year pH history of Woods, Sagamore, and Panther lakes in the Adirondack Mountains, New York State," 1988. The aluminum concentrations here are total monomeric aluminum, including the inorganic and organic fractions.

came from deeper, less acid soil layers that were able to neutralize the acids from precipitation.

In snowmelt, when several months of accumulated precipitation were released in a few weeks, the flows were quite different. During snowmelt the rate of melting exceeded the ability of the lower soil to conduct the water, and the meltwater in both watersheds moved through the upper soil or over the surface. At Woods Lake, which was below pH 5 for much of the year, this made very little difference to the pH of the lake. At Panther Lake, where the pH was around 7 for much of the year, the pH decreased over two full units to about 4.7 during snowmelt.

This last result was of considerable importance because it showed that lakes that were neutral or alkaline in the summer could suffer highly acid episodes during spring runoff. This was to become an important theme in much subsequent research and remains one today.

Interestingly, even though sulfuric acid was the main acid in deposition, the principal acid in snowmelt peaks was often nitric acid. This suggested that nitric acid might be more important in lake acidification than had previously been realized. Since nitrogen emissions had been only weakly controlled by the Clean Air Act Amendments of 1970 (p. 98), this was a finding of some considerable importance and one that we will return to at length in Chapter 5.

The work on the ILWAS lakes suggested a general model of how the chemistry of groundwater is modified as it moves through soils. Because forest soils are layered, and because each layer has a different chemistry, the chemistry of groundwater depends on which layers it has moved through. In particular, the surface and near-surface flows that occur during snowmelt are chemically very different from the deeper flows that occur at other times:

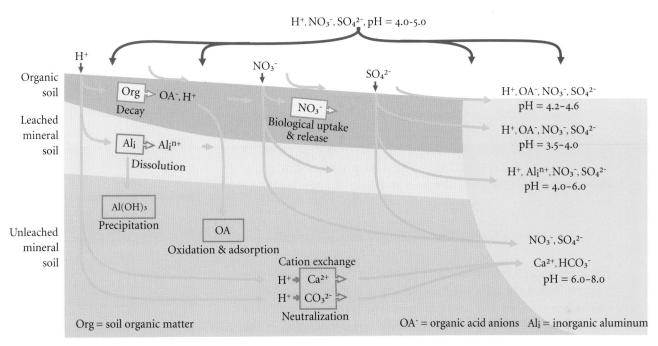

Water that moves over the surface typically has a chemistry near that of precipitation but is somewhat more acid because of nitrates and organic acids from the forest floor.

Water that moves through the upper organic layer acquires substantial amounts of organic acids and nitrates from the decay of leaves and wood and is also more acid than precipitation.

Water that moves vertically from the organic layer into the leached mineral layer below loses some of its acidity and gains inorganic aluminum, which is released when hydrogen ions are adsorbed.

And water that moves through the lower layer of unleached mineral soil loses both acids and its aluminum and gains base cations and bicarbonate in exchange.

The ILWAS was important for subsequent Adirondack research because it suggested that there were two major populations of Adirondack lakes – thin-till lakes that were sensitive to acidification and deep-till lakes that weren't – and that any study that sought to measure the severity of acidification was going to have to differentiate the two. Otherwise the study ran the risk of confounding the effects of soil depth and the effects of deposition. If it examined mostly thick-till lakes, it could underestimate acidification; if it examined mostly thin-till lakes, it could overestimate it.

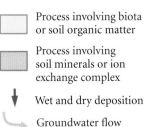

Process involving biota or soil organic matter

Process involving soil minerals or ion exchange complex

Wet and dry deposition

Groundwater flow

Adapted with permission from Driscoll and Newton, "Chemical characteristics of Adirondack lakes," copyright 1985 American Chemical Society; and Chen et al., "Hydrologic analyses of acidic and alkaline lakes," copyright 1984 American Geophysical Union. The uptake and release of nitrates and the production of natural organic acids take place in the biologically active layer near the surface, where plant growth and decay occur. The release of aluminum occurs in the uppermost layer of mineral soil, where the base cations have been largely leached out. It involves either the dissolution of aluminum containing minerals or the release of aluminum ions bound to surfaces. The neutralization of hydrogen ions and their exchange for base cations occurs mostly in the lower, unleached layers of mineral soil. It involves either the reaction of a hydrogen ion with a bicarbonate ion or the exchange of a hydrogen ion for a base cation.

The flowpath model developed by the ILWAS said that to understand lake acidification, it was first necessary to understand lake hydrology. Unfortunately, this was difficult to do. The direct hydrogeological methods used in the ILWAS were slow and expensive. Using them on even a few dozen lakes would have been very hard, and using them in the large-scale surveys of 1,000 or 1,500 lakes then being planned would have been impossible.

What was needed, then, was a proxy for flowpaths – some sort of chemical or physical diagnostic that would separate lakes with surface flow from lakes with deep flow. The system of chemical lake classification developed in the RILWAS provided this proxy and was the key that made the interpretation of large-scale lake surveys possible.

The RILWAS Lake Classification: Drainage and Seepage Lakes

The Regionalized Integrated Lake-Watershed Acidification Study, which followed the ILWAS and used many of the same techniques, was designed to test the ILWAS flowpath model on a larger group of lakes. It examined 12 lakes in a single large watershed in the western Adirondacks and another 8 lakes in other parts of the Adirondacks.

The first major finding of the RILWAS was that there were at least six major hydrological types of Adirondack lakes rather than two. Woods, Sagamore, and Panther, the ILWAS lakes, are examples of *drainage* lakes. Drainage lakes – lakes that drain by outlets – are connected to a watershed of significant size. They are usually fed by both surface runoff and groundwater and so have chemistries that are controlled by the kind of watershed processes just described.

Drainage lakes fall into three main groups: *thick-till drainage lakes,* like Panther Lake; *thin-till drainage lakes,* like Woods Lake; and *bog drainage lakes,* which are surrounded by wetlands and so, except for any inlet stream, isolated from the surrounding groundwater.* As a group they are by far the commonest sort of lake; about 87% of the lakes studied by the Adirondack Lakes Survey were drainage lakes.

Lakes without outlets, which lose water by evaporation or seepage, are *seepage lakes.* Hydrologically, they are to some extent disconnected from the watersheds they lie in. All receive water from precipitation, and some receive significant amounts of groundwater as well. None receive substantial amounts of surface runoff. Their chemistry tends to be controlled by in-lake processes and the composition of the precipitation that they receive and is often independent of the chemistry of the surrounding watershed. Because they derive much of their water from precipitation, they are often very sensitive to acid deposition.

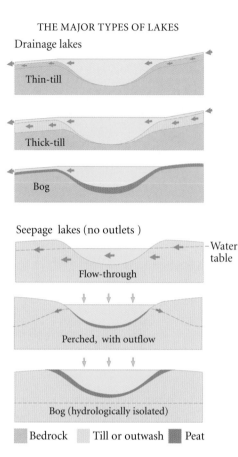

THE MAJOR TYPES OF LAKES

Drainage lakes

Thin-till

Thick-till

Bog

Seepage lakes (no outlets)

Water table

Flow-through

Perched, with outflow

Bog (hydrologically isolated)

Bedrock   Till or outwash   Peat

The types of Adirondack lakes, adapted from Driscoll and Newton, "Chemical characteristics of Adirondack lakes," 1985. The drainage lakes, though quite variable, are often on bedrock in concave terrain; effectively, they are lakes with a large enough watershed to feed an outlet stream. The seepage lakes, in contrast, tend to be in deep soils and on flat or convex terrain. Effectively, they are lakes that are more or less isolated from other surface waters and so have either small watersheds or none at all. Flow-through seepage lakes are strongly connected to the water table and influenced by groundwater flow. Perched and bog seepage lakes may be largely disconnected from the groundwater as well.

* Adirondack wetlands typically have relatively impermeable peat soils that prevent groundwater from reaching the lake.

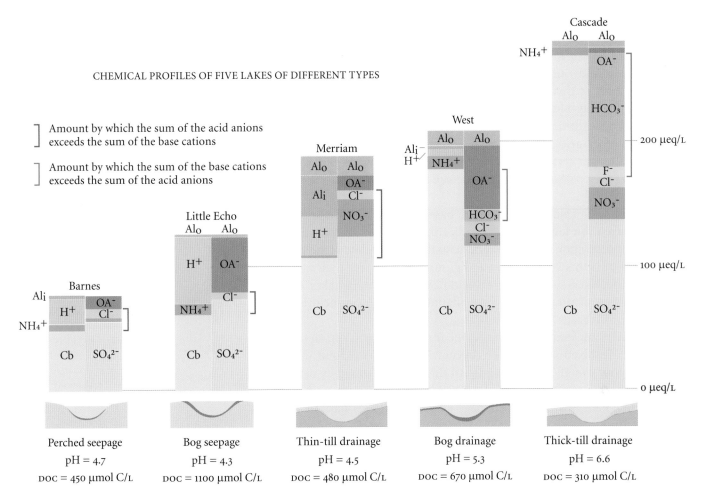

CHEMICAL PROFILES OF FIVE LAKES OF DIFFERENT TYPES

] Amount by which the sum of the acid anions
exceeds the sum of the base cations

] Amount by which the sum of the base cations
exceeds the sum of the acid anions

Barnes
Perched seepage
pH = 4.7
DOC = 450 μmol C/L

Little Echo
Bog seepage
pH = 4.3
DOC = 1100 μmol C/L

Merriam
Thin-till drainage
pH = 4.5
DOC = 480 μmol C/L

West
Bog drainage
pH = 5.3
DOC = 670 μmol C/L

Cascade
Thick-till drainage
pH = 6.6
DOC = 310 μmol C/L

Seepage lakes also come in three types. Those fed by groundwater are *flow-through seepage lakes.* Typically they are young lakes with sandy bottoms and little vegetation. Older seepage lakes that have developed a peat layer lie above the water table and so are isolated from incoming groundwater. If water can seep out along their edges, they are *perched seepage lakes.* If they are completely surrounded by bog mats or peat and no groundwater moves in or out, they are *bog seepage lakes.*

Seepage lakes are found throughout the Adirondacks but are commonest in the relatively flat valleys of the north and northwest where there are extensive deposits of glacial sands and gravels. They are much less common than drainage lakes. Only 6% of the lakes surveyed by the Adirondack Lakes Survey were flow-through seepage lakes; another 7% were perched seepage lakes.

The Chemical Signatures of Different Lake Types

Each of these lake types turns out to have a fairly characteristic chemical profile. The graph above shows five characteristic examples.

Ionic composition of lakes of five different types, redrawn with permission from Driscoll and Newton, "Chemical characteristics of Adirondack lakes." Copyright 1985 American Chemical Society. OA⁻ is the concentration of organic acid; it cannot be measured directly and is inferred from the difference between the sum of the cations and the sum of the other anions. The small bars to the right of the main bars show the difference between the sum of sulfate and nitrate, the acid anions, and the sum of the base cations. In the lakes in which the sum of the acid anions exceeds the sum of the base cations (red brackets on right) a significant part of the acidity is likely to be of atmospheric origin, and there are likely to be significant concentrations of inorganic aluminum. In the lakes in which the sum of the base cations exceeds the sum of the acid anions (blue bars), the atmospheric acids probably have been neutralized in the watershed, and any acidity that is present is probably from natural organic acids.

Barnes and Little Echo, the two seepage lakes, are both dilute lakes with low silica and aluminum concentrations. This suggests that most of their water comes from precipitation and relatively little from groundwater. Barnes Lake has low concentrations of dissolved organic carbon (DOC) and organic acids, indicating that most of its acidity comes from acid deposition; Little Echo has much higher concentrations of DOC and organic acids, indicating that at least part of its acidity is derived from the bog mats around it.

Both lakes have relatively low base concentrations and high hydrogen ion concentrations, indicating that they receive much direct deposition of atmospheric acids and little inflow of ground-water. It is this lack of bases and groundwater inflow that makes seepage lakes so sensitive to acidification: drainage lakes also receive acids directly from precipitation but often can neutralize them with bases from groundwater.

Merriam, West, and Cascade, the three drainage lakes, all have more dissolved silica, higher concentrations of bases, and water of higher overall ionic strength. All this suggests that they derive significant amounts of water from groundwater.

Merriam is a thin-till drainage lake. Like Woods Lake, it has relatively high concentrations of inorganic aluminum and hydro-gen ion, indicating that there are few bases in the soil to neutral-ize the acids from deposition and that the acids are either passing through unneutralized or being exchanged for aluminum. There are also significant amounts of organic acids, organic aluminum, nitrate, and DOC, all produced by the forest floor and suggesting that the flowpaths lie close to the surface. The sulfate concentra-tion exceeds the concentration of base cations, suggesting that much of the acidity results from atmospheric acids.

West Pond is a bog drainage lake with a higher pH and brown water with much more DOC than Merriam. It has far more organic acid and far less inorganic aluminum than Merriam but still a sig-nificant amount of sulfate; its acidity derives from a mixture of atmospheric acids from precipitation and natural organic acids from wetlands.

Cascade Lake is a thick-till drainage lake that is relatively insen-sitive to acidification. The sulfate concentration indicates that the watershed receives significant amounts of atmospheric acids. The large amounts of base cations and bicarbonate suggest that the hydrogen ions from the acids are being neutralized or exchanged for base cations before they reach the lake.

The lake classification developed by these studies–seepage lakes versus drainage lakes, clear-water lakes versus brown-water lakes, thick-till lakes versus thin-till lakes–was used in almost all subsequent studies of the acidification of Adirondack lakes. In particular, it was the main tool that the Adirondack Lakes Survey

1 The mineral acid anions sulfate or nitrate, rare in pristine waters, indicate that the watershed is receiving acid deposition.

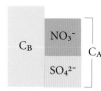

2 If the base-acid difference $C_B - C_A$ is positive, the mineral acids from acid deposition are being neutralized in the watershed.

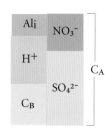

3 If the base-acid difference $C_B - C_A$ is negative, some of the mineral acids from acid deposition have not been neutralized and some of the acidity in the water is mineral acidity and aluminum.

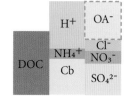

4 If significant amounts of DOC are present, and if the sum of the cations exceeds the sum of the inorganic anions, organic acids are assumed to be present.

The RILWAS used a variety of diagnostics to separate different types of lake acidity. Nitrate and sulfate indicated mineral acidity; DOC or inorganic anion deficits indicated organic acidity. The difference between acid anions and basic cations, $C_A - C_B$, was a measure of watershed response. When it was negative, the watershed was neutralizing all the mineral acid deposited on it. When it was positive, the watershed was passing mineral acids into surface water and likely releasing aluminum as well. See page 31 for a further discussion of these and other ion diagnostics.

The Adirondack Lakes Survey refined these diagnostics further by using the ratio $(C_A - C_B)/H+$ as an estimate of the percentage of the total acidity that was mineral acidity (pp. 73-75).

(Chapter 4) used to organize and interpret the results of its survey of the fisheries and chemistry of 1,469 Adirondack lakes.

The Chemical Signature of Atmospheric Acids

The results of the RILWAS suggested several important diagnostic principles to determine whether lakes are being affected by atmospheric acids:

> When substantial amounts of sulfate and nitrate are present, atmospheric acids are being deposited in the watershed.

> When the amount of sulfate and nitrate is less than the amount of base cations, the atmospheric acids are being neutralized in the watershed, and the lake is relatively insensitive to acid deposition.

> When the amount of sulfate and nitrate exceeds the amount of base cations, the atmospheric acids are not being completely neutralized in the watershed. Some of the acidity in the water is mineral acidity, and inorganic aluminum is likely to be present.

> If significant amounts of DOC are present, and if the sum of the cations exceeds the sum of the anions, organic acids are assumed to be present.

These ion diagnostics, illustrated on the opposite page, are now widely used to characterize watersheds and distinguish natural acidity from acidity caused by atmospheric acids.

Which lakes have high inorganic aluminum concentrations?

Because inorganic aluminum is toxic to fish (p. 180), there was considerable interest in the mid-1980s in determining which lakes had high concentrations of inorganic aluminum. The results from the RILWAS, shown in the upper graph, suggested that the more acid a drainage lake was, the more inorganic aluminum it had. This was consistent with the model of watershed processes just described, which said that the aluminum comes from the soil and is mobilized only after the soil is depleted of base cations and so less able to neutralize atmospheric acids.

If this model is correct, then the ratio of strong acid anions (which tell us how much acid the watershed is receiving) to base cations (which tell us how much of that acid is being exchanged or neutralized in the soil) should predict how much hydrogen ion and inorganic aluminum will be transported from the watershed to the lake. When the acid-base ratio is less than 1, most of the acid is neutralized in the soil and little is available to mobilize aluminum

INORGANIC ALUMINUM VS. pH

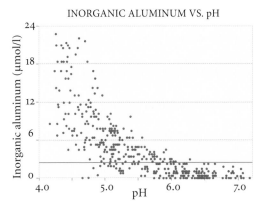

INORGANIC ALUMINUM AND THE ACID-BASE RATIO

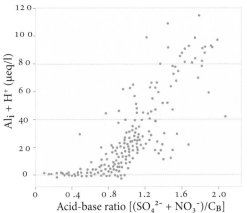

Relations between inorganic aluminum, pH, and the acid-base ratio. The upper graph, for 12 subbasins in the watershed of the North Branch of the Moose River, is redrawn with permission from Driscoll, Yatsko, and Unangst, "Longitudinal and temporal trends in the water chemistry of the North Branch of the Moose River." Copyright 1987 Springer Science and Business Media. The red line at 2 μmol/L is the lower threshold for biological toxicity; concentrations above this line are potentially harmful to fish. The lower graph, which is for all the RILWAS lakes, is from Driscoll and Newton, "Chemical characteristics of Adirondack lakes." Copyright 1985 American Chemical Society. The acid-base ratio is the ratio of acid anions to base cations. When it is above 1, the supply of acids to a watershed exceeds the watershed's ability to neutralize them. Elevated concentrations of inorganic aluminum are restricted to waters where the pH is low and the acid-base ratio is greater than 1 and thus largely to waters that have been acidified by atmospheric acids.

or enter the lake. When the ratio is greater than 1, then unneutralized hydrogen ions are available to mobilize aluminum and acidify lakes.

The second graph on page 51 shows that this is indeed the case; when C_A/C_B is greater than about 0.8, free acid and aluminum appear in lake water. This is strong support for the basic model and leads to another important diagnostic:

> If either a lake is either highly acid, or if the sum of the strong acid anions exceeds that of the base cations, toxic inorganic aluminum is likely to be present.

A Watershed-Scale Example: The North Branch of the Moose River

The North Branch studies, begun by Driscoll et al. as part of the RILWAS in 1982, were designed to provide a watershed-scale test of the ILWAS model of lake-watershed interactions. The study site was the watershed of the North Branch of the Moose River. This watershed contains a variety of soil types and lake types and so was an excellent site to test the hypothesis that soil types and flowpaths control lake chemistry. In addition, its fish populations

Both maps from Schofield and Driscoll, "Fish species distribution in relation to water quality gradients in the North Branch of the Moose River basin," 1987. The former spawning areas were in use in the 1950s. The graph of fish species includes both natives and introductions. Other things being equal, a large lake will have more fish species than a small one. Hence when small, high-ANC lakes have more fish than larger more acid ones, this is strong evidence that acidity is effecting biological diversity.

The RILWAS also did extensive in-stream toxicity studies of caged fish. Fish placed in streams in the northeastern part of the watershed, where fish diversity was low and acidity and aluminum high, had very high mortality. Fish placed in streams in the southern part of the drainage, where acidity and aluminum were lower, had much lower mortality.

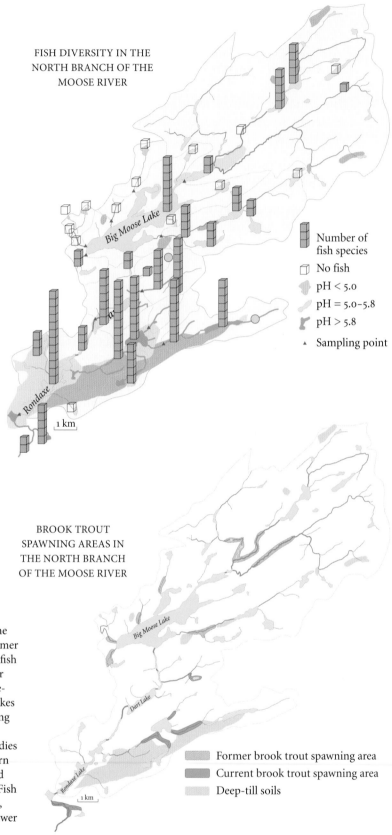

FISH DIVERSITY IN THE NORTH BRANCH OF THE MOOSE RIVER

Number of fish species
No fish
pH < 5.0
pH = 5.0–5.8
pH > 5.8
Sampling point

BROOK TROUT SPAWNING AREAS IN THE NORTH BRANCH OF THE MOOSE RIVER

Former brook trout spawning area
Current brook trout spawning area
Deep-till soils

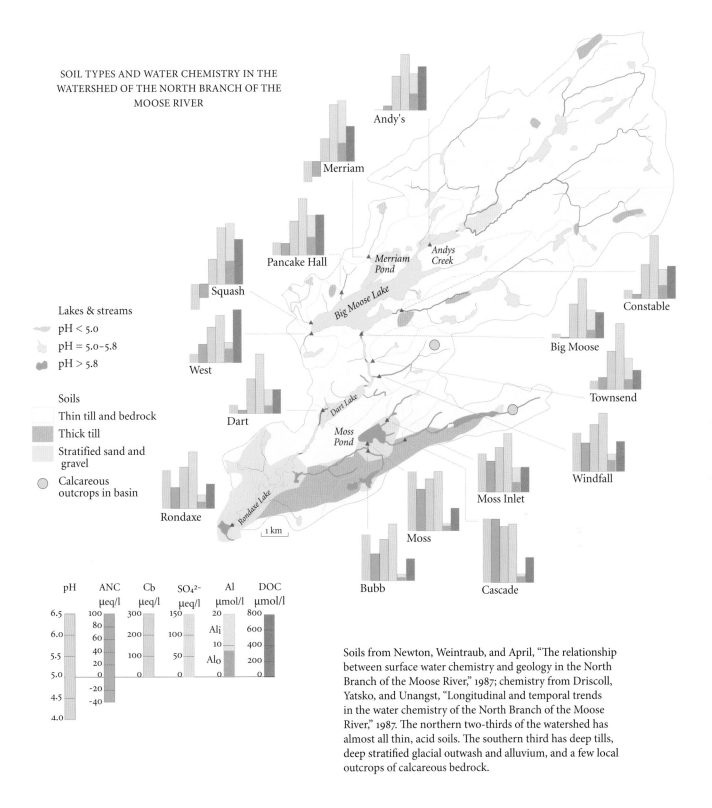

SOIL TYPES AND WATER CHEMISTRY IN THE
WATERSHED OF THE NORTH BRANCH OF THE
MOOSE RIVER

Andy's

Merriam

Pancake Hall

Squash

West

Dart

Merriam
Pond

Andys
Creek

Big Moose Lake

Dart Lake

Moss
Pond

Constable

Big Moose

Townsend

Windfall

Moss Inlet

Moss

Lakes & streams

pH < 5.0

pH = 5.0–5.8

pH > 5.8

Soils

Thin till and bedrock

Thick till

Stratified sand and
gravel

Calcareous
outcrops in basin

Rondaxe Lake

1 km

Rondaxe

Bubb

Cascade

pH	ANC μeq/l	Cb μeq/l	SO₄²⁻ μeq/l	Al μmol/l	DOC μmol/l
6.5	100	300	150	20	800
6.0	80 / 60	200	100	Ali	600 / 400
5.5	40 / 20	100	50	10	
5.0	0	0	0	Alo 0	200
4.5	-20				0
4.0	-40				

Soils from Newton, Weintraub, and April, "The relationship
between surface water chemistry and geology in the North
Branch of the Moose River," 1987; chemistry from Driscoll,
Yatsko, and Unangst, "Longitudinal and temporal trends
in the water chemistry of the North Branch of the Moose
River," 1987. The northern two-thirds of the watershed has
almost all thin, acid soils. The southern third has deep tills,
deep stratified glacial outwash and alluvium, and a few local
outcrops of calcareous bedrock.

had been extensively sampled in the past, which made it possible to test the further hypothesis that changes in lake acidity were affecting fish populations.

Both hypotheses were supported by the study. Preliminary geological studies showed that, except for two small areas of calcareous rock, the bedrock didn't vary much and had only a minor influence on the water chemistry. The depth of the till, on the other hand, varied greatly and had a great influence on the chemistry.

In the northern parts of the watershed, where the soils were thin, the lakes were highly acid; acid-neutralizing capacities were low, and the ratio of sulfate to base cations was high. Aluminum concentrations were high and, except in a few boggy ponds with high levels of dissolved organic carbon, most of the aluminum was in the toxic inorganic form.

In the southern parts of the watershed, where the till was thicker and calcareous bedrock was sometimes present, the chemistry was different. The lakes were mostly neutral or only slightly acid; acid-neutralizing capacities were high and base cation concentrations were comparable to sulfate concentrations; aluminum concentrations were low, and much of the aluminum was in nontoxic organic complexes.

The fisheries in the watershed were strongly related to the chemistry. Fish diversity was higher in the neutral than in the acidic lakes, and many of the most acidic northern lakes had no fish at all. Smallmouth bass and several other acid-sensitive native species had contracted their ranges since 1931, and several introduced, acid-tolerant species had expanded theirs. Brook trout had ceased to spawn in at least seven former spawning areas in the northern part of the watershed and were now restricted to the five high-pH streams in the southern part of the watershed.*

Soil Depth and Acid-Neutralizing Capacity

The North Branch study found a strong relation between the acid-neutralizing capacity of a lake and the percentage of the watershed covered by deep soils. The main exceptions are Bubb-Sis Pond, which is probably isolated from groundwater; West Pond, in which some ANC is generated by sulfate reduction; and Windfall and likely Cascade ponds, which have calcareous bedrock in their watersheds. If these four are excluded, the correlation coefficient for the remaining ten is a striking 0.89.

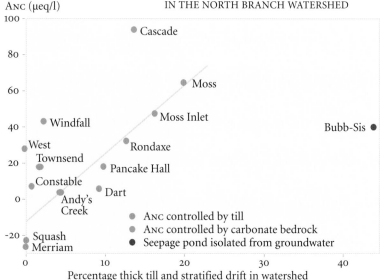

SOIL DEPTH AND ACID-NEUTRALIZING CAPACITY IN THE NORTH BRANCH WATERSHED

The relation between ANC and the extent of deep soils in the watershed of the North Branch of the Moose. Redrawn with permission from Newton, Weintraub, and April, "The relationship between surface water chemistry and geology in the North Branch of the Moose River." Copyright 1987 Springer Science and Business Media. Since lakes with ANCs of less than 50 are considered sensitive to acidification (Colquhoun, Kretser, and Pfiefer, 1984), the regression line predicts that any lake with less than about 17% thick till in its watershed will be extremely sensitive to acidification.

* For the RILWAS studies of fish mortality and aluminum toxicity, see page 180.

Observations at Hubbard Brook Experimental Forest in the 1970s had shown that mountain streams were most acid in the spring and that nitrates were more important in spring runoff than at other times of the year. The ILWAS and RILWAS found that this was true in Adirondack lakes as well.

In both cases, the spring acidity peaks seemed to be controlled by the seasonal balance of biological uptake and decay. Uptake, associated with new growth, was highest in the spring and summer. Decay occurred whenever soil temperatures were above freezing and was much less seasonal. As plant growth in the watersheds decreased in the fall, the concentrations of ammonium and dissolved organic carbon – both products of decay – began to increase. Atmospheric acids were stored in the snow in the winter; nitric acid, produced by the microbial oxidation of ammonium, accumulated in the forest floor. The accumulated acids, along with dissolved organic carbon and inorganic aluminum, were released in snowmelt.

The spring acidity peaks could be striking: a lake that was nearly neutral in the summer might have spring pH declines of more than 1 unit, ANC declines of more than 50 µeq/l, and peaks of nitrate and aluminum that were four times or more the summer levels. Interestingly, sulfate concentrations changed much less than nitrate concentrations: snowmelt acidification appeared to be a nitrate- and aluminum-dominated phenomenon.

The North Branch study added an interesting new detail to the general pattern. It found that the acidity peaks were more pronounced in the circumneutral lakes than in the extremely acid ones. This was partly because of hydrology and partly because of buffering. The circumneutral lakes tended to switch from deep flowpaths to shallow ones in the spring, which lowered their ANCs; the acidic lakes were buffered by dissolved aluminum, which stabilized theirs.

These seasonal acidity peaks, which were to receive much additional study in the late 1980s (Chapter 5), were noteworthy for several reasons. The high aluminum levels suggested, and later work (p. 180) confirmed, that the peaks could kill fish. The high nitrate levels and seasonal timing suggested that biological cycling was involved. And the magnitude of the dif-

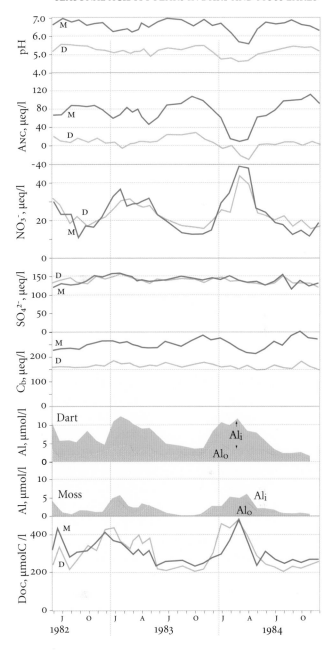

The seasonal pattern of acidity in Dart and Moss lakes, in the watershed of the North Branch of the Moose. From Driscoll, Yatsko, and Unangst, "Longitudinal and temporal trends in the water chemistry of the North Branch of the Moose River." Copyright 1987 Springer Science and Business Media. Moss Lake has thick soils and carbonates in its watershed and is circumneutral. Dart Lake has thin soils and is moderately acid with high average inorganic aluminum levels and spring peaks of nitrate. Note that Moss Lake, which has a higher baseline pH than Dart, has a smaller spring aluminum peak, a comparable nitrate peak, and greater spring decreases in pH and ANC.

ferences between spring and summer ANCs suggested that the large synoptic lake surveys like the ELS and ALS, which were conducted in the summer and could not detect lakes with spring acidity peaks, had probably underestimated the number of lakes with biologically significant acidification.

Which properties of watersheds predict lake chemistry?

The RILWAS had clearly shown that local variations in soils and bedrock were correlated with local variations in lake chemistry. In 1986, C.T. Hunsacker and his colleagues at the Oak Ridge National Laboratory tried a similar approach on a regional basis. Their goal was to develop a way of predicting which watersheds were most vulnerable to acidification. They examined 463 Adirondack headwaters lakes for which chemical data existed and tried to predict their pHs and ANCs from a set of 80 variables that described the watersheds.*

The variables they tested included physical, chemical, biological, and cultural features. Unfortunately, the data available to them were limited, and many of the important features of the watersheds – the extent of soils of different depths, the presence of calcareous bedrock, the extent of wetlands, and the local variations in deposition rates – were only approximately known.

The study was only moderately successful. Although, as the RILWAS had showed, it was possible to predict chemistry quite accurately *within* a single watershed from a few carefully measured variables, it was much harder to predict the differences between watersheds from a large set of approximately measured variables. As a result, even though amount of precipitation and the amount of acid deposited were relatively good predictors of acidification, other features that might have been expected to be important – elevation, soil porosity, cation exchange capacity, neutralizing capacity of bedrock – were not. Because of the known variability of lakes and the coarseness of the physical data, this is not an unexpected result: it may well be that many of these factors are very important in a particular type of lake in a particular watershed, and none of them are important in all types of lakes or all watersheds.

RECONSTRUCTING LAKE HISTORIES

Using the chemical diagnostics and lake classifications just described, the synoptic surveys that will be described in Chapter 4 established conclusively that many Adirondack lakes had been acidified by acid deposition. But they could not determine how much those lakes had changed or how fast the changes had been. And thus it was not clear whether acid deposition was making large chemical and biological changes or only small ones – whether it

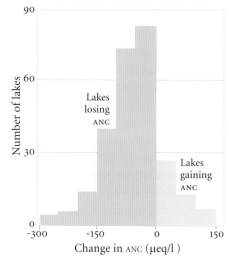

CHANGES IN ANC OF 269 ADIRONDACK
LAKES BETWEEN 1934 AND 1985

Historical ANC changes in 269 Adirondack lakes, redrawn with permission from Asbury et al., "Acidification of Adirondack lakes." Copyright 1989 American Chemical Society. The historical ANCs, measured between 1929 and 1934, were corrected for differences in the way the endpoint of the ANC titration was determined and compared with modern ANCs measured between 1975 and 1985. More than three times as many lakes have lost ANC as have gained it, and the average magnitude of the losses is more than twice that of the gains.

*Hunsaker et al., "Empirical relationships between watershed attributes and headwater lake chemistry in the Adirondack region," 1986. Most of the variables they examined either were not correlated to pH and ANC or had correlation coefficients of less than 0.3. Lake elevation and the percentage of conifers in the watershed had correlation coefficients of 0.3–0.5; total precipitation and runoff had correlation coefficients of 0.3–0.5. Total deposition rates and concentrations of acid in precipitation had correlation coefficients of 0.5–0.6. Their best multivariate model had a correlation coefficient of 0.61, not much better than could be done from deposition alone.

was eliminating fish populations from productive lakes, or only making lakes that were already acid and unproductive slightly worse.

To answer these questions, lake histories were needed. When historical records were available, as in the study by Asbury (p. 56), the changes could be determined directly. When records were not available, the history had to be reconstructed from the lake sediments using paleolimnological methods. A sediment core was collected and divided into samples, which were then dated and analyzed for indicators of acidification.

The use of sediment cores was a well-established of reconstructing gradual changes in lake biology over hundreds or thousands of years. What was new in the 1980s was the use of cores to detect the relatively fast chemical changes associated with acidification.

The key was the development of the indicators. The *onset* of acid deposition could be determined fairly easily from the presence of combustion products like soot particles and polycyclic aromatic hydrocarbons and from increases in the deposition rates of lead and mercury, both of which are released by combustion. The *progress* of acid deposition, on the other hand, was much more difficult to measure. Sediment cores do not preserve historical pHs but do preserve microfossils whose abundance can be used as an indicator of the pH at the time the sediments were deposited. The microfossils are thus proxies for pH and other chemical variables, and the pHs determined from them are called inferred pHs, to indicate that they have been reconstructed rather than directly measured.

Proxy methods for reconstructing historical chemistry are now standard limnological techniques and the backbone of much global change research. Many of these were first developed in the 1980s, and many, like Donald Charles's method for inferring pH by counting the number of diatoms in different ecological groups, were first developed or tested in the Adirondacks.

Direct Historical Comparisons

Historical data on Adirondack lakes are limited but valuable. We have some early fisheries information from the 1880s, an extensive survey of fisheries and chemistry from the 1930s, and modern fishery surveys from 1948 to 1975. The pH information in the early studies can probably not be compared accurately with modern pH determinations, but both the fisheries data and ANCs can be.

Comparisons using these data show clear evidence of recent acid-related changes. Schofield showed that 17 of 36 high-elevation lakes that had fish populations in the 1930s had lost them by 1975 (p. 41). Asbury et al. compared the historical and modern ANCs of 274 Adirondack lakes and found that more than three-quarters of

PLANKTONIC DIATOMS IN ADIRONDACK LAKES

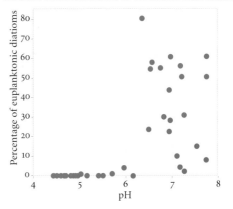

MEASURED & INFERRED pHS OF ADIRONDACK LAKES

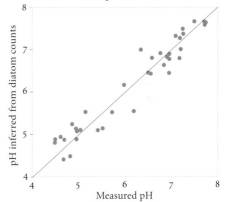

Redrawn from Charles, "Relationships between surface sediment diatom assemblages and lakewater characteristics in Adirondack lakes." Copyright 1985 Ecological Society of America via the Copyright Clearance Center. The upper graph shows one of the relationships between diatoms and pH in the contemporary lakes that were used to derive "transfer functions" for inferring historical pHs and ANCs from the percentages of different species of diatoms in sediment cores. The euplanktonic diatoms, one of five ecological groups of diatoms used to infer pH, are sharply pH-limited and only found in circumneutral and alkaline lakes. Other groups are limited to moderately or strongly acidic lakes.

The lower graph shows a test of these transfer functions in which the measured pHs are compared with those inferred from the diatoms at the top of a sediment core. The inferred pHs differ, on average, by less than 0.4 pH units from the measured pHs and capture about 90% of the variation in the measured pH.

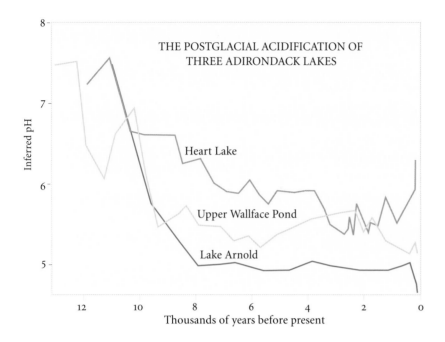

THE POSTGLACIAL ACIDIFICATION OF
THREE ADIRONDACK LAKES

Inferred pH

Heart Lake

Upper Wallface Pond

Lake Arnold

Thousands of years before present

The natural postglacial acidification of three high-elevation lakes, redrawn with permission from Whitehead et al., "The developmental history of Adirondack (N.Y.) lakes." Copyright 1989 Springer Science and Business Media. The study, which was done in the early 1980s, was the first reconstruction of the chemical history of any Adirondack lake. The lakes were neutral to alkaline immediately after the glaciers melted, acidified at different rates, and then stabilized at pHs between 5 and 6.

the lakes had decreased in ANC and that the median decrease was about 50 µeq/l.

Paleolimnological Techniques

Paleolimnological reconstructions of lake history are more versatile than direct comparisons because they afford more information and can, in principle, be used on any lake with a good sedimentary record. The principal techniques involved – radioisotope dating, microchemical analysis, and microfossil analysis – were well established by 1980 and had been widely and successfully used in limnology and oceanography. All that was required was to adapt them to the specific problem of determining the effects of acid deposition on softwater lakes.

By the middle 1980s this had been done. Lead-210 dating, developed in the 1970s, was found to give reliable dates from 1800 on, the period of most interest in acidification studies. Polycyclic aromatic hydrocarbons, soot particles, and trace metals were found to be good indicators of the input of combustion products and hence of the onset of acid deposition. Diatoms and chrysophytes, two species-rich groups of algae that are common in Adirondack lakes, were found to be sensitive indicators of pH and acid-neutralizing capacity. Diatom-inferred pHs, in particular, correlate very well with measured pHs and have become a standard paleolimnological tool, now used in hundreds of studies in North America and Europe.

The Early Chemical History of Three High Peaks Ponds

The first paleolimnological study in the Adirondacks, by Whitehead, Charles, and their collaborators, provided baseline information about the rate of natural acidification. This was important because in 1980, there was very little understanding of the comparative rates of natural and anthropogenic acidification. It was known, for instance, that natural forest and bog development could acidify lakes and watersheds by immobilizing base cations and generating organic acids. But no one knew whether this took a hundred or a thousand years, and so no one knew for sure whether the recent changes in the ANCs of Adirondack lakes (p. 56) were natural or man-made or both.

The first part of the answer came from a reconstruction of the pH and vegetation history of three high-elevation lakes in the High Peaks by Whitehead et al. All three lakes had similar histories. They were alkaline and productive in the early postglacial period when the soils in their watersheds were newly deposited and still rich in minerals. There was a further productivity and pH increase during a brief period in which alder (a nitrogen fixer) was dominant, followed by pH declines as forests developed. Once the forests were in place, the pHs tended to stabilize and then remained stable for 4,000 to 6,000 years.

These results, which were corroborated by those from Scandinavian lakes, suggested that natural processes like forest growth and base cation depletion can only acidify lakes very gradually. The fastest rates of change observed were about 1 pH unit per 500 years, and the lowest pHs attained were rarely less than 5.0.

Thus, as many researchers had suspected, the natural acidification of Adirondack lakes appeared to be a slow process that did not produce pHs as low as those currently observed in many lakes. And this, in turn, suggested that those pHs were the result of acid rain.

The Recent Chemical History of Big Moose Lake

A few years later, a paleolimnological reconstruction of chemical history of Big Moose Lake by Charles and his associates showed that this was almost certainly the case. The reconstruction showed that the acidification of Big Moose had occurred roughly ten times faster than the natural acidification studied by Whitehead and Charles and was associated with markers of fossil fuels. By-products from combustion first appeared in the sediments about 1850 and peaked around 1945. Inferred ANC and pH were fairly

RECONSTRUCTED CHEMICAL HISTORY OF BIG MOOSE LAKE

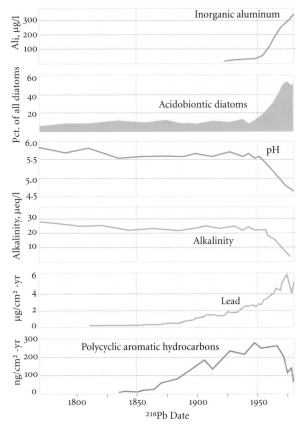

Redrawn with permission from Charles, "Recent pH history of Big Moose Lake (Adirondack Mountains, USA) inferred from sediment diatom assemblages." Copyright 1984 Verh. Internat. Verein. Limnol.; see http://www.schweizerbart.de for more information. Last panel redrawn with permission from Charles et al., "Paleolimnological evidence for recent acidification of Big Moose Lake, Adirondack Mountains, N.Y. (USA)." Copyright 1987 Springer Science and Business Media. The "acidiobiontic" diatoms are a group of species that dominate at pHs below 5.0. The increased deposition rates of lead and polycyclic aromatic hydrocarbons, both by-products of combustion, in the late 1800s reflect the increased use of fossil fuels by industry.

steady for most of the 19th and early 20th centuries. About 1925 they began a gradual decline. About 1950 the decline accelerated dramatically, as indicated by a sharp increase in the percentage of acid-lake diatoms in the core. Inorganic aluminum, an important indicator of acidification by strong acids, began to increase rapidly about the same time. By 1978, when the record ends, the pH had declined about 1 pH unit and the ANC about 20 µeq/l.

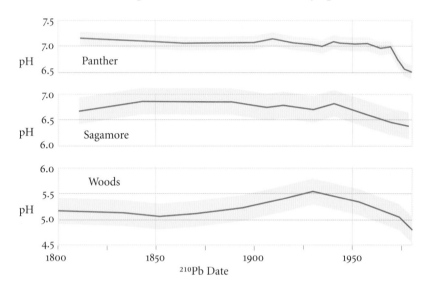

RECONSTRUCTED pH HISTORIES OF THE THREE ILWAS LAKES

Redrawn with permission from Davis et al., "Two-hundred-year pH history of Woods, Sagamore, and Panther lakes in the Adirondack Mountains, New York State." Copyright 1988 ASTM International. The dates were determined from lead isotopes and confirmed by pollen markers. The pink bands give the mean standard error when reconstructed pHs are compared with measured pHs; they do not give the standard error of individual points on the curve.

The most striking result of this study was the size and sharpness of the post-1950 pH decrease and its association with combustion products. Charles and his colleagues considered several alternative explanations and concluded,

> The recent decrease in the pH of Big Moose Lake cannot be accounted for by natural acidification or processes associated with watershed disturbance. The magnitude, rate, and timing of the recent pH and alkalinity decreases and their relationship to indicators of coal and oil combustion, indicate that the most reasonable explanation for the recent acidification is increased atmospheric deposition of strong acids derived from combustion of fossil fuels.

Thus, for the first time in the Adirondack literature, acid rain was judged by a scientific jury and found guilty as charged.

The Chemical Histories of Panther, Sagamore, and Woods Lakes

In the same period, Davis et al. examined cores from the three ILWAS lakes.

The results were similar to those from Big Moose but showed less total acidification. All three lakes had acidified, with the most rapid changes between 1950 and 1980. The acidification had not changed their relative acidities. Panther Lake, the least acid of the three, had acidified by 0.6 pH unit and was still the least acid. Sagamore, the middle lake, had acidified by 0.3 pH unit. The pH of Woods lake, the most acid of the three, rose by about 0.3 pH unit between 1900 and 1925 and then declined 0.7 pH units after 1925, for a net change of -0.4 units. Its initial pH rise may well have been associated with watershed disturbance: the Woods Lake watershed was both logged and burned in this period, while the watersheds of the other two lakes were undisturbed.

An interesting chemical feature of the Woods Lake core is the decrease in the calcium concentration of sediments over the past hundred years. This resembles the declines of exchangeable calcium in acidified watersheds recently simulated by Chen and Driscoll (p. 139). The authors note that similar calcium declines have been observed in some New England lakes and that they may result from the leaching of calcium from soils or sediments by acid rain. This may be one of the earliest mentions of the possibility of cation depletion in the Adirondacks.

The inferred pH declines, evidenced by what the authors called "qualitatively unique" changes in the diatom flora in all three cores, strongly suggest recent acidification. As had been the case with the Big Moose core, the authors looked for recent watershed disturbances that would explain the declines and found none. Echoing the verdict of the Big Moose study, they concluded,

> We have been unable to explain the unprecedently low mIpHs [mean inferred pHs] for the top samples in terms of recent changes originating in the watersheds and therefore propose that acid deposition is the likely cause.

This conclusion would not have surprised any of the acid rain researchers of the middle 1970s. But it had taken 15 years of research and some rather arcane investigations into the taxonomy and ecology of two microscopic groups of algae before it could finally be made publicly and confidently.

SUMMARY

At the start of the 1980s, there was a strong geographic association between acid deposition, acidic lakes, and fishless lakes. Researchers wanted to quantify this association and make it causal. To do this, they needed to explain how a fairly uniform cause – deposition – could result in the great variety of lake chemistries they were encountering. And they needed to separate naturally acidic lakes from artificially acid ones and show that the latter began to acidify only when they received acid deposition.

The first problem, accounting for the variety of lakes, was solved by the hydrological models and lake classification developed by the ILWAS and RILWAS. Using them it was possible to explain why some lakes acidified and others didn't, to identify the lakes that were most susceptible to acidification, and to describe how a population of lakes of varying hydrologies and chemistries might respond to acid deposition.

With these models came several scientific bonuses and at least one scientific puzzle. The bonuses were a set of chemical diagnostics that made it possible to separate the different hydrological types of lakes without detailed watershed studies and distinguish organic acidity from mineral acidity. These diagnostic tools were immediately put to work in the large synoptic lake studies that began in the middle 1980s.

The puzzle was that the hydrological models only partly explained the spring acidity peaks that affected many lakes and streams. The springtime peaks, it appeared, involved nitrates in addition to sulfates and biological processes in addition to flowpaths and soils. This realization led to much research, and thus to the new results described in Chapter 5 and the new problems described in Chapters 9 and 10.

The second problem facing researchers at the start of the 1980s was how to establish, beyond a reasonable doubt, that the acidic lakes were newly acid. The lake-watershed studies could not do this: they could show that there was mineral acid in the most acidic lakes, but they could not show that those lakes had not been acid before the mineral acids arrived.

What was needed was historical evidence of acidification. Paleolimnological methods, using isotope dating and microfossils, supplied this. They reconstructed the original pHs of acidified lakes, dated the onset of acidification, and determined its rate and extent. Before the first lake cores were analyzed, skeptics could still argue – though not demonstrate – that natural causes might be responsible for most of the observed acidification. By 1990, after a dozen or more cores from the Adirondacks and elsewhere had been analyzed, this was no longer tenable. Naturally acidic lakes of course existed and had existed for a long time. But acid rain, as researchers had long suspected, was the major cause, and in many cases the only cause, of recent lake acidification.

NOTES

General: for a detailed summary of the state of acid rain research in the 1980s see Charles, *Acidic Deposition and Aquatic Ecosystems,* 1991, and especially Chapter 6: "Adirondack mountains," by Driscoll et al.

p. 40 For the early history of acid rain, see Gorham, "Acid deposition and its ecological effects: A brief history of research," 1998. Gene Likens's original acid rain papers include Likens, Bormann, and Johnson, "Acid rain," 1972; Cogbill and Likens, "Acid precipitation in the northeast U.S.," 1974; Likens and Bormann, "Acid rain, a serious regional problem," 1976.

p. 41 The first reports of the mobilization of aluminum were Wright et al., "Impact of acid precipitation on freshwater ecosystems in Norway," 1976, and Cronan and Schofield, "Aluminum leaching response to acid precipitation: Effects on high-elevation watersheds in the Northeast," 1979. For early Adirondack reports of aluminum toxicity, see Driscoll et al., "Effect of aluminium speciation on fish in dilute acidified waters," 1980, and Baker and Schofield, "Aluminum Toxicity to Fish in Acidic Waters, "1982.

pp. 41-42 For the DEC's early studies of lake and stream acidity and its effects on fisheries, see Pfeiffer and Festa, "Acidity status of lakes in the Adirondack region of New York in relation to fish resources," 1980; Colquhoun et al., *Preliminary Report of Stream Sampling for Acidification Studies – 1980,* 1981, plus a 1982 supplement; and Colquhoun, Kretser, and Pfeiffer, *Acidity Status Update of Lakes and Streams in New York State,* 1984. Colquhoun and his collaborators began their studies of stream acidity during a study of the effects of methoxychlor, an insecticide used to kill black-fly larvae; the original study is described in Colquhoun et al., *Nontarget Effects of the Adirondack Black-fly* (Simuliidae) *Treatment Program,* 1983.

pp. 45-47 For the design and results from the ILWAS, see Goldstein et al., "A framework for the Integrated Lake-Watershed Acidification Study," 1980; Johannes and Altwicker, "Atmospheric inputs into three Adirondack lake watersheds," 1980; Johannes, Galloway, and Troutman, "Snowpack storage and ion release," 1980; April, "Mineralogy of the ILWAS watersheds," 1983; Newton, *Distribution and characteristics of surficial geological materials in the ilwas watersheds,* 1983; and Chen et al., "Hydrological analyses of acidic and alkaline lakes," 1984.

p. 48-55 For results from the RILWAS, see Cronan, Conlan, and Skibinski, "Forest vegetation in relation to surface water chemistry in the North Branch of the Big Moose River," 1987; Driscoll and Newton, "Chemical characteristics of Adirondack lakes," 1985; Driscoll, Yatsko, and Unangst, "Longitudinal and temporal trends in the water chemistry of the North Branch of the Moose River," 1987; Goldstein et al., "Lake-watershed acidification in the North Branch of the Moose River," 1987; Johnson et al., "In situ toxicity tests of fishes in acid waters," 1987; Newton, Weintraub, and April, "The relationship between water chemistry and geology in the North Branch of the Moose River," 1987; Peters and Driscoll, "Hydrogeological controls of surface water chemistry in the Adirondack region of New York State," 1987; Rasher, Driscoll, and Peters, "Flux of solutes during snowmelt from snow and forest floor during snowmelt," 1987; Schofield and Driscoll, "Fish species distribution in relation to water quality gradients in the North Branch of the Moose River Basin," 1987; Gherini et al., "Regional Integrated Lake-Watershed Acidification Study (RILWAS): Summary of major findings," 1989; Schaefer et al., "The episodic acidification of Adirondack lakes during snowmelt," 1990; and the discussion later in this chapter.

p. 44 For the PIRLA studies, see Chapter 4 and Charles and Whitehead, "The PIRLA Project: Paleoecological investigations of recent lake acidification," 1986; Charles and Smol, "The PIRLA II Project: Regional assessment of lake acidification trends," 1990; Charles et al., "Paleolimnological evidence for recent acidification of Big Moose Lake, Adirondack Mountains, N.Y. (USA)," 1987 .

p. 47 For the ILWAS model of flowpaths in different soil layers, see Goldstein et al., "A framework for the Integrated Lake-Watershed Acidification Study," 1980. An important feature of the model is that each layer has a different flow capacity, and once the rate at which water is supplied by precipitation or melting exceeds that capacity, the incoming water can no longer enter that layer and must either move through the layers above it or flow over the surface. Thus in low-flow periods, when the deep layers are not filled to capacity, the main flowpaths are deep in the soil, and the atmospheric acids are adsorbed or neutralized. At high-flow periods after storms or during snowmelt, the deep layers can only transport a fraction of the water, and the rest flows over or near the surface, transmitting the atmospheric acids directly to lakes and streams.

1983 The Paleoecological Investigations of Recent Lake Acidification (PIRLA) project is organized by White-head and Charles. It is sponsored by the Electric Power Research Institute and involves investigators from 11 U.S. and Canadian universities. In the next three years they collect sediment cores from 30 lakes and sediment surface samples from another 164 lakes.

1984 The U.S. Environmental Protection Agency begins the National Surface Water Survey. Its northeastern component, the Eastern Lake Survey, samples 1,592 lakes, including 128 in the Adirondack Park, between 1984 and 1986.

1984 The New York State Department of Conservation and the Empire State Electrical Energy Research Corporation create the Adirondack Lakes Survey Corporation (ALSC), a not-for-profit corporation charged with doing an extensive survey of the chemistry and biology of Adirondack lakes. Under the direction of Walt Kretser, the ALSC conducts field surveys of 1,459 lakes in the next three years.

1986 The Environmental Protection Agency publishes the results of the first phase of the Eastern Lake Survey. The Adirondacks have the highest percentage of acidified lakes in any of the five regions in the survey: in EPA's Adirondack Region (which includes lakes outside the Adirondacks) the survey estimates that 20% of the lakes have pHs below 5.5 and 38% have summer ANCs below 50 µeq/l .

1986 The second phase of the Eastern Lake Survey resamples 154 lakes, taking spring, summer, and fall samples from each lake.

1987 Driscoll and his collaborators in the Regionalized Integrated Lake-Watershed Study of the North Branch of the Moose River show that stream acidity is controlled by soil depth and hydrology and that the most acidic lakes and streams have the lowest fish diversity and highest fish mortality.

1988 The PIRLA-II project collects sediment cores from an additional 37 statistically selected Adirondack lakes.

1989 Kretser, Gallagher, and Nicolette publish the first summary of the biological and chemical results of the Adirondack Lakes Survey. They find that 39% of the lakes they surveyed have pHs below 5.5 and a remarkable 50% have summer ANCs below 50 µeq/l. They confirm that fish diversity decreases as acidity increases. They find that 22% of the lakes they survey have no fish and estimate that at least a third of these previously had fish and have lost them because of acidification.

1990 Baker et al. publish the *Interpretive Analysis,* a summary and analysis of the findings of the Adirondack Lakes Survey.

1990 Charles summarizes the results of the PIRLA-I studies; he notes that the lake acidification detected by the surveys is occurring too fast to be the result of natural causes and concludes that acid deposition has acidified lakes in the Adirondack Mountains, New England, Ontario, Quebec, the Atlantic provinces of Canada, the upper Midwest, and Florida.

1991 Charles edits *Acidic Deposition and Aquatic Ecosystems,* the first book-length treatment of the effects of acid rain in North America. Driscoll et al. prepare a chapter on the Adirondack mountains, summarizing the major studies of the 1980s, for this volume.

1990 The National Acid Precipitation Assessment Program produces its first *State of Science and Technology* assessment, containing 27 separate reports on the production, deposition, effects, and control of atmospheric acids.

1990 Herlihy and his collaborators publish the results of the second phase of the Eastern Lake Survey.

1992 Charles and his collaborators summarize the PIRLA-II reconstructions of lake histories. They estimate that 25 to 35% of Adirondack lakes whose current ANC is less than 400 µeq/l have acidified recently and that prior to acid deposition only about 15% of these lakes had pHs less than 5.5 and none had pHs less than 5.0.

THE BIG SYNOPTIC STUDIES, 1984–1991

LAKE ACIDIFICATION IS MEASURED AND MAPPED

4

In the early 1980s it was known that acid deposition had affected at least some northeastern lakes. But it was not known how many lakes had been affected, or how much they had been acidified, or how much of the acidity was natural and how much the result of acid deposition. The tools described in the previous chapter – lake classifications, chemical signatures, and paleolimnological reconstructions – were developed to answer these questions. By 1985 three projects were using these tools to assess lake acidification on a large scale. The first two, the Eastern Lake Survey and the Adirondack Lakes Survey, were large synoptic surveys of current lake chemistry and biology. The third, the Paleoecological Investigations of Recent Lake Acidification project, was a smaller but still synoptic survey of lake histories. By 1990, these surveys had created a clear regional picture of the geography and timing of lake acidification. This chapter describes that picture.

THE EASTERN LAKE SURVEY, 1984–1986

The Eastern Lake Survey (ELS) was one of seven regional surveys that made up the National Surface Water Survey, a federal project coordinated by the Environmental Protection Agency. The ELS covered the Northeast, Southeast, and upper Midwest. Like the other regional surveys, it was a statistical survey of lakes that used measurements from a randomly selected study set of lakes to estimate the condition of a much larger target population of lakes of interest. Thus, from a study set of about 18,000 lakes in New York and New England that were shown on 1:250,000 topographic maps, 2,681 lakes were randomly selected for study. About 40% of these were determined to be too small (under 4 hectares), shallow, salty, or inaccessible to be sampled. The remaining 1,592 lakes were sampled and used to estimate the chemistry of the total set of 18,000 lakes.

Like the Adirondack Lakes Survey (p. 69), the ELS was designed as a complete chemical survey that would examine all the major ions in lake water. It analyzed for ten elements (Al, Ca, Cl, F, Fe, K, Mg, Mn, Na, P,); four ions (H^+, NH_4^+, SO_4^{2-}, and NO_3^-); silica, inorganic carbon, and organic carbon; and color, conductivity, and acid-neutralizing capacity. It determined total and monomeric aluminum but did not separate the inorganic and organic fractions of the monomeric aluminum.*

In upstate New York, the ELS chose 155 lakes, 128 in the Adirondack Park and 27 outside it, to represent what it called

EASTERN LAKE SURVEY "ADIRONDACK REGION" STUDY LAKES

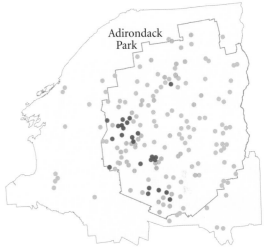

Fall pH: ● < 5.0   ● 5.0–5.9   ● 6.0 or greater

From Driscoll et al., "Adirondack mountains," 1991. The Eastern Lake Survey chose its study lakes by dividing its study area into subregions and then taking a random sample of the target population of potentially suitable lakes in the region. In northern New York this resulted in a study set of 155 randomly selected lakes that were used to represent a target population of 1,290 lakes. To these were added 49 "special interest" lakes that were sampled but not used to make inferences about the target population, making a total of 203 lakes. Somewhat controversially, the area that the ELS called the Adirondack Region included 27 study lakes (17% of the total) outside the Adirondack Park. None of these lakes were strongly acidified. Had the study been restricted to lakes within the park, its estimate of the number of acidified lakes would have been about 20% higher.

* The Adirondack Lakes Survey added analyses for Cu, Pb, and Zn and took the crucial step of separating the toxic (inorganic) and nontoxic forms of monomeric aluminum.

the Adirondack Region. Both drainage and seepage lakes were included, but bog lakes were excluded. In the first phase of the survey (ELS-1) each lake was sampled once, in the fall of 1984, 1985, or 1986. The results were first reported in 1986 and given a detailed comparative analysis in 1990.

The results of the ELS-1 paralleled those from the smaller studies described in Chapter 3.* The Adirondacks had the lowest median acid-neutralizing capacity and the highest percentage of acidic lakes of any of the five subregions in the Northeast. The median ANC was just over 100 µeq/L; 38% of the lakes had fall ANCs under 50 µeq/l, and 14% of the lakes had ANCs less than 0. Ten percent of the lakes had pH values below 5.0, and 20% had values below 5.5. The lakes within the Adirondack Park were more acid than those in Adirondack Region as a whole, with a median ANC of 69 µeq/l and 16% with ANCs less than 0.

Seventy-eight percent of the lakes sampled by ELS were drainage lakes. Their average chemistry was similar to that of the RILWAS drainage lakes discussed on p. 50. Sulfate was the principal acid anion in most of the lakes and was, on average, three to four times as abundant as the anions of natural organic acids. Nitrate and ammonium concentrations were very low, as would be expected in fall samples, and do not show on the composition graphs. Aluminum concentrations were variable but, on average, higher than in any other region the ELS studied. Again as expected, most lakes with pHs below 5.5 had significantly elevated aluminum concentrations, and the highest concentrations were in the most acidic lakes.

As predicted by the RILWAS results (p. 52), the acid-neutralizing capacities were strongly related to the sum of base cations and to the acid-base ratio. This strongly suggested that it was the degree to which atmospheric acids were being neutralized in the watersheds that was controlling the variation in ANC from lake to lake.

The Eastern Lake Survey had important limitations, and these must be remembered when comparing its results with those of other surveys or using it as a measure of the extent of lake acidification. It was a fall survey and so missed the early-season peaks of snowmelt acidity. It was limited to lakes of 4 hectares or larger, which were, on average, less acid than the smaller lakes studied by the Adirondack Lakes Survey. It did not separate inorganic and organic aluminum and so could not estimate the concentration of the toxic inorganic aluminum directly. And it did not separate the different types of lakes and so mixed results from lakes whose intrinsic sensitivity to acidification varied greatly.

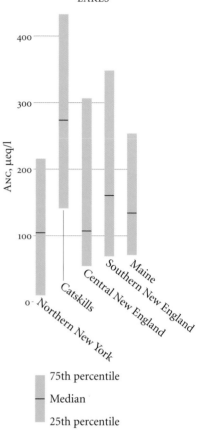

ANCS OF EASTERN LAKE SURVEY LAKES

ANC, µeq/l

- 75th percentile
- Median
- 25th percentile

From Baker et al., "Current status of surface water acid-base chemistry," 1990. The Adirondack Region had the lowest fall ANCs of any of the five regions studied. Median ANCs were around 100 µeq/l and median pHs about 6.5, but significant numbers of lakes had pHs under 5.5 and ANCs near or below 0 µeq/l.

* The results of the ELS-1 were first published in Linthurst et al., *Characteristics of Lakes in the Eastern United States Volume I: Population Descriptions and Physico-Chemical Relationships,* 1986; and Overton et al., *Characteristics of Lakes in the Eastern United States Volume II: Lakes Sampled and Descriptive Statistics for Physical and Chemical Variables,* 1986. The graphs on these pages are from two useful analyses of the data: Baker et al., "Current status of surface water acid-base chemistry," 1990; and Driscoll et al., "Adirondack mountains," 1991.

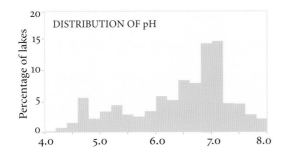

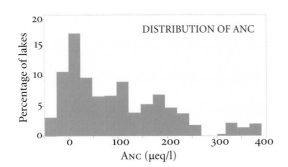

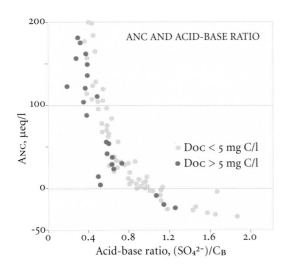

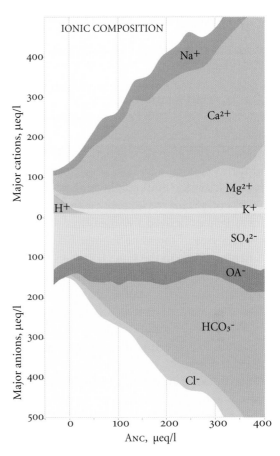

All figures redrawn with permission from Driscoll et al., "Adirondack Mountains." Copyright 1991 Springer Science and Business Media and used with its permission. The ion distribution diagram is dominated by bicarbonate and base cations at high ANCs but by sulfate, organic acid ions, and hydrogen ions at low ANCs. The watersheds have uniformly high sulfate concentrations, indicating that they all are receiving significant amounts of sulfuric acid. The extent to which the sulfuric acid has been neutralized in the watershed, measured by the amount of base cations or the acid-base ratio, varies from watershed to watershed and determines the ANC. The amounts of dissolved organic carbon and organic acids are relatively low and, at least in the nonbog lakes considered in the ELS, do not seem to be having a large influence on ANC. Lakes with elevated aluminum concentrations are common but only in the southwestern Adirondacks, where ANCs are very low.

The first of these problems was addressed in the second phase of the ELS, in 1986. The last three of these problems were addressed in the Adirondack Lakes Survey.

The Second Phase of the Eastern Lake Survey, 1986

The first phase of the Eastern Lake Survey (ELS-I) took a single fall sample from each lake. The second phase (ELS-II), which was designed to detect spring acidification and measure the errors associated with single samples, resampled 145 of the ELS-I lakes in spring, summer, and fall of 1986. Fifty of these were then resampled twice more in the same fall.

By comparing these results with the ELS-I results from 1984, the investigators derived five measures of variability: between different analyses of the same sample, between different samples from different places in the same lake, between the same lake in different seasons, between the same lake in different years, and between different lakes. The results provided the first regional picture of how lake chemistry varies within lakes and between seasons.

We show the results for ANC; those for other variables are generally similar. The differences between lakes show the greatest variance, followed by the differences between seasons. The seasonal differences are particularly important because many lakes that are nearly neutral in the summer become acidic in the spring. The spring measurements, which were taken several weeks after ice-out and thus did not capture the most acid conditions, still showed 24% more lakes with ANCs less than 0 µeq/l than did summer or fall measurements.

The differences between years were smaller and in most cases would not have changed the total number of lakes classified as acid. The differences between different locations in the same lake and different analyses of the same sample were smaller still.

Thus, even though lakes are complex and the analysis of dilute waters technically difficult, it appears that single samples give a surprisingly accurate picture of the overall chemistry of a given lake in a given season. But single samples cannot predict how the lake will change from season to season. Only monthly sampling, which is the current gold standard in lake monitoring, can do this.

The results from ELS-II have been very important for the design of subsequent surveys. What they say, in essence, is that most of the variability in lake chemistry is between lakes and between seasons, and so the more lakes you sample and the more seasons you sample them in, the more you will learn. Sampling different points in the same lake is probably unnecessary, and sampling in multiple years, though essential for detecting long-term trends, is probably unnecessary for determining the overall distribution of acidic lakes.

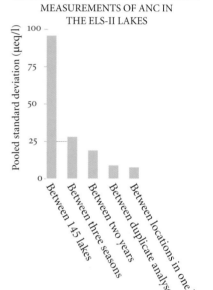

Both graphs from Herlihy et al., *Temporal Variability in Lakewater Chemistry in the Northeastern United States: Results of Phase II of the Eastern Lake Survey, 1990.* The results are for all 145 lakes that were resampled, not just for the 36 in the Adirondacks. Spring ANCs are consistently lower than fall ANCs. The difference is greatest in the high-ANC lakes, which are both acidified and diluted in the spring, and less in the low-ANC lakes, which are already dilute and acid. The pooled variance between individual lakes is about four times larger than the variance between years and 20 times larger than the variance within a single lake.

THE ADIRONDACK LAKES SURVEY, 1984-1987

The Adirondack Lakes Survey was designed to determine, by as exhaustive a survey as possible, how many Adirondack lakes had been acidified, and how fish populations had been affected by acidification.

This was a daunting task. The ILWAS and RILWAS had established that there were at least ten different populations of Adirondack lakes, each physically and chemically different from the others. The existence of these distinct groups of lakes means that a randomly selected lake is not representative of Adirondack lakes in general but only of lakes of similar type and size. Thus, for example, the high acidities and depauperate fish populations that Schofield observed in his 1976 survey (p. 41) were probably representative of other small, high-elevation lakes like those he surveyed but not of larger lakes at lower elevations. And likewise, the set of lakes studied by the ELS, which was dominated by medium-sized drainage lakes, was probably not representative of some parts of the western Adirondacks, where small seepage lakes were common.

What this meant was that any survey that wanted to present an accurate picture of the state of Adirondack lakes would have to treat each of the main types of lakes separately. It would have to divide the Adirondack lakes into classes, determine how common each class was in the Adirondacks, and sample enough members of each class to determine the chemistry and biology of that type of lake.

The Adirondack Lakes Survey was designed to do exactly that. It began in 1984, finished its field work in 1987, and issued its major *Interpretive Analysis* in 1990. It surveyed 1,469 lakes, including examples of every hydrological class; gathered enough physical and chemical data to classify every lake it studied; and did a semi-quantitative fishery survey of each lake. It is the only Adirondack survey, before or since, that has surveyed this many lakes and characterized them this thoroughly, and one of the only surveys anywhere to do parallel biological, physical, and chemical surveys on about half the lakes in a region of six-million acres.*

The Design of the Survey

The field work for the ALS began in 1984 and continued through 1987. In the first three years 1,247 lakes in the large northern and western watersheds of the park were surveyed. In the fourth year 222 lakes from the southern and eastern watersheds were surveyed. Altogether, 1,469 lakes were surveyed, or about 53% of the estimated population of 2,760 Adirondack lakes in the desired size range.

WATERSHEDS INCLUDED IN THE
ADIRONDACK LAKES SURVEY

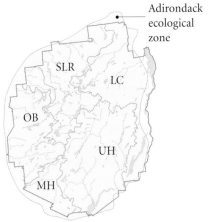

LC Lake Champlain
MH Mohawk-Hudson
OB Oswegatchie-Black
SLR St. Lawrence-Raquette
UH Upper Hudson

The ALS focused on five major watersheds within the Adirondack ecological zone, defined as the portion of those watersheds above the 1,000-foot contour. There are about 2,760 lakes larger than 0.2 hectares within this zone. The ALS excluded lakes over 203 ha, lakes that had been disturbed by recent fisheries work or liming, and lakes that were too shallow, weedy, or filled with snags to sample, giving it a set of about 2,500 candidate lakes. From these, 1,469 were chosen for sampling; 1,247 lakes in the three northern and western watersheds were sampled between 1984 and 1986 and 222 lakes in the two southern and eastern watersheds in 1987.

*The methods and results of the ALS are documented in Kretser, Gallagher, and Nicolette, *Adirondack Lakes Survey 1984-1987, An Evaluation of Fish Communities and Water Chemistry*, 1989; and Baker et al., *Adirondack Lakes Survey: An Interpretive Analysis of Fish Communities and Water Chemistry, 1984-1987*, 1990.

Each selected lake was visited twice: once in the spring or fall for mapping and biological sampling, and once in midsummer for chemical sampling. In the spring and fall surveys the lake was measured, notes were taken on vegetation and aquatic invertebrates, and fish were collected and identified in a standardized manner, using gillnets, seines, and traps. Single surface-water samples were also taken. In the midsummer surveys, both surface and deep chemical samples were taken and field determinations of temperature, pH, and dissolved oxygen were made. In addition, a blank (distilled water) sample for quality control was prepared at each lake, and triplicate samples, also for quality control, were taken from about 5% of the lakes.

All of this created a very large data set: the ALS database contains 11,000 entries on 1,469 waterbodies and includes about 220,000 laboratory determinations. The consistency of the data, as measured by chain-of-custody records, duplicate and blank analyses, and calculations of charge balance, ANC, and conductance, was quite high: fewer than 1% of the laboratory analyses failed quality-control tests.

General Chemical Results

The overall results of the ALS paralleled those of earlier surveys. About 40% of the lakes were at least moderately acidic, with summer pHs below 5.5. Twenty-six percent, representing 8% of the

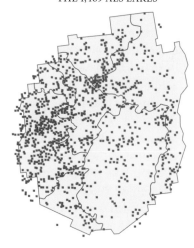

The ALS used a semirandom sampling design. About two-thirds of the lakes were chosen randomly. The remaining third were chosen from lakes within 2 km of a randomly selected lake so that travel time would be minimized and each size class and elevation well represented. This design was a compromise between the desire to have a statistically unbiased sample, the desire sample each size class evenly, and the need to use helicopter and crew time efficiently.

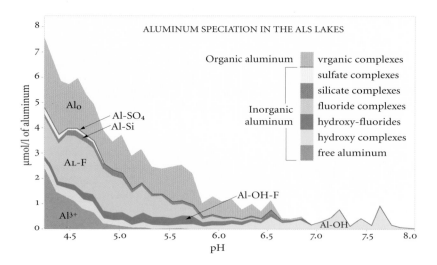

Aluminum and pH. From Munson, Driscoll, and Gherini, "Phenomenological analysis of ALSC chemistry data," in Baker et al., *Adirondack Lakes Survey: An Interpretive Analysis of Fish Communities and Water Chemistry, 1984–1987,* 1990. The ALS was the first large-scale survey to separate monomeric aluminum into organic and inorganic fractions. Inorganic aluminum reacts with proteins and so is toxic to fish and other aquatic animals. Both its total concentration and its importance relative to other forms of aluminum increase with decreasing pH. At pH 6.0, typical of a well-buffered lake, it is a relatively minor component, representing about a third of all monomeric aluminum. At pH 4.5, typical of a highly acidified lake, it is eight times more concentrated and represents three-quarters of all monomeric aluminum.

total lake area, were strongly acidic, with pHs below 5.0. Strongly acid waters were found throughout the Adirondacks but were most common in the west and south, where precipitation is high and the ability of the soils to neutralize acids generally low.

As expected, low acid-neutralizing capacities and significant amounts of inorganic aluminum were associated with low pHs.

About 50% of the lakes had summer ANCs below 50 ueq/l and so were considered potentially sensitive to pulses of acidity following storms; 26%, representing 11% of the total lake area, had summer ANCs below zero and so were chronically acid. Inorganic aluminum was common in most acidic lakes and, as in the RILWAS and ELS lakes, began to reach biologically significant levels when the pH dropped below 6.

Sulfate was the most abundant acid anion in summer, with a median concentration of 106 ueq/l in drainage lakes; thus it was clear that atmospheric sulfate was reaching most lakes and was likely the cause of at least some of the observed acidification. But neither the variations in sulfate nor the variations in the sum of sulfate plus nitrate correlated with the variations in ANC, suggesting that although the atmospheric acids were clearly causing lake acidification, other factors might still be controlling it.

The total amount of base cations, on the other hand, correlated extremely well with the ANC. This was consistent with the ILWAS model, in which cation exchange processes in watershed soils neutralize atmospheric acids by immobilizing hydrogen ions and releasing base cations (p. 47). The extent of this neutralization varied from watershed to watershed and was responsible for much of the ANC variation from one lake to another. Put another way, while acid deposition guaranteed that *some* lakes would be acid, the different amounts of cation exchange in different watersheds apparently determined *which* lakes will be acid and how acid they would be.

The Geography of Acidification

Lake acidification in the Adirondacks has a clear geographic pattern. Nonacidic lakes are more common than acidic ones and are found throughout the park. Acidic lakes are largely restricted to the western half of the park, where rainfall and deposition are higher and the bedrock is lower in bases (p. 42). Within the western Adirondacks, the distributions of slightly and strongly acidic lakes are similar, suggesting that the degree of acidification is locally controlled: any western watershed that has slightly acidic lakes also has strongly acid ones.

Lake Classification

The ALS developed a working classification of 12 lake types that could be recognized from a combination of physical and chemical data. The results both showed the complex chemical variation in Adirondack lakes and let researchers identify the lakes that were most sensitive to acidification.

THE pHS OF THE ALS LAKES

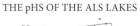

pH >6.0

pH 5.5 to 5.9

pH 5.0 to 5.4

pH < 5.0

Maps from Gallagher and Baker, "Current status of fish communities in Adirondack lakes," in Baker et al., *Adirondack Lakes Survey: An Interpretive Analysis of Fish Communities and Water Chemistry, 1984–1987*, 1990. Circumneutral lakes (with pHs over 6) are found throughout the Adirondacks; low-pH lakes are mostly in the west and north.

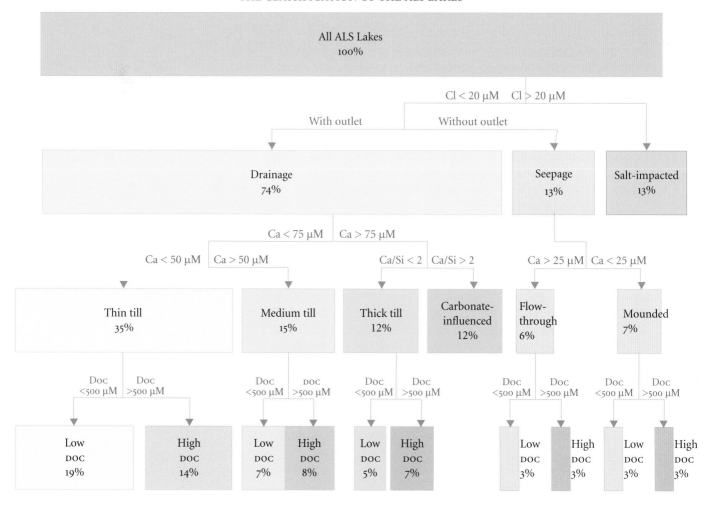

The major results of the classification are shown in the graphs on the next three pages. Drainage lakes are much more common than seepage lakes overall and come in all sizes. About half of them, mostly in the thick-till and carbonate-influenced groups, have summer ANCs over 50 ueq/l and are considered relatively insensitive to acidification. Another quarter have ANCs between 0 and 50 ueq/l and are considered sensitive. The final quarter have summer ANCs below 0 ueq/l and are considered chronically acid.

Seepage lakes – lakes without outlets – are much less common than drainage lakes and were to some extent neglected in lake surveys before the ALS. But because they are easily acidified, they contribute disproportionately to the geography of acidification. And because they are locally common in some parts of the Adirondacks and are chemically different from drainage lakes, they need to be considered in any account of Adirondack acidification.

The ALS was the first survey to provide a detailed picture of seepage lakes. The ones it studied were, on average, smaller, deeper, and more acid than drainage lakes. It found that they made up about

From Newton and Driscoll, "Classification of ALSC Lakes," in Baker et al., *Adirondack Lakes Survey: An Interpretive Analysis of Fish Communities and Water Chemistry, 1984–1987,* 1990. The ALS classification developed from the RILWAS (p. 48) and was designed to separate the lakes into groups that respond to acidification in similar ways. The lakes are first divided by hydrology. Drainage lakes are further divided by the average depth of the soil. Then all lakes are divided by the amount of dissolved organic carbon, separating naturally acid (high-DOC) lakes from the rest. The salt-impacted lakes are mostly lakes near roads that are affected by road salt. Because the salt increases the concentration of acid anions in these lakes and makes it difficult to determine the amount of acid contributed by acid deposition, they were usually excluded from analyses of the causes of acidification.

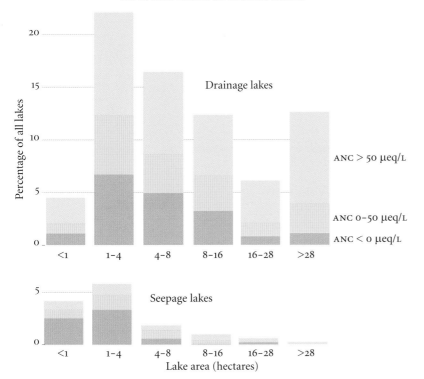

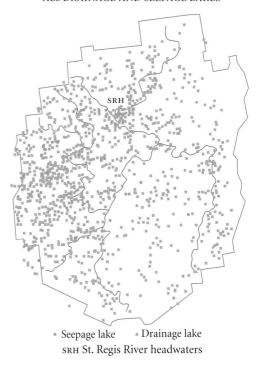

- Seepage lake   · Drainage lake
SRH St. Regis River headwaters

13% of all the lakes studied and averaged only a third of the size of drainage lakes. Three-quarters of them were under 4 hectares, the smallest size studied in the Eastern Lake Survey. Their watersheds averaged only 28 hectares, a fifth that of the drainage lakes, but their average depth of 2.7 meters was a third greater than that of the drainage lakes.

As small, deep lakes with little surface inflow, many had water budgets dominated by precipitation and chemistries controlled by acid anions. But even so there were significant differences in chemistry – and hence in sensitivity to acidification –among them. More than half of them, mostly perched seepage lakes with little groundwater inflow (p. 48), had ANCs below 0 µeq/l and so were chronically acid. Another quarter had ANCs between 0 and 50 µeq/l and were likely very sensitive to atmospheric deposition. The remaining quarter, mostly flow-through seepage lakes with some groundwater inflow, had summer ANCs over 50 µeq/l, significant amounts of base cations, and at least some capacity to resist further acidification.

The Sources of Lake Acidity

Because lakes contain both natural acids and atmospheric (mineral) acids, and because the hydrogen ions from these sources are identical, the pH or ANC of a lake, by itself, tells us nothing about where the acidity came from or whether it is the result of natural

Graph from data in Kretser, Gallagher, and Nicolette, *Adirondack Lakes Survey: 1984-1987,* 1989. Map from Newton and Driscoll, "Classification of ALSC lakes," in Baker et al., *Adirondack Lakes Survey: An Interpretive Analysis of Fish Communities and Water Chemistry, 1984-1987,* 1990. Drainage lakes are found throughout the park but are least common in the eastern mountains and commonest in the broader and flatter valleys of the north and west. Seepage lakes, which commonly form in glacial outwash, are uncommon in the south- and east-draining watersheds, more common in those that drain west and north, and especially concentrated near the headwaters of the St. Regis River.

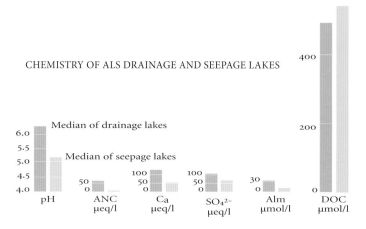

CHEMISTRY OF ALS DRAINAGE AND SEEPAGE LAKES

Median of drainage lakes

Median of seepage lakes

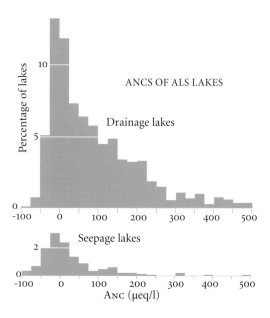

ANCS OF ALS LAKES

Drainage lakes

Seepage lakes

ANC (µeq/l)

Bar graph from data in Kretser, Gallagher, and Nicolette, *Adirondack Lakes Survey: 1984-1987,* 1989; histograms from Newton and Driscoll, "Classification of ALSC lakes," in Baker et al., *Adirondack Lakes Survey: An Interpretive Analysis of Fish Communities and Water Chemistry, 1984-1987,* 1990. Seepage lakes, on average, are higher in DOC than drainage lakes but lower in pH, ANC, sulfate, base cations, and aluminum.

processes or acid deposition. This must be inferred from either historical reconstructions or ion-balance diagnostics (p. 50).

The PIRLA studies described later in this chapter used historical reconstructions. The ALS used ion balances and was in fact the first survey to compute them for a large sample of acidic lakes. The results were interesting and somewhat unexpected.

The ion balance method compares C_B, the sum of the concentrations of base cations, to C_A, the sum of the concentrations of the acid anions. The underlying assumption is that C_A tells you how much mineral acid has been deposited in the watershed, and C_B how much of that acid has been neutralized. Thus, for lakes with a pH equal to or less than 5,

> if $C_B > C_A$, all the mineral acid has been neutralized in the watershed and only organic acids are present;

> if $C_A > C_B$, mineral acid is present; if in addition $C_A - C_B$ is less than H^+, organic acids are present as well and the fraction of the total acidity derived from mineral acids is at least $(C_A - C_B)/[H^+]$.

The upper graph on the opposite page plots the distribution of the base-acid difference $C_A - C_B$. Lakes to the right of the red line have only organic acids; lakes to the left of the red line have a mixture of organic and mineral acids, and the farther to the left they are, the more mineral acid they have. The center of the distribution is near the red line, suggesting that lakes with organic acidity and lakes with mineral acidity are both common.

The lower graph on the opposite page, which plots the number of lakes in which a given fraction of acidity is balanced by organic anions, gives a more precise picture of the relative importance of mineral and organic acids. Interestingly, most lakes are dominated by one or the other but not by an equal mixture of both. In 43% of the low-pH drainage lakes, 80% or more of the acidity is associated with organic anions. In 36%, less than 20% of the acidity is. This is a very nonrandom distribution. Apparently some features of hydrology or chemistry, which to our knowledge have not yet

DISTINGUISHING ORGANIC AND MINERAL ACID

Only mineral acids present

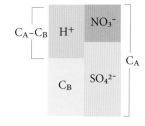

The excess of acid anions $C_A - C_B$ equals the concentration of hydrogen ion, H^+; all of the hydrogen ion is assumed to be from mineral acids from acid deposition.

Both mineral & organic acids present

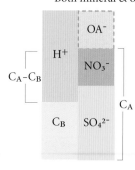

The excess of acid anions $C_A - C_B$ is less than the concentration of hydrogen ion, H^+; some of the hydrogen ion is assumed to be from organic acids with organic anions OA^-. The fraction of the hydrogen ion from minerals acids is assumed to be $(C_A - C_B)/H^+$.

Only organic acids present

$C_A < C_B$ and all the hydrogen ion is assumed to be from organic acids with organic anions OA^-.

been explained, make it unlikely that both kinds of acidity will coexist in significant amounts.

It is important to realize that although the ion balance method was historically useful for demonstrating that mineral acids were present, it gives, at best, a minimum estimate of their importance. In particular, any lake or watershed process that generates base cations or removes acid anions will reduce the apparent fraction of the acidity associated with mineral acids. Since such processes are common, the actual importance of mineral acids is probably considerably greater, and the actual importance of organic acids correspondingly less, than the graphs on this page indicate.

Nonetheless, the association between organic acids, dissolved organic carbon (DOC), and low pHs in some of the ALS lakes was something of a scientific surprise. It had been known for a long time that DOC was produced by the decay of organic material and contained significant amounts of organic acids. But it had been assumed that these were all weak acids, which would be "fully protonated" (undissociated) at low pHs and so would not contribute to acidity at pHs much below 5 or 5.5. The ALS found otherwise: apparently some natural organic acids are quite strong and capable of contributing to acidity at pHs of 4.5 or even 4.0. They are rarely the dominant acids at low pHs but their presence is biologically interesting and raises some interesting questions about the impacts of wetlands on lake chemistry, to which we will return in Chapter 7.

Fish and Acidity

It had been known since the middle 1970s that some acidic lakes had no fish but not whether fishlessness was the rule or the exception. The fishery surveys conducted by the Adirondack Lakes Survey were designed to investigate this question on a large scale. The goal was to map the occurrence and, more generally, the diversity of fish throughout the Adirondacks and then relate the results to the summer chemistry of the lakes and the overall geography of acid deposition.

Scientifically, this was a difficult job. The chemistry of any given lake is fairly uniform and, as the ELS-II had shown, can be sampled in a few minutes with a single bottle. Fish populations, on the other hand, can only be sampled with many hours of seining and trapping. Furthermore, the absence of fish species can have many causes. An acidic lake with low fish diversity might have lost fish species to acid rain. But it also might have lost them to fishermen, beavers, otters, introduced pickerel, or fishery management. Or, especially in seepage lakes that do not have outflows, it may never have had them at all.

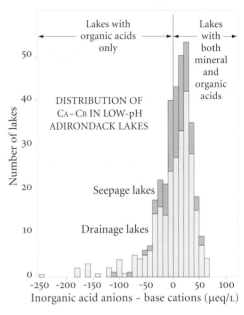

TYPES OF ACIDS IN LOW-pH ALS LAKES

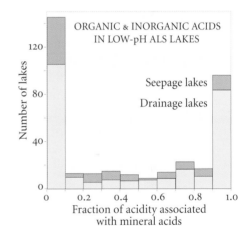

From Munson et al., "Integrated analysis," in Baker et al., *Adirondack Lakes Survey: An Interpretive Analysis of Fish Communities and Water Chemistry, 1984-1987,* 1990. The data are for lakes with pH ≤ 5; in the original publication the x-axis is C_B - C_A. When C_A, the sum of the nitrate and sulfate concentrations, exceeds C_B, the sum of the base cation concentrations, at least some of the hydrogen ion is derived from acid deposition. As noted in the text, this analysis provides a minimum estimate of the importance of mineral acids and is now believed to overemphasize the importance of organic acids; the number of low-pH lakes whose hydrogen ion comes mostly from mineral acids is probably considerably greater than shown in the graphs.

Given both the scale of the project – ALS biologists caught and identified some 202,000 fish from 1,469 lakes – and the number of variables involved, the analysis of the results was necessarily complex. The details are given in two major reports cited on p. 69. Fortunately, and gratifyingly, the Adirondack Lakes Survey scientists who analyzed the data were able to find some simple relations between fish and acidity, which we present here.*

The ALS found a total of 50 fish species and 3 hybrids in their surveys. Thirty-eight of these were native species; the 12 remaining species and the 3 hybrids were introduced. Seventy-six percent of the lakes surveyed had fish; 24% were fishless. The commonest fish caught were brown bullhead, brook trout, and white sucker, all native, acid-tolerant species. The maximum number of fish species caught in any lake was 13. The median number of species varied widely between watersheds. For the less-acidified Champlain, Hudson, and St. Regis watersheds it was four to five species; for the more-acidified Oswegatchie, Black, and Upper Mohawk watersheds it was one species.

Most Adirondack fish species prefer neutral or slightly acid conditions and do not tolerate low pHs well. The majority occurred over a range of 2.5 pH units or less and had an optimum range, in which the central 50% of the population occurred, of less than 1 pH unit. Only four of the 15 most common species were regularly found below pH 5, and only one had an optimum range that extended below pH 5.5. There are, in other words, no acidiphilic fish in the Adirondacks: pH 5.5 seems to be a stress point beyond which most species do not function well, and pH 5.0 a limit below which most species cannot survive.

A striking result of the preference of most fish for near-neutral pHs is that as pH decreases, fish diversity also decreases and the number of lakes without fish increases. Lakes with pHs of 6.5 or more average six species of fish; the number decreases by about one species for every 0.5 unit decrease in pH. Very few lakes with pHs above 5.5 are fishless. Between pH 5.0 and 5.5, about a fifth of the lakes are fishless. Below pH 5.0, more than three-quarters of the lakes are without fish.

At the low end of the diversity curve are the lakes with no fish at all. A second important result of the fish studies was that there was a clear relation between acidity and fishlessness. Most fishless lakes were acid, and many were located in the regions of the park where acid deposition was highest.

Because the pHs of Adirondack lakes are lowest in the western and southwestern watersheds, this is where the majority of fishless lakes are found. The weakly acidified Hudson watershed has only 9% fishless lakes, and the Champlain and St. Regis watersheds

pH RANGES OBSERVED IN THE ALS

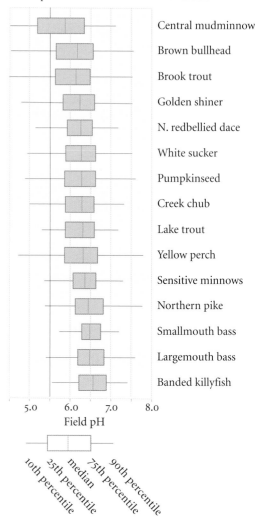

From Gallagher and Baker, "Current status of fish communities in Adirondack lakes," in Baker et al., *Adirondack Lakes Survey: An Interpretive Analysis of Fish Communities and Water Chemistry, 1984–1987*, 1990. If the optimum range of the species is defined as the range over which the central 50% of the records occur, then only one species has a pH optimum below 5.5 and none have pH optima below 5.0.

*The principal biologists involved in the analysis of the ALS results were Joan Baker, Sigurd Christensen, James Gallagher, William Warren Hicks. Walt Kretser, Kenneth Reckhow, and Carl Schofield.

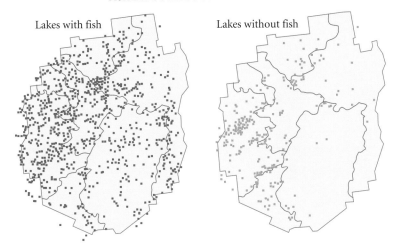

Lakes with fish   Lakes without fish

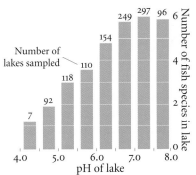

about 14% each. The strongly acidified Oswegatchie, Black River, and Upper Mohawk watersheds have about 38% each.

Fish in Different Types of Lakes

As we would expect, there are clear correlations between the presence and diversity of fish and the type of lake (graphs on p. 78). Seepage lakes and thin-till drainage lakes, the most easily acidified types of lakes, average about two to three fish species per lake less than the less easily acidified drainage lakes with thicker till or carbonate influence.

High-elevation lakes, the group in which Schofield originally demonstrated a relation between acidity and fish populations (p. 41), show almost no relation between elevation and the presence of fish. But they only rarely have fish if the pH is below 5.5 and never have fish if the pH is below 4.8. And in the lakes with pHs less than 5.5, those whose acidity is dominated by mineral acids are less likely to have fish than those whose acidity is dominated by organic acids.

A clear conclusion results from this work: anything that increases the mineral acidity of a lake (and hence increases aluminum and decreases ANC) is going to affect fish populations. Small increases in acidity eliminate individual species and decrease diversity; large changes can eliminate fish entirely.

Historical Changes in Fish Diversity

One of the goals of the ALS was to determine which lakes had recently lost fish populations and whether these losses were related to acid deposition. A large quantity of systematically gathered his-

Maps from Gallagher and Baker, "Current status of fish communities in Adirondack lakes," in Baker et al., *Adirondack Lakes Survey: An Interpretive Analysis of Fish Communities and Water Chemistry, 1984–1987,* 1990. Graph from Kretser, Gallagher, and Nicolette, *Adirondack Lakes Survey: 1984–1987,* 1989. Most fishless lakes have pHs below 5.0 and are in the western part of the park. Fishy lakes tend to have pHs above 5.0 and are found throughout the park.

NUMBER OF FISH SPECIES IN ALS LAKES

Graph from Kretser, Gallagher, and Nicolette, *Adirondack Lakes Survey: 1984–1987,* 1989. The average number of fish species in a lake decreases from six in slightly alkaline lakes to one in lakes at pHs below 4.5. The decline is fairly uniform: about 0.8 species is lost for every 0.5 unit decrease in pH.

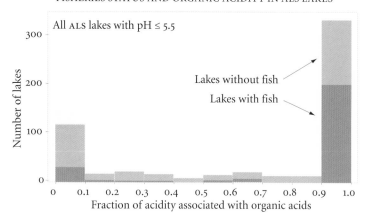

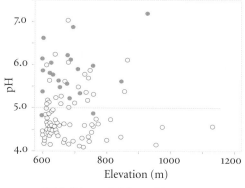

● With fish ○ Without fish

torical data was available from the statewide biological surveys conducted between 1929 and 1934, and more scattered data from other surveys since then. But unfortunately, none of these surveys were comparable, in either completeness or intensity, to the ALS. The previous surveys tended to sample less thoroughly and may have missed species that the ALS found. Further, they tended to concentrate on large lakes at low elevations and so missed many of the small, sensitive lakes that are currently fishless.

As a result, the historical data needed to be used with great care. The clearest cases involved historical records of species that are no longer found. There were, for example, 17 fishless lakes that had historical surveys. Nine of them, or roughly half, had fish in 1929–34; the other eight did not. There are 409 lakes that are known to have had brook trout before 1970; in the 1980s 282 (69%) still had them and 127 (31%) had lost them. Likewise, of the lakes that formerly had brown bullheads and northern red-bellied dace, 15% no longer had the relatively tolerant bullheads and a noteworthy 71% no longer had the relatively sensitive dace.

For several reasons, these estimates of species losses almost certainly underestimate the true loss rate. First, historical records are not random samples. Fisheries biologists tend to sample large lakes with significant fisheries; many small, acid-sensitive lakes that may have lost their fish populations were not sampled in previous surveys. And second, people tend to replace lost populations of sport fish, and thus the deliberate restocking of native species could be masking the effects of acidification.

The historical data may also be analyzed for net changes in the total number of species in individual lakes. This analysis is more difficult because of problems from introductions and incomplete surveys, but it is also more interesting ecologically because it looks at groups of species rather than individual species.

The ALS data have been analyzed for diversity changes twice, both times by Joan Baker and her associates. In their 1990 attempt,

Both graphs from Gallagher and Baker, "Current status of fish communities in Adirondack lakes," in Baker et al., *Adirondack Lakes Survey: An Interpretive Analysis of Fish Communities and Water Chemistry, 1984-1987*, 1990. Most lakes with pHs below 5.6 are fishless except those in which 90% of the acidity or more is organic. (See also p. 75.) Likewise, high-elevation lakes tend to be ecologically difficult, and the higher they are the lower their pHs and the less likely they are to have fish. But pH can to some extent offset the disadvantages of elevation: over half the lakes with pHs of 5.5 or more have fish, versus 1 lake in 14 of those with pHs below 5.5.

FISH DIVERSITY IN LAKES OF DIFFERENT TYPES

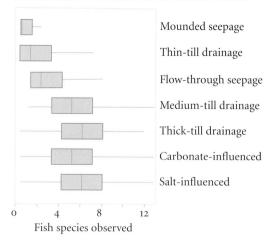

From Kretser, Gallagher, and Nicolette, *Adirondack Lakes Survey: 1984-1987*, 1989. The seepage and thin-till drainage lakes, which are the lake types most sensitive to acid deposition, have the lowest number of fish species.

they compared diversity changes to the current pH of the lake and found no evidence that lakes that were currently acid had lost more species than lakes that were not (p. 79). In their 1993 attempt, in which they compared diversity changes to the pH changes estimated by paleolimnological studies, they got a very different result (pp. 183-184).

Why do some lakes lack fish?

The 346 fishless lakes found by the Adirondack Lakes Survey are of particular interest because they provide some of the best evidence for the biological effects of acid deposition. But this evidence is of value only if we can separate the lakes that are naturally fishless from those that have been made so by mineral acids.

The ALS did this in a clever and objective way. The researchers compared the lakes that didn't have fish to those that did and tried to determine how many fishless lakes, *even in the absence of mineral acids*, might be ecologically unsuitable for fish.

Thus from the 346 fishless lakes they eliminated 46 bogs, 13 high-elevation lakes, 145 lakes whose acidity was dominated by natural organic acids, and 30 lakes that did not have significant amounts of mineral acid. The remaining 113 lakes, totaling 32% of the fishless lakes and 8% of all the lakes sampled by the ALS, they considered to be fishless primarily because of mineral acids and acid deposition.

Ecologically, the lakes believed to have lost fish because of acid deposition were a consistent group and clearly differentiated from the lakes that still supported fish. They were mostly thin-till drainage or perched seepage lakes – the two lake types believed most sensitive to acid deposition – and they tended to occur at higher elevations, have lower pHs, and have more inorganic aluminum than lakes that still had fish.

Although the fishless lakes have received a considerable amount of attention and are certainly a cause for concern, it is important to realize that they are indicators of a larger problem. For every lake that has lost all its fish species to acidification, there are several others, less visible but equally affected, that have lost their sensitive species and retained their tolerant ones. It is this second, larger group of lakes – the lakes whose faunas have been depleted – that is the true measure of the biological effects of acidification.

How many lakes are acidic?

The two major Adirondack surveys of the 1980s, the ELS and the ALS, gave very different estimates of the number of lakes that were acidic. In 1990, the differences between these estimates were politically important and quite controversial. Now, 15 years

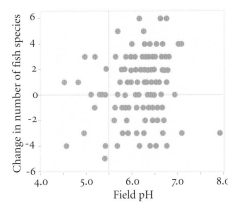

HISTORICAL CHANGES IN FISH DIVERSITY
IN THE ALS LAKES

From Baker et al., "Historical changes in fish communities in Adirondack lakes," in Baker et al., *Adirondack Lakes Survey: An Interpretive Analysis of Fish Communities and Water Chemistry, 1984-1987,* 1990. The change in the number of fish species is the difference between the number of species caught by the ALS and the number caught in earlier surveys. Altogether the analysis shows little relation between the current pH and historical gains or losses. There is a weak tendency for high-pH lakes to gain rather than to lose species but no tendency for low-pH lakes to lose rather than to gain them.

Any analysis of fish diversity changes is very sensitive to the effects of stocking and introduced species. Stocking can maintain the diversity of lakes where populations can no longer reproduce naturally. And acid-tolerant alien species like the golden shiner and central mudminnow have replaced acid-sensitive native ones like the Cyprinid minnows and so conceal the effects of acidification on native species diversity.

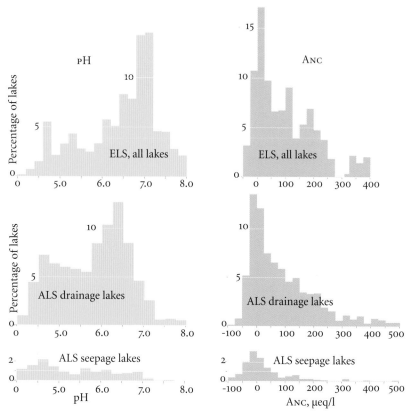

The individual distributions of the pHs and ANCs of the ELS and ALS lakes, based on data from Driscoll et al., "Adirondack mountains," 1990, and Newton and Driscoll, "Classification of ALSC lakes," in Baker et al., *Adirondack Lakes Survey: An Interpretive Analysis of Fish Communities and Water Chemistry, 1984–1987,* 1990. Note how different the pH and ANC distributions are; the most common pH is near 6.5, and the most common ANC near 0 µeq/l . The distributions are of fairly different shapes and suggest that the two surveys were sampling two different populations. The ELS distributions are more concentrated in the center; the ALS sampled many more low-pH and low-ANC lakes and also a few more high-ANC lakes. The ELS sampled relatively few seepage lakes and consequently, as the ALS data show, missed many low-pH and low-ANC lakes.

later, it is easy to see them as a logical consequence of the way the studies were designed and the way they defined acidification.

The ELS, as noted earlier in this chapter, was a statistical survey that used a sample of 155 lakes to infer the properties of a target population of 1,290 lakes. The ALS was a much more exhaustive survey, examining 1,469 lakes from a population of 2,770. It simply described the lakes it examined and did not try to extend its conclusions to the lakes it didn't examine.

The graphs above compare the percentages of lakes in the two surveys for given ranges of pH and ANC. The overall results for the two surveys are similar but with important differences. The ALS, because it sampled more small lakes, detected about twice as many low-pH and low-ANC lakes as did the ELS. The ELS, because it sampled larger lakes and included lakes from outside the Adirondack Park, sampled nearly three times as many near-neutral lakes as did the ALS. The individual distributions of pH and ANC of the ELS lakes are more clustered around their peaks and have shorter tails than those of the ALS. The ALS pH distribution is almost bimodal (two-peaked), suggesting one population of lakes with pHs near

AREAS AND ANCS OF THE ALS LAKES

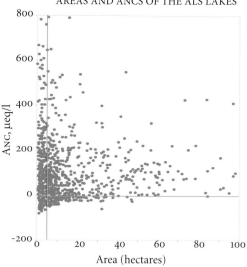

Redrawn from Sullivan et al., "Variation in Adirondack, New York, lakewater chemistry as a function of surface area." Copyright 1990 American Water Resources Association via the Copyright Clearance Center. The red vertical line is at 4 ha, the lower size limit of the lakes surveyed by the ELS. The lakes above 20 ha are fairly uniform, with ANCs mostly between 0 and 200 µeq/l. The lakes below 20 ha are more variable, with many ANCs above 400 µeq/l or less than 0 µeq/l.

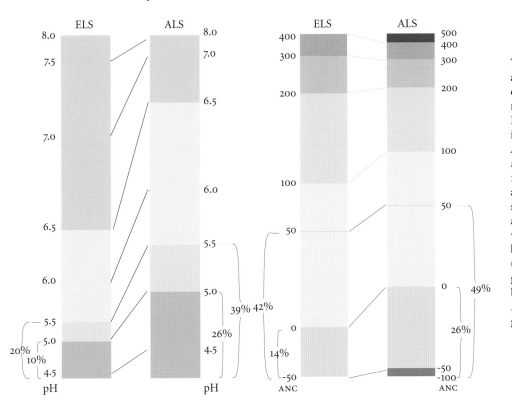

The cumulative distributions of the pHs and ANCs of the ELS and ALS lakes, based on data from Driscoll et al., "Adirondack mountains," 1990; and Newton and Driscoll, "Classification of ALSC lakes," in Baker et al., *Adirondack Lakes Survey: An Interpretive Analysis of Fish Communities and Water Chemistry, 1984-1987*, 1990. The ELS bars represent 155 lakes, and the ALS bars, 1,469 lakes. The ELS survey found more lakes with high pHs and high ANCs than did the ALS and fewer with low pHs and low ANCs. This is partly because the ELS did not survey small lakes (lakes to the left of the red line on the graph on the opposite page) and partly because it included lakes from outside the Adirondacks in areas where the soils have greater reserves of base cations.

6.5 and another with pHs near 4.5. Both surveys produced results that are consistent with their sampling methods and design, but clearly the ALS design looked for, and found, a wider spectrum of variation.

THE PIRLA PROJECT

While the ELS and ALS had shown conclusively that many Adirondack lakes were acidified by mineral acids, because they did not know what the lakes were like before the onset of acid deposition, they could not describe the process of acidification itself. They could not say how much the lakes had acidified, or how fast the acidification had happened, or whether other factors like fires and storms had contributed to it. To learn these things, paleoecological reconstructions of historical pHs were required. The two PIRLA projects supplied these.

PIRLA-I

The first Paleoecological Investigation of Recent Lake Acidification (PIRLA-I) project, which began in 1983, used diatoms,

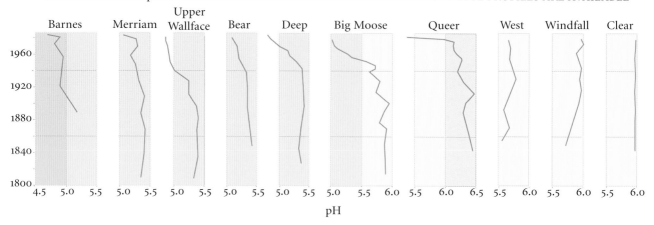

chrysophytes, and chemical markers of combustion from lake sediments to reconstruct the chemical histories of 35 lakes in four regions of the eastern United States (pp. 57-58). Methods were carefully standardized and tested, and separate regression equations for inferring pH and ANC were developed for each region. In the Adirondacks, for example, contemporary diatom and chrysophyte samples from a set of 37 calibration lakes were used to generate the predictive equations applied to the 12 study lakes.

The diatom-based results from ten of the PIRLA-I Adirondack lakes are shown above. Seven of the ten, most of them moderately acid to begin with, show recent acidification. The other three, all with pHs between 5.5 and 6.0 in 1850, have not acidified.

The rates of acidification shown in the cores suggest a strong association between acid deposition and lake acidification. The most sensitive lakes began to acidify about 1880, when sulfate deposition is believed to have increased and chemical markers of combustion like soot, lead, and aromatic hydrocarbons first appeared in the sediment cores. The less sensitive lakes began to acidify about 1930 or 1940, in peak periods of fossil fuel use. Many lakes showed an accelerated rate of acidification after 1950 as acid deposition intensified. And no lake showed a substantial amount of acidification before 1880, suggesting that natural acidification, if it was occurring in these waters at all, was happening very gradually.

The PIRLA researchers looked for, but did not find, evidence that watershed disturbances like logging and fires were causing acidification. In some cases acidification began before the watersheds were disturbed; in others disturbed and undisturbed watersheds were acidifying at the same rates. Their conclusion was that watershed disturbances might be modifying the rate of acidification but were never the primary cause of acidification.

The pH changes inferred from the cores are substantial but not enormous. The median change, for the lakes that acidified at all, is

The pH histories for 10 of the 12 Adirondack lakes included in the PIRLA-I project, from Sullivan et al., *NAPAP Report 11: Historical Changes in Surface Water Acid-Base Chemistry in Response to Acidic Deposition*, 1990, Section 4.2.1.2, and based on Charles and Smol, "New methods for using diatoms and chrysophytes to infer past pH of low-alkalinity lakes." Copyright 1988 American Society of Limnology and Oceanography via the Copyright Clearance Center. The dates are obtained by lead-isotope dating, the pHs from the number of diatoms. The average standard error of the inferred pHs is about 0.25 pH units; the standard deviation of the dates is about five years. pH estimates based on chrysophytes are similar but, probably because chrysophytes better reflect the springtime acidity peaks than diatoms, show somewhat greater acidification.

about 0.5 pH unit (p. 86). Only three lakes of ten changed by 0.7 of a pH unit, and only one by more than 1 pH unit. But given the sensitivity of fish and other aquatic animals to pH (pp. 177-178), and given that pH changes are closely tied to increases in inorganic aluminum (p. 51), these changes were clearly large enough to have had substantial biological effects.

Thus the PIRLA-I results confirmed all the significant features of what had become the standard model of lake acidification: that much or all of the recent lake acidification of clear-water lakes coincided with and was probably caused by acid deposition; that the resulting pH changes were sufficiently large to be biologically significant; and that the changes, which had occurred in decades rather than centuries, were much faster than any that had been observed in long-term cores from undisturbed lakes.

Interestingly, however, the PIRLA-I results also confirmed the premise of the RILWAS and ILWAS studies: because of differences in soils, different lakes respond very differently to the same amount of acid deposition. None of the lake acidification curves follow the sulfate deposition curve exactly. Instead, the differing abilities of watersheds to store and neutralize acids modulate the way the lakes respond. Some watersheds pass a pulse of incoming acid directly to the lakes; others delay it for many years. Subsequent studies based on the PIRLA-II results (p. 88) were to show that there are at least four kinds of Adirondack lake histories, each reflecting a different combination of watershed and lake processes.

The First North American Synthesis, 1990

By 1989, pH reconstructions were available for about 100 lakes in the United States and eastern Canada (p. 84). The geographic association between acid deposition and acidification was striking, and the absence of acidification in areas without deposition equally striking. Donald Charles, who reviewed the data, was able to conclude,

> Paleoecological data now available are sufficient to conclude that lake acidification has occurred in the Adirondack Mountains (New York), New England, Ontario, Quebec, the Atlantic Provinces, the Upper Midwest, and Florida … Based on palaeolimnological and other data, the primary cause of recent lake acidification in most of the above regions is acidic deposition derived from combustion of fossil fuels, although catchment changes and natural long-term processes may play a minor role … It is clear that pH declines in most areas cannot be accounted for by natural processes (the rates of change are too fast) or by catchment changes, although these probably contributed to the process in some areas.

ESTIMATED WET DEPOSITION OF SULFATE IN THE ADIRONDACKS

From Sullivan et al., *NAPAP Report 11: Historical Changes in Surface Water Acid-Base Chemistry in Response to Acidic Deposition*, 1990, Section 2.4.1. Sulfur emissions began to increase with the widespread introduction of coal-fired boilers and furnaces in the 1880s and internal combustion engines in the 1900s. They decreased during the Depression, increased during World War II, peaked in 1973, and then decreased as the Clean Air Act regulations went into effect.

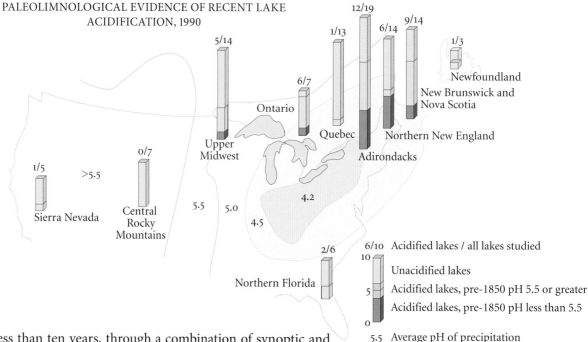

PALEOLIMNOLOGICAL EVIDENCE OF RECENT LAKE
ACIDIFICATION, 1990

12/19

1/13

6/14

9/14

1/3

Newfoundland

New Brunswick and
Nova Scotia

5/14

6/7

Ontario

Quebec

Northern New England

Upper
Midwest

Adirondacks

0/7

1/5

>5.5

Sierra Nevada

Central
Rocky
Mountains

5.5

5.0

4.5

4.2

2/6

6/10 Acidified lakes / all lakes studied
10

Unacidified lakes

5

Acidified lakes, pre-1850 pH 5.5 or greater

0

Acidified lakes, pre-1850 pH less than 5.5

Northern Florida

5.5 Average pH of precipitation

Area with average pH less than 5.0

In less than ten years, through a combination of synoptic and paleolimnological studies, many using methods and classifications first developed in the Adirondacks, the atmospheric acidification of lakes had gone from being a scientific hypothesis to a scientific fact. The next step was to quantify the historical changes. This was the goal of the PIRLA-II.

PIRLA-II and the Regional Picture

The purpose of the PIRLA-II study was to supplement the PIRLA-I study with additional, randomly selected lakes from which an extrapolation could be made to the Adirondacks as a whole. Thirty-seven drainage lakes and 11 seepage lakes were selected. The drainage lakes had previously been studied in the Eastern Lake Survey and the Direct Delayed Response Project (pp. 68, 96); they were all 4 hectares or larger and together were assumed to represent a total population of 675 Adirondack lakes.

The map on the opposite page shows the overall geography of drainage-lake acidification as reconstructed by the two PIRLA projects. The pattern is very similar to the distributions of low pHs found by the ELS and ALS (pp. 65, 71). Low contemporary pHs in drainage lakes are apparently a good predictor of recent acidification, and significant acidification is largely confined to the southwestern Adirondacks, where the deposition rates are high and current pHs are highly acid.

The PIRLA-I study had suggested that it was mostly the lakes that were originally acid that acidified further. The PIRLA-II study confirmed this. In the pooled PIRLA-I and PIRLA-II data shown on

Based on Charles, "Effects of acidic deposition on North American lakes: Palaeolimnological evidence from diatoms and chrysophytes," 1990. This was the first map to show the relation between acid deposition and lake acidification on a continental scale. Lakes are considered to have acidified if their pHs, as inferred from diatom or chrysophyte assemblages, dropped by 0.2 units or more between 1850 and 1980. The 101 lakes included were chosen from the roughly 150 North American lakes for which inferred pHs were available in 1989. The lakes studied were usually the most acidic in the region; they were not randomly chosen and are not statistically representative of their regions, but still the association of acidification and acid deposition is clear: of the 42 acidified lakes on the map, only one is in a region that does not receive significant acid deposition.

Overall, more lakes with preindustrial pHs over 5.5 acidified more frequently than those with preindustrial pHs below 5.5. This is partly because preindustrial pHs below 5.5 were uncommon and partly because lakes with naturally low pHs are often buffered by organic acids and hard to acidify further.

DIATOM-INFERRED pH CHANGES IN
THE PIRLA-II LAKES

Lake Francis

Bear Pond
Trout Lake   Dry Channel Pond
                  Middle Pond
                  Little Echo   Kiwassa Lake
                  Pond

Nicks Pond   Mt. Arab Lake   Upper Wallface Pond
                                   Lake Arnold
          John Pond

Middle Pond   Clear Pond
          Partlow Lake
      Hawk Pond
                              Zack Pond
Hitchcock Lake   Cheney Pond
                                 Nate Pond
              Big Moose   Unknown Pond
              group

Grass Pond
    Woodhull Lake   Wolf Lake   Long Pond
Barnes Lake   Whitney Lake
    Fourth Lake   Deep Lake   Fish Ponds
    South Lake
    Wilmurt Lake   St. John Lake
          Trout Lake
Curtis Lake
    N. Branch Lake   Mud Pond
                    Duck Lake
                              Woods Lake
                      Chub Lake
                    Nine Corner Lake
          Mud Pond

Big Moose group

Merriam ○   ◐ Gull
Big Moose ◑   ● Constable
West ○   ◐ Queer
        Windfall

Diatom-inferred pH change
● > -0.6
◑ -0.35 to -0.6
○ -0.3 to 0.3
◐ > 0.3

page 86, 27 lakes (55% of those studied) originally had pHs below 6.0. Twenty-five of the 27 acidified at least mildly, and 12 of these acidified sufficiently for their pHs to fall below 5.0. In contrast, of the remaining 22 lakes with initial pHs of 6.0 or higher, only 10 acidified, and the remaining 12 either stayed the same or became less acid.

Much the same turned out to be true of ANC. Lakes whose current ANC is below zero have acidified fairly: their median increase in total acidity (which includes decreases in ANC and increases in aluminum) is 37 µeq/l. Lakes whose current ANC is between 0 and 25 µeq/l also acidified but more weakly; their median increase in total acidity is 7 µeq/l. Lakes whose current ANC was more than 25 µeq/l have usually become less acidic; their median *decrease* in total acidity is 23 µeq/l.

Based on Sullivan et al., "Quantification of changes in lakewater chemistry in response to acidic deposition," 1990, with additional data from Sullivan et al., *NAPAP Report 11: Historical Changes in Surface Water Acid-Base Chemistry in Response to Acidic Deposition*, 1990, Section 4.2.1.2. The inferred pH change is the difference between the contemporary pH inferred from the diatom assemblages at the top of the core and the pre-1850 pH inferred from those at the bottom of the core. The PIRLA-II used essentially the same methods as the PIRLA-I but examined only the uppermost and lowermost parts the core and developed new calibration equations using correspondence analysis rather than linear regression.

Seepage lakes, shown in the lower panel of the chart at right, tended to be quite acid already and, perhaps because they are often buffered by organic acids, did not show great changes.

The relation between the initial pH and the extent of acidification suggested an important conclusion: acid deposition has had the largest effects on lakes that were at least slightly acidic when it began. It has thus had a great effect on lakes of moderate pHs and ANCs and hence on the regions like the Adirondacks where such lakes were common. But it has not been able to turn high-pH or high-ANC lakes into acidic lakes and has had relatively little effect on the most acid seepage lakes, though it may at times have converted organic acidity to mineral acidity.

Further Lessons from Paleolimnology

When paleolimnological inferences are combined with contemporary chemical and ecological data, it is possible to estimate some quantities and relationships that cannot be obtained any other way. In an aside from our main story we give two examples, the first a determination of f-factors and the second an examination of the relationship between lake histories and watershed properties. Both use somewhat complex analyses and are correspondingly uncertain but also give interesting views of some of the details of acidification that could not be obtained in other ways.

In 1990, Sullivan and his colleagues calculated f-factors for base cations from the Adirondack PIRLA data. An f-factor is the ratio of the changes in two ions as a lake acidifies or deacidifies. The f-factor for base cations, $\Delta C_B/\Delta SO_4^{2-}$, is the change in the total sum of base cations for a given change in sulfate. It is of interest because it is a quantitative measure of how much the watershed is affecting the rate of acidification. It tells us the approximate fraction of the incoming hydrogen ions that have been exchanged for base cations (pp. 31, 50). When it is near or above 1, the watershed is able to sequester or neutralize most of the incoming acid; when it is near 0, the watershed is doing very little, and most of the incoming hydrogen ions are passing directly into surface water.

The f-factors for the PIRLA data can be calculated from the current lake chemistry, an assumed background value for preindustrial sulfate (20 μeq/l), and the inferred changes in ANC and aluminum obtained from sediment cores. The graph on page 87 shows that, as expected, f-factors decrease with the current acid-base ratio of the watershed, and that, contrary to many expectations, they are surprisingly high. In even the most base-poor Adirondack watersheds, one new base ion appears in the lake for every two new sulfate ions.

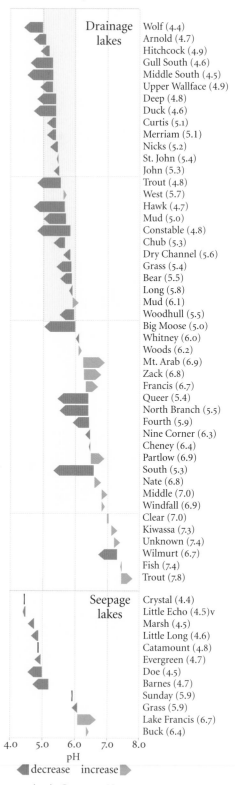

ESTIMATED pH CHANGES IN THE PIRLA LAKES, Ca. 1800-1980

Drainage lakes
Wolf (4.4)
Arnold (4.7)
Hitchcock (4.9)
Gull South (4.6)
Middle South (4.5)
Upper Wallface (4.9)
Deep (4.8)
Duck (4.6)
Curtis (5.1)
Merriam (5.1)
Nicks (5.2)
St. John (5.4)
John (5.3)
Trout (4.8)
West (5.7)
Hawk (4.7)
Mud (5.0)
Constable (4.8)
Chub (5.3)
Dry Channel (5.6)
Grass (5.4)
Bear (5.5)
Long (5.8)
Mud (6.1)
Woodhull (5.5)
Big Moose (5.0)
Whitney (6.0)
Woods (6.2)
Mt. Arab (6.9)
Zack (6.8)
Francis (6.7)
Queer (5.4)
North Branch (5.5)
Fourth (5.9)
Nine Corner (6.3)
Cheney (6.4)
Partlow (6.9)
South (5.3)
Nate (6.8)
Middle (7.0)
Windfall (6.9)
Clear (7.0)
Kiwassa (7.3)
Unknown (7.4)
Wilmurt (6.7)
Fish (7.4)
Trout (7.8)

Seepage lakes
Crystal (4.4)
Little Echo (4.5)v
Marsh (4.5)
Little Long (4.6)
Catamount (4.8)
Evergreen (4.7)
Doe (4.5)
Barnes (4.7)
Sunday (5.9)
Grass (5.9)
Lake Francis (6.7)
Buck (6.4)

4.0   5.0   6.0   7.0   8.0
pH
◀ decrease   increase ▶

(5.0) Current pH

Based on Sullivan et al., *NAPAP Report 11: Historical Changes in Surface Water Acid-Base Chemistry in Response to Acidic Deposition*, 1990, Section 4.2.1.2. Both the PIRLA-I and PIRLA-II are included. The arrows show the change in diatom pH from the bottom (ca. 1850) to the top (ca. 1985) of the core.

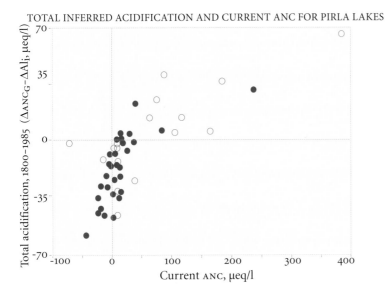

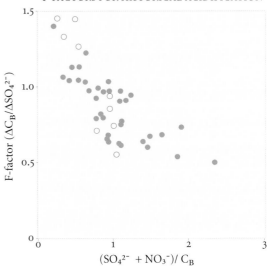

- ● Undisturbed watershed
- ○ Watershed with logging or other disturbance

The high f-factors indicate that these watersheds are exporting significant amounts of base cations and raise the question of whether the cumulative effects of base cation losses are important. In 1990 these cumulative losses, which we now speak of as base cation depletion, were not thought significant. Since then they have become a major topic of research. We discuss recent research on cation depletion in Chapter 6 and the connection between depleted cation reserves and the slow responses of waters to decreases in deposition in Chapter 9.*

In both graphs at the top of the page the open circles represent lakes whose watersheds have had fires, windstorms, or other disturbances. If these disturbances had caused significant acidification, the open circles would lie below the closed ones, indicating that disturbed watersheds had greater ANC changes or lower f-factors than ones. Instead they lie among or above the closed circles, suggesting that watershed disturbances either have not affected acidification or, in a few cases at least, may have in fact decreased it. This was a controversial finding; in 1990, acid rain skeptics were claiming that lake acidification, when it had occurred at all, was most likely the result of watershed disturbances and not acid deposition.

In Cumming and his collaborators, returned to this issue, using 18 cores taken from southwestern Adirondack lakes during the PIRLA-I project (p. 88). The lake histories derived from the cores were grouped using cluster analysis and then displayed in a two-dimensional ordination, along with several contemporary environmental variables.

The results suggest that there are at least four kinds of southwestern Adirondack lake history, and that each is characteristic

Redrawn from Sullivan et al., "Quantification of changes in lakewater chemistry in response to acidic deposition" and based on data from the Adirondack PIRLA lakes. Copyright 1990 Nature Publishing Group via the Copyright Clearance Center. The left graph shows that the total inferred acidification from 1850 to the present (including both decreases in ANC and increases in inorganic aluminum) is greatest in lakes whose current ANCs are low. The right graph compares the f-factors (change in base cations from preindustrial times per unit change in sulfate) to the current acid-base ratio. As expected, when the acid-base ratio is high, the f-factor is low. In both graphs the open circles are lakes whose watershed has had some recent disturbance.

* Base cation depletion has important implications for forest ecology, a topic that lies outside the scope of this book.

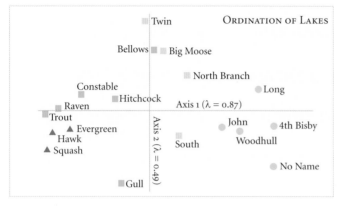

ORDINATION OF LAKES

- ▲ Original pH below 5.5, further pH decline after 1900
- ■ Original pH 5.5-6.0, further pH decline after 1900
- ▥ Original pH about 6.0, rapid pH decline after 1930
- ● No pH decline or slight decline and recovery

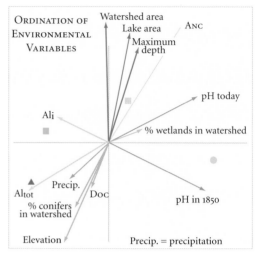

ORDINATION OF ENVIRONMENTAL VARIABLES

Precip. = precipitation

▲ ■ ▥ ● Midpoints of groups from left graph

of a different sort of lake. Small, high-elevation, brown-water lakes that receive large amounts of precipitation (brown triangles) tended to be naturally acid but acidified further after 1900. Larger and somewhat lower lakes in high-deposition regions (red squares) tended to be somewhat less acid originally but also acidified rapidly after 1900. Even larger lowland lakes, typically with large watersheds and in lower-deposition areas (tan squares), did not start to acidify until after 1930 but often acidified rapidly after that. And a group of high-pH lakes, usually with deep till or limy bedrock in their watersheds, has not acidified at all.

SUMMARY: HOW MANY ADIRONDACK LAKES ARE ACIDIC AND HOW MUCH HAVE THEY ACIDIFIED?

The three large studies – ALS, ELS, and PIRLA – that were completed in the late 1980s and early 1990s each attempted to give an overall picture of Adirondack acidification. They worked on different groups of lakes, using different methods. The ALS made contemporary measurements on a large set of both small and large lakes. The ELS made contemporary measurements on a smaller but more randomly selected set of lakes that excluded very small lakes. The PIRLA project studied a subset of the ELS lakes and used paleolimnological methods to infer historical pHs.

Given the differences in scope and methods, it is neither surprising nor important that the three projects produced somewhat different estimates of the number of acidic Adirondack lakes. What is important is that the estimates are reasonably consistent with each other and that where they differ, they differ in ways that reflect the methods they used. Thus the chrysophyte-based

Redrawn with permission from Cumming et al., "When did acid-sensitive Adirondack lakes (New York, U.S.A.) acidify and are they still acidifying?" Copyright 1994 National Research Council of Canada. Sediment cores were taken from 18 Adirondack lakes. pH histories, expressed as the pH change per decade, were inferred from chrysophyte assemblages. The histories were divided into four groups by cluster analysis and then ordinated by canonical variates analysis. The analysis identified three "active" variables (elevation, current pH, and preindustrial pH) that best separated the four different histories. As in other ordination diagrams, the longer an arrow is, the more of the total variation it explains, and the more nearly parallel two arrows, the more the variables they represent are correlated.

studies, which can detect snowmelt acidity, show, on the whole, more acidic lakes than the diatom-based studies, which can't. The ALS, which included lakes under 4 hectares, estimated a higher percentage of acidic lakes than did the ELS, which studied only larger ones.

The graphs to the right suggest that the studies agree on most important points, and that we can combine them to produce an overall picture of the historical changes in Adirondack lakes. This picture has four principal elements:

Currently, between 20% and 40% of Adirondack lakes are moderately acid, with pHs below 5.5, and 10%–25% of Adirondack lakes are highly acid, with pHs below 5.0.

Most of the lakes with pHs currently below 5.5 have probably acidified in the past 100 years.

Low-pH lakes were uncommon or rare in the preindustrial Adirondacks: the number of lakes with pHs less than 5.5 has at least doubled and the number with pHs less than 5.0 has increased by five to ten times.

The timing and chemistry of all the recent pH decreases suggest that they are principally caused by acid deposition, with watershed disturbances playing a secondary role, and natural acidification unimportant.

With the completion of this picture, all the original questions posed in the early 1980s about the chronic acidification of lakes had been answered. The scientific community now knew how intense and prevalent it was, when it first had occurred, and most important, what had caused it. To have gotten answers this clear to a problem this difficult in less than a decade was a remarkable scientific achievement; that many of the answers came from Adirondack lakes and Adirondack researchers should make us all proud.

But this was far from the end of the story. If lake acidification was better understood, forest acidification was still largely a mystery. In 1990 we knew very little about the effects of acidification on trees and soils, or whether these effects were cumulative or reversible, or how they related to the transient but increasingly severe acidification caused by spring peaks of nitrates. The investigation of these questions, which are still only partially answered, occupied the next decade.

ESTIMATES OF PREINDUSTRIAL & CONTEMPORARY ABUNDANCE OF ACID LAKES

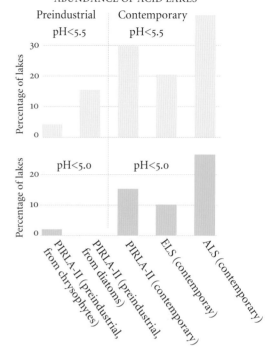

ESTIMATED FREQUENCIES OF ACIDIFICATION

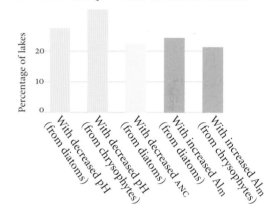

PIRLA-II data from Cumming et al., "How much acidification has occurred in Adirondack region lakes (New York, USA) since preindustrial times?" 1992; ALS data from Kretser, Gallagher, and Nicolette, *Adirondack Lakes Survey 1984-1987*, 1989; ELS data from Driscoll et al., *Adirondack Mountains*, 1990. Chrysophytes are believed to be more sensitive to snowmelt acidity than diatoms, and chrysophyte-based pHs suggest somewhat larger and more extensive historical changes than diatom-based pHs.

1980 The average sulfate concentration in wet deposition at Huntington Forest is approximately twice that of nitrate.

1980 Johannes, Galloway, and Troutman discover that snowmelt acidity is dominated by nitric acid rather than sulfuric acid.

1982 David, Mitchell, and Scott study sulfur cycling in a hardwood forest at Huntington Forest; they find that most of the sulfur in the soil is in organic form and that the forest is releasing more sulfur than it receives from deposition.

1984 Rascher, Driscoll, and Peters collect snowmelt water near Twitchell Lake and find that the leachate from melting snow is more acid than the snow itself, and the leachate from the forest floor more acid still.

1985-1990 Friedland et al. study nitrogen cycling in spruce-fir forests on Whiteface Mountain. They estimate that the forest is retaining 71% of the nitrogen it receives from deposition.

1986-1987 Schaefer et al. find that spring decreases in ANC in ten Adirondack lakes are controlled by dilution in low-ANC lakes and by nitrates in high-ANC lakes.

1986-1987 Schaefer and Driscoll estimate the contributions of new meltwater and old groundwater to the spring runoff in 11 Adirondack watersheds. They find that old water is richer in acids, aluminum, and base cations than new water.

1987 Driscoll and Peters suggest that some of the acidity of spring runoff comes from nitrogen-cycle acidification.

1988-1990 The Episodic Response Project monitors four Adirondack streams and finds sharp drops in pH and ANC and sharp increases in aluminum in high-water episodes.

1989 The Direct Delayed Response Project estimates that most northeastern watersheds are not retaining sulfur.

1989 Aber et al. hypothesize that forests exposed to nitrogen deposition go through four progressive stages of nitrogen saturation.

1990 McNulty et al. show that the more nitrogen a spruce forest receives in deposition, the more organic nitrogen it converts to nitrate.

1991-1993 Mitchell et al. prepare nitrogen budgets for three Adirondack hardwood forests and find that the stands retain most of the ammonium they receive but only 13% to 58% of the nitrate.

1992-1993 Samples from red spruce forests show that the more deposition the stand receives, the more sulfur and nitrogen are stored in the soil.

1994 Stoddard suggests that the stages of nitrogen saturation can be recognized by characteristic seasonal patterns of nitrogen release. He finds that many Adirondack and Catskill watersheds are at saturation Stage 1.

1995 The average sulfate concentration in wet deposition at Huntington Forest is 1.2 times that of nitrate.

1995 Diese and Wright show that European watersheds receiving more than 10 kg/ha-yr of nitrogen begin to approach nitrogen saturation and lose increasing amounts of nitrogen.

1996 Mitchell et al. review 1983-1993 monitoring data for watersheds in Maine, New Hampshire, and New York and find that periods of high nitrogen release are synchronized and associated with climate.

1997 Sullivan et al. find that summer levels of nitrates in Adirondack lakes, though small, correlate better with lake ANCs than do sulfate levels.

2000 Stoddard, Traalen, and Skelkvåle find that all European watersheds receiving more than 10 kg/ha-yr of nitrogen are at saturation Stage 2 or higher.

2003 Aber et al. examine data from 83 watersheds and 354 waterbodies in the northeastern United States and find that at deposition rates higher than 6-8 kg N/ha-yr, spring nitrate levels rise rapidly and the amount of nitrogen retained in the watershed drops from more than 90% to less than 60%. They conclude: "it seems clear that N deposition is altering the N status of, and NO_3^- leaching from, forests in the northeastern United States."

THE CYCLING OF SULFUR AND NITROGEN

HOW THE TWO MAJOR ATMOSPHERIC ACIDS ARE STORED AND TRANSFORMED IN WATERSHEDS

5

In the next four chapters, we consider how the picture of acidification that emerged from the synoptic studies of the 1980s was enlarged and made more complex by continuing research in the 1990s. Chapters 5 and 6 consider nutrient cycling and are specifically concerned with how the natural element cycles in forests, wetlands, and lakes have been altered by acid deposition. Their theme is that acid deposition has produced cumulative changes in watershed soils and that these cumulative changes, in turn, are now altering the ability of the watersheds to neutralize acid deposition. Watersheds, in other words, not only transform atmospheric acids but have themselves been transformed by them.

Chapter 7 is concerned with wetlands and mercury, two emerging and interconnected areas of research. Wetlands turn out to be highly active chemical storehouses and transformers. Mercury, of great concern because of its toxicity and ability to bioaccumulate, turns out to be one of the elements they store and transform.

Chapter 8, in contrast, looks backward at one of the original questions of acid rain research and asks what we have learned about fish and aquatic ecology in the 15 years since the Adirondack Lakes Survey.

Sulfur and nitrogen are have dual roles: they are essential nutrients of great biological importance and also the two major acids of acid rain. Nitrogen is the most abundant inorganic element in plant tissue, making up 1% by dry weight of living tissue. It is required for proteins, nucleic acids, alkaloids, and a variety if other specialized plant products. Sulfur is equally essential and is required for phospholipids, proteins, and vitamins. It is about a tenth as abundant as nitrogen in plant tissue, making up about 0.1% of the dry weight of living tissue.

Both sulfur and nitrogen are extensively cycled in the biosphere. The two cycles are generally similar. They involve atmospheric and geological sources, storage in the soil and in living and dead tissue, assimilation by green plants, microbially mediated decay, and a variety of microbially mediated transformations between oxidized and reduced forms. Both sulfur and nitrogen are eventually exported in surface water and groundwater, and both can be volatilized and lost as gases.

Although the sulfur and the nitrogen cycles are similar in outline, they differ greatly in relative magnitude. An Adirondack hardwood forest studied by David, Mitchell, and Scott in the early 1980s

STORAGE OF SULFATE AND NITROGEN IN SOILS

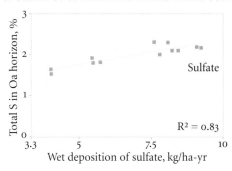

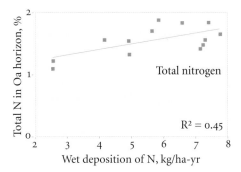

The relation between deposition rates and the amount of sulfate and nitrogen stored in the soils of red spruce stands in Maine, New Hampshire, New York, and Vermont. Redrawn with permission from Lawrence, "Persistent episodic acidification of streams linked to acid rain effects on soil." Copyright 2002 Elsevier. The samples were collected in 1992 and 1993. The higher the deposition rate, the more sulfur and nitrogen are stored. The stored sulfur and nitrogen can be mineralized to nitric and sulfuric acids, which then leach soil calcium and mobilize aluminum. They are thus a source of continuing acidity that will be increasingly important as acid deposition declines.

(pp. 93-95) was estimated to have a pool of about 150 kg S/ha in living and dead biomass and to require about 12 kg S/ha every year for new growth. This particular forest was receiving 8.2 kg S/ha per year in wet deposition and an unknown but possibly smaller amount in dry deposition. It was losing 14.4 kg S/ha every year to groundwater. Thus the amount of sulfur added by acid deposition was comparable to the biological demand and so, when added to the sulfur released by decay, was more than the forest could use. Most of the sulfur deposited every year passed though the system and was exported in drainage water.

In contrast, a study of nitrogen cycling in a spruce forest on Whiteface Mountain found a pool of about 3,000 kg N/ha in living and dead biomass, 20 times the size of the sulfur pool in the hardwood forest (p. 101). The nitrogen demand for new growth was about 50 kg/ha per year, and the inputs from acid deposition about 16 kg N/ha per year. Here the biological demand was greater than the input, and the forest could use a significant amount of the atmospheric nitrogen it received. This is probably even more true of lower-elevation deciduous forests, in which nitrogen demand for new growth (on the order of 100 kg N/ha-yr) exceeds atmospheric nitrogen inputs (4–10 kg N/ha-yr) by 10 to 25 times.

These numbers illustrate a general point. As the atmospheric acids enter watersheds, they are often assimilated into organic matter and, at least for a time, immobilized. This process keeps acids from entering the groundwater, which in the short term is good. But it also means that acids are being stored in the watershed. Thus some of the acids that were deposited on a forest in 1960 may still be in that forest today and may reappear in groundwater in the future. They are, in a sense, a chemical debt: putting them into storage ameliorated the effects of acid deposition in the past but makes it harder for the watershed to recover in the future.

Watersheds as Transformers

The notion that the properties of watersheds depend on the biological cycling and storage of elements is relatively new. During the first period of Adirondack research, from the ILWAS through the Adirondack Lakes Survey, watersheds were conceived of more simply and mechanistically. In essence they were chemical transformers. They neutralized acids, exchanged hydrogen ions for base cations, assimilated ammonium, reduced and immobilized sulfates, and generated aluminum. They stored some sulfur and much nitrogen, but the storage was a fixed property that didn't change the future behavior of the watershed.

In this view a watershed was equivalent to a factory of fixed capacity: deposition supplied acids, the factory transformed them as best it could, and drainage water carried the products away. The

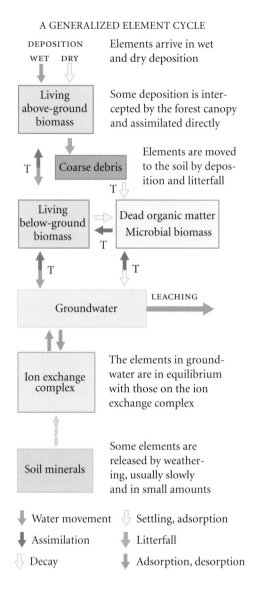

A GENERALIZED ELEMENT CYCLE

DEPOSITION — Elements arrive in wet and dry deposition

Some deposition is intercepted by the forest canopy and assimilated directly

Elements are moved to the soil by deposition and litterfall

The elements in groundwater are in equilibrium with those on the ion exchange complex

Some elements are released by weathering, usually slowly and in small amounts

Water movement   Settling, adsorption
Assimilation   Litterfall
Decay   Adsorption, desorption

A generalized element cycle for a nutrient element that is supplied by deposition and is also present in soil minerals. Such elements are typically stored both in organic forms and also on the ion exchange complex. The transfers between compartments often involve biologically mediated transformations, indicated by the letter *T*. The groundwater compartment links the other compartments but turns over quickly and does not store elements in significant amounts.

The principal cumulative effects of deposition are to change the amounts of elements stored in the compartments and the rates at which elements move between them. Nitrogen deposition, for example, increases the uptake of nitrogen, the amount stored in vegetation and soil, and the amount released to groundwater.

job of acid rain research was to characterize these transformations and use the results to predict the effects of a given amount of deposition or, even more important, of a given reduction in deposition.

Many of the theoretical studies of acid rain in the 1980s were, in effect, attempts to describe the capacity of the factory. The input-output ratios (f-factors) describing the extent to which acids were exchanged for bases were one such attempt (p. 87). The sulfate-adsorption capacities calculated by the Direct Delayed Response Project (p. 96) were another.

Calculating these ratios and capacities required a decade of research and was a significant achievement. For the first time, it was possible to make reasonable predictions about how a specific watershed might respond to a specific input of atmospheric acids. But what this represented was not so much the solution of a problem as the emergence of a new way of looking at watersheds and, to the researchers' surprise, the discovery of a new problem.

Watersheds Have Histories

By the early 1990s, about the same time as f-factors and sulfur retention capacities were first being computed, it was becoming increasingly clear that the responses of watersheds to atmospheric acids depended not only on the amount of acid they were currently receiving but also on the total amount of acid they had received in the past. Their ability to neutralize acids depended on their pools of available bases: if the bank was low on cash, it couldn't make change. Their ability to retain nitrogen depended on the growth rate of the forest and would decrease if the forest's growth rate decreased or if its assimilative capacity was exceeded.

In the new view, watersheds were still factories, but now they were factories with warehouses, and their behavior depended critically on what was stored in the warehouses and whether there was room to store more.

The past ten years of research have confirmed and developed this view and produced what we might describe as a second synthesis of acid rain research. Acid rain, it is now believed, has both short-term and cumulative effects. In the short term, acids are supplied to a watershed, which then processes them in some way characterized by input-output ratios. In the long term, the acids change the watershed itself, depleting its stores of some ions and increasing its stores of others. As the stores change, the biology and nutrient cycling of the watershed also change, and with them its input-output ratios. In particular, the more acids it has already stored or neutralized, the lower its ability to neutralize or store any new acids that are deposited.

SULFUR POOLS IN A HARDWOOD
FOREST

LOCATION OF POOL

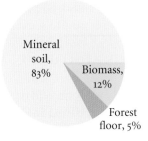

CHEMICAL FORM

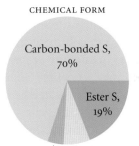

From David, Mitchell, and Scott, "Importance of biological processes in the sulfur budget of a northern hardwood ecosystem," 1987. The sulfur in the ecosystem is divided among three compartments, biomass, forest floor, and mineral soil. It cycles rapidly through the biomass and forest floor compartments but is mostly stored in the mineral soil.

Sulfur occurs in organic forms, ester sulfur and carbon-bonded sulfur, and inorganic forms, mostly sulfate and sulfides. The sulfates are highly mobile and, at least in the Northeast, not much retained in soils. Even though most of the sulfur inputs to the ecosystem are sulfates, almost all of the stored sulfur, even in the mineral soil, is organic sulfur that has been assimilated by plants and microbes.

This chapter and the next are about these sorts of changes – which is to say, about the cumulative chemical histories of watersheds and how these histories affect the watershed's short-term ability to process acids. We begin with sulfate, the most abundant anion in acid rain. Every hectare of Huntington Forest, according to the deposition history reconstructed by Chen and Driscoll (p. 215), has received more than 1,500 kilograms of sulfur in wet deposition in the past hundred years. Where has this sulfur gone, and when might we expect to see it again?

SULFUR ADSORPTION AND SULFUR CYCLING

The early work on acid deposition assumed that much of the sulfate that was deposited in Adirondack watersheds remained as inorganic sulfate and moved relatively quickly through the soil and into surface water and groundwater. Sulfate was, in this view, mobile and unreactive; the sulfate that entered the top of a watershed was supposed to come out the bottom, not long after and not much changed in quantity or form.

This was, of course, an oversimplification. Sulfur is both stored inorganically in watersheds and assimilated by biota. Both processes occur in the Adirondacks and both are consequential.

Inorganic storage occurs in the soil and involves a mixture of direct chemical bonding and anion exchange (adsorption) on the surface of iron and aluminum oxides. The exchange releases hydroxyl ion, which is a base and so deacidifies the groundwater.

The inorganic binding of sulfur in soils is to a large extent reversible. If less sulfate is deposited and groundwater sulfate concentrations decrease, sulfate will be released from the ion exchange sites and hydrogen ions produced. Just how much sulfate will be released depends on the type of the soil and how much of it is chemically (covalently) bonded and how much just held on ion exchange sites. Ion exchange sulfate is easily released, chemically bonded sulfate much less so.

The organic binding of sulfur occurs when it is incorporated into living tissue. Both plants and microbes assimilate sulfate directly, producing carbon-bonded and ester-bonded sulfur compounds. In northeastern forest soils, which have relative little ability to bind inorganic sulfur, 80% or more of all the stored sulfur is in organic form.

In wetland soils, sulfur is often stored in reduced form. Under anaerobic conditions, bacteria use sulfate to oxidize organic matter, reducing the sulfate to insoluble sulfides or thiosulfates, which are stored in the soil. Under aerobic conditions the process reverses: other bacteria use oxygen to oxidize the sulfides, regenerating sulfate. Thus sulfate reduction remove sulfates from groundwater and stores them in the soil; sulfide oxidation reverses the process. Sulfate

SIZE OF SULFUR POOLS IN A HARDWOOD FOREST

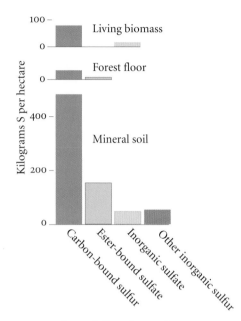

From David, Mitchell, and Scott, "Importance of biological processes in the sulfur budget of a northern hardwood ecosystem," 1987. The sulfur in the ecosystem is mostly incorporated in organic matter (carbon-bonded or ester-bonded)

MICROBIAL REMOVAL & REGENERATION
OF SULFATE FROM WETLAND SOILS

1 In wet anaerobic soils, microbes use sulfate as as an electron acceptor to oxidize organic matter.

$$SO_4^{2-} + 2\ H^+ + 2\ CH_2O$$
$$\rightarrow 2\ CO_2 + H_2S + 2\ H_2O$$

The sulfate is reduced to hydrogen sulfide, elemental sulfur, or other sulfides, all of which tend to be retained in the soil. The reaction consumes sulfate and hydrogen ions and so deacidifies the groundwater and increases its ANC.

2 If a soil containing reduced sulfur dries out, microbes reoxidize the stored sulfur or sulfides to sulfate, generating hydrogen ions in the process.

$$S + H_2O + 1.5\ O_2 \rightarrow SO_4^{2-} + 2\ H^+$$

This reaction produces sulfate and hydrogen ions and so acidifies the groundwater and reduces its ANC.

reduction, like other anaerobic process, is most common in lake sediments and wetland soils. But forest soils can also be wet, and reduced inorganic sulfides can be a significant part of the forest sulfur pool.

Several recent studies have looked at sulfur budgets in the Adirondacks, and another has reviewed 34 years of sulfur studies at Hubbard Brook. Because of uncertainties in the amounts of sulfur provided by dry deposition and weathering, none present an exact budget. Nonetheless, all show sulfur outputs greater than the known inputs and raise the strong possibility that at least some of the net output is coming from the release of previously stored atmospheric sulfur.

Sulfur Cycling in a Hardwood Forest

In the early 1980s David, Mitchell, and Scott studied the distribution and cycling of sulfur in a hardwood stand at Huntington Forest (pp. 93-95). They divided the stand into compartments – leaves, branches, bark, litter, roots, different layers of soil, groundwater at different depths – and estimated the amount of sulfur in each compartment and the annual fluxes of sulfur from one compartment to another. Such studies are always somewhat uncertain but nonetheless valuable because they give us a sense of the complexity of the system and way elements are transferred within it.

By their reckoning, the forest stored 860 kg of sulfur per hectare, 88% in the soil and 12% in biomass. Surprisingly, 89% of the sulfur was organic and only 11% inorganic. They suggested that the large amounts of organic sulfur were a result of the wet climate and soils. Warmer, drier, and better-oxidized soils would have less organic matter and more ability to store inorganic sulfur.

As noted above, the inputs of sulfur from acid deposition were small compared with the total pool of sulfur but large compared with the biological demand.

The forest received 8.2 kg of sulfur per hectare per year from wet deposition; inputs from dry deposition were believed to be low because the throughfall (water filtering through the canopy) had only slightly more sulfur than wet deposition. The bedrock contained very little sulfur, and so inputs from weathering, though unknown, were believed to be small.

The main biologically active pool of sulfur was the forest floor. The turnover of sulfur within this pool was rapid; a total pool of 43 kg received inputs of about 21 kg every year and lost roughly the same amount to assimilation and leach-

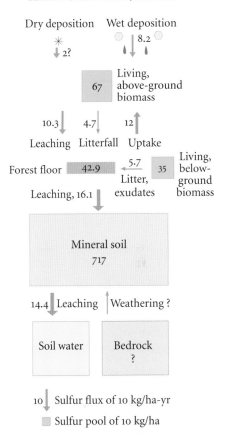

SULFUR POOLS AND CYCLING IN A HARDWOOD FOREST, 1982-1983

Data from David, Mitchell, and Scott, "Importance of biological processes in the sulfur budget of a northern hardwood ecosystem," 1987. The authors did not estimate dry deposition or release from weathering but noted that throughfall contained only 7% more sulfur than wet deposition and so dry deposition was likely small. Later estimates at Huntington Forest suggest that dry deposition is about 25% of wet deposition, giving the 2 kg/ha-yr shown here. The "net hydrological flux" (wet deposition - outputs in soil water) is -6.2 kg/ha-yr.

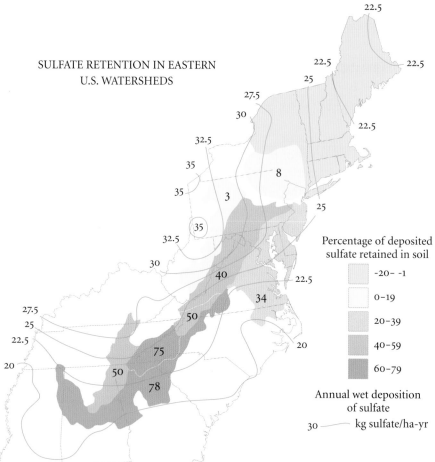

SULFATE RETENTION IN EASTERN
U.S. WATERSHEDS

Percentage of deposited
sulfate retained in soil

	-20– -1
	0–19
	20–39
	40–59
	60–79

Annual wet deposition
of sulfate

30 ——— kg sulfate/ha-yr

From Church et al., "Future effects of long-term sulfur deposition on surface water chemistry in the Northeast and southern Blue Ridge province," 1989 preprint. The map shows the DDRP estimate of the percentage of the sulfur added by wet deposition that is retained in the watershed. The deposition rates given were medians for the mid-1980s; the current rates are significantly lower. In the southern Appalachians deposition rates are moderate, and the soils, which are rich in iron and aluminum oxides, are quite retentive. In the Northeast, where the deposition rates are higher and the soils less retentive, sulfur is being released rather than retained.

ESTIMATED NUMBER OF LOW-ANC
LAKES UNDER A REDUCED-DEPOSITION
SCENARIO

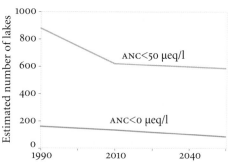

From Church et al., "Future effects of long-term sulfur deposition on surface water chemistry in the Northeast and southern Blue Ridge province," 1989 preprint. The DDRP prediction of the number of low-ANC lakes under a scenario in which sulfur deposition decreases by 30% between 1990 and 2015. The predictions were done by calibrating the MAGIC watershed model for 123 watersheds and then applying the model to the 3,227 northeastern lakes whose ANCs were predicted by the National Surface Water Survey. The model is old-fashioned by today's standards but of some historical interest because it provided, for the first time, a realistic description of the way soils immobilized sulfate and exchanged hydrogen ions for base cations.

ing. Clearly, the roots and microbes were busy. As a consequence, essentially all the sulfur in the forest floor was organically bound and almost no free sulfate occurred.

Almost all of the forest's relatively small store of inorganic sulfur was in the mineral soil. About half of it was sulfate and half reduced sulfur. Organic sulfate dominated here as well: even in the mineral soil there was six times as much organic sulfur as inorganic sulfur.

The overall balance suggested that 14.4 kg of sulfur leached out for every 8.2 kg that arrived in wet deposition, producing a net sulfur release of 6.2 kg per year. The exact balance was uncertain but still suggested, as have subsequent studies at this forest and elsewhere, that the watershed might be releasing previously stored sulfur.

Sulfur Retention and Loss: The Direct Delayed Response Project, 1984–1989

By the early 1980s it was known that variations in the ability of watersheds to store sulfate would influence their long-term behavior as sulfur inputs changed. The goal of the Direct Delayed Response

Project (DDRP) was to measure these variations and incorporate them in a process-based model that would predict how watersheds would respond to changing inputs of sulfate.

The DDRP was in many ways a larger-scale version of the RILWAS (pp. 48-54). It studied a total of 216 watersheds, 145 in the Northeast, 36 in the middle Appalachians, and 35 in the southern Blue Ridge. Measurements were made of acid deposition, soil depth, soil and water chemistry, and watershed hydrology. The measurements were then incorporated in MAGIC, the Model of Acidification of Groundwater in Catchments, a process model that connected watershed properties with surface water chemistry.

The DDRP soil studies showed that the highly oxidized southern soils had a much greater capacity for immobilizing sulfur than the more reduced northern ones. The difference in soils created a sharp south-to-north gradient in sulfate retention. In the Appalachians, watersheds were still retaining sulfate; in the Northeast they were producing sulfate.

Sulfur Budgets at Arbutus Lake and Hubbard Brook

Two watershed studies, one in the Arbutus Lake watershed of Huntington Forest in the Adirondacks and the other at Hubbard Brook Experimental Forest in the White Mountains of New Hampshire, have long-term records of sulfur deposition and export. Both made on-site measurements of dry sulfur deposition; at Arbutus dry deposition is about 37% of wet deposition, and at Hubbard Brook, about 21% of wet deposition. At Hubbard Brook, where there is known to be some sulfur in the bedrock, sulfur inputs from weathering are estimated at 1.6 kg per hectare per year. At Huntington Forest there is believed to be very little sulfur in the bedrock but no estimate of weathering is available.

The budgets for the two forests are generally similar but with some important differences. Hubbard Brook is more mountainous and receives about 30% more deposition; when the estimated sulfur contribution from weathering is added, its outputs are only about 20% above its inputs. Likens and his colleagues made a careful analysis of the uncertainties and concluded that the forest was most likely releasing sulfur that had been stored in organic form in the upper layers of the soil. But the difference between inputs and outputs was small, and it is also possible that the additional sulfur in the output came from dry deposition or weathering rather than stored sulfur.

The Arbutus Lake watershed is similar in deposition rates but strikingly different in output: it is believed to receive 7.8 kg of sulfur per hectare-year from deposition and to discharge 15.8 kg, or 103% more than it receives. The difference between inputs and outputs is 8 kg per hectare-year, just about what it receives in deposition. It

AVERAGE ANNUAL SULFATE FLUXES AT
ARBUTUS LAKE WATERSHED, 1995–1998
(kg S/ha-yr)

Deposition on watershed
wet   dry
5.7   2.1

Released from watershed 8.0

Inflow to lake   15.8

Stored in Arbutus Lake -2.5

Outflow from lake   13.3

From Mitchell et al., "Role of within-lake processes and hydrobiogeochemical changes over 16 years in a watershed in the Adirondack Mountains of New York State, USA," 2001; dry deposition is an earlier estimate from Shepard et al., "Measurements of wet and dry deposition in a northern hardwood forest," 1989. The sulfate from deposition is apparently augmented by substantial amounts of sulfate from within the watershed. About 16% of the sulfate is retained in the lake by biological uptake and microbial reduction; the rest leaves the watershed in stream water.

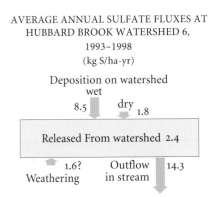

AVERAGE ANNUAL SULFATE FLUXES AT
HUBBARD BROOK WATERSHED 6,
1993–1998
(kg S/ha-yr)

Deposition on watershed
wet
8.5   dry   1.8

Released From watershed 2.4

1.6?   Outflow   14.3
Weathering in stream

From Likens et al., "The biogeochemistry of sulfur at Hubbard Brook," 2002. The estimates of dry deposition and weathering are uncertain but reasonably consistent with other observations. The sulfur released by the watershed appears to originate in the upper, largely organic layers of the soil; the authors argue that this makes it most likely that it is being generated by the mineralization of organic sulfur rather than desorption of sulfate from the mineral soil.

is very difficult to see how this could be accounted for by weathering or additional dry deposition; the likeliest hypothesis, though still only a hypothesis, is that it represents the release of previously stored sulfur.

NITROGEN CYCLING AND NITROGEN BALANCES

Nitrogen Neglected

At the beginning of acid rain research, nitrogen was considered the less important of the two main atmospheric acids. Although nitrogen deposition was substantial – in 1980 roughly one equivalent of nitrate was deposited for every two of sulfate – summer nitrate concentrations in lakes were only a small fraction of summer sulfate concentrations, and researchers assumed that most of the nitrogen deposited was being taken up and immobilized by soils and vegetation. The chemical characterizations of different lake types developed by the RILWAS (p. 49) showed 10 to 20 times less nitrate than sulfate in drainage lakes and almost no nitrate in seepage lakes. The fall nitrogen concentrations measured by the Eastern Lake Survey were so low that they do not show on the ion distribution graph of major ions (p. 67) at all. As a result, many researchers believed that sulfur was the main acidifying agent and the one that had to be regulated first. If nitrogen deposition was a problem at all, it was a problem that could be addressed later.

Because sulfate was believed more acidifying than nitrate, it followed that air quality regulations should focus on sulfur emissions. This was welcome news because sulfur is easier to control than nitrogen. Sulfur emissions come from sulfur-containing fuels and are largely produced by large, coal-burning boilers. They can be reduced by switching fuels, or removed by scrubbing stack gases or passing them over catalysts. Nitrogen emissions, on the other hand, are an intrinsic part of the combustion process itself. They come from furnaces and engines of all sizes, fixed and mobile. They cannot be ameliorated by switching fuels and are difficult to remove with scrubbers and catalysts. Any significant attempt to control nitrogen emissions will likely require the replacement of existing boilers and engines with cooler and more efficient ones. This, of course, will be both slow and expensive.

Because nitrogen emissions were both more difficult to control and deemed less worth controlling, they have been less regulated than sulfur emissions. The 1970 Clean Air Act Amendments set nitrogen emissions standards for vehicles, which resulted in lower nitrogen emissions per mile. The 1990 Clean Air Act Amendments required industrial boilers to reduce the amount of NO_x generated per BTU of heat produced and further reduced the allowable emissions per mile. But neither set a cap on total NO_x production; as

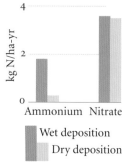

AVERAGE ADIRONDACK NITROGEN DEPOSITION, CA. 1990

Data from Driscoll and Schaefer, "The nitrogen cycle and its role in soil and drainage water acidification," 1991. Nitrogen is deposited in two chemical forms by two routes. The graph shows a total deposition of about 10 kg N/ha-yr, or about 830 eq/ha-yr. The rate of wet deposition is easy to measure and fairly well known; the rate of dry deposition requires complex instrumentation to measure and has been measured only at a few sites. Driscoll and Schaefer estimated total Adirondack nitrogen deposition at 10.6 kg/ha-yr, of which 78% was nitrate and 22% ammonium; 59% of this was wet deposition and 41% dry deposition.

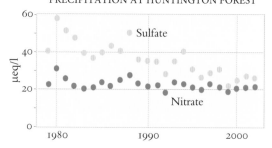

CONCENTRATION OF SULFATE AND NITRATE IN PRECIPITATION AT HUNTINGTON FOREST

Wet deposition data from the National Trends Network station at Huntington Forest. In 1980 the concentration of sulfate was approximately twice that of nitrate. By 1995, as a result of the Clean Air Act Amendments, the sulfate concentration was only 1.2 times the concentration of nitrate.

long as the emissions per BTU and per mile are within limits, there is no restriction on the total amount of fuel burned or miles driven. In consequence, while the total U.S. emissions of SO_2 have decreased by 13 million metric tons (33%) since 1983, the total U.S. emissions of NO_x are believed to have decreased by only 3.4 million metric tons (15%, p. 13).

Nitrogen Acidification Appears

Nitrogen, however, is not a benign pollutant. It is indeed taken up by vegetation in relatively large quantities – forests use at least ten times as much nitrogen each year as they do sulfur – but it is also regenerated by decay in relatively large quantities. The uptake of nitrate consumes acidity, but the regeneration of nitrate produces acidity. Nitrate-related acidity can accumulate in soils in the winter, when the vegetation is dormant and there is little nitrate uptake, and then be flushed into streams and lakes by spring runoff.

By the 1980s there were already indications that nitrogen was a more important acidifying agent than was previously thought.

In 1978 Likens and his collaborators at Hubbard Brook Experimental Forest reported that when the regrowth of a logged watershed was suppressed with herbicide, elevated concentrations of nitrogen appeared in stream water.

In 1980 Johannes, Galloway, and Troutman reported that nitrate was three times more abundant than sulfate in the snowpack around Sagamore Lake (p. 42).

In 1981-1982 Driscoll and Schafran mapped the seasonal distribution of base-neutralizing capacity in Dart Lake and found that it agreed closely with the distribution of nitrate but not with the distribution of sulfate.

Sometime in the early 1980s the curves of falling sulfur emissions and stable nitrogen emissions met, and total U.S. NO_x emissions (about 25 million metric tons) equaled SO_2 emissions for the first time (p. 13).

In 1987, Rascher, Driscoll, and Peters reported that the ions in snowpack concentrate in the melting phase, and so acids can be more concentrated in meltwater than in the snowpack itself (p. 107).

Also in 1987 Driscoll, Yatsko, and Unangst described pronounced spring peaks of nitrate in Moss and Dart lakes (p. 55).

These observations did not go unnoticed. By the late 1980s the Episodic Response Project, a major regional study of short-term acidity peaks, was under way (p. 109). By the early 1990s nitrogen saturation was being widely discussed, and

DISTRIBUTIONS OF NITRATE, HYDROGEN ION, AND ALUMINUM IN DART LAKE, 1981-1982

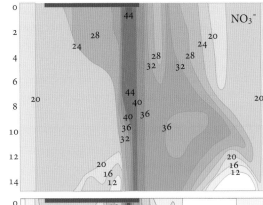

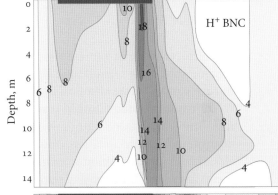

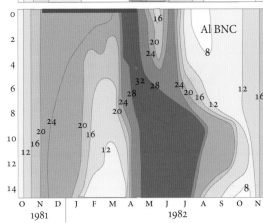

All contours in µeq/l.   ▬▬▬▬ Lake frozen

Redrawn Driscoll and Schafran, "Short-term changes in the base-neutralizing capacity of an acid Adirondack lake, New York." Copyright 1984 Nature Publishing Group via the Copyright Clearance Center. In late winter nitrate is injected near the surface of the lake by runoff and groundwater. It is mixed throughout the lake during spring runoff and then gradually replaced with low-nitrate water near the surface in the summer. The distributions of hydrogen ion and aluminum are quite similar, suggesting that their concentrations are in part controlled by the concentration of nitrate. See page 105 for more discussion.

many nitrogen budget and nitrogen cycling studies were undertaken (p. 112). By the late 1990s it had become clear that nitrogen saturation was at least locally important in the Adirondacks and that lake nitrogen was certainly associated with and perhaps more responsible for the observed seasonal patterns of acidification than anyone had previously believed.

In next six sections we describe a series of studies on nitrogen cycling and nitrogen saturation. The sequence is causal rather than strictly historical. We first describe nitrogen cycling in forests and the spring nitrogen peaks caused by this cycling. We then turn to the mechanism and geography of nitrogen saturation and finish with several recent studies of the relation between nitrogen and lake acidification.

Nitrogen in Forests

The nitrogen cycle in a forest is generally like the sulfur cycle but is somewhat more complicated because there are more forms of nitrogen and so more chemical transformations between them.

Human-generated nitrogen is supplied to forests in two chemical forms, nitrate and ammonium ion, and by three paths, wet deposition from precipitation, cloudwater deposition from fog and clouds, and dry deposition from gases and particulates. Measurements at CASTNET monitoring stations in our area suggest that dry deposition at low and middle elevations is about a third to a half of wet deposition (p. 7); nearer the sources of pollution it is relatively more important, and farther away, less so. Cloudwater deposition is important at high elevations and there may equal or exceed wet deposition.

Much of the nitrogen deposited on forests is intercepted by the leaves and branches of trees. Part of this is assimilated directly by the trees; the remainder falls to the ground as throughfall and stemflow. The concentration of nitrogen in throughfall usually exceeds that in wet deposition and is often used as a minimum estimate of total deposition.

Much of the nitrogen reaching the soil is assimilated by vegetation and microbes. Depending on the form of nitrogen, this may acidify or deacidify the soil. The assimilation of ammonium releases hydrogen ions; the assimilation of nitrate releases bases that consume them.

Natural inputs of nitrogen also occur, though they are small compared with those from acid deposition. In habitats where nitrogen-fixing bacteria are active, nitrogen gas (N_2) may be assimilated directly into microbial tissue. Nitrogen fixation is believed to be relatively important in wetlands and unimportant in forests but is difficult to measure directly and has been little studied.

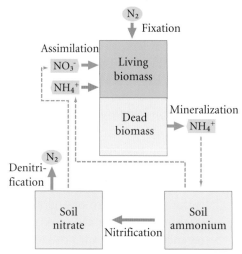

NITROGEN CYCLING WITHIN A FOREST

→ Process generating hydrogen ions
→ Process consuming hydrogen ions
→ Process neither generating nor consuming hydrogen ions

Within a forest, nitrogen is assimilated into living tissue, mineralized to ammonium by decay, and then either assimilated again or nitrified to nitrate. Nitrogen is added to the forest by deposition and nitrogen fixation and lost to the forest by denitrification and groundwater flow.

Within the cycle, the oxidative steps (red arrows) generate hydrogen ions and acidify groundwater; the reducing steps (green arrows) consume hydrogen ions and deacidify groundwater. Any complete path around the cycle – say, nitrate to biomass to ammonium to nitrate again – has no overall effect on acidity. But any incomplete path in which the transfers of hydrogen ions are unbalanced – say, ammonium to biomass to ammonium to nitrate that is lost in groundwater – will acidify or deacidify.

The net production of acidity for the forest as a whole is calculated from the inputs and outputs:

$$H^+ \text{ generated} = NH_4^+ (in) - NH_4^+ (out) + NO_3^- (out) - NO_3^- (in).$$

In June, when forests are taking up significant amounts of nitrate and consuming almost all the ammonia they produce, this sum is negative, and the forest is also consuming hydrogen ions. And in December, when the forest is taking up very little and when the ammonia produced by decay is getting oxidized to nitrate, the sum is positive, and the forest is generating hydrogen ions.

The nitrogen assimilated by trees is used for new growth. At the end of the growing season, some of this growth falls as litter and becomes part of the pool of dead plant material in the forest floor.

The bacterial and fungal decay (mineralization) of dead organic matter produces ammonium ions and consumes hydrogen ions. Decay occurs at all seasons but is faster in the summer than in the winter.

Because ammonium is the preferred nitrogen source for most plants, during the growing season most ammonium produced by decay is immediately reassimilated by plants. But during the dormant season a portion of the ammonium is oxidized by bacteria to nitrate (nitrified), producing hydrogen ions. Some of the nitrate is reassimilated and some is reduced by microbes to nitrogen gas, which then escapes into the atmosphere. The rest is exported in the groundwater.

Nitrogen-Cycle Acidification

Nitrogen cycling is of central interest in acid rain research because the nitrogen cycle can either produce or consume acid. Which it does depends on the inputs and outputs and on the balance between growth and decay. The principles are simple:

When, as in the annual cycle of an undisturbed forest, uptake and decay are balanced and nitrogen cycles continuously between the plants and the soil, there is no net production or consumption of hydrogen ions and no acidification or deacidification.

When, as in the summer months, growth exceeds decay and the forest is consuming nitrate, it is also consuming hydrogen ions and deacidifying groundwater.

When, as in the winter months or after disturbance, decay exceeds growth and the forest is generating nitrate, it is also generating hydrogen ions and acidifying groundwater.

And when deposition is high and the forest is converting ammonia inputs to nitrate outputs, it is also generating hydrogen ions and acidifying groundwater.

The hydrogen ions produced by the nitrogen cycle are called nitrogen-cycle acidity, and the process is called nitrogen-cycle acidification.

Nitrogen Cycling on Whiteface Mountain

As mentioned on page 98, in the first decade of acid rain research it was widely assumed that most of the nitrogen deposited on forests

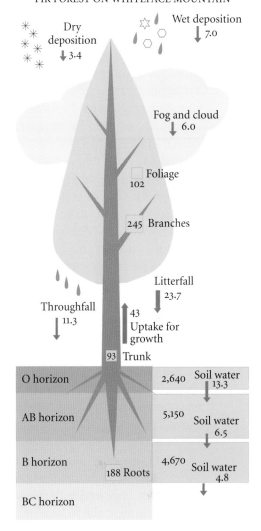

NITROGEN CYCLING IN A SUBALPINE SPRUCE-FIR FOREST ON WHITEFACE MOUNTAIN

From Friedland et al., "Nitrogen deposition, distribution, and cycling in a subalpine spruce-fir forest in the Adirondacks, New York, USA," 1991. Cloudwater, which is a major source of nitrogen at high elevations, was collected on Teflon fibers; dry deposition was measured with air filters. Soil water was sampled with lysimeters. The quantity of soil water was estimated, with some uncertainty, from calculations of evapotranspiration.

was assimilated by the vegetation and hence that nitrogen-cycle acidification was relatively unimportant. It was, then, something of a surprise when the first Adirondack studies of forest nitrogen cycles found otherwise.

The most detailed study of nitrogen cycling in an Adirondack forest was a compartment study done on Whiteface Mountain by Friedland and his collaborators. This was part of a major cooperative study, the Forest Ecosystem Research Program, that studied deposition, nutrient cycling, and forest dynamics in high-elevation spruce-fir forests. The study ran from 1986 to 1999 and produced the longest and most detailed picture of the effects of acid deposition on forests that we have for any place in the park. It measured total atmospheric deposition for 14 years, quantified the effects of elevation on deposition, quantified red-spruce decline and showed that it was related to the deposition of acid cloudwater, and provided the first Adirondack estimates of mineral weathering rates and the first evidence for nitrogen saturation in an Adirondack forest.

The nitrogen cycling studies were done in subalpine spruce-fir forests. Friedland et al. measured stand composition, growth, deposition, litterfall, throughfall, mineralization, and soil and groundwater chemistry. They assumed that nitrogen fixation and denitrification were small but did not try to measure them.

The forests they studied were heavily affected by acid deposition. They estimated that, on average, 16 kg of nitrogen was deposited on each hectare of forest every year, 40% as ammonium and 60% as nitrate. Only 43% of this came in wet deposition; the rest was dry deposition (21%) and cloudwater (36%).

Thirty percent of the incoming nitrogen, including about two-thirds of the ammonium, was assimilated in the canopy. The rest, about 11 kg, appeared as throughfall.

In addition to the 16 kg of nitrogen from deposition, the forest had available about 40 kg of nitrogen per year from the decay of organic matter. This made a total of 56 kg of nitrogen available for plant growth every year. About 43 kg of this was used for new forest growth. Another 4.8 kg was exported from the lower soil by groundwater, leaving 8 kg unaccounted for.

Compared with the amounts of nitrogen stored in the system – 13,100 kg per acre, including 650 kg in biomass, 2,640 kg in the upper soil, and 9,800 kg in the lower soil – the 16 kg added annually by deposition and the 4.8 kg exported in groundwater appear small. But remember that most of the stored nitrogen is immobilized and unavailable for growth. Compared with the 40 kg released by decay, the 16 kg of nitrogen supplied by deposition represents a 40% increase in the nitrogen available for growth. And the overall nitrogen balance – 16 kg per hectare in and 4.8 kg per hectare out – suggests that at least 29% of the nitrogen received by the forest is being exported to groundwater.

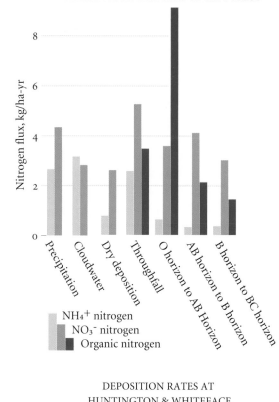

ANNUAL NITROGEN FLUXES IN THE WHITEFACE MOUNTAIN SPRUCE-FIR FOREST

NH₄⁺ nitrogen
NO₃⁻ nitrogen
Organic nitrogen

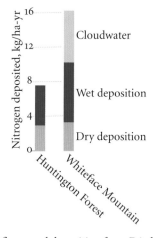

DEPOSITION RATES AT HUNTINGTON & WHITEFACE

Whiteface fluxes and deposition from Friedland et al., "Nitrogen deposition, distribution, and cycling in a subalpine spruce-fir forest in the Adirondacks, New York, USA," 1991. Huntington deposition from Shepard et al., "Measurements of wet and dry deposition in a northern hardwood forest," 1989. Dry deposition is similar at Huntington and Whiteface; wet deposition is about 45% higher at Whiteface; and cloudwater deposition, which is assumed absent at Huntington, almost equals wet deposition on Whiteface. The authors found that the most heavily affected montane forests may receive four to five times as much S and N as low-elevation ones.

The Nitrogen Balance of the Arbutus Lake Watershed

Like the work on Whiteface Mountain, the nitrogen balance studies of the Arbutus watershed at Huntington Forest are part of a larger study. The Arbutus watershed has been studied continuously since 1983 and is the only Adirondack watershed – and indeed one of only a few in the Northeast – where deposition, flow, and surface water chemistry are simultaneously monitored. Much important work on element cycling has been and continues to be done there. We mentioned the Arbutus sulfur budget on p. 97 and will present other results from the watershed later in this chapter and in Chapter 7 and Chapter 8.

In 2001, Mitchell, Raynal, and Driscoll summarized the results of the first ten years of monitoring at Arbutus. The nitrogen balance is shown at right.

Total nitrogen deposition at Arbutus is about 7.7 kg, about half that of Whiteface. Sixty-one percent of the deposition is wet and 39% dry; cloudwater deposition was not measured but is assumed to be low. Seventy-seven percent of the nitrogen is nitrate, 23% ammonium.

The forest stores 94% of the ammonia and 64% of the nitrate in the watershed and another 32% of the nitrate in the lake. The total nitrogen storage in the watershed is 70% of deposition, and in the watershed plus the lake, 84% of deposition.

Nitrogen Cycling in Hardwood Forest Floors

As part of a 1991–93 study on the effects of nitrogen additions on nutrient cycling, Mitchell and his colleagues constructed nitrogen budgets for the forest floors of three Adirondack study areas. They measured the nitrogen in throughfall and at two different depths in the soil and used a computer model to estimate drainage. By combining their observations and the modeled movement of water, they could calculate the nitrogen flux through the forest floor and the amount retained by the vegetation and the soil.

At the study site at Huntington Forest, for example, the forest received a total of 5.3 kg of nitrogen per hectare per year from deposition. It retained 0.7 kg (13%) of this in the canopy and passed 4.6 kg on to the forest floor. The forest floor, in turn, retained 3.1 kg (67%) of this and passed the remainder on to the deeper soil. As expected, ammonium was assimilated preferentially: 92% of the ammonium reaching the forest floor was retained, but only 58% of the nitrate.

The two other study sites, at Woods Lake and Pancake Hall Creek, were in the southwestern portion of the park, where deposition is higher. Their forest floors received more than twice as much nitrate and ammonium as those at Huntington Forest. Interest-

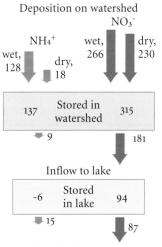

ANNUAL NITROGEN FLUXES AT THE ARBUTUS LAKE WATERSHED, 1983-1992

From Mitchell et al., "Role of within-lake processes and hydrobiogeochemical changes over 16 years in a watershed of the Adirondack Mountains of New York State, USA," 2001; dry deposition from Shepard et al., "Measurements of wet and dry deposition in a northern hardwood forest," 1989.

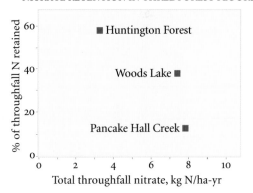

NITRATE RETENTION IN THREE FOREST FLOORS

From Mitchell et al., "Nitrogen biogeochemistry of three hardwood ecosystems in the Adirondack region of New York," 2001. The y-axis is the percentage of the nitrate arriving in throughfall that is stored in the forest floor or assimilated by vegetation.

ingly, they still retained more than 90% of the ammonium they received but retained only 38% and 13% of the nitrate. Nitrate retention, the graph suggests, might have a threshold in the vicinity of 8–10 kg/ha-yr. In the next ten years, studies in Europe and North America would explore similar terrain and encounter a similar threshold (pp. 116–119).

Estimates of Nitrogen-Cycle Acidification

We can use the amounts of nitrate and ammonium retained at these sites to calculate the proton balance, which is the amount of acidity generated or consumed. The rule (p. 100) is that retaining ammonium generates acidity and retaining nitrate consumes it.

The results are illustrative rather than general. Nitrogen cycling is closely linked to both forest growth and forest hydrology, and these in turn are linked to and vary greatly with the average temperature, the amount of precipitation, and the timing and duration of snowmelt.

With this caveat, the results suggest that at most sites nitrate retention exceeds ammonium retention and so, over the course of a year, the nitrogen cycle consumes more acid than it generates, though at three sites the difference is small. At Pancake Hall Creek, however, ammonium retention exceeds nitrate retention and the forest floor generates about 160 equivalents of nitrogen-cycle acidity per hectare-year.

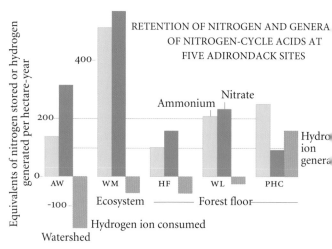

RETENTION OF NITROGEN AND GENERA OF NITROGEN-CYCLE ACIDS AT FIVE ADIRONDACK SITES

AW Arbutus watershed   WM Whiteface Mt.   HF Huntington For
WL Woods Lake   PHC Pancake-Hall Creek

Above, net ammonium and nitrate storage and hydrogen ion generation for five Adirondack sites, calculated from data in the studies described on pages 102–103. The green bars give the ammonium and nitrogen retained in the system per ha-yr. The amount of hydrogen ion generated or consumed is the difference between the two; when ammonium retention exceeds nitrate retention, hydrogen ion is generated; when nitrate retention exceeds ammonium retention, it is consumed.

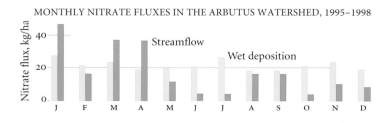

MONTHLY NITRATE FLUXES IN THE ARBUTUS WATERSHED, 1995–1998

Left, average monthly fluxes of nitrate supplied to the Arbutus Lake watershed by wet deposition and exported from it in streamflow. Deposition is fairly uniform; export is highly seasonal, with peaks in the winter and early spring and very low values in summer. From Mitchell et al., "Role of within-lake processes and hydrobiogeochemical changes over 16 years in a watershed of the Adirondack Mountains of New York State, USA," 2001.

The Nitrogen Cycle Generalized

The results just described, plus similar ones from outside the Adirondacks, suggest three general observations about nitrogen cycling:

> First, though the amount of nitrogen stored in forests is large, the amount cycled between vegetation and soils is much smaller. As a result, the amounts of nitrogen in acid deposition are often enough to alter natural cycling.

Second, the ammonia from deposition is assimilated and retained efficiently, but the nitrate is not. As a result, nitrates are often exported from forests, especially in winter.

And third, the ability of forests to retain nitrogen is limited. As a result, the more they receive, the less they retain.

These observations led, inevitably, to the concept of nitrogen saturation, to which we will turn in a few pages. Before that, however we need one more piece of the puzzle: if the nitrogen is leaving the forests, where is it going and what is it doing?

NITROGEN PEAKS IN LAKES, MELTWATER, AND STREAMS

Acid Episodes in Adirondack Lakes

To follow the nitrogen that is exported from forests, we backtrack a bit and look at the first studies of the sources and chemistry of spring runoff.

In the Adirondacks, more than 50% of the annual runoff often occurs in March, April, and May. By the mid-1980s it was clear that the runoff period was chemically and ecologically important: many lakes and streams experienced acid episodes during snowmelt in which their pHs and ANCs decreased and their aluminum concentrations increased. These episodes were chemically different from the chronic acidification of lakes with high sulfate concentrations: they often involved peaks of nitrate and could occur in waters that were neutral or only weakly acidic in summer and fall.

The first two Adirondack studies to look at the details of runoff chemistry were on lakes. A 1981–1982 study of Dart Lake by Driscoll and Schafran prepared isopleth maps (p. 99) showing the concentrations of different elements at different depths and times. The maps show a plume of high-nitrate water entering the upper parts of the lake in early April and then mixing through the profile during the spring overturn. The high-nitrate water is also high in aluminum and hydrogen ion. After examining the correlations between these and other ions, the authors concluded, "Our results suggest that much of the variation in hydrogen ion and aluminum concentration can be attributed to changes in nitrate concentration and not to variations in sulfate, chloride, or organic anion concentrations."

That conclusion was important at the time and remains true today. Sulfate is clearly responsible for much of the chronic acidification of lakes (pp. 73–74), but nitrate, which is relatively more variable than sulfate, plays a larger role in the seasonal acidity peaks.

In the second study of the spring acidification, Schaefer and his collaborators examined the long-term monitoring data for 1986–

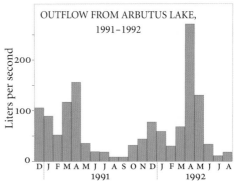

Average monthly water flows at the outlet of Arbutus Lake, from Mitchell et al., redrawn with permission from "Biogeochemistry of a forested watershed in the central Adirondack Mountains: Temporal changes and mass balances." Copyright 1996 Springer Science and Business Media. The spring runoff peak begins with snowmelt in late March. In 1991, 47% of the annual runoff occurred in March, April, and May.

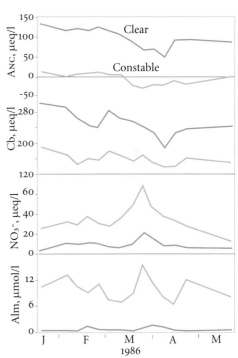

Adapted with permission from Schaefer et al., "The episodic acidification of Adirondack lakes during snowmelt." Copyright 1990 American Geophysical Union. Medium-ANC Clear Pond, with a baseline ANC of around 100 µeq/l, shows a strong dilution of base cations (C_B) and a corresponding drop in ANC. Acidic Constable Pond, with a baseline ANC near 0 µeq/l, shows higher nitrate and aluminum peaks but a smaller drop in ANC.

1987 from ten Adirondack lakes. They confirmed the importance of nitrogen in the spring acidification of low-ANC drainage lakes but found that other mechanisms were at work in high-ANC lakes.

The graph at right shows the seasonal chemistry at two representative lakes from the study. Constable Pond is a highly acidic pond in the southwestern Adirondacks with a baseline ANC just slightly above 0 µeq/l. In the spring it had sharp increases in nitrate and aluminum but gradual and relatively small decreases in base cations. Its ANC decrease was also small (-25 µeq/l), probably because the acidifying effects of the changes in nitrates and base cations were moderated by the buffering effects of aluminum.

Clear Pond, a less acid pond with a baseline ANC near 100 µeq/l, responded quite differently. It had a large spring decrease in base cations, probably caused by an influx of dilute surface water, but only a small increase in nitrate and almost no change in aluminum. The resulting change in ANC, driven largely by the decrease in base cations, was about twice that of Constable Pond.

A comparison of the ten lakes in the study showed that the differences between Clear and Constable ponds are part of a general pattern. Lakes with thin-till watersheds, like Constable Pond, are chronically low in base cations. Because their normal cation concentrations are already very low, they have only small changes in base cation concentrations during spring runoff. They tend to have strong nitrate and aluminum peaks but, because of aluminum buffering, only moderate springtime decreases in ANC.

Lakes like Clear Pond, which are in medium-till watersheds and derive their water from a mixture of surface water and deep groundwater, have moderate amounts of base cations and thus large decreases of ANC when their base cation supply is diluted by meltwater during the spring runoff.

And finally, a few high-ANC lakes with very deep soils in their watersheds usually show only slight spring changes in ANC. Black Pond, for example, derives much of its water from groundwater year-round. It has a baseline ANC of over 200 µeq/l, and even during spring runoff its ANC remains over 150 µeq/l.

Thus another consequence of lake classification emerged: apparently there were two mechanisms of spring acidification and hence two sorts of acid episodes. In nitrate-driven events in thin-till lakes, the actual ANC changes were not very large, but the aluminum peaks were severe and the ANC often became negative. In dilution-driven events in medium-till lakes, the ANC changes were large but aluminum was not a problem and the ANC rarely became negative.

Clearly then, spring runoff was carrying nitrogen and, with the nitrogen, aluminum and acids. But what nitrogen was it carrying? Was it atmospheric nitrogen that had been stored in the snowpack, or biogenic nitrogen produced by nitrogen cycling in the forest

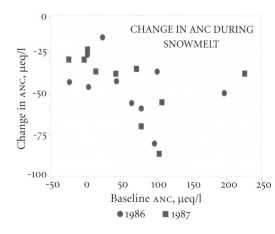

CHANGE IN ANC DURING SNOWMELT

● 1986   ■ 1987

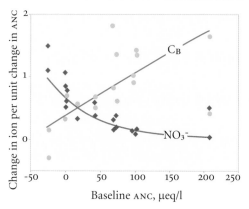

CONTRIBUTIONS OF BASE CATIONS AND NO₃⁻ TO SPRING ANC DECREASES IN ADIRONDACK LAKES

From Schaefer et al., "The episodic acidification of Adirondack lakes during snowmelt." Copyright 1990 American Geophysical Union. The upper graph compares the average baseline ANC of ten ALTM lakes with their springtime drop in ANC. Both high-ANC and low-ANC lakes are partially buffered against ANC changes, the high-ANC lakes by base cations and the low-ANC lakes by aluminum. The largest springtime drops in ANC are in the middle-ANC lakes.

The second graph plots the concentration change ratios $\Delta C_B/\Delta$ANC (blue circles) and $\Delta NO_3/\Delta$ANC (red diamonds), where Δ indicates the change in the concentration of the ion from the baseline, again for two years of data from the ten ALTM lakes. In very low-ANC lakes most of springtime decrease in ANC is associated with changes in nitrate. In high-ANC lakes most of the decrease is caused by the dilution of base cations. In lakes with ANCs near 0 µeq/l, both base cations and nitrate are important.

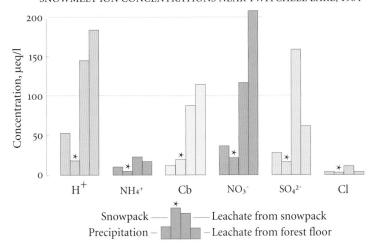

SNOWMELT ION CONCENTRATIONS NEAR TWITCHELL LAKE, 1984

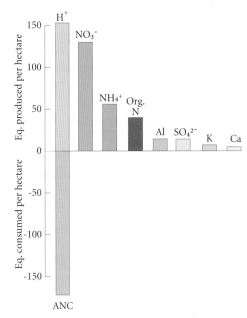

ION BUDGET OF THE FOREST FLOOR NEAR
TWITCHELL LAKE DURING SNOWMELT, 1984

floor? Or were the two connected, and was snowpack nitrogen feeding the biological cycling in the soil?

Snowmelt Chemistry at Twitchell Lake

Two Adirondack papers of the mid-1980s did much to clarify these questions.

The first, by Rascher, Driscoll, and Peters, compared the chemistry of precipitation and snowpack with the chemistry of water leaching out of the forest floor. Their work showed that while the Adirondack snowpack is surprisingly dilute, the meltwater from snow is significantly more concentrated than the snowpack, and the spring leachate from the forest floor more concentrated still.

When the study began in January 1984, the precipitation contained about 40 µeq/l nitrate and 30 µeq/l sulfate. The high nitrate concentration was normal: precipitation chemistry in the Adirondacks varies seasonally, and nitrate is most abundant, both absolutely and relative to sulfate, in the winter. The chemistry of the snowpack (starred bars in the graph above) was similar to that of the precipitation but, probably because of partial melting in thaws, considerably less concentrated: it had less than a third of the hydrogen ion and only about 60% of the nitrate and sulfate.

Thus the snowpack was actually less concentrated than normal rain or snow. If it had melted all at once, it might have produced a dilution event rather than a peak in acidity.

Snowmelt, however, is a gradual process. During gradual melting the ions in the snow migrate to the melting phase, and as a result the early spring meltwater is much more concentrated than either the precipitation or the snowpack (third bars in each set above). Nitrate and hydrogen ion concentrations were 2.5 to 3 times higher

Both graphs based on data from Rascher, Driscoll, and Peters, "Concentration and flux of solutes from snow and forest floor during snowmelt in the west-central Adirondack region of New York," 1987. The study ran from 29 March to 15 April, 1984. At the start the winter snowpack contained the equivalent of 18 cm of water. By the end of the winter 70% of the original snow cover had melted and an additional 4.5 cm of rain had fallen, producing a total of about 16 cm of runoff.

The left graph shows that the leachates from melting snow and the forest floor were several times more concentrated and more acidic than either precipitation or the snowpack itself. Sulfate is most concentrated in the leachate from the snowpack, nitrate most concentrated in the leachate from the forest floor.

The right graph gives the total amounts of various ions leached from the forest floor during the runoff period. During snowmelt the forest generates nitric acid, ammonium, and organic nitrogen and consumes ANC.

in meltwater than in the snowpack; sulfate concentrations were fully 5 times higher.

Concentration by partial melting is not, however, the whole story. The leachate from the forest floor was even more concentrated and more acid than the meltwater from the snowpack (fourth bars in each set above). It had somewhat more base cations, twice as much nitrate, and only half the sulfur. It also had acquired significant amounts of organic carbon and nitrogen, which were largely absent in the snowpack.

The changes in composition between meltwater and leachate indicated that the forest floor was biochemically active during the winter. It was producing significant amounts of DOC, hydrogen ion, nitrate, ammonium, dissolved organic nitrogen and aluminum, and smaller amounts of sulfate and base cations.

The large amounts of nitrate coming from the forest floor and the large amounts of hydrogen ion associated with them were the most striking findings. The forest floor at Twitchell Lake produced 150 equivalents per acre of hydrogen ion in two weeks, equal to an annual rate of 3,900 equivalents per hectare-year and 25 times faster than the highest average rate of acidification in the watersheds discussed on page 104.

The quantity of nitrogen involved suggested that much of the nitrate and hydrogen ion was generated by nitrogen cycling. Some nitrates certainly arrived in winter precipitation and some may have been produced by the oxidation of the ammonium in precipitation, but neither source was sufficient to account for the amounts observed. "In particular," the authors said in summary, "forest floor processes resulted in a fivefold enrichment in H$^+$ and NO$_3^-$ over snowpack inputs."

Thus the generation of snowmelt acidity was found to involve more than melting snow. It required a concentrating mechanism – differential melting – to turn dilute ice into concentrated meltwater. And it required a good deal of microbial activity under the snowpack to turn stored nitrogen into nitrates and hydrogen ions.

New and Old Water in the ALTM Watersheds

The Twitchell Lake study had left investigators with an important observation – that forest floors export nitrogen and acidity during snowmelt – and a hydrologic problem. If spring runoff, as its name suggested, was meltwater moving over the surface, how did the acids from within the soil get into streams and lakes?

One possible hypothesis was that spring runoff consisted of two sorts of water: new water from melting snow and old water from within the soil. The new water, which was fairly dilute, would both run over the surface and act as piston pushing down on the old

ELEMENT FLUXES IN 11 ADIRONDACK WATERSHEDS DURING SNOWMELT, 1986

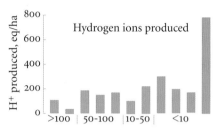

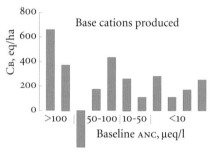

Based on Schaefer and Driscoll, "Identifying sources of snowmelt acidification with a watershed mixing model," 1993. The lakes are arranged by the baseline (late winter) ANCs. The lower the baseline ANC, the more N-cycle acidity and the fewer base cations the watershed produces during snowmelt.

The mixing model used in this analysis works from measurements of the concentrations of "conservative tracers," in this case sodium and sulfate, that are not produced or retained in the soil. From the concentrations of the tracers in surface water, groundwater, and lake water, the mixing ratio of surface water and groundwater can be calculated. From the mixing ratio and the composition of lake water, the fluxes of nonconservative elements can be calculated; these fluxes can then be compared with the deposition rates to find out which elements the watershed is producing and which it is consuming.

A recent study using similar techniques is McHale et al., "A field-based study of soil water and groundwater nitrate release in an Adirondack forested watershed," 2002. The authors found that most of the nitrate reaching streams moves in groundwater flowing through till, both in dry periods and after storms.

water. The old water, which was enriched with nitrogen, aluminum, and acids, would be driven down into the soil profile and then downslope into lakes and streams.

In the springs of 1986 and 1987, Schaefer and Driscoll tested this hypothesis in 11 Adirondack watersheds. They analyzed meltwater, lake water, and groundwater from the forest floor and then used a mixing model to estimate the amounts of meltwater and groundwater reaching the lakes. The results were somewhat variable and the authors warn that they are only semiquantitative. But they are consistent enough to suggest some interesting and otherwise invisible details about hydrology and chemistry. In particular:

> Some 66% to 90% of the water arriving in lakes during snowmelt is old groundwater.

> The old water is richer in hydrogen ion, nitrate, aluminum, and base cations than the new water and creates a significant flux of these ions from the watershed to the lake.

> High-ANC watersheds tend to export base cations; low-ANC watersheds export nitrogen-cycle acids and aluminum.

> The amounts of acids exported are significant, averaging 150 equivalents per hectare or more in low-ANC watersheds.

The results of this study were part confirmation, part qualification, and part surprise. The old idea that deep flowpaths neutralize most of the acids moving through them was qualified, and the new ideas about the importance of nitrogen-cycle acidification and old groundwater during snowmelt were confirmed. The surprise was that – as the results of the authors' concurrent study of lake chemistry (p. 106) were also suggesting – the spring ANC losses in high-ANC and low-ANC lakes were driven by different mechanisms. In low-ANC lakes they were mostly the result of the transport of acids that had been generated or stored in the watershed. In high-ANC lakes they were mostly the result of the dilution of the normal flow of bases and involved relatively little generation of new acids at all.

Acid Episodes on Four Adirondack Streams

The three studies just described established that Adirondack watersheds export an interesting mixture of snowmelt and groundwater in the spring and that this mixture travels to lakes and, depending on the lake, dilutes or acidifies them. A fourth study, the Episodic Response Project (ERP), looked at what the meltwater does to streams along the way.

When the ERP began in 1988, much less was known about Adirondack streams than about Adirondack lakes. This was not because the streams were less important but because stream sam-

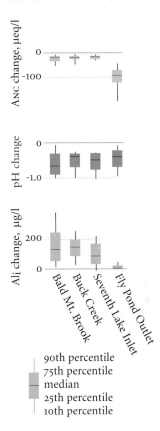

CHEMICAL CHANGES DURING ACID EPISODES ON FOUR ADIRONDACK STREAMS, 1988-1990

90th percentile
75th percentile
median
25th percentile
10th percentile

The distribution of the magnitudes of the chemical changes during acidity peaks on four Adirondack streams, redrawn from Wigington et al., "Episodic acidification of small streams in the northeastern United States: Ionic controls of episodes." Copyright 1996 Ecological Society of America via the Copyright Clearance Center. Bald Mountain Brook, which is nearly neutral in summer, had both the largest decrease in pH and the largest increases in aluminum. Fly Pond Outlet, a highly buffered stream with abundant base cations, had the highest baseline ANC and the largest ANC decreases but the smallest changes in aluminum. Its large ANC change was dramatic but, because of its high baseline, of less biological importance than the smaller changes on the more acidic streams.

pling is more difficult than lake sampling. Lake chemistry varies slowly and, even in the spring, weekly or monthly samples are usually adequate to capture the seasonal pattern. Streams vary quickly, and daily or even hourly samples are required to catch the rapid pulses of acidity during snowmelt and after storms. This kind of sampling is difficult even under the best circumstances; when, as in the Adirondacks, the streams are remote, it creates major technical and logistical problems.

The Episodic Response Project was a two-year cooperative federal project that monitored 13 streams in New York and Pennsylvania. Its purpose was to measure chemical changes during high-water episodes and determine their effects on fish. The ERP built gauging stations on the streams and connected them to automatic water samplers. Water levels were recorded every 15 minutes. Samples were collected automatically during high-water periods, either every hour or more frequently when the stream levels were changing rapidly.

Four western Adirondack streams were studied from summer 1988 through spring 1990. (Three of them later became ALTM waters in 1992; their long-term chemical trends are discussed on p. 203.) All were streams with watersheds of 700 hectares or less, elevations between 550 and 850 meters, and annual median flows between 0.01 and 0.06 cubic meters per second. In addition, all had extant brook trout populations, making them suitable for studies of fish mortality. Buck Creek was the most acid (1989 median pH 5.4, median ANC 10 µeq/l); Bald Mountain Brook and Seventh Lake Outlet are somewhat less acid (median pHs 6.2 and 5.7, ANCs 26 and 21 µeq/l, respectively), and Fly Pond Outlet neutral (median pH 7.1, ANC 225 µeq/l). The streams are in the southwestern Adirondacks, where deposition is high; a nearby deposition station at Moss Lake reported 8.2 kg of sulfur and 7.7 kg of nitrogen in wet deposition in 1989.

The record for Bald Mountain Brook, which is generally typical of all the sites, shows two protracted periods of high water in late winter and eight other shorter high-water periods in other seasons. In these periods flows increased 20 to 160 times, pHs decreased by an average of three-quarters of a unit, acid-neutralizing capacities decreased by around 25 µeq/l or more, and inorganic aluminum rose by an average of 150 µg/l.

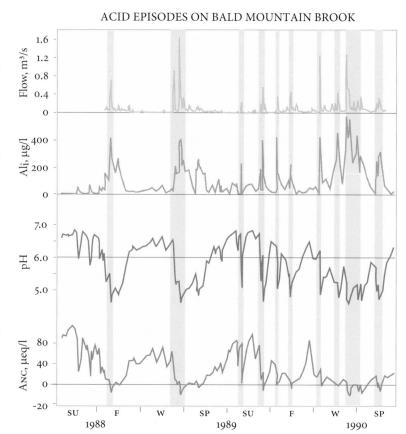

Redrawn from Wigington et al., "Episodic acidification of small streams in the northeastern United States: Ionic controls of episodes." Copyright 1996 Ecological Society of America via the Copyright Clearance Center. Bald Mountain Brook had the largest ANC changes of the four Adirondack streams studied by the Episodic Response Project. The acid peaks (gray bands) are marked by sharp increases in inorganic aluminum and sharp decreases in pH and ANC.

Like the North Branch studies (p. 52), the ERP used bioassays with caged fish to determine whether the aluminum peaks were biologically significant. The results, which are discussed in more detail in Chapter 8, were unequivocal: changes of this magnitude, even when of short duration, are more than sufficient to kill fish. Whenever the median aluminum concentration in the peak was more than 100 micrograms per liter, or whenever the peak lasted for more than six days, the survival of the test fish dropped from nearly 100% to under 20% (p. 180).

The Nitrate Balance of the ERP Streams

The ERP researchers computed approximate nitrate balances for the four watersheds they studied. The streams receive about 5.0 kg/ha-yr of nitrogen in nitrate and 2.7 kg/ha-yr of nitrogen in ammonium. Dry deposition is unknown but, judging from the rates measured at Huntington Forest (p. 102), is at least another 3 kg N per ha-yr or more.

The ERP data suggest that the Fly Pond Outlet watershed, where ANC was high, consumed about 3 kg of nitrate per ha-yr in 1989 and thus retained 39% of the total nitrogen deposited in wet deposition. The other three watersheds actually exported more nitrogen than they received in wet deposition and had negative nitrate balances of 10–12 kg N/ha-yr. This was a striking finding: either the inputs from

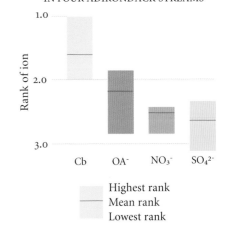

CONTRIBUTIONS OF DIFFERENT IONS TO SPRINGTIME ANC DEPRESSION IN FOUR ADIRONDACK STREAMS

Highest rank
Mean rank
Lowest rank

From data in Wigington et al., "Episodic acidification of small streams in the northeastern United States: Ionic controls of episodes," 1996. The authors ranked the ions by the amount they changed in each episode; no attempt was made to separate high-ANC and low-ANC streams.

From Simonin and Kretser, "Nitrate deposition and impact on Adirondack streams," 1997. The blue line is nitrogen deposition, the other lines, nitrogen export. All four watersheds store nitrogen in the summer, when vegetation is active, and export it during the winter. The switch from export to retention seems to occur in May; Bald Mountain Brook, for example, exported 73% of its total annual nitrate output between January 1 and May 1. The fall switch from retention to export is more variable; in a wet year nitrogen export may start soon after the vegetation becomes dormant in the fall; in a dry one nitrogen may be retained until early winter.

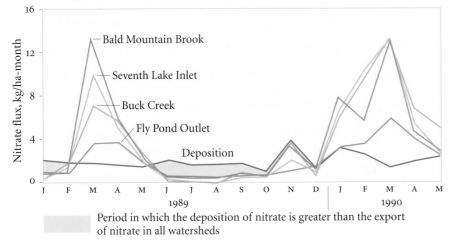

NITRATE DEPOSITION & EXPORT IN FOUR ADIRONDACK LTM WATERSHEDS

 Period in which the deposition of nitrate is greater than the export of nitrate in all watersheds

dry deposition were 1.3–1.5 times as high as wet deposition (which would be unprecedented), or some western Adirondack watersheds had reached nitrogen saturation and were releasing more nitrogen than they receive.

Which ions control acid episodes?

The pictures of the chemistry of acid episodes given by the water-shed and lake studies of Schaefer and his collaborators and the stream studies of the Episodic Response Project are generally similar but differ in some details. They agree that:

> The dilution of groundwater by meltwater, resulting in decreases in base cation concentrations, is the principal cause of ANC depressions in moderate-ANC and high-ANC waters.

> The introduction of pulses of acid from snowmelt and the forest floor is an important mechanism of episodic acidification in low-ANC streams and in the most severe acid episodes.

> The pulses of acids involve nitrate, sulfate, and organic acids. Sulfate is important in establishing the baseline acidity but, at least in the Adirondacks, varies relatively less than nitrate and is less correlated with the acidity changes during the pulse.

The differences between the two groups of researchers are mostly matters of emphasis and technical detail. The Episodic Response Project researchers ranked the absolute changes in ions (graph on p. 111) and included an estimate of organic acids in their calculations; their conclusion was that base cation dilution and organic acid production are the most important ion changes in acid episodes. Other researchers, particularly Sullivan and his colleagues, have looked at proportional rather than absolute changes. In their work the importance of changes in nitrate, especially in low-ANC waters, becomes evident. Their graph at the right, for example, shows that the lower the baseline ANC at the start of an acid episode, the more important nitrate is relative to sulfate.*

THE NITROGEN SATURATION OF WATERSHEDS

By the late 1980s, the nitrogen cycle and acid episode studies described above had made it clear that nitrogen-related acidification mattered. Nitrogen compounds were being deposited in significant quantities, especially in the winter when biological uptake was very low. They were also being produced, again significantly, by the mineralization of organic matter. They were accumulating in snowpack and in the forest floor and contributing to snowmelt episodes in lakes and streams. The resulting nitrogen loss was larger than had previously been thought: far from retaining most of the nitrogen deposited on them, many ecosystems were exporting 25% to 50% of the nitrogen that arrived in precipitation.

These concerns were given a conceptual focus in 1989, when John Aber and his colleagues introduced the concept of nitrogen saturation. They hypothesized that forests have a maximum

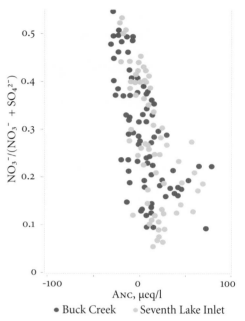

$NO_3^-/(NO_3^- + SO_4^{2-})$

ANC, µeq/l

● Buck Creek   ● Seventh Lake Inlet

A reanalysis of the ERP data showed that the relative importance of nitrate, measured by the ratio of nitrate to nitrate plus sulfate, increases as the episode becomes more acid. Redrawn with permission from Sullivan et al., "Increasing role of nitrogen in the acidification of surface waters in the Adirondack Mountains, New York." Copyright 1997 Springer Science and Business Media.

* An interesting regional finding of the Episodic Response Project was that the ion changes involved in acid episodes differ regionally. In Pennsylvania, where sulfate deposition is high and the snowpack almost nonexistent, large sulfate pulses controlled the most severe acid episodes and nitrate pulses were unimportant. In the Catskills and Adirondacks, where snowpack is significant and the forests older and perhaps closer to nitrogen saturation, nitrate pulses were very important and sulfate pulses nonexistent. Organic acid pulses were important in all three areas but relatively more important in the coniferous and mixed forests of the Adirondacks than in the largely deciduous forests of the Catskills and Pennsylvania.

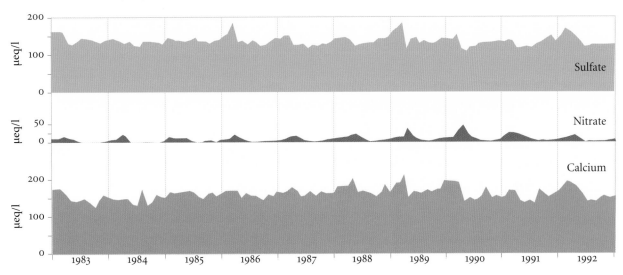

capacity to store nitrogen that is determined by their composition, age, and physical structure. When the nitrogen inputs exceed this capacity, the excess nitrogen first accumulates in biomass and soils and then is released to groundwater. As this happens, the forests pass through four stages of increasing nitrogen saturation (pp. 114-115). The stages are marked by increasing releases of nitrogen and an increasing annual period of nitrogen release: nitrogen is first released only in the winter, then in both winter and spring, and finally year-round. The last stage in the progression, where forests are actually releasing more nitrogen than they are receiving, is associated with an overall decline in biomass and productivity. This may be the result of the natural aging and senescence of the stand, or of changes in soil chemistry and microbiology, or of the toxic effects of large amounts of acid deposition.

Diagnosing the Stages of Nitrogen Saturation

In 1994, John Stoddard suggested that the four stages of nitrogen saturation recognized by Aber and his colleagues were associated with characteristic patterns of stream nitrate concentrations (diagrams on pp. 114-115). The key idea was that even without detailed information on nitrogen retention, the stage of saturation can be recognized by the annual pattern of nitrogen concentrations in surface water. In undisturbed watersheds (Stage 0), nitrogen is only released in runoff peaks. The peak concentrations are low, and the baseline concentrations during the rest of the year are near zero.

As nitrogen inputs increase, two things happen: the peaks become higher and the period of elevated baseline concentrations becomes longer. In Stage 1, baseline concentrations are above zero,

Redrawn with permission from Mitchell et al., "Biogeochemistry of a forested watershed in the central Adirondack Mountains: Temporal changes and mass balances." Copyright 1996 Springer Science and Business Media. The Arbutus watershed has calcium-rich bedrock and the runoff is high in ANC and bases. Each spring the lake receives a pulse of nitrate, bases, and sometimes sulfate. The changes in sulfate and base cations are sharp and of significant size but, because the baseline concentrations are high, represent relative changes of less than 50%. The changes in nitrate are somewhat smaller but, because the baseline is much lower, represent changes of several hundred percent. The nitrate peaks of the early 1980s, which are separated by periods when nitrate concentrations fall to near 0, would represent Stoddard's Stage 0. The less separate nitrate peaks of the late 1980s, if they were not caused by cold winters or watershed disturbance, would represent his Stage 1.

STAGE 0: NITROGEN LIMITING FOR MOST OF YEAR

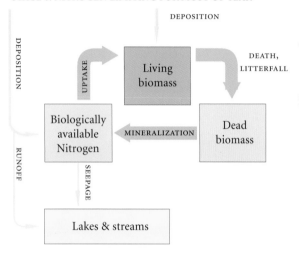

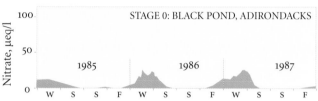

In Stage 0 nitrogen inputs are low and inorganic nitrogen is in biological demand for most of the year. The biological nitrogen cycle is almost closed. Most of the inputs are used in growth, and the outputs are a small fraction of inputs. Nitrate appears in stream water only in winter and early spring, and even then the concentrations are lower than those in precipitation and the net nitrogen storage (nitrogen in – nitrogen out) is positive year-round.

STAGE 1: EXCESS NITROGEN IN WINTER AND SPRING

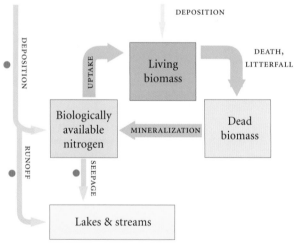

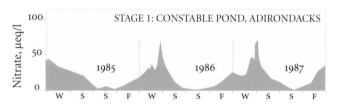

Diagrams adapted with permission from Stoddard, "Long-term changes in watershed retention of nitrogen: Its causes and aquatic consequences." Copyright 1994 American Chemical Society. The red circles (●) denote a pathway that increases in this stage.

In Stage 1 nitrogen inputs are greater and there are excesses of inorganic nitrogen in winter and in spring. The biological nitrogen cycle now starts to leak. Only a part of the inputs can be used in growth, and outputs are a significant fraction of inputs. Spring nitrate peaks reach concentrations several times those in precipitation and last for much of the spring; only in summer does the demand of the vegetation for nitrogen exceed the supply, and growth becomes nitrogen-limited. The net nitrogen storage, though positive overall, is negative in the winter and spring, indicating seasonal nitrogen loss.

STAGE 2: EXCESS NITROGEN IN ALL SEASONS

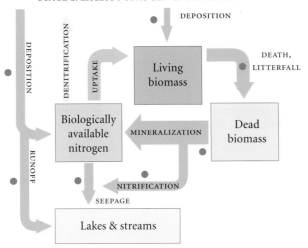

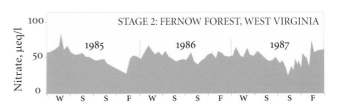

In Stage 2 inputs are still greater, and there is an excess of biologically available nitrogen for much of the year. Nitrification now occurs year-round, and excess nitrates leave the root zone and enter groundwater. As a result, stream nitrate concentrations are elevated year-round. Spring nitrate peaks, though equally high, are less sharply defined. The watershed loses nitrogen for much of the year and its net storage balance, though still positive, is near zero.

STAGE 3: GROWTH DECREASES, OUTPUTS EXCEED INPUTS

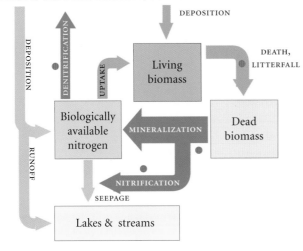

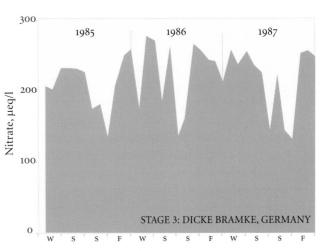

In Stage 3 the nitrogen balance is negative and the forest is losing more nitrogen each year than it receives. Essentially it is reversing the nitrogen accumulation process and exporting the nitrogen it has previously accumulated. Uptake has decreased, and nitrification and denitrification are now the dominant processes. Nitrate concentrations in stream water are now high for the whole year and have lost a clearly defined seasonal cycle.

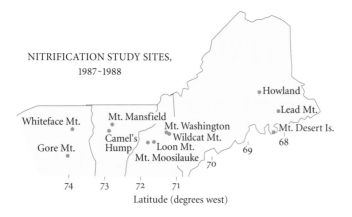

NITRIFICATION STUDY SITES,
1987–1988

Whiteface Mt.

Mt. Mansfield

Howland

Lead Mt.

Gore Mt.

Camel's
Hump

Mt. Washington
Wildcat Mt.
Loon Mt.
Mt. Moosilauke

Mt. Desert Is.

74   73   72   71   70   69   68

Latitude (degrees west)

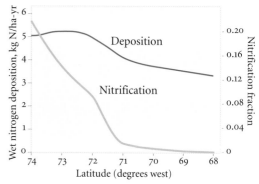

DEPOSITION & NITRIFICATION

Deposition

Nitrification

Latitude (degrees west)

even in summer. In Stage 2, summer baseline concentrations are half as high as peak concentrations. In Stage 3, baseline concentrations are almost as high as peak concentrations, and a seasonal pattern can no longer be recognized.

Aber, Stoddard, and their colleagues felt that the saturation stages were progressive and that once nitrogen inputs exceeded a forest's capacity to use them, the forest would gradually move to higher stages of saturation. In their view Stage 2 was a critical stage in which the excess nitrogen and its associated acidification began to damage the forest and reduce its capacity for growth. This, in turn, would reduce nitrogen demand and accelerate the progression to Stage 3.

What is the evidence for nitrogen saturation?

The evidence for the existence of the different saturation stages is compelling. Recent work has confirmed that forests do, as Aber and Stoddard suggested, have very different patterns of nitrogen export. Patterns vary with nitrogen loading and, as the nitrogen saturation hypothesis suggests, are characterized by increasing rates of nitrogen mineralization and export.

The graphs show several examples. In 1987 McNulty et al. collected soil samples from 11 high-elevation spruce-fir forests with differing inputs of atmospheric nitrogen. They incubated the samples in the laboratory and determined the increases in ammonium and nitrate as the organic matter in the samples decayed. The nitrification fraction, the fraction of the mineralized nitrogen oxidized to nitrate and hence available to be exported in groundwater, increases from east to west with increasing deposition.

Similarly, studies in 1994 and 1995 by Stoddard and his collaborators found clear associations between nitrogen loading and both the concentrations of nitrate in streamflow and the total nitrogen exports. In both North America and Europe there appears to be a threshold near 5–10 kg N/ha-yr of wet deposition above which nitrogen exports increase rapidly. Once forests exceed these

Map and graph from McNulty et al., "Nitrogen cycling in high-elevation forests of the northeastern US in relation to nitrogen deposition," 1990. Both curves are smoothed. The nitrification fraction is the proportion of the nitrogen released by decay that is converted into nitrate; it is calculated as $NO_3^-/(NH_4^+ + NO_3^-)$, where the quantities are the net increases in ammonium and nitrate when the soil is incubated. At wet deposition loads of 4–5 kg /ha-yr, nitrification increases abruptly, suggesting that the forest is retaining less nitrogen.

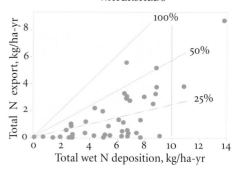

EXPORT OF NITROGEN FROM U.S.
WATERSHEDS

100%

50%

25%

Total wet N deposition, kg/ha-yr

From Stoddard, "Long-term changes in watershed retention of nitrogen: Its causes and aquatic consequences." Copyright 1994 American Chemical Society. The lines indicate exports of 25%, 50%, and 100% of inputs from wet deposition. Dry deposition rates are unknown for most of these sites. As wet deposition increases from about 3 to 10 kg N/ha-yr, the percentage of sites exporting nitrogen and the average percentage of the nitrate that is exported both increase.

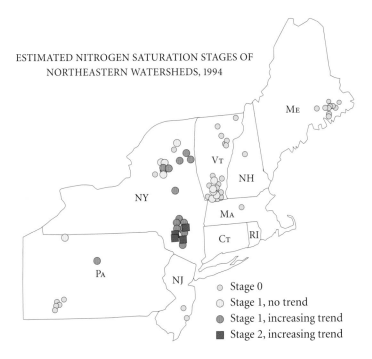

Stage 0
Stage 1, no trend
Stage 1, increasing trend
Stage 2, increasing trend

ESTIMATED NUMBER OF WATERS AT
DIFFERENT SATURATION STAGES, 1994

Saturation stage

	0	1	2
Maine	9		
New Hampshire	1	1	
Vermont	18	6	
Massachusetts	1		
Adirondacks		16	
Catskills		19	7
Pennsylvania	4	2	
New Jersey	1		

Map and table from Stoddard, "Long-term changes in watershed retention of nitrogen: Its causes and aquatic consequences." Copyright 1994 American Chemical Society. The map shows the general distribution of saturation stages but, because many study areas are close together, not every individual site.

EXPORT OF NITROGEN FROM EUROPEAN
WATERSHEDS

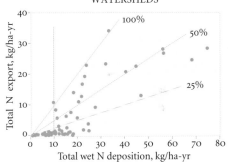

From Dise and Wright, "Nitrogen leaching from European forests in relation to nitrogen deposition." Copyright 1995 Elsevier. Note the difference in vertical scale between this and the graph of American watersheds on the opposite page. The lines indicate exports of 25%, 50%, and 100% of inputs from wet deposition. European watersheds, many of which receive much more nitrogen than American watersheds, show an abrupt increase in exports at a wet deposition input of about 10 kg N/ha-yr.

thresholds, the percentage of nitrogen exported increases and the percentage retained decreases.

The Extent of Nitrogen Saturation

In 1994 Stoddard estimated the level of nitrogen saturation in about 85 watersheds in the Northeast; in 2001 he and two collaborators did the same thing for 144 watersheds in Europe. The estimates were mostly based on monthly or seasonal nitrogen levels and, in some cases, on multiyear trends. Mass balances and the percentages of nitrogen retained were only available for a few of the watersheds.

Of the 85 northeastern watersheds Stoddard examined in 1994, 34 (40%) were estimated to be in saturation Stage 0, 44 (52%) in Stage 1, and 7 (8%), all in the Catskills, in Stage 2. In about half the Adirondack watersheds and most of the Catskill ones, stream nitrate concentrations were apparently increasing, but Stoddard warned that in some cases the period of record was limited and the trends uncertain. This proved to be the case with the Adirondack sites, all of which lost their increasing trends in the 1990s (p. 207).

Nitrogen deposition is substantially higher in Europe than in North America, and nitrogen saturation apparently more advanced. In Stoddard's 1994 review of North American watersheds (opposite page), only two watersheds received more than 10 kg N/ha-yr from wet deposition. In Dise and Wright's 1995 review of European watersheds, three-quarters received more than 10 kg N/ha-yr in wet deposition and several had more than 50 kg/ha-yr. In Stoddard's 2001 review, more than half of the International Cooperative Program's European study sites were at Stage 2 or higher, and a few

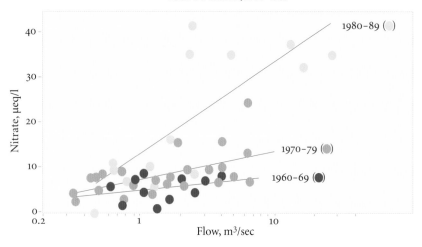

From Stoddard, "Long-term changes in watershed retention of nitrogen: Its causes and aquatic consequences." Copyright 1994 American Chemical Society. Long-term monitoring on several Catskill streams showed increasing nitrate levels, especially at high flows, from the 1960s through the 1980s. The increases could reflect either increasing rates of nitrate deposition or progressive decreases in the forest's ability to assimilate nitrogen.

Stage 3 sites were known. Stage 0 sites were limited to the low-deposition areas of northern Scandinavia, Britain, and Ireland.

Do forests progress through the nitrogen saturation stages?

The theory of nitrogen saturation proposed that the saturation stages were progressive. Above some critical level of nitrogen input, forest health was assumed to decline, resulting in progressive decreases in nitrogen uptake and progressive increases in nitrogen release. This is biologically logical: nitrogen is, after all, a powerful fertilizer, and we know from agronomy that plants will decline if they are overfertilized.

But just what the critical level is and how close particular forests are to it are unknown. On the one hand, the pool of nitrogen stored in dead biomass in the lower horizons of the soil can be very large (p. 105), suggesting a large storage capacity for surplus nitrogen. But on the other hand, declining forests don't assimilate much nitrogen, and so the rate at which the forest can add to this pool may well be limited, even if the pool itself is not.

Currently, the only way to tell whether a forest is progressing through the series of saturation stages is to look for an increasing trend in nitrogen export. This is possible only at the relatively few watersheds for which there are long-term monitoring data. And it is difficult even at these watersheds, both because nitrogen deposition rates have been changing, and because nitrogen cycling is influenced in complex ways by climate and forest disturbance as well as by deposition.

Thus far, we have much evidence that nitrogen saturation is occurring but no conclusive evidence that it is progressive. In the Catskills, with four decades of data, there were clear changes in stream nitrate levels between the 1960s and the 1980s. This, how-

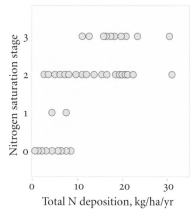

From Stoddard, Traaen, and Skjelkvåle, "Assessment of nitrogen leaching at ICP-waters sites (Europe and North America)," 2001. Above a threshold of 10 kg N/ha-yr total deposition, all European watersheds were classified as Stage 2 or Stage 3.

ever, was a period in which nitrogen deposition was also increasing, and so the stream increases are not conclusive. There were also some increases in nitrate levels in Adirondack streams during the 1980s, but as noted above, these seem to have leveled out or reversed slightly. In Europe, of 49 sites studied in 1990 and 1998, 36 were at the same nitrogen saturation stage, 5 had moved to a higher stage, and 8 had dropped to a lower stage.

Thus the case for progressive saturation, as it stands today, is undecided. While it seems clear that increases in deposition translate into increases in nitrogen export, at present we do not know whether constant levels of deposition will produce constant or increasing levels of export.

A Synoptic Study of Nitrogen Retention

Researchers have wanted for some time to be able to do synoptic studies of nitrogen retention in watersheds, much as they did synoptic studies of lake acidification in the 1980s. The question was what measure of nitrogen retention to use. The four nitrogen saturation stages described on pages 114-115 are qualitative and inexact. The percentage of nitrogen retained is more exact, but only available for watersheds with full monitoring programs.

What was needed was a set of diagnostic indicators, akin to the ion diagnostics used by the synoptic surveys (p. 74), that would allow researchers to assess the nitrogen status of watersheds that were not continuously monitored.

The first attempt to provide such indicators was made in 2003 by a group of researchers led by John Aber. Their goal, again like the synoptic surveys, was a regional assessment: they wished, simply, to determine whether "nitrogen deposition is altering the nitrogen status of eastern forests."

To do this, they reanalyzed the results of some 40 studies involving 354 waterbodies, 83 monitored watersheds, and 251 forest plots. They examined three indicators of nitrogen status: foliar chemistry, soil chemistry, and surface water chemistry. The premise was that sites with more nitrogen deposition would be storing more nitrogen in foliage, mineralizing more nitrate in their soils, and exporting more nitrate to surface waters. They expected that because many factors besides deposition influence nitrogen status, any relationships they found would be statistically noisy. But they also hoped that a metanalysis of data from many watersheds and sample plots could overcome the noise and show general patterns in nitrogen chemistry.

In the foliar chemistry data, the first of three indicators they analyzed, the noise overcame them. The nitrogen levels in needles and leaves varied greatly and somewhat confusingly with elevation, temperature, longitude, and precipitation. Nitrogen deposition,

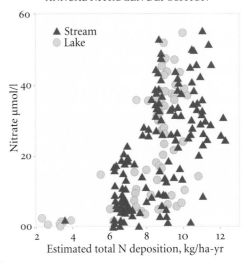

SUMMER NITRATE CONCENTRATIONS AND ANNUAL NITROGEN DEPOSITION

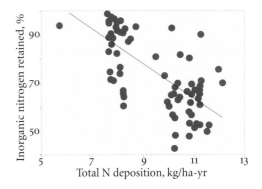

NITROGEN RETENTION IN NORTHEASTERN U.S. WATERSHEDS

Both graphs from Aber et al., "Is nitrogen deposition altering the nitrogen status of northeastern forests?" Copyright 2003 American Institute of Biological Sciences via the Copyright Clearance Center. The paper is a metanalysis of data sets collected in the 1990s. The summer nitrate concentrations are from 212 waterbodies in Maine, New Hampshire, Vermont, New York, and West Virginia. Above a threshold of 8 kg N/ha-yr, summer nitrate levels rise rapidly.

The nitrogen retention data come from 83 watersheds across the Northeast. The total deposition was estimated from a regional computer model. When the estimated deposition exceeds about 8 kg/ha-yr, the amount of inorganic nitrogen retained in the watershed drops rapidly.

unfortunately, depends on the same variables, and there was no convincing way to separate the effects of deposition from the effects of climate and geography.

In the surface water chemistry, on the other hand, there were clear relationships between nitrogen deposition and nitrogen export. In some 350 lakes and streams, summer nitrate concentrations increased rapidly with increasing deposition above a threshold of about 6 kg N/ha-yr total deposition. Likewise, in the 83 waters for which the annual nitrogen balance had been measured, above a threshold of about 8 kg N/ha-yr the average nitrogen retention fell rapidly from around 90% to less than 60%.

These are significant results. Summer nitrate concentrations and nitrogen retention are two of the defining indicators for nitrogen saturation (pp. 114-115). The presence of elevated summer nitrogen concentrations and reduced nitrogen retention in a majority of the watersheds with deposition above the threshold level suggests that the early stages of nitrogen saturation are now widespread in the Northeast.

The soil chemistry results were more variable, probably because the number of samples was limited, but nonetheless paralleled the surface water chemistry. Soil carbon-nitrogen ratios, an indicator of the amount of nitrogen stored per unit of organic matter, fell as nitrogen deposition increased. Further, the relative nitrification rose as the C/N ratio fell, indicating that the more nitrogen a forest had stored, the more it was likely to convert organic nitrogen to nitrate and export it in groundwater.

The authors concluded that although the soil data were interesting, it was the surface water data that sent the clearest and most general message: "Using surface waters as a indicator of the degree of N saturation, it seems clear that N deposition is altering the N status of, and NO_3^- leaching from, forests in the northeastern United States."

Summer Nitrate Levels in the Adirondacks

Summer nitrate levels in Adirondack lakes are often quite low – typically 0–30 µeq/l – because forests are retaining nitrate and because much of the nitrate that does reach lakes is used by algae and aquatic plants. In most cases nitrate concentrations are less than 1% of sulfate concentrations; in consequence nitrates, however important in acid episodes, were thought to contribute little to the chronic acidification of Adirondack lakes.

In 1997 Sullivan and his collaborators wrote a paper challenging this. They pointed out that though sulfate concentrations were much higher than nitrate concentrations they did not vary much from lake to lake. Nitrates not only varied but varied in the same

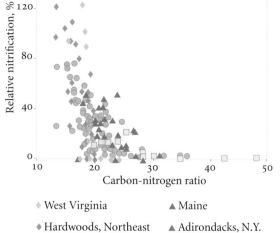

◆ West Virginia ▲ Maine
◆ Hardwoods, Northeast ▲ Adirondacks, N.Y.
● White Mountains, N.H. ☐ Spruce-fir, Northeast
● Catskills, N.Y.

From Aber et al., "Is nitrogen deposition altering the nitrogen status of Northeastern forests?" Copyright 2003 American Institute of Biological Sciences via the Copyright Clearance Center. The soil data are taken from 251 forest plots in Maine, New Hampshire, Vermont, Massachusetts, New York, and West Virginia. The relative nitrification is the ratio $NO_3^-/(NH_4^+ + NO_3^-)$, where the quantities are the net increases in ammonium and nitrate when the soil is incubated in the laboratory. A high relative nitrification indicates that most of the nitrogen released from decaying is appearing as nitrate, which is highly mobile and easily exported in groundwater.

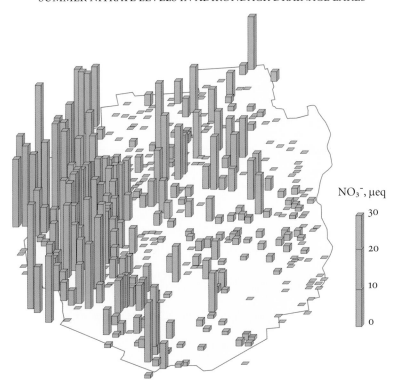

NO₃⁻, μeq

30

20

10

0

Redrawn with permission from Sullivan et al., "Increasing role of nitrogen in the acidification of surface waters in the Adirondack Mountains, New York." Copyright 1997 Springer Science and Business Media. The data are from the 1984-87 Adirondack Lakes Survey. The summer nitrate concentrations in circumneutral lakes are very low. In the most acidic lakes they are considerably higher, typically in the 10-30 μeq/l range and often 30-50% of the levels during spring acidity peaks. The distribution of high summer nitrate concentrations is similar to the distribution of low-pHs (p. 71) and historical acidification (p. 85). A related study of summer nitrate levels is Momen et al., "Determinants of summer nitrate concentration in a set of Adirondack lakes, New York," 1999.

way as lake acidity. Furthermore, the concentrations of nitrates, though low, were on the same order as the changes in hydrogen ion inferred from the PIRLA studies of historical acidification and might be sufficient to account for the levels of historical acidification. Their map, on page 121, has a striking resemblance to the pH and historical acidification maps on pages 71 and 85 and suggests that there is a good bit more about the importance of nitrogen that we need to know.

Perhaps the most interesting of the unknowns is the relative importance of deposition and nitrogen cycling in controlling summer nitrate concentrations. Sullivan and his associates suggested that in summer and early fall, when most of the nitrogen deposited on forests is retained within the watershed, the direct deposition of nitrogen to lakes might account for the observed differences in both nitrate concentrations and acidity. They estimated the amount of nitrate that could be supplied by direct deposition for 34 lakes and found that the amounts of sulfate and nitrate directly deposited to the lake surface were comparable. Thus, in many lakes, direct deposition to the lake surface could account for most or all of the summer nitrate in the lake.

If their interpretation is correct, in about half the lakes summer acidification may be controlled by direct deposition to the lake surface, and nitrate and sulfate have roughly equal roles. In the remainder of the lakes, acids from the watershed, predominantly associated with sulfates, contribute to or dominate summer acidification.

SUMMARY: NITROGEN AND SULFUR CYCLES

This chapter is the longest and one of the most important in this book. Accordingly, we provide a detailed summary.

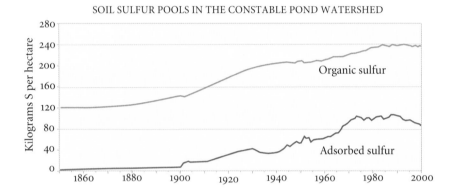

SOIL SULFUR POOLS IN THE CONSTABLE POND WATERSHED

A simulation of the organic and mineral sulfur pools in the Constable Pond watershed, redrawn with permission from Chen and Driscoll, "Modeling the response of soil and surface waters in the Adirondack and Catskill regions of New York to changes in atmospheric deposition and historical land use disturbance." Copyright 2004 Elsevier. The simulation is generated by a watershed model (PNET-BGC) that uses deposition history, climate, weathering rates, and disturbance history to simulate the biogeochemical processes in a watershed. The graph shows the storage of sulfur from acid deposition in watershed soils and biomass. Currently, the watershed is estimated to contain about three times as much sulfur as it did in 1850. The watershed has released some stored sulfur since sulfur deposition peaked in 1973, but the amount released so far has been only a small fraction of the amount stored.

1 *Sulfur and nitrogen* are essential nutrients that participate extensively in biogeochemical cycles. They are assimilated by plants and microbes, stored in biomass, oxidized and reduced biologically, and released by decay.

Their oxidized forms, sulfate and nitrate, are the most important anions in acid deposition and the main inorganic anions in acidified soils and waters. In the early 1980s the Adirondacks were receiving roughly twice as many equivalents of sulfur as of nitrogen in wet deposition. Over the past 20 years nitrogen deposition has been nearly constant and sulfur deposition has decreased, and now the quantities of each in precipitation are close to equal.

2 *Sulfur* is a relatively minor nutrient, which in the Adirondacks is stored mostly in organic matter in the soil. It cycles rapidly through biomass, with a turnover time of about five to six years and even faster through the forest floor, with a turnover time of about two years.

In undisturbed Adirondack forests, the cycling was probably very tight, with very little sulfur being added by deposition or weathering and equally little exported in groundwater.

Because preindustrial inputs of sulfur were very low, acid deposition has greatly increased the rates at which sulfur arrives in and moves through northern forests. In the Adirondacks the annual sulfur inputs from acid deposition are comparable to the total biological demand. Thus between deposition and decay, many forests have at least twice as much sulfur available as they can assimilate. Some of the excess sulfur has stored in the watersheds, mostly in organic form. The rest has been exported to surface waters.

3 As the *deposition* of sulfur declines, many northeastern water-sheds are releasing more sulfur than they receive. The Arbutus Lake watershed, for example, is releasing more than twice as much sulfur as it receives in deposition. The extra is suspected to be sulfur that was stored in biomass and soils when sulfur deposition was higher.

The release of stored sulfur will slow the recovery of streams and lakes as acid deposition declines. The first estimates of recovery, made by the DDRP IN 1989 using the MAGIC model, were that about a third of the waters whose ANCs are now less than 50 µeq/l would have ANCs over 50 µeq/l in 50 years. More recent models, with less optimistic assumptions about continuing base cation supplies and nitrogen retention, predict less recovery.

4 *Nitrogen* resembles sulfur in that it is an essential nutrient that cycles rapidly through biomass and is stored largely in soil organic matter. It differs from sulfur in that it is ten times or more as con-centrated in biomass, and so the annual biological demand is higher. It also differs in that it is deposited in two chemical forms, ammonium and nitrate. Nitrate is more abundant, but ammonium is assimilated preferentially by plants.

5 Currently the *total nitrogen deposition* at the Huntington Forest is about 8 kg/ha-yr. This is, very roughly, a fifth of the annual nitrogen demand of a conifer forest and a tenth the nitrogen demand of a hardwood forest.

Because nitrogen inputs are much less than the annual biological nitrogen demand, forests assimilate much of the ammonium and at least some of the nitrate that is deposited on them during the grow-ing season. The assimilation of ammonium releases hydrogen ions; the assimilation of nitrate consumes hydrogen ions.

6 The *decay of organic matter*, which occurs year-round, releases ammonium and consumes hydrogen ions. If the ammonium exceeds what the forest can use, some of it can be oxidized to nitrate (nitrified), producing hydrogen ions.

7 The hydrogen ions produced when ammonium is assimilated or converted to nitrate are called *nitrogen-cycle acidity*. Nitrogen-cycle acidity can be produced at any time of year but is most important in the winter, when decay and nitrification exceed assimilation.

Whether the nitrogen cycle as a whole produces or consumes acids depends on the balance of inputs and outputs. If a forest

SULFUR EXPORTS FROM ADIRONDACK WATERSHEDS

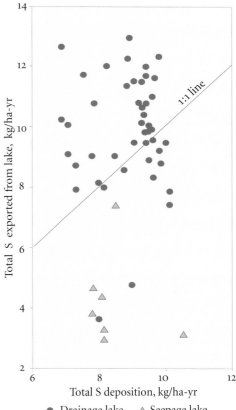

From Driscoll et al., "The response of lake water in the Adirondack region of New York to changes in acidic deposition." Copyright 1998 Elsevier. Most Adirondack LTM lakes have been exporting more sulfur than they receive, suggesting that either dry deposition has been greatly underestimated or that they are releasing sulfur stored in soil organic matter. The seepage lakes are a clear exception: they are less influenced by watershed processes and, because they often have long hydraulic residence times and extensive shoreline wetlands, have more ability to store sulfur than the drain-age lakes.

is consuming nitrates, the nitrogen cycle will help deacidify the groundwater. If it is consuming ammonium, the cycle will acidify the groundwater. And if, as in some forests with high nitrogen loading, it is consuming ammonium and producing nitrates, the cycle will be even more acidifying.

8 The *nitrogen cycle* has been studied in four forest plots and four experimental watersheds in the Adirondacks. The results are not strictly comparable because of differences in methods and uncertainties in the amount of dry deposition. Studies at Arbutus and Whiteface in which both wet and dry deposition were measured showed about 70% retention of total deposited nitrogen; four studies of the forest floor at a variety of sites found that 34% to 68% of the nitrogen in throughfall was retained; and four studies of ERP watersheds found that one was retaining 39% of the nitrogen in wet deposition and the others were generating 10-12 kg/ha-yr more nitrogen than they received.

9 In the early discussions of acid rain it was assumed that *sulfate*, because it was more abundant than nitrate and less assimilated by forests, was the most important atmospheric acid. But by the middle 1980s a series of new findings had changed this view. Sulfate was still thought important, particularly in chronic acidification, but nitrate was thought equally or more important in episodic acidification.

10 The resulting picture of *nitrate-related acidification* drew heavily on studies of snowmelt chemistry and acid episodes. The principal findings were that:

> Most Adirondack drainage lakes and streams receive a large pulse of water, often equal to 50% of their total annual water budget, in February, March, and April. This water is often chemically different – lower in pH and ANC and often higher in aluminum – than the water they receive at other times of the year.
>
> The water in the springtime pulse comes from two sources: new water from melting snow and old groundwater mobilized by the weight of the meltwater above it.
>
> Both the meltwater and the groundwater contain acids. The meltwater contains acids deposited during the winter, often concentrated by differential melting. The groundwater contains sulfate, nitrogen-cycle acids, and organic acids from the forest floor and often significant amounts of inorganic aluminium as well.

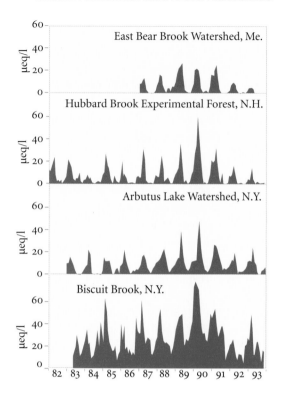

Reprinted with permission from Mitchell et al., "Climatic control of nitrate loss from forested watersheds in the northeast United States." Copyright 1996 American Chemical Society. All the watersheds release nitrogen during the dormant season. At Bear Brook and Hubbard Brook the peaks are narrow and well separated, indicating that these watershed are in saturation Stage 0. At Arbutus Lake the peaks are broader and the summer baseline levels slightly elevated, indicating that the watershed is in or approaching Stage 1. At Biscuit Brook, in the Catskills, the summer baseline levels are strongly elevated, indicating that the watershed is in Stage 2.

The year-to-year variations in the heights of the peaks of the four watersheds are generally similar. In particular, all show an increase in the late 1980s and three of the four show a peak in 1990, which the authors suggest was caused by the freezing of forest soils in the dry and extremely cold December of 1989.

The chemistry of the springtime pulse depends on the mix of old and new water and the baseline chemistry of the stream or lake involved.

Low-ANC waters show sharp springtime peaks in nitrates and aluminum but smaller changes in pH, ANC, and base cations. The increases in aluminum moderate the pH and ANC changes but greatly increase the lethality of the episodes.

Higher-ANC waters tend to show larger snowmelt changes in ANC and base cations but smaller changes in pH and aluminum.

In high-ANC waters with substantial amounts of base cations, the decreases in ANC result largely from the dilution of base-rich groundwater by snowmelt. In low-ANC waters there are few base cations to dilute, and the decreases in ANC result from acids stored in the snowpack or produced by nitrogen cycling in the forest floor.

Sulfates change relatively little in acid episodes. They probably have little influence on ANC depression during the episode but do determine the ANC baseline from which the episode starts and so influence its biological severity.

11 Although forested watersheds are good at retaining small amounts of added nitrogen, there is considerable evidence from both the United States and Europe that above a threshold of 8–10 kg /ha-yr of nitrogen deposition, they retain progressively less of the added nitrogen and export progressively more.
   This has been interpreted as evidence for the theory of *nitrogen saturation*, which states that forests have a finite capacity for storing nitrogen and that when this capacity is exceeded, nitrification rates increase, spring nitrate peaks in surface waters become higher and last longer, and summer and fall nitrate levels become elevated.

12 Aber and his associates have defined four *stages of nitrogen saturation*, which can be recognized qualitatively by baseline levels of nitrates during the summer and by the height and duration of the spring nitrate peaks. The degree of nitrogen saturation can also be quantified by measuring carbon-nitrogen ratios, nitrification rates, and nitrogen retention rates.

13 Records of *nitrate levels* in the runoff for several hundred watersheds in North America and Europe confirm the basic premises of the nitrogen saturation hypothesis: nitrogen export is linked to nitrogen loading, and as the loading increases, the percentage of the atmospheric nitrogen that the watershed retains decreases. There are also clear correlations between nitrogen loading and soil

nitrogen chemistry, also as predicted by the nitrogen saturation hypothesis.

14 *Monitoring data* suggest that most watersheds in the eastern United States and Canada are in Stage 0 or Stage 1 of nitrogen saturation. In some areas in the Catskills and southern Appalachians many watersheds are in Stage 2. In central Europe, where nitrogen loads are several times those in the United States, many watersheds are in Stage 2, and a significant number are in Stage 3.

15 In the first nitrogen saturation analyses of the 1990s, increasing nitrate concentrations in many watersheds suggested that nitrogen saturation might *increase with time,* even at constant levels of nitrogen deposition. By 2000, when many of these trends had vanished (and a few had reversed) and only a few watersheds had been observed to progress from one stage to another, the hypothesis of increasing saturation was in doubt, and it seemed as likely that nitrate exports might remain constant if nitrogen deposition remained constant.

16 Although the *summer concentrations of nitrate* in Adirondack lakes are low, they correlate in an interesting way with acidity and estimates of historical acidification. An analysis by Sullivan et al. suggested that lake chemistry in the summer may be controlled more by direct deposition to the lake surface than by inputs from the watershed and that nitrates are just as important as sulfates in summer deposition.

17 Summarizing, *sulfate deposition* currently exceeds biological demand and so sulfate fluxes are not much affected by differences in biological uptake. Many watersheds are currently producing more sulfate than they receive in wet deposition, perhaps because they are releasing sulfate that they stored when deposition rates were higher, or perhaps because dry deposition and weathering are higher than current estimates.

Nitrate deposition is currently less than biological demand, and nitrate fluxes are strongly affected by biological uptake and by the reactions of the nitrogen cycle. At low levels of deposition, forests retain most of the added nitrogen. At higher levels, outputs of nitrates and nitrogen-cycle acids increase. These releases of nitrates and acids, which were neglected in much of the original research on chronic acidification, now appear to be the main control of the biologically damaging spring acidity peaks in low-ANC streams and may play a role in chronic lake acidification as well.

NOTES

General references for this chapter are Aber et al. "Nitrogen saturation in northern forest ecosystems–hypotheses and implications," 1989; Driscoll and Schaefer, "The nitrogen cycle and its role in soil and drainage water acidification," 1991; Driscoll et al., "Nitrogen pollution in the northeastern United States: Sources, effects, and management options," 2003; Aber et al., "The nitrogen cascade," 2003.

p. 99 The papers on the importance of nitrogen are Bormann and Likens, *Pattern and Process in a Forested Ecosystem*, 1978; Johannes, Galloway, and Troutman, "Storage and release of ions from snowpack," 1980; Driscoll and Schafran, "Short-term changes in the base-neutralizing capacity of an Adirondack lake, New York," 1984; Rascher, Driscoll, and Peters, "Concentration and flux of solutes from forest during snowmelt in the west-central Adirondack region of New York," 1987; and Driscoll, Yatsko, and Unangst, "Longitudinal and temporal trends in the water chemistry of the North Branch of the Moose River," 1987.

p. 102 The Ecosystem Research Program on Whiteface Mountain produced more than 20 research papers. Representative examples are Scott et al., "Decline of red spruce in the Adirondacks, New York," 1984; Friedland et al., "Nitrogen deposition, distribution, and cycling in a subalpine spruce-fir forest in the Adirondacks, New York, USA," 1991; Battles et al., "Red spruce death: Effects on forest composition and structure on Whiteface Mountain, New York," 1992; Miller, Blum, and Friedland, "Determination of weathering rates and soil exchangeable cation loss using Sr isotopes," 1993; and Johnson et al., "Acid rain and the soils of the Adirondacks, II: Evaluation of calcium and aluminum as causes of red spruce decline on Whiteface Mt., New York," 1994.

p. 103 Several other papers on nitrogen cycling in the Arbutus watershed have appeared too recently to cover fully here. These include McHale et al., "Nitrogen solutes in an Adirondack forested watershed: Importance of dissolved organic nitrogen," 2000; Hurd, Raynal, and Schwintzer, "Symbiotic N_2 fixation of *Alnus incana* ssp. *rugosa* in shrub wetlands of the Adirondack Mountains, New York, USA," 2001; Park et al., "Impacts of changing climate and atmospheric deposition on N and S losses from a forested watershed of the Adirondack Mountains, New York State," 2003; and Bischoff et al., "N storage and cycling in vegetation of a forested wetland: Implications for watershed N processing," 2001.

p. 109 The results of the Episodic Response Project are given in Simonin et al., "In situ bioassays of brook trout (*Salvelinus fontinalis*) and blacknose dace (*Rhinichthys atratulus*) in Adirondack streams affected by episodic acidification," 1993; Wigington et al., "Episodic acidification of small streams in the northeastern United States: Episodic Response Project," 1996; Wigington et al., "Episodic acidification of small streams in the northeastern United States: Ionic controls of episodes," 1996; Van Sickle et al., "Episodic acidification of small streams in the northeastern United States: Fish mortality in field bioassays," 1996; and Baker et al., "Episodic acidification of small streams in the northeastern United States: Effects on fish populations," 1996.

1985 The Lake Acidification Mitigation Project experimentally limes Woods Lake and Cranberry Pond.

1989 Federer et al. show that six eastern forests are all losing calcium at a significant rate.

1989 The Experimental Watershed Liming Study applies 1,000 tons of lime to the watershed of Woods Lake.

1990 The DEC issues an environmental impact statement and suggested policy on liming Adirondack lakes.

1990 Bondietti et al. discover a widespread "calcium mobilization signal" in the rings of red spruce laid down between 1945 and 1970.

1992 Shortle and Bondietti find that contemporary measurements of base cations in conifer stands are half or less of historical ones.

1993 Yanai and Siccama report soil calcium declines of 20% to 30% in Watershed 6 of Hubbard Brook between 1970 and 1987.

1994 Hedin et al. confirm decreases of 25% in the amounts of base cations in precipitation at many stations in Europe and the eastern United States.

1994 Johnson, Andersen, and Siccama resample forest soils on plots sampled by Heimberger in the 1930s and find decreases in extractable calcium in the forest floor.

1994 Johnson et al. find that spruce-fir forests on Whiteface Mountain are losing forest floor base cations at a rate of 2.8% per year, several times higher than the average rate for the previous 50 years.

1995 Lawrence, David, and Shortle report that in acidified soils aluminum can migrate from the mineral soil to the forest floor and there accelerate base cation loss.

1995 Kirchner and Lydersen report that because of decreases in base cations, the acid-neutralizing capacities of Norwegian streams have not increased as sulfate deposition decreases.

1995 Wesselink et al. find that pools of exchangeable calcium in spruce forests in Solling, Germany, decreased strongly from 1968 to 1990.

1995 The concluding report of the International Conference on Acid Rain states that we know "with confidence" that sulfur deposition has caused the depletion of base cations on soil exchange sites.

1996 Bailey et al. use strontium isotopes to trace the movement of calcium in the Cone Pond watershed in New Hampshire. Each year the watershed loses twice as much calcium as it gains, which represents a loss of about 1% of the calcium stored in the soil.

1996 Likens, Driscoll, and Buso show that as sulfate inputs to Hubbard Brook have fallen, base cation concentrations in stream water have fallen faster than sulfate concentrations, preventing any recovery of ANC.

1997 Lawrence et al. examine spruce forest soils across the northeastern United States and show that as sulfate deposition increases, soil sulfate concentrations increase and base saturation decreases.

1998 Likens et al. estimate that the forest floor at Hubbard Brook lost 47% of its exchangeable calcium between 1970 and 1990 because of a mixture of forest growth, decreased calcium deposition, and leaching by acid rain.

1998 Sullivan et al. find weak correlations between Adirondack blowdowns and historical lake acidification and between Adirondack fires and lake deacidification. Logging shows no correlation.

1999 Lawrence et al. show that in the Catskills sulfate deposition, soil cation losses, and stream acidity are strongly correlated.

2000 Lawrence shows that the ANCs of streams decrease as the pool of exchangeable calcium in their watershed is depleted.

2003 Gbondo-Tugbawa and Driscoll use a simulation model to estimate that between 1875 and 1995 the forests at Hubbard Brook lost 60% of their exchangeable calcium.

2004 Chen and Driscoll use the same model to estimate that between 1900 and 2000 the Constable Pond watershed in the western Adirondacks lost 78% of its exchangeable calcium and had its base saturation decrease from 22% to 6%.

THE CYCLING AND LOSS OF CALCIUM

HOW ACID DEPOSITION DRIVES THE LOSS OF BASES

6

The three previous chapters, like much of the acid rain research of the 1970s and 1980s, focused on sulfur and nitrogen. Chapters 3 and 4 showed how sulfur, nitrogen, and hydrogen ion arrive in precipitation, are partially neutralized in watersheds, and then migrate to lakes and acidify them. Chapter 5 explained that the ability of watersheds to neutralize acids was related to the biological cycling of nitrogen and sulfur and that there was considerable evidence that the natural nitrogen and sulfur cycles were being altered by the cumulative effects of acid deposition.

Biochemical cycles do not, however, operate independently. They are linked by shared reactants, by their effects on pH, and by their effects on ion exchange sites. When one cycle changes, especially a major cycle like nitrogen or sulfur, other cycles like aluminum and calcium will change as well. In this sense, the changes in nitrogen and sulfur cycles are the primary effects of acid deposition and the changes in, say, aluminum or calcium, secondary effects. But because the changes in aluminum or calcium may be as important than the primary changes in nitrate and sulfate that caused them, we may also want to speak of an acidification cascade and emphasize the ways that acidification propagates through an interconnected system.

In this chapter we examine the effects of the acidification cascade on calcium. We look at two types of linkages: the mobilization of stored cations by strong acids, and the contribution of stored cations to the ANCs of streams and lakes.

CALCIUM CYCLING AND CALCIUM DEPLETION

About Calcium

Calcium is, after magnesium, the second commonest alkali metal, making up about 3% of the earth's crust.* It is commonly found in carbonate minerals like calcite and even more commonly in aluminum silcate minerals, particularly plagioclase feldspar, which is 14% calcium by weight. It is released from these minerals by weathering. The weathering of calcite is relatively rapid, and soils derived from calcitic bedrock often have little residual calcite. The weathering of plagioclase and other silicate minerals is much slower. Typical Adirondack soils often contain large amounts of unweathered plagioclase and other silicates.

TOTAL WET DEPOSITION IN THE ARBUTUS LAKE WATERSHED, 1985-1998

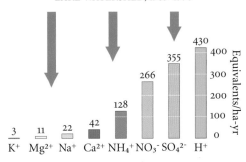

From Mitchell et al., "Role of within-lake processes and hydrobiogeochemical changes over 16 years in a watershed in the Adirondack Mountains of New York, USA," 2001. Element cycling in the Arbutus Lake watershed is dominated by the relatively large inputs of nitrogen, sulfur, and hydrogen ion. The watershed is currently storing nitrogen and hydrogen ion but releasing sulfur. Calcium inputs to the watershed are low, but calcium outputs, averaging 1,384 eq/ha-yr from 1995 to 1998, are large. The high calcium outputs are partly from the natural weathering of calcareous bedrock and partly from the coupling of the nitrogen, sulfur, and calcium cycles. The hydrogen ions arriving in acid deposition and produced by the nitrogen and sulfur cycles release calcium from ion exchange sites and allow it to be exported in groundwater.

* Calcium is the most abundant and most biologically important of the base cations in biomass and soils, and so we focus on it here. Much of what we say about calcium and calcium depletion applies to magnesium and the other base cations as well, and the problem can be called, collectively, base cation depletion.

Calcium is an essential nutrient for all animals and plants. Structurally, it is used in shells, bones, and connective tissues in animals and as part of the secondary cell walls in plants. Metabolically, it is essential for the functioning of cell walls, membrane channels, and several enzymes. It is, after nitrogen and phosphorus, the most important mineral nutrient in forests. Its overall concentration in forest trees is around 0.3%, rising to 0.5–1.0% in the leaves, and falling to less than 0.1% in the wood.

Within Adirondack watersheds calcium has two roles, which are to some extent competitive. As an alkali metal, it is a source of acid-neutralizing capacity: dissolution and ion exchange, the two main processes freeing inorganically bound calcium within soils, both neutralize hydrogen ions. As an essential nutrient, it is required for forest growth and, because pools of available calcium are often limited in northern forest soils, often cycles rapidly between vegetation and the forest floor.

The competition between these roles arises because calcium pools in soils are limited. To support growth, calcium must be stored on the ion exchange complex and incorporated into plant tissue. To neutralize acids and support the ANC of surface waters, it must be freed from its bound forms and be exported from the forest and into lakes and streams. Because supplies are limited, every atom of calcium that has been used for growth is an atom that is no longer available to neutralize acid deposition, and every calcium ion that has been exported from the forest in the past is no longer available for growth.

Calcium Pools in a Forest

Within forests, calcium exists in three forms: *organic calcium,* incorporated in living and dead biomass; *exchangeable calcium,* held on the surface of soil particles by electric charges; and *mineral calcium,* chemically incorporated in bedrock and the mineral grains within soils.

Though mineral calcium is by far the largest pool of calcium in most forests, because of the slow weathering rates of silicate minerals it is relatively unavailable for biological cycling in most Adirondack watersheds. Weathering rates are not known very accurately but are believed to be a few hundred equivalents per hectare per year or less in watersheds with silicate bedrock.

Organic and exchangeable calcium – collectively called *labile calcium* – are much more available. Exchangeable calcium is available almost instantaneously. Organic calcium is made available through decay, which for calcium-rich tissues like leaves and bark can occur within a few months after the litter falls. As a result the total release of organic calcium is often much greater than the

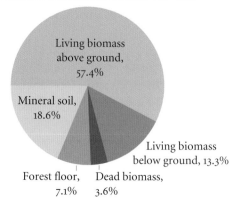

DISTRIBUTION OF LABILE CALCIUM IN FORESTS AT HUBBARD BROOK, 1987–1992

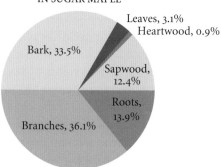

CALCIUM DISTRIBUTION IN SUGAR MAPLE

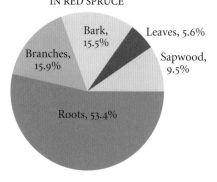

CALCIUM DISTRIBUTION IN RED SPRUCE

Based on data from Likens et al., "The biogeochemistry of calcium at Hubbard Brook," 1998. Labile calcium is the calcium that is either incorporated in organic matter or held on the soil ion exchange complex. About three-quarters of it is in biomass, mostly in living trees, and the rest in the soil. Within living trees, it is principally in the branches, bark, and roots. Leaves, though relatively rich in calcium, are low in total weight; sapwood and heartwood, though a large part of the weight of the tree, are very low in calcium.

release of mineral calcium and can result in calcium fluxes of several thousand equivalents per hectare per year.

Our most detailed information about calcium pools comes from the reference watershed, W6, at the Hubbard Brook Experimental Forest in New Hampshire. The watershed is dominated by sugar maple and beech, with spruce, fir, and birch in the upper parts. In the period 1987–1992, the forest was estimated to contain 32,000 moles per hectare of labile calcium, of which 60% was in living and dead biomass, 21% in exchangeable calcium, and 19% in organic calcium in the forest floor. It also contained a much larger amount, estimated at 245,000 moles, of mostly mineral calcium in the mineral fraction of the soil.

These are very significant amounts: they are equivalent to 1.3 metric tons of calcium per hectare in the labile pool and another 9.8 metric tons of calcium per hectare in the nonlabile pool in the mineral soil. They indicate both the biological and geological abundance of calcium and, judging from the disparity between the mineral calcium and the organic and exchangeable, the difficulty of converting from one to the other.

Calcium Cycling

Compared to the cycles of nitrogen and sulfur, which involve a variety of chemical species, the cycling of calcium is very simple. Biologically available calcium is supplied to forests by deposition and weathering, assimilated by vegetation, released by decay, and stored in organic material and on the soil ion exchange complex. In undisturbed forests most of the calcium released by decay is reassimilated rapidly, and only small amounts are exported in groundwater.

Although neither the dry deposition rate nor the weathering rate can be determined directly, both are believed to be relatively small in most northern forests. At Hubbard Brook the total input from weathering and wet and dry deposition was estimated as 100 moles per hectare per year or less for the period 1987–1992.

Compared to either the pool of biologically available calcium or the rate at which calcium is cycled, the input rate is small. It would

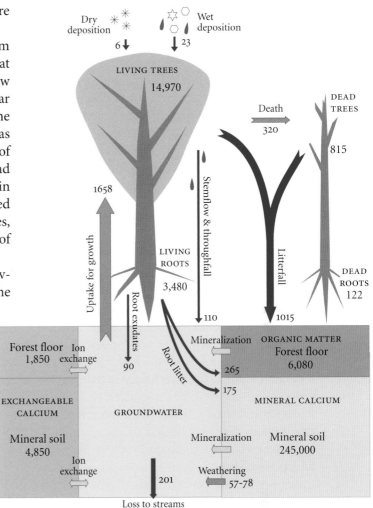

Based on data from Likens et al., "The biogeochemistry of calcium at Hubbard Brook," 1998. The largest pool of labile calcium, about 19,400 moles, is in living and dead biomass; the ion exchange pools and soil organic matter pools (the latter mostly in the forest floor) are considerably smaller. The dominant fluxes are uptake and litterfall. Uptake is 35 times greater than inputs and 8 times greater than outputs. Ion exchange, weathering, and mineralization occur simultaneously and can't be determined directly; weathering, believed to be quite small, has been estimated from sodium fluxes and assumptions about the chemistry of weathering.

take 193 years for the current inputs to supply the amount of calcium currently stored in biomass and another 80 years to supply the biologically available calcium in the forest floor. The annual biological uptake is about 16 times the inputs from deposition and weathering, and the annual return of calcium from litterfall is about ten times the inputs from deposition and weathering.

The large amounts of calcium in biomass suggest that disturbances like fires and logging, which alter the amount of biomass, can affect calcium cycling. Fires free calcium and can result in both large exports of calcium in surface water and a large pool of soil calcium that is available for new growth. Logging removes calcium from the system. The amount removed depends on the type of logging. It is low in some chipping operations in which the bark and twigs are left in the forest, higher when logs and bark are removed, and highest when whole trees are removed.

The rates of biological uptake and return in the calcium cycle are not only high in themselves but also high relative to the calcium pools they draw from. A tree drops, on average, about 7% of its above-ground calcium in litter every year. To replace this, it absorbs about a quarter of the exchangeable calcium from the soil every year. In consequence, the turnover rate of the biologically active layers of the soil is quite high: the average residence time of a calcium atom in the forest floor is estimated to be less than six years.

Forest soils lose calcium when more is taken up by plants for new growth than is returned by decay and when it is exported by stream water. At Hubbard Brook in the period 1987–1992, the forests were growing quite slowly and consuming only about 100 moles per hectare per year for net growth. Stream exports, however, were moderately high, about 200 moles per hectare per year. Since inputs were around 100 moles per hectare per year, this meant that the net loss to the forest floor was about 200 moles per hectare per year, or twice the rate of input.

Compared to other biogeochemical cycles, the calcium cycle in acidified forests is characterized by its fast turnover, its high storage in biomass, and its high losses relative to inputs. It is, in effect, a fast-running machine with a serious leak. As such, it could easily be disturbed if the stored calcium, and particularly the relatively small pool of available calcium stored in the forest floor, were depleted.

This could happen in a variety of ways. It might occur slowly through natural causes, as the calcium in young glacial soils gradually leaked out of the system or was sequestered in biomass. It might occur much more rapidly if enough calcium was removed by repeated harvesting. And it might, as many researchers began to think in the 1990s, occur from the accelerated calcium losses caused by acid rain.

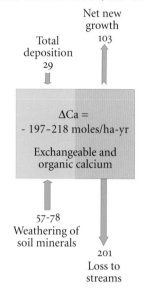

AVERAGE SOIL CALCIUM BALANCE AT HUBBARD BROOK, 1987–1992

Net new growth 103

Total deposition 29

$\Delta Ca = -197–218$ moles/ha-yr

Exchangeable and organic calcium

57-78 Weathering of soil minerals

201 Loss to streams

Based on data from Likens et al., "The biogeochemistry of calcium at Hubbard Brook," 1998. The input from deposition and the loss to streams have been measured directly. The input from weathering has been estimated from weathering rate calculations, and the net uptake by forests (the amount the calcium used each year in new growth exceeds that returned in litter) from measurements of above-ground growth and estimates of root growth. The net loss of around 200 moles per year is about 2.5% of the calcium in the forest floor and 1.6% of the labile calcium in the soil.

Can acid deposition deplete calcium pools?

Acid deposition is a major disturber of the calcium cycle. The hydrogen ions from atmospheric acids free bases, particularly calcium, from the ion exchange complex. The bases enter groundwater and migrate with the mobile anions from the atmospheric acids into lakes and streams.

This export of cations is good for lakes, which receive base cations and neutralized drainage water. But it can be quite bad for the forests that lose the cations. Unscripturally, to neutralize is less blessed than to be neutralized.

The loss of base cations from forest soils can create two problems. The first is that the lost cations are taken from the same pool of labile calcium that supplies forest growth. When this pool is small, forest growth may suffer. The second is that streams need a supply of base cations to maintain their baseline ANCs and neutralize acids during peak flows. If a watershed's soils have been depleted of base cations, its streams are likely to be chronically acid and to have severe acid peaks during high flows.

The first papers on calcium depletion in the late 1980s focused on forest growth. But it was this second issue, the stubbornly chronic acidity of streams, that drew the attention of many acid rain researchers to cation depletion in the early 1990s.

The problem was that acid deposition was decreasing but streams were showing little or no recovery. By 1990 the sulfate levels in lakes and streams had declined substantially but, contrary to expectation, pHs and ANCs had not increased (p. 199). Long-term monitoring studies, like the Hubbard Brook data shown at right, suggested that the problem was the base cation supply. As sulfate concentrations fell, base concentrations fell with them or even faster. Because ANC equals the difference between base cations and acid anions, this meant that the ANCs stayed the same or even decreased.

As a result of these and other studies, researchers starting looking for evidence of base cation depletion. Finding it was not easy. Soil chemistry is notoriously variable over short distances, and there were, in any event, few historical data available for comparison. Furthermore, there were confounding factors: depletion might be real but caused by forest growth or decreased cation inputs and not by acid deposition.

Despite the difficulties, a number of important cation depletion studies have led to a growing consensus that cation depletion is both widespread and important. The chronology at the start of the chapter lists some of the important studies, and the gallery of graphs on the next two pages illustrates some of the major results.

STREAM CHEMISTRY AT HUBBARD BROOK

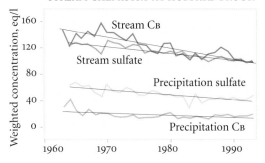

Redrawn with permission from Likens, Driscoll, and Buso, "Long-term effects of acid rain: Response and recovery of a forest ecosystem." Copyright 1996 American Association fort the Advancement of Science. Watershed 6 at Hubbard Brook Experimental Forest in New Hampshire has shown long-term declines in stream base cations and sulfate, paralleling declines in cations and sulfate in precipitation. As a result, ANC has not increased, even though sulfate has decreased.

CALCIUM IN THE RINGS OF A RED SPRUCE FROM BIG MOOSE LAKE

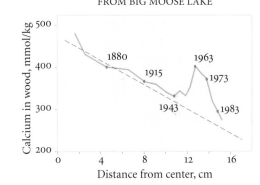

- - - Predicted decline in calcium with age

Redrawn with permission from Shortle and Bondietti, "Timing, magnitude, and impact of acid deposition on sensitive forest sites." Copyright 1992 Springer Science and Business Media. The concentration of calcium in the wood of trees normally declines as a tree ages because the growth rate declines. The 1940–1980 peak, which has been observed in several species of trees, is thought to represent calcium mobilized by the rapid increase in acid deposition after 1940.

A BASE CATION DEPLETION GALLERY

CALCIUM INPUTS AND OUTPUTS FROM SIX FORESTED WATERSHEDS

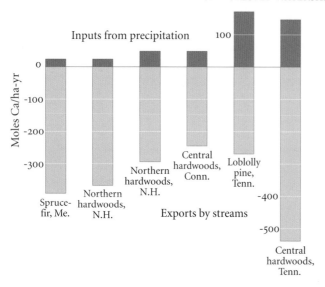

From Federer et al., "Long-term depletion of calcium and other nutrients in eastern US forests," 1989. This was the first paper to draw attention to the possibility of base cation depletion in eastern U.S. forests. The dark blue bars are the annual calcium input from precipitation; the light bars are the calcium losses in stream water. Inputs from weathering were not calculated. All the forests were in areas affected by acid deposition. Losses in stream water were 2 to 16 times the input from precipitation, strongly suggesting that unless inputs from weathering were unusually high, cation depletion was likely occurring. The authors also noted that a whole-tree harvest could remove as much calcium as 10 to 100 years of leaching and so double the rate of calcium loss over a 40- to 60-year forest rotation.

CALCIUM BALANCES AT HUBBARD BROOK, 1965–1992

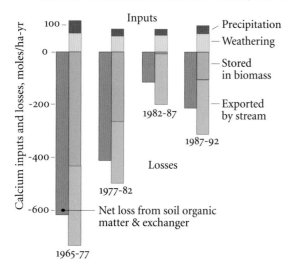

From Likens et al., "The biogeochemistry of calcium at Hubbard Brook," 1998. Over the past 40 years, calcium inputs from precipitation have decreased while weathering is believed to have remained fairly constant. Storage in biomass has declined greatly, and stream exports have declined slightly. The soil has lost calcium throughout the period, though at a decreasing rate. See also the mass-balance and stream results from Hubbard Brook on pages 132–133.

DECLINES IN STREAM CATIONS IN BIRKENES, NORWAY

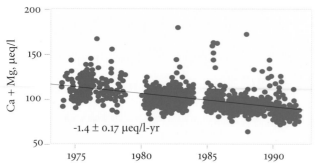

Redrawn with permission from Kirchner and Lydersen, "Base cation depletion and potential long-term acidification of Norwegian catchments." Copyright 1995 American Chemical Society. The graph shows the decline in base cations after the effects of reductions in sulfate deposition and changes in precipitation volume have been removed. The residual decline is believed to be caused by the gradual depletion of the pool of exchangeable calcium and magnesium in the soil.

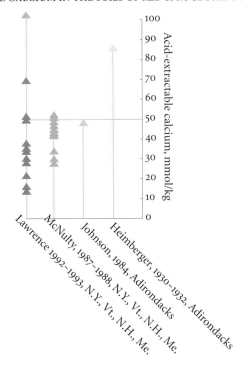

Redrawn with permission from Lawrence et al., "Assessment of soil calcium status in red spruce forests in the northeastern United States." Copyright 1997 Springer Science and Business Media. The graph compares the mean calcium concentrations in the forest floor at sites sampled at different times. The 1930 and 1984 results were corrected for differences in laboratory methods. The calcium concentrations measured in the 1950s were higher than any measured in the 1980s and 1990s, except for one site (green triangle) on calcareous bedrock.

As a result of these studies, by the late 1990s acid-induced cation depletion had been suggested by at least five different lines of investigation:

Historical comparisons, showing decreases in the base cation content of forest soils.

Tree-ring chemistry, showing the mobilization of calcium in periods of high acid deposition.

Strontium isotope studies, suggesting that the inputs of calcium from the weathering of soil minerals in watersheds with noncalcareous bedrock are quite low.

Mass-balance studies, showing that calcium outputs exceed inputs for many watersheds affected by acid deposition.

Stream-watershed studies, showing slow changes in stream-ANCs as sulfate deposition decreases.

Thus in 1999 base cation depletion was regarded in much the way that acid deposition had been regarded in 1980: there was a general feeling that it was likely widespread and ecologically consequential, but there were no synoptic data that would allow its extent and severity to be mapped. The participants in a Ecological Society of America workshop that year reported high agreement on the statement "Some forest sites show depletion of labile pools of calcium and magnesium due to acid deposition," and moderate agreement that cation deficiencies were associated with mortality of maple and spruce in Pennsylvania, and aluminum mobilization with red spruce decline throughout the Northeast.

In 2005, as we write this, cation depletion is still largely unmapped but somewhat better understood. The connections with forest health, which lie outside the scope of this book, have had significant research. The history of cation depletion has been examined with a new generation of biogeochemical models, which show considerable promise as investigative tools (p. 139). And the empirical connections between cation depletion and stream chemistry have been demonstrated by several studies, to which we now turn.

Calcium and Streams

The goal of these studies was to determine whether the slow response of streams to decreases in acid precipitation was related to cumulative calcium losses from their watersheds.

In theory, there should be a close relation. For a stream to have a positive ANC, it must receive a baseline flux of calcium and other base cations from its watershed, in addition to any bases that are released by neutralizing acid deposition. Otherwise, as acid deposition decreases, its base cation concentrations will also decrease, and there will be no change in ANC.

Thus, depleted pools of base cations in forest soils should mean low baseline flows of cations to streams, and low baseline cation flows should mean little recovery from acidification.

By the late 1990s, it appeared that this was exactly what was happening (p. 133). Despite 25 years of substantial decreases in sulfur deposition, northeastern streams were recovering slowly if at all. Sulfates had decreased greatly and pHs had increased slightly, but base cation concentrations had decreased almost as much as sulfates and so ANCs had changed very little.

Although there was clearly a cation supply problem, it was not at all certain that it was caused by acid rain. Cation exports, after all, are linked to deposition and were supposed to fall as acid deposition decreased. What was required was to show that they were also linked to the base saturation – the percentage of cation exchange sites occupied by bases – and that as the base saturation of a watershed decreased, so did the ANCs of its streams.

Two studies by Lawrence and his colleagues in the U.S. Geological Survey did just this.

The first study examined the relation between acid deposition, base concentrations, and stream chemistry at different elevations in the watershed of the Neversink River in the Catskills. The idea

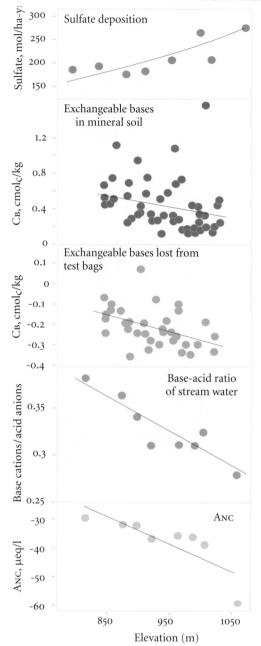

Redrawn from Lawrence et al., "Soil calcium status and the response of stream chemistry to changing acidic deposition rates." Copyright 1999 Ecological Society of America via the Copyright Clearance Center. This was the first study to show a direct connection between base cation depletion and stream acidification. At higher elevations in the watershed, sulfate deposition is higher, base cation reserves lower, and streams more acid. Bags of test soil placed at different elevations show cation losses that are proportional to sulfate deposition.

was to find a watershed with fairly uniform soils and vegetation where sulfate deposition varied with elevation. Then, if base cation reserves and stream chemistry also varied with elevation, it was likely that sulfate deposition was controlling cation reserves, and cation reserves were controlling stream chemistry.

The Neversink was such a watershed. Its higher elevations had more sulfate deposition than its lower but were otherwise similar. Long-term records showed a decline of about 25% in stream calcium since 1968, paralleling the declines observed at Hubbard Brook and in Norway (pp. 133, 134) and suggesting that calcium depletion might be occurring.

The results from the Neversink study suggested strongly that sulfate deposition was depleting exchangeable cation pools and that the exchangeable cation pools were affecting stream chemistry. As expected, the higher parts of the watershed, where sulfate deposition was greatest, had the lowest base cation concentrations in the forest floor and the lowest base-acid ratios in streams. Also as expected, the total reserves of available cations decreased as sulfate deposition increased, and stream acidity increased as the cation reserves decreased.

As a bonus, it turned out to be possible to demonstrate cation depletion experimentally. When bags of test soil were placed at different elevations, the bags at higher elevations lost more cations, and, clinching a good argument, the cation saturation of the soil in the bags controlled the base-acid ratio of water percolated through them in just the way the depletion theory predicted it should.

These results, though not conclusive, were very important. They established that acid rain was capable of causing the kind of calcium depletion observed in many watersheds and hence the slow improvement of many acidic streams. The authors concluded, "Worldwide, there are no published long-term data that directly relate acidic deposition to measurements of soil Ca depletion and resulting changes in stream chemistry. In the absence of such data, the spatial patterns measured in [the] Winnisook watershed uniquely demonstrate how soil and stream chemistry vary together in response to variations in acidic deposition."

Thus, as many other times in the baseline-starved world of environmental science, a strong geographic pattern substituted for missing historical detail.

Lawrence's second study looked at the relation between cation depletion and acid episodes (figure at right). Acid episodes either result from or are exacerbated by the dilution of base cation fluxes at high flows (pp. 106, 109). Thus, they should be very sensitive to the supply of base cations from the watershed and should be most severe where the watershed reserves of base cations are the lowest.

CALCIUM IN THE NEVERSINK RIVER, 1968-1996

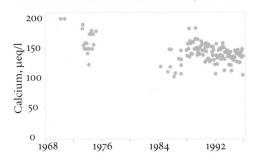

From Lawrence et al., "Soil calcium status and the response of stream chemistry to changing acidic deposition rates." Copyright 1999 Ecological Society of America via the Copyright Clearance Center. The chemistry of the Neversink has been measured since 1952. Prior 1968, total base cation concentrations were between 200 and 300 µeq/l.

STREAM ANC AND EXCHANGEABLE CALCIUM

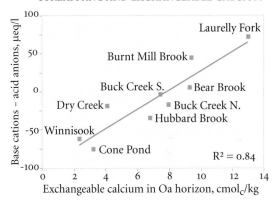

Redrawn with permission from Lawrence, "Persistent episodic acidification of streams linked to acid rain effects on soil." Copyright 2002 Elsevier. The streams are located in Pennsylvania, New York, Vermont, New Hampshire, and Maine; the cation difference, which approximates the ANC, was measured by automatic samplers during high flows. In a striking demonstration of the link between soil cation pools and acid episodes, the difference between the base cations and the acid ions is low in watersheds with low amounts of calcium in the forest floor.

To test this, Lawrence and his colleagues studied eight creeks in four states at various times between 1991 and 2000. They collected soil samples throughout the watersheds and monitored acidity peaks with stage-sensitive recorders that took water samples automatically when the flow rose above a critical level or increased at a critical rate.

ACIDIC SEGMENTS OF THE WEST BRANCH OF THE NEVERSINK RIVER, CATSKILL MOUNTAINS, N.Y.

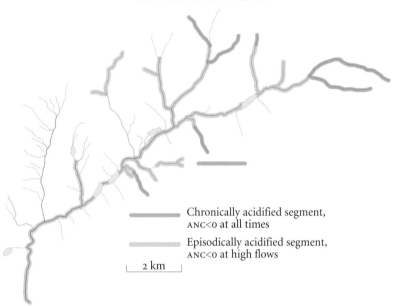

Chronically acidified segment, ANC<0 at all times

Episodically acidified segment, ANC<0 at high flows

2 km

Redrawn with permission from Lawrence, "Persistent episodic acidification of streams linked to acid rain effects on soil." Copyright 2002 Elsevier. The Neversink is an acidified watershed in the Catskills with low soil calcium reserves. In the West Branch watershed, 16% of the stream segments are chronically acidified; they receive little or no groundwater flow and are acidic at all times. Another 66% are episodically acidified. At low flows they receive high-ANC groundwater from deep mineral soils where there are base cation reserves. At high flows they receive water from the forest floor and upper layers of the soil where cation depletion has occurred. Note that episodic acidification extends much farther downstream than chronic acidification. Chronic acidification is limited to a few headwaters streams, while episodic acidification extends all the way to the mouth of the stream.

Their results, graphed on page 137, showed a surprisingly regular relationship between calcium reserves and acid episodes: where forest floor calcium levels were high, ANCs remained above zero, even at peak flows. Where forest floor calcium levels were low, peak-flow ANCs were negative and acid peaks were severe.

This was also an important result. It confirmed the central role of the forest floor – where forest litter accumulates, where most calcium cycling takes place, and where the high-water flowpaths lie – in controlling acid episodes. And it suggested that acid episodes, which were controlled by the easily depleted forest floor, would affect many more miles of stream than acid baseline flows, which were controlled by the much less depletable mineral soil.

The differing extent of chronic and episodic acidification is shown dramatically in the Neversink watershed, which Lawrence et al. studied intensively. At low flows, 16% of the stream miles in the basin were acid; at high flows, 82% of the stream miles were. If this result holds true for other streams, acid episodes and the damaged fisheries associated with them (p. 180) may be extremely

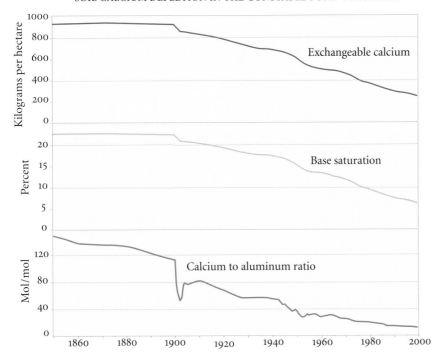

A simulation of the loss of soil calcium from the Constable Pond watershed, redrawn with permission from Chen and Driscoll, "Modeling the response of soil and surface waters in the Adirondack and Catskill regions of New York to changes in atmospheric deposition and historical land use disturbance." Copyright 2004 Elsevier. The simulation uses a dynamic biogeochemical model, which couples a forest growth model (PNET) to a model of element cycling in soils (BGC). Acid deposition, beginning after 1850, depletes the pool of exchangeable calcium, reduces the base saturation, and mobilizes aluminum. By 2000 more than three-quarters of the available soil calcium is gone, and the base saturation and calcium-to-aluminum ratio have fallen to levels believed detrimental to forest growth. Constable Pond is part of the much-studied and modeled North Branch watershed in the southwestern Adirondacks. The chemical geography of the watershed is shown on pages 52–53. The spring acidity peaks in the pond are shown on page 105 and other modeling results for it on pages 112, 221, and 222.

common, if not nearly universal, in other areas with calcium-depleted soils.

How much calcium has been lost from forest soils?

To measure the impact of acid deposition on soils, we need to know what the soils were like before deposition began. Unfortunately there are no paleoecological proxies, analogous to the diatoms in lake sediments, that can be used to reconstruct the chemical history of soils. But we do know emission rates for the past 100 years, and from these we can reconstruct, with reasonable accuracy, deposition rates (pp. 13, 215). From deposition rates, weather records, and soil data it is possible to compute element fluxes, and from the element fluxes it is possible to reconstruct the presettlement chemistry of the soils.

The first such reconstructions have recently been prepared by Chen and Driscoll for watersheds in the Adirondacks and the Catskills, and by Gbondo-Tugbawa and Driscoll for the reference watershed at Hubbard Brook. We show a reconstruction for the Constable Pond watershed in the Adirondacks. According to the simulation, exchangeable calcium concentrations in the watershed were initially about 900 kilograms per hectare and the base saturation about 22%. The calcium concentrations began to decline in about 1900 and have decreased ever since. Currently the exchangeable calcium concentrations are near 200 kg/ha and the base

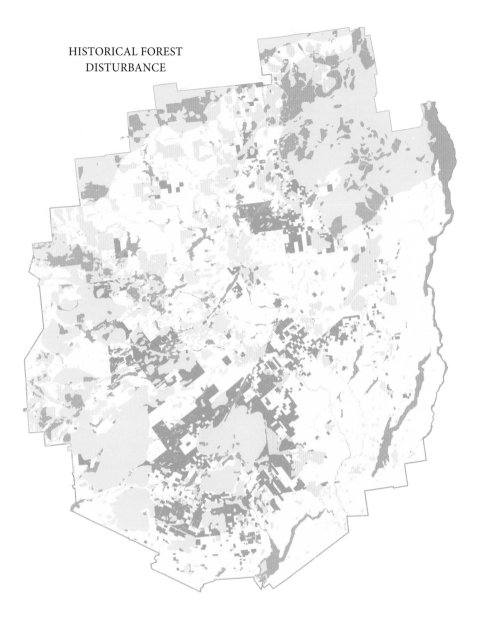

HISTORICAL FOREST
DISTURBANCE

Historical forest disturbance in the Adirondack Park, reprinted with permission from Jenkins, *The Adirondack Atlas,* copyright 2004 Wildlife Conservation Society. The map is a composite of known disturbances; see the original for maps and discussions of the individual events involved. Major fires affected the western and northern parts of the park, where heavy softwood logging was occurring, between 1900 and 1915. There have been no major fires since. Major blowdowns occurred in the west in 1950 and 1995, and in the north in 1998. Logging, which began in the early 1800s, has affected the whole park except for the 10% to 15% that was acquired for the state Forest Preserve (where logging is not permitted) prior to 1900.

Historical forest disturbances,
with percentage of park

Storm damage, no fires: 23.9%

Fire damage, no storms: 10.3%

Both storms and fires: 5.3%

Logging, no storms or fires: 50.9%

Possible old-growth; no logging, storms, or fires: 9.6%

saturation about 5%, both about a quarter of their presettlement values.

There are, of course uncertainties in this analysis, particularly concerning weathering rates, forest growth, and calcium deposition. But if the model is even approximately correct, it suggests that there have been major long-term soil changes in the most acidified watersheds and that these soil changes will have to be reversed before the watersheds can recover fully.

Do forest disturbances remove calcium or acidify surface waters?

Many forests have had complex histories of disturbance. In the past 150 years the Adirondacks been disturbed by major storms, extensive fires, and widespread logging. Our best (though necessarily approximate) estimate is that fires have affected at least 15% of the park, windstorms have affected at least 30%, and logging at least 80%. Only about 10%, mostly in scattered tracts in the western and southern portions of the park, has not been burned, blown over, or logged.

The chemical effects of these disturbances have been little studied. From work elsewhere and from the few Adirondack studies that we have, we can make a few general observations:

1 Normal forest growth, which removes cations and generates organic acids, is believed to be acidifying over long periods. Both American and European studies have shown the slow acidification of lakes, over hundreds or thousands of years, as forests developed following glaciation (p. 58). Researchers have also observed rapid acidification in polluted areas where new conifer forests have increased the deposition of acids by increasing the interception of dry deposition. But thus far no example is known of forests in unpolluted areas causing the rapid acidification of soils or surface waters (p. 61).

2 Forest fires, which drive sulfur and nitrogen off as gases and free base cations from soil organic matter, are almost always deacidifying. The ashes from fires are always alkaline, and in the short term fires always raise the pH of soil and surface water. A sediment core from Mud Pond in Maine, for example, showed abrupt pH increases of about 1 pH unit associated with historical fires, followed by gradual decreases in pH as the forests regrew.

3 The effects of logging are more complex than those of either fire or normal growth and not very well studied. They involve the removal of biomass, the generation of dead biomass, and the stimulation of regrowth. Logging is generally believed to acidify watersheds, at least temporarily, but there is very little direct evidence on this point.

4 Our most detailed study of logging was of a clear-cut done in Watershed W5 at Hubbard Brook in 1983. The cut, which involved whole-tree harvest, removed 3,480 moles of calcium per hectare directly and elevated stream calcium levels, resulting in the export of another 3,420 moles of calcium per hectare in the next eight years. Stream nitrate levels were also elevated, and stream pHs decreased. Stream nitrates and pHs returned to their baseline values within 3 years after cutting but, somewhat unexpectedly, stream calcium levels are still elevated 25 years later.

5 Blowdowns are in some ways like a kind of natural logging in which the dead trees are left on the ground instead of

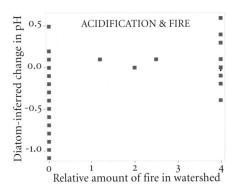

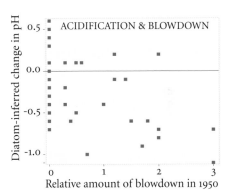

Redrawn with permission from Sullivan et al., "Relationship between landscape characteristics, history, and lakewater acidification in the Adirondack Mountains, New York." Copyright 1999 Springer Science and Business Media. In these graphs, historical changes in lake pH, inferred from sediment cores, are plotted against indices of disturbance compiled from historical records. The pHs of lakes have tended to increase in watersheds that have had fires and decrease in watersheds that have had blowdowns, but neither relationship is particularly strong. See text, page 143.

being removed. As with logging, there has been much discussion in the literature of their possible acidifying effects. Only recently has this been confirmed: in a study of the effects of the 1998 ice storm in New Hampshire, Houlton et al. found greatly increased rates of nitrate export at 8 of 11 monitored watersheds that had ice storm damage. At Hubbard Brook, the increased nitrate losses began in August, about seven months after the ice storm. The total loss was 349–522 moles per hectare per year, comparable to losses observed after insect defoliation and severe soil freezing but much less than the losses associated with experimental clear-cuts.

Correlating Disturbance and Acidification

Lacking direct evidence of the effects of disturbance, another approach is to try to correlate historical records of disturbance and acidification. Several groups, most notably Sullivan and his collaborators, have done this for the Adirondacks.

Their studies are of considerable scientific importance because it is likely that both watershed disturbance and acid deposition have influenced the recent acidification of lakes. Though the studies described in Chapters 3 and 4 suggest that most recent acidification is the result of acid deposition, it would be scientifically very satisfying to have an independent confirmation.

Satisfying or not, the analysis of Adirondack disturbance histories is a daunting task, for two reasons.

First, the history itself is complex. While the general history of Adirondack forest disturbance is well known (p. 141), its detailed geography is not, and it is often very difficult, especially in the small watersheds that are of interest in acidification studies, to reconstruct the local disturbance history and determine how much of the watershed has been disturbed.

Second, Adirondack disturbances overlap and are correlated with physical factors and with each other. Logging tends to occur at low elevations, where acid deposition is less; blowdown tends to be most intense on ridgetops and thin-soil areas, where acid deposition is relatively high. The big historical fires almost all started along railroads, where the cutting was also heaviest. Two of the largest blowdowns came from the west, where deposition is the highest. These correlations make the problem of the historical causes of acidification statistically intractable: it is relatively easy to come up with possible explanations but almost impossible to come up with unique ones.

The work of Sullivan and his collaborators illustrates both the difficulty of the problem and the amount that can be learned from a systematic approach. They selected 44 lakes for which they had

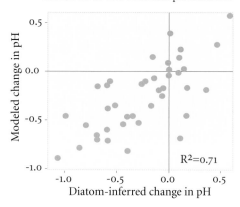

A MODEL OF HISTORICAL pH CHANGE

CORRELATIONS BETWEEN ACIDIFICATION AND
FEATURES OF THE WATERSHED

Contemporary conditions

Average precipitation	0.57**
Nitrate deposition	0.42**
Sulfate deposition	0.42**
Elevation	0.39*
Mean slope	−0.41*
Hydraulic residence time	−0.33*
Percentage of riparian wetlands	−0.49**
Hemlock-birch forests	−0.35*
Spruce-birch forests	0.42*

Historical disturbance

Blowdown in 1950	0.48**
Logging	n.s.
Fire	−0.49**
Lakeshore cabins	n.s.
Timing of logging	n.s
Total watershed development	−0.35

Redrawn with permission from Sullivan et al., "Relationship between landscape characteristics, history, and lakewater acidification in the Adirondack Mountains, New York." Copyright 1999 Springer Science and Business Media. The graph shows the predictions of a model in which changes in lake pH are predicted from a model that uses precipitation, the hydraulic residence time of the lake, and the amount of blowdown in the watershed. The table gives the Pearson correlation coefficients between the historical and environmental variables and the reconstructed pH changes in the 44 lakes studied by the PIRLA project (p. 86). The higher the correlation coefficient, the stronger the correlation. * = significant at 0.05; ** = significant at 0.001; n.s. = not significant. Other variables such as lake area and watershed area were tested and not found significant.

paleolimnological estimates of historical acidification (p. 86) and, using reconstructions of forest history supplied by the late Barbara McMartin, compared the historical acidification with 15 variables characterizing the watershed and its history. These variables included precipitation, deposition rates, slope, elevation, and vegetation type but did not include any information on soils or geology, which are major determinants of the degree of acidification.

As expected, correlations with precipitation and present-day watershed characteristics were moderately strong. There is a 0.57 correlation between acidification and rainfall, a 0.39 correlation between acidification and elevation, and somewhat surprisingly, a 0.49 correlation between acidification and shoreline wetlands.

Interestingly, correlations with fires and the 1950 blowdown were equally strong. The amount of historical blowdown had a 0.48 positive correlation with acidification; blowdowns, at least some of the time, seem to be associated with acidification. The amount of historical fire has a negative correlation of 0.49. Fire, as suspected, often decreases acidification. Logging, perhaps because it is hard to quantify, did not have a statistically significant effect. Total development, represented by roads and houses, had a weak deacidifying effect.

While this is certainly interesting, because the variables representing disturbance are correlated and because they have odd and discontinuous distributions, very few of them are of much predictive use. A model using only precipitation and hydraulic residence time, the two best physical variables, accounted for a respectable 58% of the variance in acidification. A model using only blowdown, a very messy variable, accounted for a meager 37% of the variance in acidification and could not be improved by adding any other historical variables. The best combination of physical and historical variables, which accounted for 71% of the variance and produced a fairly respectable agreement between the predicted acidifications and the acidification estimated from sediment cores, still used only three variables – precipitation, hydraulic residence time, and blowdown.*

At the time we write, the influence of historical disturbance on acidification is still uncertain. We can say with some confidence that the degree of acidification varies with precipitation and hydraulic residence time. Blowdowns and fires also seem important but less so and with less predictive power. The physical and historical variables are statistically correlated, and thus far, despite fairly good historical information and careful analysis, it has not proved possible to separate them.

*From a theoretical point of view, this kind of exercise shows both the possibilities and limits of regression models. On the one hand, a lot can be predicted with only three variables. A model using precipitation, hydraulic residence time, and blowdown can account for 71% of the variance in lake acidification. But on the other hand, beyond three variables the regression models flounder. Adding other variables – even relevant ones like nitrate or sulfate loading, topography, vegetation, fire, and logging – does not improve the estimate at all.

What this probably means is that landscape variables are linked in complex ways that linear models don't capture. More complex models that include soil chemistry and forest growth have recently been developed and are yielding some interesting results. One of these models has been applied to Adirondack watersheds. Its reconstructions of historical soil chemistry are shown on page 139, and its predictions of soil and water chemistry under different deposition scenarios on page 215.

MANIPULATING CALCIUM

Long before acid rain was found to be a problem, acidic lakes were being limed – sweetened, the fishery biologists called it – to increase their productivity and improve their fisheries. It was only natural that liming would be used to offset atmospheric acidification: by the mid-1980s, acidic lakes were being limed in the United States, Canada, and Scandinavia. By 1988, approximately 103 Adirondack lakes had been limed, 29 on private land and 74 in the Forest Preserve.

In the Adirondacks, lake liming attracted both scientific and regulatory interest.

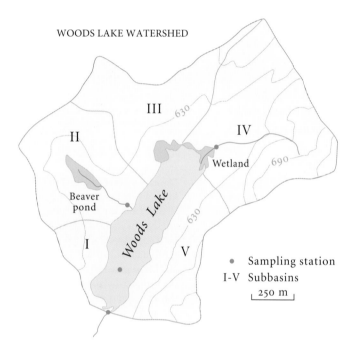

WOODS LAKE WATERSHED

III

II

IV

Wetland

Beaver pond

Woods Lake

I

V

• Sampling station

I-V Subbasins

⊢ 250 m ⊣

The Woods Lake watershed, originally studied in the ILWAS and subsequently used for lake liming experiments in 1985 and 1986 and a watershed liming experiment in 1989. Map redrawn with permission from Driscoll et al., "The experimental watershed liming study: comparison of lake and watershed neutralization strategies." Copyright 1996 Springer Science and Business Media. The lake liming studies applied ground lime directly to the water. The watershed-liming experiments spread lime over subbasins II and IV. The Woods Lake liming projects produced at least 15 scientific papers; for general references, see the references in this section and the note on page 149. For the effects of liming on the beaver pond northwest of the lake, see page 159.

Scientifically, liming raised both practical and theoretical questions. Working biologists with acidic lakes to manage wanted to know how much lime to use, when to add it and how long the effects would last. Acid rain researchers who were trying to unravel lake budgets wanted to know what liming actually did: where the added calcium went, what effects it had on other ions, and how the ANC it generated was eventually exported or consumed.

The scientific questions were addressed by a series of studies, particularly the Lake Acidification Mitigation Project (LAMP), which began in 1985, and its successor, the Experimental Watershed Liming Study, which ran to 1992. The LAMP began by treating the water columns of Woods Lake and Cranberry Pond with a calcium carbonate slurry. The slurry produced dramatic chemical effects but washed out of the lakes very rapidly. The researchers then treated Woods Lake with a coarser suspension that sank to the bottom and had somewhat more long-lasting effects, and then finally, determined to find a treatment that would last, treated the whole Woods Lake watershed.

The regulatory questions arose because the Department of Environmental Conservation had, on the one hand, the statutory mission of protecting the wildlife of the state and, on the other hand, the constitutional requirement that it keep the lands of the New York State Forest Preserve "forever wild." Both fishery biologists and managers of private lands wanted to use liming to mitigate acidification. But the DEC was also obligated keep the public waters in as natural condition a as it could and was also required to obtain wetlands permits before it treated any lake with associated wetlands or significant amounts of aquatic vegetation.

The regulatory questions were first addressed on a case-by-case basis, in which managers asked whether the lake was a good candidate for liming and whether an important fishery was involved. The process was formalized in 1990, when the DEC presented an impact statement summarizing the results of its studies on liming and suggested criteria for selecting lakes for treatment and guidelines for applying lime.*

Liming a Lake

Liming research in the Adirondacks began with the experimental liming of Woods Lake on May 31, 1985.

Woods Lake is a small, thin-till drainage lake at an elevation of 606 meters south of Stillwater Reservoir in the watershed of the Beaver River. It is about a kilometer long and has an area of 25 hectares, an average depth of 3.5 meters, and a maximum depth of 11 meters. Its watershed is 207 hectares, about eight times the lake surface, and is fairly steep. As a result, it receives almost twice its own volume in runoff every year, and its hydraulic residence time is only 174 days. The bedrock in the watershed is a typical west-Adirondack hornblende gneiss, which produces thin, acid soils with frequent outcrops.

Woods Lake was initially studied by the Integrated Lake-Watershed Acidification Study in the early 1980s (p. 46) and has been monitored by the Adirondack Lakes Survey Corporation since 1992. In the early 1980s its summer pH was often less than 5 and its ANC less than 0 µeq/l. Summer aluminum concentrations were around 8 µeq/l, and DOC concentrations around 200 µmol/l. The concentration of acid ions exceeded the concentration of base cations, suggesting that much of its acidity was derived from acid deposition.

Its size and acidity made it a good candidate for a liming experiment. Because it was small, the quantities of lime involved were

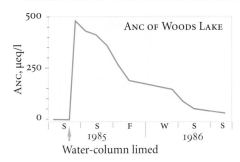

ANC CHANGES IN WOODS LAKE AFTER LIMING

From Driscoll et al., "Chemical response of lakes treated with CaCO3 to reacidification," 1989. When Woods Lake was limed in early summer, the ANC rose abruptly and then started to decline. By a year after liming it was only slightly above where it had started.

* For the DEC impact statement on liming, see Simonin, "Final generic environmental impact statement on the New York State Department of Environmental Conservation program of liming selected acidified waters," 1990. Currently, permits for liming are handled by the Adirondack Park Agency (APA). Following standards proposed by the DEC in 1990, the APA now requires that a lake proposed for liming have a summer pH below 5.7 or an ANC below 20 µeq/l; that it either contain a heritage strain of fish or have a "seriously degraded" aquatic ecosystem or have had in the past an excellent fishery; that it not be a bog lake or brown-water lake, or flush more than two times per year; and that it have oxygen and temperature levels suitable for the fish that managers wish to preserve.

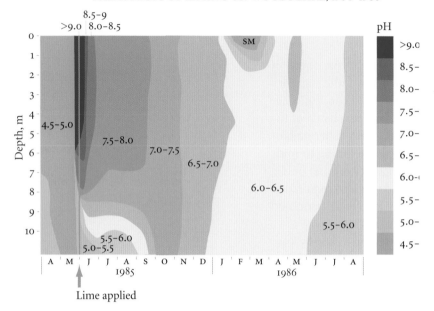

Lime applied

From Driscoll et al., "Chemical response of lakes treated with CaCO3 to reacidification." Copyright 1989 National Research Council of Canada. The diagram is an isopleth plot and shows the average pH of the lake as a function of depth and time. (Isopleth plots look like cross sections but are space × time rather than space × space.) Note that the lime did not reach the bottom of the lake until the fall overturn in September and that a surface plume of highly acid snowmelt water (SM) entered the lake under the ice in February. For other effects of the liming and the second liming in 1987, see Bukaveckas, "Effects of calcite treatment on primary producers in acidified Adirondack lakes. I. Response of macrophyte communities," 1988; Driscoll et al., "Short-term changes in the chemistry of trace metals following the calcium carbonate treatment of acidic lakes," 1989; and Gubala and Driscoll, "The chemical responses of acidic Woods Lake, NY, to two different treatments with calcium carbonate," 1991.

manageable; because it was quite acidic and flushed rapidly, it was a good test of what liming could do for a severely altered lake.

The research at Woods Lake included both chemical and biological studies. We focus on the chemical studies here. In May 1985 the lake was treated with 22.6 tons of calcium carbonate (limestone). The limestone was in the form of small (2 micron) particles, mixed with a weak detergent solution to make a slurry.

The lake was weakly stratified when the lime was applied, with a thermocline at 8 meters. Most of the lime did not penetrate the thermocline and remained suspended in the water in the upper eight meters of the lake.

Because the lake was acid and the calcium carbonate particles small, the immediate chemical response was rapid. Eighty percent of the lime dissolved in the first month after treatment. Within a few days, the pH rose by 4 pH units and the ANC by about 500 μeq/l, and the surface layers of the lake became nearly saturated with calcium carbonate. Zooplankton and phytoplankton populations, either shocked by the pH change or injured by the slurry, fell rapidly. Dissolved organic carbon, perhaps released by dying plankton, increased abruptly and then decreased abruptly. Carbon dioxide from the atmosphere entered surface layers, restoring the carbonate-bicarbonate equilibrium and dropping the pH from 9 to about 8.

Over the next two months there were noteworthy though considerably slower changes in toxic metal concentrations. Aluminum, manganese, and zinc concentrations all decreased by ten times or more, probably because of the precipitation of aluminum and manganese and the adsorption or coprecipitation of zinc. The equilibrium between the different forms of aluminum shifted as well, and some polymeric aluminum that had formed during the abrupt initial changes in pH was changed into monomeric aluminum.

Because the lake had a short hydraulic residence time, the calcium flushed out steadily, and none of the chemical ameliorations lasted long. By October, when the streamflow increased and the lake turned over, only about 50% of the calcium added in May remained in the lake. The pH had now fallen to around 7 and the ANC was 250, half of what it had been in June. The lake remained near neutral until snowmelt the following spring, when nitrate-rich runoff drove the surface pH below 5 and the surface ANC below 0 μeq/l.*

By August 1986, when the first phase of the experiment ended, the effects of the liming had almost vanished. Only about 2.5% of the added calcium carbonate remained in the lake, the average pH had fallen below 6.0, and the ANC was near 0 again. Some effects of the liming remained, but for most purposes the lake was, physically and biologically, once again an acidic lake.

In September 1986, Woods Lake was relimed in an attempt to get more lasting effects. This time researchers applied 43 tons of lime, twice the previous amount, about half of which was finely ground and half coarse. The coarse particles were supposed to fall to the bottom and dissolve gradually, prolonging the effects of the treatment.

The ANC contours (p. 148) show that this was exactly what happened. Immediately after the treatment a pool of high-ANC water developed near the bottom of the lake. The sediments continued to release ANC for the next 15 months but then apparently ran out of lime. By 24 months after the treatment, the lake had largely reacidified.

These results, though not perhaps what had been hoped for, were in fact a confirmation what the ILWAS had said about this lake (p. 45). It was the watershed and not the water column that was in fact controlling the acidification process. Sixty-six tons of lime (2,800 kilograms or 50,000 equivalents per hectare) had been applied to the water of a single small lake. The result was 36 months of positive acid-neutralizing capacity, after which the lake was acidic again. Clearly what mattered in lakes with short residence times was not the acidity of the lake but the acidity of the watershed. No matter how much lime was added to the lake, it flushed out quickly, and once it flushed out the watershed was back in control.

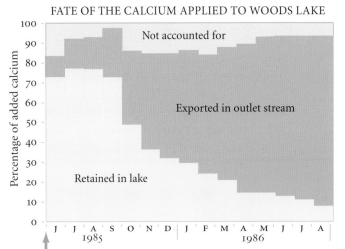

FATE OF THE CALCIUM APPLIED TO WOODS LAKE

Redrawn with permission from Driscoll et al., "Chemical response of lakes treated with CaCO3 to reacidification." Copyright 1989 National Research Council of Canada. The figure shows the sum of the total calcium in the lake water ("retained in lake") and the amount that had been exported from the outlet. The calcium that could not be accounted for had probably been deposited in the lake sediments.

Initially, almost all the calcium was in the lake water. But because Woods Lake has a short hydraulic residence time, the lime that was applied began to flush out almost immediately; four months after the lime was applied, 50% of the added calcium was gone.

* Interestingly, brook trout that had been stocked when the lake was limed proved very sensitive to the decreases in pH. When the springtime pH reached 6, almost all the trout left the lake and moved into the tributary streams.

Liming a Watershed

Logically enough, the next step was to lime the watershed. As with the previous treatment, this was done both as a management experiment and as a test of the current scientific understanding of how watersheds work. The expectation was that an application of lime to the soil surface would increase the pHs of soils and surface water, stimulate decay, increase base cation fluxes, and decrease aluminum concentrations and spring acidity peaks.

ANC CONTOURS OF WOODS LAKE, 1984–1991

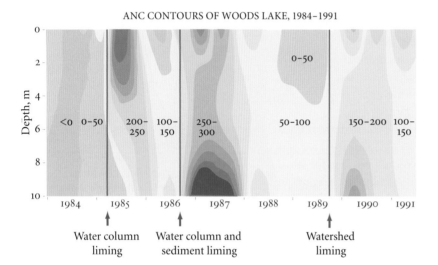

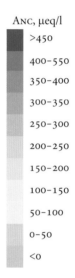

Redrawn with permission from Driscoll et al., "The Experimental Watershed Liming Study: Comparison of lake and watershed neutralization strategies." Copyright 1996 Springer Science and Business Media. The plot shows how the average ANC at different depths changed during the three liming experiments. The added lime (darkest blue) was mostly near the top of the lake after the first treatment, at the bottom of the lake after the second treatment, and spread throughout the lake after the third. Note the rapid reacidification after the water column and the sediment treatments, compared with the slow changes after the watershed liming.

Testing these expectations was a large project, involving 7 institutions, more than 20 investigators, and 3 years of field research. In October 1989, 1000 tons of pelletized limestone, enough to neutralize 300 years of acid rain, was applied to 100 hectares of the Woods Lake watershed by helicopter. The target application rate was 10 tons per hectare (= 200,000 equivalents per hectare), roughly ten times greater than the original water column treatment and six times greater than the water column and sediment treatment.

The results confirmed most of the expectations. Compared to the earlier experiments, the lime applied to the forests dissolved relatively slowly. Some was taken up by vegetation, and much was bound to exchange sites in the soil. Some was assimilated by microbes, stimulating decay and the mineralization of nitrogen. Much of the mineralized nitrogen was apparently used by vegetation, and nitrate exports did not increase. Only a little of the new calcium was lost as surface runoff, and very little by deep groundwater.

Because the lake was originally very dilute, the relatively small amounts of calcium exported to the streams and the lake had significant effects. The fall pH of the lake rose slightly, from 6.3 to 6.8; the ANC increased from 53 to 138 µeq/l; dissolved calcium

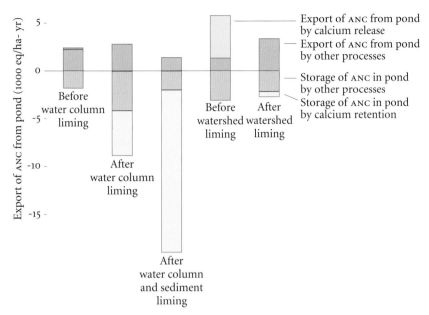

The ANC budget of Woods Lake, showing the effects of the three liming treatments, redrawn with permission from Driscoll et al., "The experimental watershed liming study: Comparison of lake and watershed neutralization strategies." Copyright 1996 Springer Science and Business Media. The bars give the difference between the inputs of ANC to the lake and the outflow of ANC in the outlet stream. Before the first liming the pond was exporting slightly more ANC than it was consuming; thus the output water had a higher ANC than the input. During two water column liming treatments it stored some of the added calcium and so was consuming ANC; later it released some of the stored calcium and exported ANC again.

The watershed liming experiment was different from the two previous treatments in that the calcium was delivered to the lake gradually and very little calcium was retained in the lake. But interestingly, nitrate and sulfate were retained, and the lake remained a producer of ANC.

The experimental watershed liming study produced a substantial literature. In addition to the paper cited above, see Blette and Newton, "Effects of liming on the soils of Woods Lake, New York," 1996; Burns, "Effects of $CaCO_3$ application to an Adirondack lake watershed on outlet stream chemistry," 1996; Geary and Driscoll, "Forest soil solutions: Acid/base chemistry and response to calcite treatment," 1996; Mackun, Leopold, and Raynal, "Short-term responses of wetland vegetation after liming of an Adirondack watershed," 1994; Newton et al., "Effect of whole-catchment liming on the episodic acidification of two Adirondack streams," 1996; Rossell, Leopold, and Raynal, "Competition among shoreline plants: Responses to watershed liming," 1995; Schofield and Keleher, "Comparison of brook trout reproductive success and recruitment in an acidic Adirondack lake following whole lake liming and watershed liming," 1996; Simmons, Yavitt, and Fahey, "Response of forest floor nitrogen dynamics to liming," 1996; and Yavitt and Fahey, "Peatland porewater chemical responses to $CaCO_3$ applications in wetlands next to Woods Lake, New York," 1996.

increased by about 50%, and aluminum concentrations dropped significantly.

The striking thing about these changes was not their size but the way they persisted. Because most of the calcium was retained in the watersheds and delivered slowly to the streams, the ANC and pH of the lake changed relatively little in the next two years. This was just the opposite of the two previous liming experiments, in which large initial increases had been followed, in less than a year, by equally large decreases. Two years after the first water column experiment, 97% of the lime had been flushed from the lake. Two years after the watershed liming experiment, 96% of the lime was still in the lake and the watershed.

The effects of the gradual release of calcium were most marked during spring runoff. Before watershed liming the lake had typically been flushed with highly acid, nitrate-dominated water in the spring, which reduced its pH and prevented fish from spawning. Water column liming had done nothing to reduce these peaks, two of which show clearly in the isopleth diagram on the opposite page. Watershed liming, by increasing the supply of base cations in the spring and reducing the export of aluminum and nitrate, reduced the acidity peaks on the inlet streams and largely eliminated them from the lake. In 1990 the surface water of the lake actually gained calcium in the spring, and brook trout, which had left the lake when the pH fell after the second water column liming experiment, returned and reproduced successfully.

The critical question, of course, was how long these effects would last. The calcium addition was large, probably five to ten times the existing pool of labile calcium in the watershed and in theory sufficient to neutralize acid deposition for several decades or more. The investigators originally intended to monitor the lake for several years but lost their funding and discontinued their studies in the fall of 1992, three years after the project began. Fortunately, the Adirondack Lakes Survey took over the monthly chemical monitoring of the lake in 1992. Their data, which are currently being analyzed but have not yet been published, show a gradual decline in pH in the 16 years since the lake was limed and suggest that the effects of the liming have persisted for some time.

SUMMARY

1 *Calcium* is a keystone element, both biologically and chemically. It is essential biologically for plant and animal growth and chemically for buffering and the generation of acid-neutralizing capacity. These functions are to some extent competitive: the more calcium is used to neutralize acids, the less it is available to support growth.

2 Watersheds have three major pools of calcium – mineral calcium, exchangeable calcium, and biomass calcium. In areas like the western Adirondacks with silicate bedrock, mineral calcium is relatively unavailable for either growth or neutralization, and most calcium cycling involves exchangeable calcium and biomass calcium.

3 Because *inputs of calcium* to Adirondack forests are low, any disturbance – fire, logging, acid deposition – that causes calcium loss can potentially have long-term effects on the total pool of biologically available calcium.

4 Prior to acid deposition, the calcium in the western Adirondacks *cycled* rapidly but tightly between biomass and the soil, with very little loss to surface water. Acid deposition has changed this by greatly increasing the rate at which calcium leaches from ion exchange sites and is exported in surface water. When the rate of leaching exceeds the calcium inputs, this results in base cation depletion, reflected in decreases in exchangeable calcium and base saturation.

5 Like the changes in watershed nitrogen and sulfur discussed in Chapter 5, cation depletion is one of the *cumulative effects* of acid deposition. It differs from those previously discussed only in that it is a deficit rather than an accumulation.

6 The concept of *acid-driven base cation depletion* entered the American literature in 1989. Since then it has been the subject of much study and has been suggested or confirmed by six separate lines of research: historical comparisons of soil chemistry, tree-ring chemistry, mass-balance studies, stream-watershed studies, isotope studies, and simulations of watershed biogeochemistry.

7 The effects of *other watershed disturbances* on calcium cycling are much less studied. Fires clearly cause short-term calcium exports and so deacidify surface waters; logging exports both nitrates and calcium and seems to acidify waters; blowdowns are thought to cause short-term acidification as well, and this has been recently documented in several New Hampshire watersheds.

8 It is much less clear what the *long-term effects of watershed disturbances* on surface waters may be. A recent statistical study found moderately strong individual correlations between blowdowns and acidification and between fires and deacidification. Logging was not correlated with either acidification or deacidification. The correlations were not strong enough, however, to explain acidification by themselves. A model using only precipitation and hydraulic residence time explained 58% of the variation in historical acidification; adding blowdown and fire explained 13% more.

9 *Lake liming* originated as a fishery management tool for naturally acidic lakes and then was applied to atmospherically acidified ones. Liming clearly benefits fish and is now occasionally and fairly selectively used in the Adirondack Park. To be eligible for liming, a lake must have clear water and a moderately slow flushing rate – conditions that disqualify many small Adirondack lakes – and must have or have had a significant fishery or other important aquatic resource.

10 Several *experiments with lake liming* established that applications of 1 to 2 tons of lime per hectare can cause immediate increases in the pH and ANC of lakes. But they also found that unless the flushing rate is slow, these changes only last for a few months to a year.

11 *Watershed liming* has been tried only once in the Adirondacks.* It seems to have had more persistent effects than lake liming. Unfortunately, the original experiment was terminated, and there has not yet been any published analysis of the long-term effects.

NOTES

p. 128 References not given with the figures in the chapter are Bailey et al., "Calcium inputs and transport in a base-poor forest ecosystem as interpreted by Sr isotopes," 1996; Gbondo-Tugbawa and Driscoll, "Factors controlling long-term changes in soil pools of base cations and stream acid-neutralizing capacity in a northern hardwood forest ecosystem," 2003; Hedin et al., "Steep declines in atmospheric base cations in regions of Europe and North America," 1994; Johnson, Andersen, and Siccama, "Acid rain and soils of the Adirondacks I: Changes in pH and available calcium, 1930-1984," 1994; Johnson et al., "Acid rain and soils of the Adirondacks III: Rates of soil acidification in a spruce-fir forest at Whiteface Mountain, New York," 1994; Lawrence, David, and Shortle, "A new mechanism for calcium loss in forest-floor soils," 1995; Rodhe et al., *Acid Reign '95? – Conference Summary Statement*, 1995; Wesselink et al., "Long-term changes in soil and water chemistry in spruce and beech forests, Solling, Germany," 1995; and Yanai, Siccama, and Arthur, "Changes in forest floor mass and nutrient content over 17 years in a northern hardwood forest," 1993.

p. 129 The best general summary of calcium cycling is Likens et al., "The biogeochemistry of calcium at Hubbard Brook," 1998.

p. 142 For the effects of logging on stream chemistry at Hubbard Brook, see Martin et al., "Impacts of intensive harvesting on hydrology and nutrient dynamics of northern hardwood forests," 2000.

* For a recent watershed liming experiment in New Hampshire, see Peters et al., "Dissolution of wollastonite during the experimental manipulation of Hubbard Brook Watershed 1," 2004.

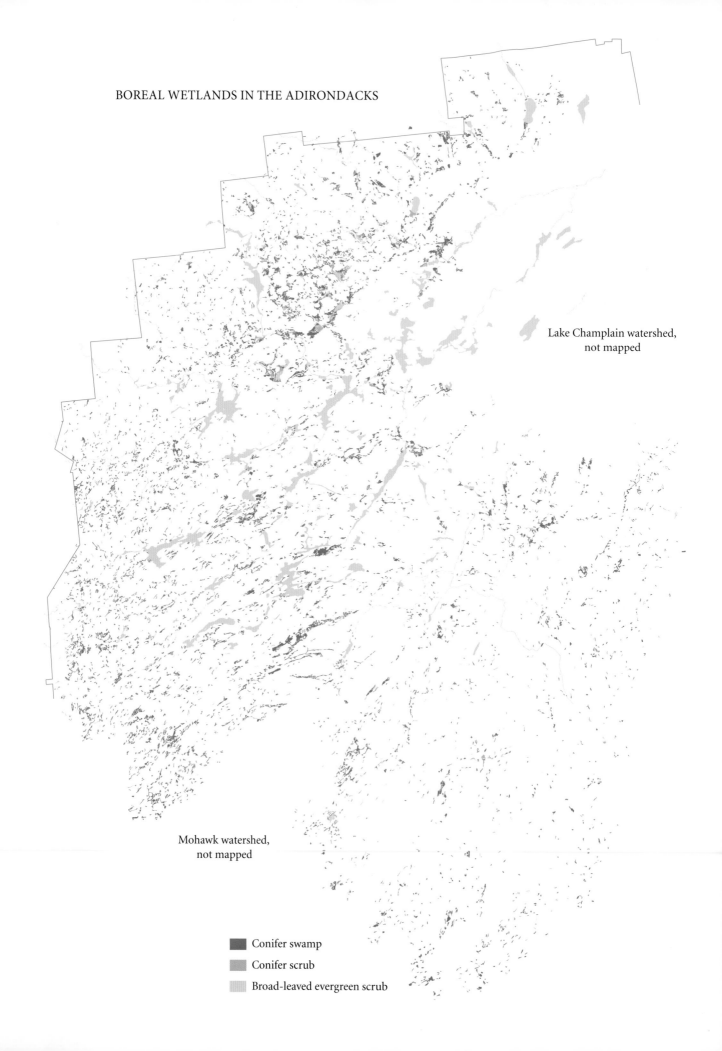

BOREAL WETLANDS IN THE ADIRONDACKS

Lake Champlain watershed,
not mapped

Mohawk watershed,
not mapped

Conifer swamp

Conifer scrub

Broad-leaved evergreen scrub

WETLANDS, CARBON, AND MERCURY

CASE HISTORIES OF STORAGE AND TRANSFORMATION

Thus far we have only touched on wetlands. We mentioned their chemical activity in Chapters 3 and 5 and also mentioned in Chapter 6 an interesting, though still unexplained, relation between the amount of wetlands near a lake and the amount it has acidified since preindustrial times. But thus far we have not dealt with them directly.

Dealing with them, however, presents a problem. They are, on the one hand, very widespread in the Adirondacks and clearly important for the acidification story. But they also are, on the other, chemically complex and still little studied.

Their geographic importance is clear. In many Adirondack watersheds, 10% of the watershed is wetlands. In some, like the upper Oswegatchie, over 20% is. Almost every Adirondack headwaters stream has one or more beaver ponds, and almost every small lake with a natural water level has some shoreline wetlands. In the low-gradient drainages of the northern and western Adirondacks, many streams have open corridors consisting of a continuous border of sedge or shrub wetlands, and almost every flat place is either a conifer swamp or an open wetland. In some of these watersheds, which are among the most acid in the Adirondacks, it is virtually impossible for water to enter a lake or stream without passing through one or more wetlands.

The chemical importance of wetlands is also clear. Adirondack wetlands have biologically active organic soils. They are places where nitrogen and sulfur are immobilized and dissolved organic carbon and organic acids are generated. They have high cation exchange capacities and both adsorb and release calcium. They also trap aluminum, reduce sulfate, mobilize iron and ammonium, and convert ionic mercury to the highly toxic methylmercury.

Because wetlands can both acidify and deacidify, their effect on stream chemistry is complex. When they retain aluminum, they decrease ANC but also make the water less toxic. When they reduce sulfates to sulfides, they increase ANC, but if they reoxidize the sulfides, they may lower it again. The organic acids they produce both acidify waters and, by binding to toxic metals like aluminum and mercury, ameliorate some of the effects of acidification.

Until more research is done on more kinds of wetlands, we cannot review Adirondack wetland chemistry as a whole. But we can describe several case histories and one "inverse modeling" study that suggest some interesting generalizations and show how much there is left to learn. Two of the case histories looked at the ion budgets of Adirondack beaver ponds, and the third at a spruce-

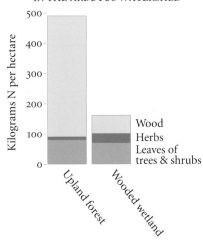

NITROGEN STORAGE IN BIOMASS
IN THE ARBUTUS WATERSHED

Above, storage of nitrogen in living vegetation at two sites in Huntington Forest. Data from Bischoff et al., "N storage and cycling in vegetation of a forested wetland: Implications for watershed N processing," 2001. The forest stores about the same amount of nitrogen in leaves as the wetland does but seven times as much in wood.

Opposite, the conifer-dominated wetland layers from digital maps produced by the Adirondack Park Agency (APA) in collaboration with the Adirondack Lakes Survey Corporation and the State University of New York at Plattsburgh. The maps allow spatially explicit studies of the relations between wetlands, land cover, and water chemistry. The model of DOC generation described on page 161 in this chapter is the first major Adirondack study to do this.

Conifer swamps are the dominant wetland type in the northwestern Adirondacks and make up a total of 15% of the area in the Oswegatchie-Black River watershed. Open peatlands appear as orange patches, often adjoining small, light green areas of conifer scrub.

Information on the APA mapping program may be found at www.apa.state.ny.us. For the chronology for this chapter, see p. 175.

white cedar swamp in Ontario. The modeling study examined the concentration of dissolved organic carbon in 428 Adirondack lakes and reconstructed the sources generating the carbon and the paths by which it was reaching the lakes.*

Case Study 1: A Beaver Pond Acts as a Chemical Transformer

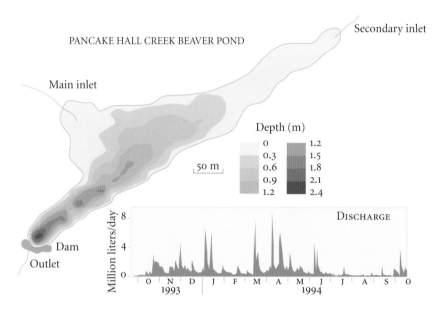

* Two recent Adirondack wetland studies that reached us too late to be included in the text are Hurd, Raynal, and Schwintzer, "Symbiotic N₂ fixation of *Alnus incana* spp. *rugosa* in shrub wetlands of the Adirondack Mountains, New York, USA," 2001; and McHale et al., "Wetland nitrogen dynamics in an Adirondack forested watershed," 2004. The first estimates that nitrogen fixation contributes 37 kg/ha-yr to the nitrogen budget of an alder swamp. The second shows that the groundwater in a streamside wetland was rich in nitrates, and that these nutrients were, in large part, being stored in accumulating peat and not being discharged into stream water.

The Pancake Hall Creek beaver pond, showing depths and the highly episodic flow. This figure and those on the opposite page redrawn from Cirmo and Driscoll, "Beaver pond biogeochemistry: Acid-neutralizing capacity generation in a headwater wetland." Copyright 1993 Society of Wetlands Scientists via the Copyright Clearance Center.

Pancake Hall Creek is a small stream that enters Big Moose Lake from the north. A few hundred meters from the lake is a small wetland basin and in it a beaver pond that has been studied since the middle 1980s. The pond, like many beaver ponds, is really just an enlarged segment of the stream. It is about 500 meters long, mostly less than 50 meters wide, and has an area of 3 hectares and an average depth of 0.4 meters. It is fed by two inlet streams and has a 2-meter-high dam at its outlet. The surrounding vegetation is mostly sedges and mosses; the sediments, both in the basin and in the pond, are organic peats. Flows through the pond vary greatly: the hydraulic residence time of the pond is 50 days in the summer, 35 days in average high flows, and 1 day in peak flows.

In 1990, Cirmo and Driscoll began a two-year study of the ion budgets of the pond. The purpose was to see what elements the pond was storing and releasing and whether the pond was generating or consuming ANC.** Gauge stations were installed above and below the lake, and water samples were taken every three weeks.

The results showed that the pond was an effective chemical transformer and that many of the transformations were connected with the biological cycling of sulfur and carbon. The pond was producing ANC by storing sulfur and nitrogen and also producing

**A pond is said to generate ANC when the ANC of its outlet is greater than that of its inlet. A pond can do this either by storing acids or by releasing bases; thus when it is generating ANC downstream, it is becoming more acid itself.

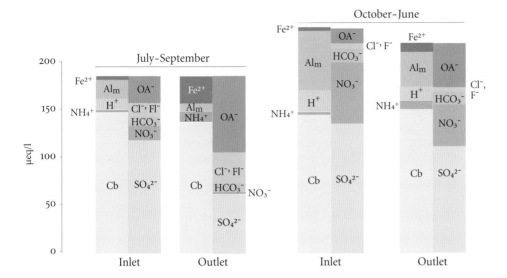

The ion balance of the Pancake Hall Creek beaver pond in different seasons. In the summer, when both the watershed and the pond are biologically active, inputs of acid anions and aluminum are relatively low, and retention of these elements is relatively high. In the rest of the year the inputs of acid anions and aluminum are higher, and the retention of them is lower. Base cation inputs are similar in both periods, but there is a slight retention of base cations in the summer and a slight loss of them from the pond in the rest of the year.

dissolved organic carbon and organic acids by the bacterial decay of organic matter.

The graph above shows the differences between inputs and outputs. The water entering the pond was typical for a thin-till Adirondack watershed, with relatively high concentrations of nitrate, sulfate, and aluminum and low concentrations of base cations. As in many similar streams, sulfate concentrations didn't vary much, and the ANC of the inlet stream was largely controlled by variations in nitrate, aluminum, and base cations.

Once the water entered the pond, it encountered a zone of high biological activity. Except at peak flows, the pond was still and shallow, and most of the water was in close contact with vegetation and organic sediments. Decaying organic matter was abundant. Where the oxygen levels were low, reducing conditions developed and microbes used nitrate, ferric iron, and sulfate as electron acceptors, producing nitrogen gas, ferrous ions, and sulfides. The ferrous ions were exported and the sulfides stored in sediments. Also because of the reducing conditions, decay was often incomplete and considerable amounts of organic acids and ammonium ion were produced.

ANC Generation in the Pancake Hall Creek Beaver Pond

As a result of these transformations, the water leaving the pond was considerably different from the water coming in. Nitrate, sulfate, aluminum, and base cation levels were lower. The nitrate was probably assimilated or denitrified, the base cations immobilized on ion exchange sites, the sulfate converted to sulfides, and the aluminum, which is soluble only at low pHs, hydrolyzed and pre-

THE ANC BALANCE OF THE PANCAKE HALL CREEK BEAVER POND

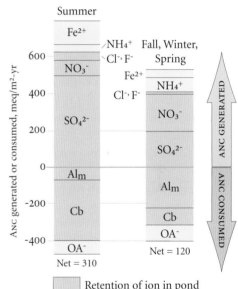

The ANC balance of the pond in different seasons. Processes with positive values increase the ANC of the water in the outlet stream; those with negative values decrease it. The pond generates ANC year-round, though more in the summer, when it is biologically active. The major processes generating ANC are the retention of nitrate and sulfate and the release of ammonium and ferrous iron.

cipitated. Other elements and compounds – organic and inorganic carbon, organic acids, ferrous iron, and ammonium, which are all products of decay and biological reductions – increased in concentration and were exported from the pond.

The net result was an increase in ANC. The retention of nitrate and sulfate in the pond and the release of ammonium and ferrous iron from it were the dominant ANC-increasing processes. The production of organic acids and retention of aluminum and base cations consumed ANC, but not enough to offset the increases.

The input-output graphs at right show an interesting and complex seasonality. The pond is most active in the summer, when temperatures are high, vegetation is growing, and flows and oxygen are low. It is least active in the spring when flows are high and residence times are short. But interestingly, there are also subsidiary peaks in iron, ammonium, and dissolved inorganic carbon in midwinter, when flows are again low and the water under the ice is largely deoxygenated.

The annual rate of ANC production is 160 meq/m2-yr, or 1,600 eq/ha-yr. Since the southwestern Adirondacks receive somewhere around 800 equivalents of nitrate and sulfate in wet deposition per hectare per year, this means that a hectare of the Pancake Hall wetland can neutralize the acid deposited on itself, plus the acid from another hectare of uplands. Since most uplands in the southwestern Adirondacks neutralize only a fraction of the acid deposited on them (p. 86), this is a surprisingly high rate of ANC production and shows just how active a small, shallow pond can be.

Case Study 2: A Swamp in Ontario Releases Pulses of Acid

There is, however, no reason to believe that all wetlands generate ANC. ANC generation in wetlands works by the same mechanisms as ANC generation in forests, and as in forests, a wetland's ability to store acids may become saturated, or its store of bases may be depleted. In either case the wetland may start to release acids and consume rather than generate ANC.

Our second case study, from a swamp in Ontario with a history of heavy deposition, shows how this happens. Plastic Lake 1 is a small forested peatland of about 2 hectares on the west shore of Plastic Lake in the Muskoka region of central Ontario. The Muskoka region is at the southern edge of the Canadian Shield and has igneous bedrock, thin glacial soils, and historically high rates of acid deposition. The Plastic Lake swamp is dominated by black spruce and white cedar and is probably biologically comparable to many of the boreal swamps in the Adirondacks shown in the map on p. 152.

A series of studies by Lazerte and his collaborators have determined the hydrology, chemical activity, and ion budgets of the

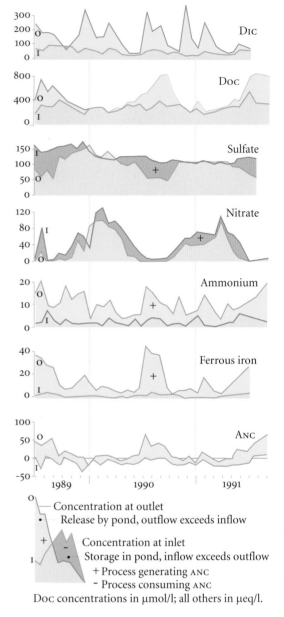

SEASONAL STORAGE AND RELEASE IN THE PANCAKE HALL CREEK BEAVER POND

Doc concentrations in μmol/l; all others in μeq/l.

Input and output concentrations for the Pancake Hall Creek beaver pond. Brown lines are concentrations in the inlet stream, blue in the outlet stream, both in μeq/l. When the brown line is above the blue, the pond is removing (storing) the ion. When the blue is above the brown, the pond is generating (releasing) it.

Each element has a different seasonal cycle. DIC and ammonium have both summer and winter peaks; DOC and iron have summer peaks only. Sulfate inputs are highest in fall and early winter; sulfate storage is highest in summer. Nitrate inputs and outputs are highest in late winter, but peaks can occur in runoff events at other times in the year.

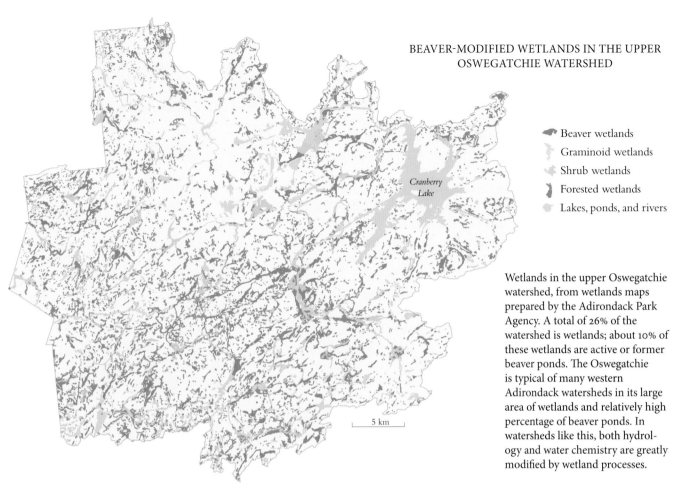

*Cranberry
Lake*

🐾 Beaver wetlands

🌾 Graminoid wetlands

🌿 Shrub wetlands

🌲 Forested wetlands

▪ Lakes, ponds, and rivers

5 km

Wetlands in the upper Oswegatchie
watershed, from wetlands maps
prepared by the Adirondack Park
Agency. A total of 26% of the
watershed is wetlands; about 10% of
these wetlands are active or former
beaver ponds. The Oswegatchie
is typical of many western
Adirondack watersheds in its large
area of wetlands and relatively high
percentage of beaver ponds. In
watersheds like this, both hydrology and water chemistry are greatly
modified by wetland processes.

Plastic Lake swamp. Their results show that the swamp receives
significant amounts of sulfate, inorganic aluminum, hydrogen ion,
and base cations from the watershed. It stores the aluminum, probably through ion exchange, releasing base cations in the process.
It also releases organic acids, generated by the decay of organic
matter, and hydrogen ions, generated variously by decay and the
oxidation of stored sulfur.

One of the most interesting findings from this study was the
extent to which the chemistry varies between wet and dry years.
In the three water years following wet summers (vertical blue bar
on graph on p. 158), the swamp exported significant amounts of
organic acids – probably, the author suggests, because of the larger
amounts of water moving through the swamp – but retained sulfate and exported only small amounts of base cations. In dry summers inorganic acids accumulated, probably from the oxidation of
stored sulfur when the peat surface was exposed to air. These were
then flushed from the wetland the following winter and spring,
generating peaks in sulfate, base cations, and hydrogen ion. In
effect, this swamp was showing signs of "sulfur saturation," storing
sulfur-cycle acids in dry seasons and then releasing them in peak
flows, much as nitrogen-saturated forests do with nitrogen-cycle
acids.

ION BUDGETS FOR THE PLASTIC
LAKE I SWAMP, 1984–1990

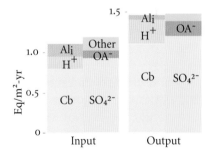

From Lazerte, "The impact of
drought and acidification on
the chemical exports from a
minerotrophic conifer swamp,"
1993. As in Pancake Hall Creek (p.
156), the ion budget is dominated
by sulfate and base cations. But
unlike the beaver pond on Pancake
Hall Creek, the Plastic Lake swamp
is exporting more base cations and
more sulfate than it receives.

WETLANDS, CARBON, AND MERCURY 157

Unlike the Pancake Hall beaver pond, the Plastic Lake swamp consumed rather than generated ANC in six of the seven years it was studied. In wet years sulfate retention almost balanced organic acid production, and the amount of ANC consumed was 500 equivalents per hectare or less. In dry years more base cations were released, but the release was offset by sulfate production and aluminum storage and the swamp consumed 1,000–1,500 equivalents of ANC per hectare per year.

The soils of conifer swamps are typically low in base cations, and Lazerte notes that the current average rate of base cation export of more than 1,500 eq/ha-yr is unlikely to be sustainable: "Eventually, if current conditions persist, the exchangeable pool of base cations in the swamp will be depleted, and more protons and some aluminum ions will be exported to compensate."

Thus the Plastic Lake swamp is currently the chemical opposite of the Pancake Hall beaver pond, consuming about half as much (about 800 eq/ha-yr) ANC as the Pancake Hall pond generates. Further, because its base cation stores are limited and being depleted, it may well export more hydrogen ion and consume even more ANC in the future.

Conifer swamps are common in the Adirondacks; the recent National Wetlands Inventory maps produced by the Adirondack Park Agency show about 70,000 hectares of conifer swamps in the Adirondack portions of the St. Lawrence, Oswegatchie-Black, and Hudson watersheds. No Adirondack conifer swamps have been studied, and so the obvious and important question of whether they are generating or consuming ANC – whether, that is, they are more like the Pancake Hall pond or the Plastic Lake swamp – has, at present, no answer.

Case Study 3: Liming a Pond Stimulates Decay and Generates ANC

As part of the Woods Lake watershed liming study (p. 148, map p. 144), the ANC budget for a beaver pond on a tributary north of the lake was determined before and after watershed liming. The pond had a total area of 2.4 hectares, of which 1.3 hectares was open water and 1.1 hectares sphagnum-sedge marsh. The average depth was 0.6 meters. Both physically and chemically, it was similar to the Pancake Hall pond (p. 154): shallow, rich in organic acids, and low in oxygen, typically retaining aluminum, sulfate, and nitrate, generating ANC, and exporting iron, ammonium, and organic acids.

In September 1989, 16 metric tons of pelletized limestone, designed for slow release, was applied to the pond and its associated wetlands. This represented 113,000 equivalents of calcium per hectare or, at the current wet-deposition rate of 40 eq/ha-yr, the calcium supplied by 2,800 years worth of rain and snow.

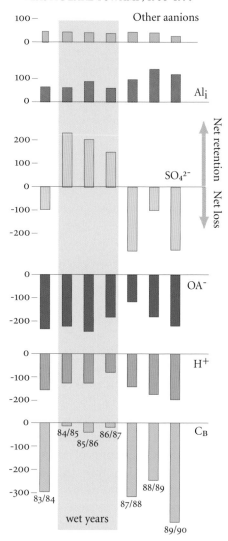

STORAGE AND LOSS OF IONS IN THE PLASTIC LAKE-I SWAMP, 1984–1990

From Lazerte, "The impact of drought and acidification on the chemical exports from a minerotrophic swamp in Ontario," 1993. Positive values are net meq/m²-yr retained in the swamp; negative values are net meq/m²-yr released from the swamp. 83/84 indicates the water year from October 1983 through September 1984. The swamp retains sulfate in wet years but releases it in dry years.

The immediate effects were striking. Like the Pancake Hall pond, the Woods Lake pond had substantial amounts of dissolved carbon dioxide and so the limestone dissolved rapidly. The ANC rose from 0 to more than 1,000 µeq/l, and the pH from less than 5 to about 7.

The changes in pH and ANC had immediate effects on other elements. There was an abrupt decrease in inorganic aluminum in the inlet stream, a somewhat slower increase in nitrate, and brief peaks in ammonium, DOC, and organic acids in the outflow from the pond. The aluminum was probably being hydrolyzed and retained in the watershed and the pond. The nitrate was likely generated by increased microbial activity in the watershed; the ammonium, DOC, and organic acids were likely generated by the decay of organic matter within the pond.

As in other liming experiments (Chapter 6), the lime in the water was much more mobile than the lime in the watershed. In the next six months 34% of the lime that was applied to the pond was flushed from the outlet, while only 1% of the lime applied to the watershed moved into the pond.

Again as in the Woods Lake liming experiment, the effects of the liming persisted for some time. A year after the liming, there was a summer peak in pH and ANC, probably associated with further dissolution of the limestone when CO_2 levels were high. The amount of calcium bound to ion exchange sites on the surface of the peat was now ten times greater than at an untreated pond. About 8% of the calcium applied to the pond appeared to be bound to ion exchange sites on living plants of sphagnum moss, and a similar but unquantified amount was assumed to be bound to the peat.

All the major postliming changes in chemistry persisted for the three years of the study. Aluminum remained very low. Inflow nitrate was still fairly high and still being retained in the pond. There were striking summer peaks in DOC, organic acids, ammonium, and iron in the outflow water, but it was uncertain whether these were consequences of the liming or part of the normal seasonal cycle.

All of this suggested that the pond, in its normal role as a chemical modifier of runoff, was also able to modify the effects of liming. The watershed released lime slowly but fairly continuously. The pond released it quickly and episodically. The watershed released nitrate and aluminum; the pond stored them and released ammonium and ferrous iron instead. The principal cation exchanger in the watershed was dead organic matter in the soil; the principal cation exchanger in the wetlands may have been living sphagnum.

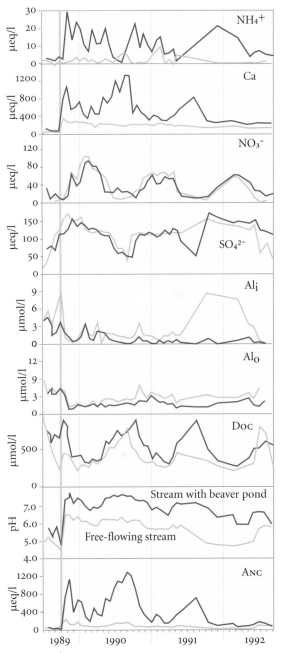

THE EFFECT OF WATERSHED LIMING ON TWO TRIBUTARIES OF WOODS LAKE, 1989-1992

↑ CaCO₃ applied to watersheds of both streams

Two tributaries of Woods Lake, with and without a beaver pond, after liming the watershed. Redrawn with permission from Cirmo and Driscoll, "The impacts of a watershed CaCO3 treatment on stream and wetland biogeochemistry in the Adirondack Mountains." Copyright 1996 Springer Science and Business Media. Note the higher pH and greater biological activity of the stream with the pond, and that the spring peaks in acidity and aluminum disappeared after liming.

About DOC

Dissolved organic carbon, has been mentioned in all the previous chapters but never emphasized. Because it is intimately connected with wetlands and because it has been the subject of some interesting new work, we now treat it in more detail.

DOC is a mixture of exudates from living plants and compounds produced by the decay of organic matter. It is chemically very heterogeneous and includes compounds of many sizes and structures. Because it is produced by the oxidative degradation of organic matter, it commonly contains acidic functional groups, particularly carboxyls, phenols, and alcohols. These acid groups, which can be either weak or strong, can release or exchange hydrogen ions and bond coordinately to metals.

DOC is also heterogeneous in its origins and reactivity. Some DOC, particularly that generated within waterbodies, is biologically labile and is consumed by heterotrophic microbes within a few weeks of its formation. Other DOC, particularly that produced by the decay of woody plants, is biologically recalcitrant and may persist for hundreds or perhaps thousands of years in deep groundwater.

And finally, because it is both chemically and physically active and easily assimilated by microbes, DOC is of major ecological importance in surface waters. Chemically, it is the most abundant solute in many undisturbed natural waters and can control pH, form metal-organic complexes, and alter the solubility and availability of a variety of inorganic ions. Physically, it affects the absorption of light and, through that, photosynthesis and water temperature. Biologically, it is the major organic carbon source for microbes in many low-productivity waters and hence the basis of many food chains.

In the early decades of acid rain research, DOC was to a great extent a complication and a problem. It was a "nonanalytical" solute of variable acidity that interfered with Gran titrations, kept ion budgets from balancing, and created discrepancies between predicted and measured ANCs. It was an important complexing agent that buffered pH changes and altered the availability of several ions that researchers were trying to study. And it was the source of much natural acidity and so had to be carefully distinguished from the unnatural mineral acidity that acid rain researchers were trying to detect.

By the early 1990s, after a very focused combination of theoretical and applied research had been brought to bear, most of the complications were untangled and the DOC nuisance abated. The three main advances, which were interlinked, were that:

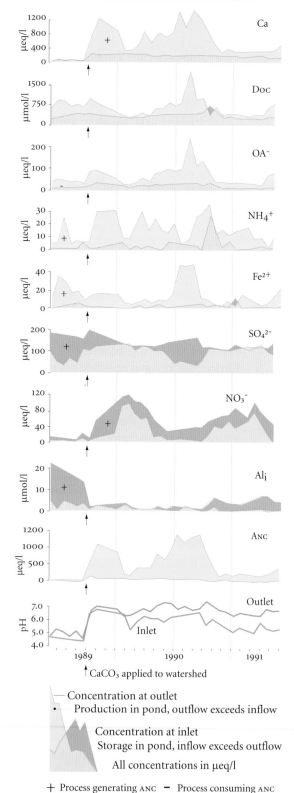

ION BUDGETS FOR THE WOODS LAKE BEAVER POND, AFTER WATERSHED LIMING

↑ CaCO₃ applied to watershed

— Concentration at outlet
· Production in pond, outflow exceeds inflow

Concentration at inlet
Storage in pond, inflow exceeds outflow

All concentrations in µeq/l

+ Process generating ANC − Process consuming ANC

DOC was realized to have functional groups of various strengths and so act as both a weak and a strong acid.

Complex but tractable models were developed that treated DOC as a triprotic acid and predicted pHs, ANCs, and the speciation of aluminum at different concentrations of DOC.

Specific diagnostics based on ion ratios (p. 50) were developed to separate natural acidity from atmospheric acidification.

Today, even after it has ceased to be a problem, DOC remains important. DOC concentrations, for unknown reasons, are usually low in lakes with mineral acidity (p. 75). Thus increases in DOC, even in advance of any increase in pH, are now considered to indicate the beginning of recovery. And less benignly, DOC is either a carrier of or a fellow-traveler with methylmercury, and lakes with high concentrations of DOC are at risk for elevated concentrations of methylmercury (p. 170).

The Sources of DOC

By 2000, much was known about the behavior of DOC – what sort of lakes it was associated with, what concentrations it was commonly found in, and how it influenced the chemistry of other elements. But less was known about where it came from and how it got to the lakes in the first place.

Certainly, some of the DOC comes from wetlands. DOC is produced by partial decay, and wetlands are filled with partially decayed plants. But watersheds contain different types of wetlands at different distances; do all the wetlands in a watershed contribute DOC equally or, as many researchers believed, do the wetlands closest to the lake contribute more than the ones farther from it?

Quite likely, some of the DOC comes from forests as well. Decay occurs in forest floors as well as wetlands, and since there are more forests than wetlands, it was certainly possible that some, perhaps even much, DOC originates in them.

These questions about DOC were both interesting in themselves and important because they led to larger questions about how watersheds work. Thus far, many field studies and essentially all modeling studies had treated watersheds as structureless – as boxes of a certain size and slope, with uniform vegetation and soils.

But since watersheds, of course, are not structureless, the question about the sources of DOC is also a question about whether the structure of watersheds matters. If it does not, then we can go on using compartment models like MAGIC and PnET-BGC (pp. 97, 122) that treat watersheds as boxes. If it does matter, then we need to construct spatially explicit models of watersheds containing the details of topography, vegetation, and soils.

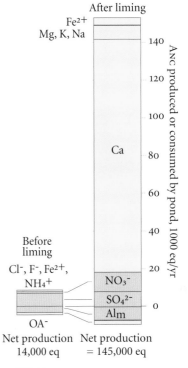

ANNUAL ANC BUDGET OF WOODS LAKE BEAVER POND

This figure and the one opposite redrawn with permission from Cirmo and Driscoll, "The impacts of a watershed CaCO3 treatment on stream and wetland biogeochemistry in the Adirondack Mountains." Copyright 1996 Springer Science and Business Media. The pond consumed acidity (generated ANC) before and after liming. Before liming it also generated organic acids and retained significant amounts of nitrate, sulfate, and aluminum. The retention of nitrate and sulfate produced ANC; the retention of aluminum consumed it. The lime added to the pond dissolved rapidly; the pond released more calcium than it received and so generated large amounts of ANC. In addition, the pond became more biologically active in a variety of ways: it retained more sulfate, nitrate, and aluminum and released more iron, ammonium, DOC, and base cations.

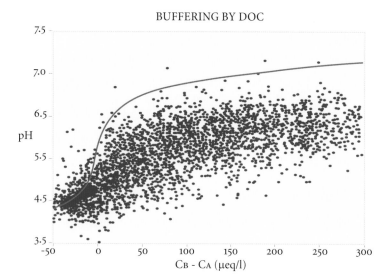

The first spatially explicit model of Adirondack watersheds is a model of DOC production created by Canham and his collaborators. It is interesting both because of what it suggests about the behavior of DOC and because it is the first Adirondack use of a computationally intense technique called inverse modeling to reconstruct element fluxes that are difficult to measure.

The inverse modeling procedure begins with data – in this case the DOC concentrations in 486 lakes and the vegetation at some 20 million grid points in their watersheds – and constructs a model that predicts the DOC contributions to a lake from different vegetation types at different distances. The model contains unknown parameters that describe how much DOC is produced by each vegetation type and how much of it is removed as it travels through the soils of the watershed.

The model is then run several million times – a process that takes a few days on a desktop computer – until it finds the values for the unknown parameters that give the best fit to the observed DOC concentrations.*

The results of the modeling were simple and surprising:

> Deciduous, evergreen, and mixed forests were very similar in their carbon outputs. All exported 37–47 kg of organic carbon per hectare year. Very little of the carbon was retained by watershed soils during transport and most of it reached the lakes.

> The main wetland types – conifer swamps and the three types of shrub swamps – were also surprisingly similar: all exported roughly four times as much organic carbon per hectare as the forests. Again, very little was lost on the way to the lakes.

The pH and the base-acid difference for the 1,469 lakes studied in the Adirondack Lakes Survey, from Munson, Driscoll, and Gherini, "Phenomenological analysis of ALSC chemistry data," in Baker et al., *Adirondack Lakes Survey: An Interpretive Analysis of Fish Communities and Water Chemistry, 1984-1987*, 1990. The red line is the theoretical curve for a solution that contains only strong acids and bases in equilibrium with atmospheric carbon dioxide. The observed values lie 0.5-1 pH unit below the theoretical curve, indicating that moderately strong organic acids associated with DOC are present; they also have a lower slope than the theoretical line, indicating that the organic acids are buffering pH changes. See the discussion on page 20 for a similar example.

AVERAGE DOC FLUXES TO MUIR POND

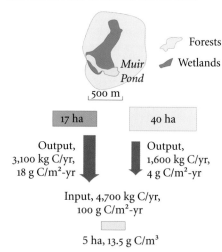

Dissolved carbon fluxes to Muir Pond, calculated from a spatially explicit model of DOC production. This and the diagram on the opposite page from Canham et al., "A spatially explicit watershed-scale analysis of dissolved organic carbon in Adirondack lakes," 2004. Muir Pond is a small lake with a high DOC loading. Its watershed is 30% wetlands, and two-thirds of the DOC reaching the pond is believed to come from these wetlands.

*Technically, the unknown parameters are obtained by maximum likelihood estimation: the model gives the likelihood of obtaining the observed data values for a given choice of the unknown parameters. The space of all possible values of the unknown parameters is then searched, using an procedure called simulated annealing, to find a value of the parameters that maximizes the likelihood.

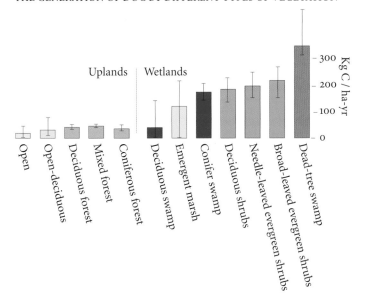

Average outputs of DOC for five types of uplands and seven types of wetlands, from a nonspatial analysis in which loading was independent of distance. From Canham et al., "A spatially explicit watershed-scale analysis of dissolved organic carbon in Adirondack lakes," 2004. The error bars are the 95% "support intervals" produced by a maximum-likelihood analysis. Considering the size of the error bars, there is relatively little difference between the different forest types and different wetland types but considerable difference between wetlands and uplands.

Emergent marshes and dead-tree swamps also exported significant amounts of carbon, but the carbon was removed by watershed soils within a few hundred meters, and so these types of wetlands only contributed to lake DOC when they were very close to the lakes.

Although wetland outputs per unit area were high, the total area of wetlands was usually less than the area of forests, and wetlands contributed, on average, only 30% of the carbon reaching lakes. Thus in most watersheds upland forests were the largest source of DOC, contributing an average of 70% of all DOC.

Because of the low loss rates for both forest and much wetland DOC, the more distant parts of the watersheds contributed as much or more DOC as the parts near the lake.

The DOC output per unit area from forests was low relative to annual production, representing at most 1%–2% of net ecosystem productivity. The output from wetlands was relatively larger, representing perhaps 10%–20% of net ecosystem productivity.

The diagrams of two sample watersheds, Clear Lake and Muir Pond, illustrate these results. Clear Lake has a moderate-sized watershed. Almost all the DOC comes from the forests. Because little is retained by watershed soils, all portions of the watershed contribute and the total load is high. But because the lake is relatively large, the loading per unit lake area is low. The concentrations in the lake are also low and the lake is in fact clear.

AVERAGE DOC FLUXES TO CLEAR LAKE

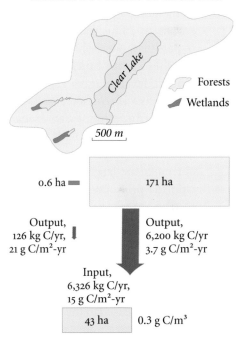

Clear Lake is larger than Muir Pond and has fewer wetlands in its watershed and only about a sixth the DOC input per unit area. The wetlands generate six times as much DOC as the forests per unit area but, because of their small total area, contribute only 2% of the DOC reaching the lake.

Muir Pond has small watershed that is one-third wetlands. The wetlands supply about two-thirds of the carbon reaching the lake. Because the pond is small, the flux per unit of pond surface is high, and the DOC concentrations in the pond are 40 times higher than those in Clear Lake. But interestingly, the DOC fluxes per unit area of forest or wetland are about the same as those in Clear Lake, indicating that long flowpaths in the large Clear Lake watershed are no less effective at transporting DOC than the shorter ones in the smaller Muir Pond watershed.

THE MERCURY PROBLEM AND THE MERCURY CYCLE

About Mercury

Mercury is a heavy, uncommon metal that, like many other heavy metals, is both toxic and useful. It is found naturally in trace quantities in air, water, coal, and many minerals. It is used commercially in medicines, amalgams, thermometers, many electronic devices, and many industrial processes. Its toxicity comes from its ability to pass through the blood-brain barrier and inhibit nerve development and nerve function. Young animals whose nervous systems are still developing are especially sensitive to mercury poisoning.

Mercury is released into the environment from natural sources, particularly volcanoes, wildfires, and weathering, and from industrial sources, particularly combustion, mining, and a variety of chemical processes. In the United States, coal-fired boilers are currently the largest single source, followed by gold mining and chlorine production. Waste incineration was a major U.S. source in 1990 but was regulated by the 1990 Clean Air Act Amendments and by 1999 had almost been eliminated.

Atmospheric mercury occurs in two forms, ionic mercury and elemental mercury. Ionic mercury is soluble in water and readily removed from the air by precipitation. Elemental mercury is relatively insoluble and can remain in the air for a year or more.

Once released in the environment, mercury has three peculiarities that make it unusually dangerous. First, unlike any of the other pollutants discussed here, it can stay in the air for long periods and cross continents and oceans. Second, it is easily converted by bacterial action to methylmercury, which is both more toxic and more easily absorbed by animals than ionic mercury. And third, the methylmercury acquired by animals binds to protein and is not readily excreted. Animals thus aquire it from the animals they eat, accumulate it through their lives, and pass it on to the animals that eat them.

Mercury's ability to bioaccumulate makes it dangerous in exceedingly small quantities. Mercury deposition rates in the Adirondacks are on the order of a 20th of a gram of mercury per

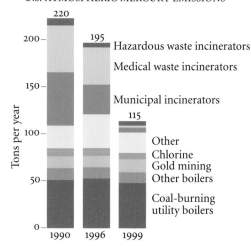

U.S. ATMOSPHERIC MERCURY EMISSIONS

Changes in U.S. mercury emissions, from EPA data available on-line at http://www.epa.gov/mercury. U.S. mercury emissions declined nearly 50% between 1990 and 1999. Almost all of the change was the result of improvements in incinerators. There was almost no change in emissions from coal-burning boilers (which now produce more than half of the U.S. mercury emissions) or the chloroalkali plants that use mercury to produce chlorine. Emissions from gold mines, which use mercury amalgams to extract gold from rocks, rose slightly.

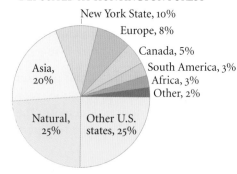

ESTIMATED SOURCES OF THE AIRBORNE MERCURY DEPOSITED AT HUNTINGTON FOREST

From Seigneur et al., "Contributions of global and regional sources to mercury deposition in New York State," 2003. The model used to estimate deposition has uncertainties but still indicates the global nature of the mercury problem.

hectare per year, equal to spreading the 10 grams of mercury from a clinical thermometer over 200 hectares. Mercury concentrations in Adirondack lakes are thus only a few parts per trillion, roughly a millionth of the sulfur concentrations, and methylmercury concentrations are roughly a tenth of this. But since animals retain much of the methylmercury they have eaten, top carnivores like loons, otters, and predatory fish may have tissue methylmercury concentrations of several parts per million, 1 million to 10 million times greater than that in the water.

The First Adirondack Mercury Studies

Until about 30 years ago mercury pollution was assumed to be a local problem of industrial areas, arising from industrial discharges to water. Thus, for example, the mercury pollution of Onondaga Lake from a chloroalkali plant had been known for many years. Much progress had been made in cleaning up industrial effluents, and in 1970 mercury pollution was to some extent regarded as an old problem, persisting near mines and in the lakes that had received the heaviest industrial discharges but still largely controlled and certainly not increasing.

That optimistic view of environmental mercury was dispelled when a DEC survey of mercury in sport fish discovered concentrations exceeding the U.S. limit of 1 part per million (ppm) in fish from wilderness lakes in northern New York. The survey collected 3,500 fish between 1969 and 1972. Ninety percent of them had mercury concentrations of less than the federal action level of 1 ppm, and most of the rest were from lakes like Onondaga that were known to be contaminated by industrial discharges. But several fish with high mercury concentrations came from Cranberry Lake and Stillwater Reservoir in the western Adirondacks.

Similar discoveries occurred elsewhere. Canadian and European researchers documented the accumulation of mercury in aquatic insects and fish; the microbial production of methylmercury in wetlands was discovered; and reports began to appear in the literature of mercury emissions from burning coal and associations between lake acidity and mercury levels in fish.

Thus by the middle 1970s there was a growing awareness that mercury could accumulate in remote lakes and a growing suspicion that the mercury was coming from the atmosphere and might be linked to acid deposition.

Two Adirondack studies in the late 1970s established that mercury pollution was widespread in the Adirondacks. In 1975 and 1977 Sloan and Schofield sampled fish and measured water chemistry in 15 small Adirondack lakes, 8 of which had recently been limed. They were trying to determine whether the liming affected the mercury concentrations in fish. They found no effect from

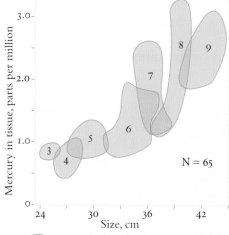

MERCURY IN SMALLMOUTH BASS FROM
CRANBERRY LAKE, 1969–1978

3 Range of values for three-year old fish

Redrawn with permission from Bloomfield et al., "Atmospheric and watershed inputs of mercury to Cranberry Lake, St. Lawrence County, New York." Copyright 1980 Springer Science and Business Media. As fish grow older, the concentration of mercury in their tissue increases, both because they retain much of the mercury they have consumed and because they take larger prey and eat higher on the food chain.

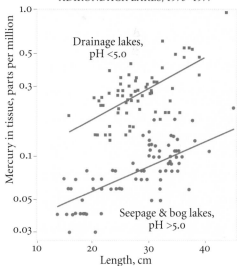

MERCURY IN BROOK TROUT FROM
ADIRONDACK LAKES, 1975–1977

From Sloan and Schofield, "Mercury levels in brook trout (*Salvelinus fontinalis*) from selected acid and limed Adirondack lakes," 1983. The mercury concentrations in tissue increase with the size of the fish and are three times greater in low-pH lakes.

liming but did find a surprising difference between lake types: the fish from the drainage lakes they studied, which even after liming had pHs below 5.0, were carrying three times as much mercury as the fish from seepage and bog lakes, which had higher pHs. Their report, in 1983, was the first to document a pH-mercury relation for Adirondack lakes.

In 1978, Jay Bloomfield and Scott Quinn of the New York State DEC and their collaborators returned to Cranberry Lake to try to identify the sources of the mercury. They performed a remarkable study, anticipating many of the questions and methods that were to become standard a decade later. They collected samples of mercury in deposition, snowpack, lake and stream water, lake sediments, and fish. They estimated mercury fluxes, documented mercury accumulation in fish and sediments, and tried to prepare a mercury budget for the lake. They were limited by the sensitivity of their methods and, as in all mercury research prior to about 1985, by problems of contamination. As a result, despite asking the right questions and making the right measurements, they were unable to show that the mercury in Cranberry Lake was coming from acid rain. "It cannot be concluded," they said in summary, "that direct atmospheric sources are responsible for the elevated mercury levels in either lake water or fish flesh." But they still suspected an acid-mercury connection and speculated that "it seems likely that the acidity of precipitation is somehow modifying the chemical nature of the mercury present in Cranberry Lake water, availing the mercury to the food web."

Mercury and Fish in the 1980s and 1990s

The mercury studies of the 1970s were limited by analytical problems. The quantities of mercury in fish, which were in the 0 to 5 parts-per-million range, could be reliably measured by the equipment then available. But the quantities of mercury in the air and in the lakes were in the parts-per-trillion range, and the quantities of methylmercury ten times lower yet. Researchers in the 1970s could make rough measurements in the parts-per-trillion range but, because of both equipment problems and contamination problems, could not perform reliable analyses at this level.

By the mid-1980s, new equipment and new ultraclean protocols had made nanogram-level analyses reliable, and it was finally possible to make accurate comparisons of mercury levels in fish and mercury levels in the lakes where the fish lived.

Two Adirondack studies immediately took advantage of the new methods. The first was a 1987 study of yellow perch in 12 Adirondack lakes by Simonin and his associates; the second, which also involved yellow perch, was a study of 16 lakes by Driscoll and his associates in 1992.

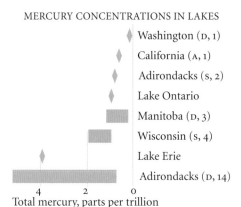

MERCURY CONCENTRATIONS IN LAKES

Washington (D, 1)
California (A, 1)
Adirondacks (S, 2)
Lake Ontario
Manitoba (D, 3)
Wisconsin (S, 4)
Lake Erie
Adirondacks (D, 14)

4   2   0
Total mercury, parts per trillion

A Alpine lake   D Drainage lakes   S Seepage lake
12 Number of lakes

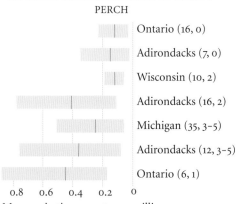

MERCURY CONCENTRATIONS IN YELLOW PERCH

Ontario (16, 0)
Adirondacks (7, 0)
Wisconsin (10, 2)
Adirondacks (16, 2)
Michigan (35, 3-5)
Adirondacks (12, 3-5)
Ontario (6, 1)

0.8   0.6   0.4   0.2   0
Mercury in tissue, parts per million

(12, 3-5) Number of lakes, age class of fish

Data for upper graph from Driscoll et al., "The mercury cycle and fish in Adirondack lakes," 1994. Bars give a range of reported values; diamonds, a single value. Because of analytical difficulties, much less information is available on mercury concentrations in lake water than in fish. In 1994, the Adirondack concentrations were among the highest ever reported in remote North American lakes.

Data for lower graph from Driscoll et al., "The role of dissolved organic carbon in the chemistry and bioavailabity of mercury in remote Adirondack lakes," 1995. Compare with the map of mercury deposition on page 173. Mercury pollution is now very widespread, and the concentrations in Adirondack fish are generally similar to those of fish of the same size elsewhere in the Northeast.

Both studies found widespread mercury contamination in fish from drainage lakes. Mercury concentrations in fish tissue ranged from 0.2 to 1.2 ppm. The first study found fish exceeding the proposed EPA action level of 0.3 ppm in 11 of 12 lakes. The second found fish exceeding the proposed level in 15 of 16 lakes and average mercury concentrations in older fish of 0.45 ppm, 50% above the proposed guidelines.

The second study also provided the first accurate Adirondack determinations of the mercury and methylmercury concentrations in the lakes from which the fish came. Total mercury concentrations were 0.8 to 5.3 parts per trillion (ppt), of which 40% was particulate mercury and 60% dissolved mercury. Methylmercury concentrations were 0.07 to 0.6 ppt; they averaged about 10% of the total mercury concentration in oxygenated lakes and 20% of the total mercury concentration in lakes with an anoxic lower layer.

Both the concentrations in water and those in fish were high by U.S. standards. Comparable concentrations of mercury in fish from remote lakes had been reported in the upper Midwest and Ontario but not elsewhere in the Northeast. Comparable concentrations of mercury in water had, thus far, been reported only from lakes with industrial pollution.

Several things about the mercury concentrations were chemically and ecologically suggestive. The overall northeastern geography of mercury pollution in remote lakes suggested a connection with acid rain; the local association between low pHs and high mercury levels made it even more likely. An association between shoreline wetlands, anoxic lake bottoms, and high methylmercury levels was consistent with the notion that methylmercury was produced from ionic mercury by bacterial reduction in oxygen-limited habitats; a parallel association between dissolved organic carbon and methylmercury suggested that organic carbon, which is produced in wetlands, was binding to methylmercury and transporting it downstream. Bloomfield and Quinn's prescient statement 15 years earlier that the acidity of precipitation was modifying the chemistry and availability of mercury was, though still not explained, strikingly confirmed.

The Mercury Cycle

As a result of these and other studies, there was by the mid-1990s a reasonable picture of the generation of atmospheric mercury and the pathways by which it was reaching lakes and entering food chains:

METHYLMERCURY AND DOC

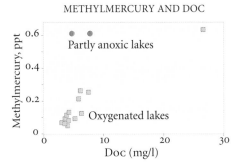

METHYLMERCURY AND pH

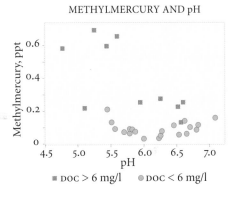

MERCURY IN YELLOW PERCH FROM ADIRONDACK LAKES

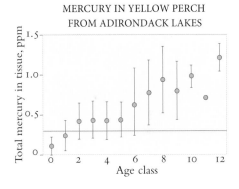

Redrawn with permission from with Driscoll et al., "The role of dissolved organic carbon in the chemistry and bioavailabity of mercury in remote Adirondack lakes." Copyright 1995 Springer Science and Business Media. The upper two graphs give methylmercury concentrations in lake water in parts per trillion. Methylmercury levels correlate with oxygen status and DOC concentrations and with pH in high-DOC lakes but not low-DOC lakes.

The third graph shows tissue mercury levels in yellow perch. The red line is the proposed EPA action level of 0.3 µg/g. Mercury concentrations increase with the size of the fish, both because older fish have had more time to accumulate mercury and because they feed higher up the food chain.

THE MERCURY CYCLE IN ADIRONDACK LAKES

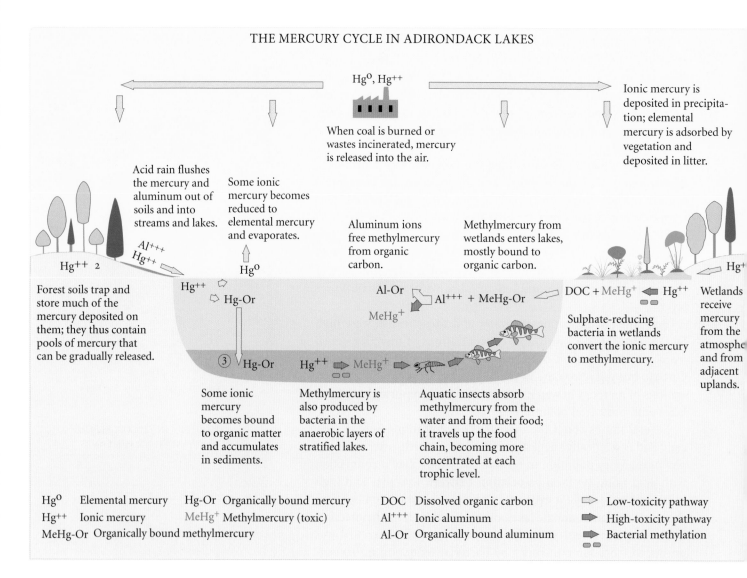

Hg°, Hg++

When coal is burned or wastes incinerated, mercury is released into the air.

Ionic mercury is deposited in precipitation; elemental mercury is adsorbed by vegetation and deposited in litter.

Acid rain flushes the mercury and aluminum out of soils and into streams and lakes.

Some ionic mercury becomes reduced to elemental mercury and evaporates.

Aluminum ions free methylmercury from organic carbon.

Methylmercury from wetlands enters lakes, mostly bound to organic carbon.

Al+++
Hg++
Hg++ 2
Hg°

Forest soils trap and store much of the mercury deposited on them; they thus contain pools of mercury that can be gradually released.

Hg++
Hg-Or

Al-Or
Al+++ + MeHg-Or
MeHg+

DOC + MeHg+ ← Hg++

Wetlands receive mercury from the atmosphere and from adjacent uplands.

Sulphate-reducing bacteria in wetlands convert the ionic mercury to methylmercury.

Hg+

③ Hg-Or   Hg++ ➡ MeHg+ ➡

Some ionic mercury becomes bound to organic matter and accumulates in sediments.

Methylmercury is also produced by bacteria in the anaerobic layers of stratified lakes.

Aquatic insects absorb methylmercury from the water and from their food; it travels up the food chain, becoming more concentrated at each trophic level.

Hg°	Elemental mercury	Hg-Or	Organically bound mercury
Hg++	Ionic mercury	MeHg+	Methylmercury (toxic)
MeHg-Or	Organically bound methylmercury		

DOC	Dissolved organic carbon
Al+++	Ionic aluminum
Al-Or	Organically bound aluminum

⇨ Low-toxicity pathway
➡ High-toxicity pathway
➡ Bacterial methylation

Mercury is emitted in very small quantities from incinerators, coal-burning furnaces, mining, and some industrial processes. Many of the sources are the same as the sources of acid rain.

Airborne mercury may be elemental mercury, a gas, or ionic mercury, which may be either dissolved or particulate.

Ionic mercury is deposited, mostly in wet deposition, within a few hundred kilometers of its source. Elemental mercury can remain in the air for a year or more and be transported completely around the world.

Elemental mercury and gaseous and particulate ionic mercury can also be deposited in dry form: they accumulate in tree crowns and are washed down in rain and snow, or bind to plant tissue and are deposited in plant litter.

Drawing based on Driscoll et al., "The mercury cycle and fish in Adirondack lakes," 1994; adapted from a drawing in Jenkins, *The Adirondack Atlas*, 2004.

Some of the deposited mercury accumulates in soil, mostly as ionic mercury. The rest is reduced to elemental mercury, evaporates, and reenters the atmosphere.

The ionic mercury stored in soils migrates, often in association with dissolved organic carbon, to lakes and wetlands.

Under reducing conditions in wetlands and the lower parts of lakes, bacteria convert ionic mercury to methylmercury. Where stored sulfates are abundant and the rate of sulfate reduction high, the rate of methylation is also high.

Methylmercury is transported from wetlands to lakes either along with or bound to DOC. Where DOC production is high, the rate of methylmercury transport is also high, but (because DOC binds methylmercury) the bioavailability of methylmercury is low.

Aluminum ions in lakes compete with methylmercury for the organic carbon, releasing free methylmercury.

Free methylmercury, which is highly toxic, enters plankton and invertebrates and then is passed up the food chain, concentrating at each step.

Methylmercury concentrations in fish tissue increase with the size and age of the fish and, either because of differences in the availability of methylmercury or because of the slow growth rates of fish in acidic lakes, are usually higher in fish from low-pH lakes than in fish from high-pH lakes. Virtually all of the mercury in fish is the highly toxic methylmercury.

The methylmercury in fish is passed up the food chain to fishing-eating birds and mammals, particularly loons, ospreys, eagles, mink, and otters.

Recent Mercury Research

In the past ten years much research has gone into quantifying each of the steps in the mercury cycle. Because of the very small quantities of mercury involved, doing this took careful sampling and very clean chemistry. But interestingly, once laboratories learned

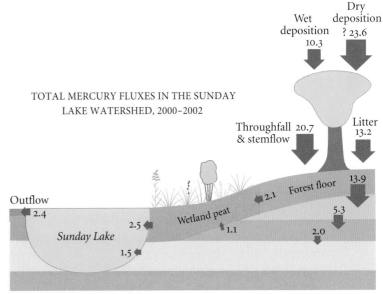

TOTAL MERCURY FLUXES IN THE SUNDAY LAKE WATERSHED, 2000–2002

◀ Annual total mercury flux, μg/m²-yr

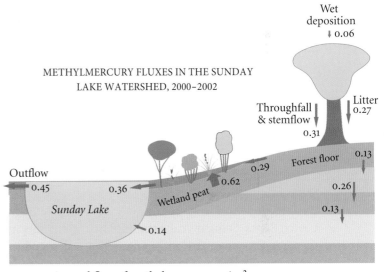

METHYLMERCURY FLUXES IN THE SUNDAY LAKE WATERSHED, 2000–2002

◀— Annual flux of methylmercury, μg/m²-yr

From Driscoll et al., "Chemical and biological control of mercury cycling in upland, wetland, and lake ecosystems in the northeastern U.S.," 2004. Sunday Lake is a small pond in the western Adirondacks with a 240-hectare watershed that is 20% wetlands. Inorganic mercury arrives in dry and wet deposition, is stored in soils, and is transmitted to wetlands and lakes. As was the case with the Pancake Hall Creek beaver pond (p. 170), the wetlands are net sources of mercury. Methylmercury is almost absent from deposition. It is generated from ionic mercury in very small amounts in the forest floor and in larger amounts (though still in the micrograms per square meter range) in wetlands.

to work reliably in the subnanogram range, it did not require any really new tools. The basic techniques – deposition studies, sediment cores, synoptic surveys, mass-balance studies – that had been used with great effectiveness in other acid deposition research proved equally effective in studying mercury.

Because of the speed at which the mercury story is developing, it is too early to give a full account of the mercury cycle. Instead, we comment briefly on what has been learned about each of the main steps.

Emissions. Current estimates are that about 60% of total mercury in the atmosphere comes from human activities and 40% from natural sources. In the United States, the EPA estimates that in 1999, 52% of emissions came from coal-fired boilers, 10% from gold mining, 7% from waste incinerators, 6% from chlorine production, and the remainder from other sources. Total U.S. emissions have been reduced greatly since 1990, mostly through emission controls on incinerators.

Long-distance transport. Because elemental mercury can remain airborne for a year or more, mercury pollution is increasingly a global problem. Mercury from Asia, which emits five times as much mercury as North America, can easily reach the United States and Canada. The EPA estimates that about half the mercury deposited in the United States originates in other countries and that only a third of the mercury emitted in the United States is deposited in the United States. Seineur et al. estimated that about 60% of the mercury deposited at Huntington Forest originated in the United States and 40% in other countries.

Wet deposition. Mercury deposition has been measured since 1995 by the Mercury Deposition Network, a part of the National Acid Deposition Network. The mercury network now has about 50 stations. Adirondack precipitation contains on average about 7 parts per trillion of mercury, roughly twice as high as average Adirondack lake concentrations. Total wet deposition for 2001 was estimated at 6.3 µg/m²-yr (p. 172), about half the maximum rate in the Midwest and along the Gulf Coast and 50% higher than the rate in northern New England.

Dry deposition. Dry deposition to tree crowns is estimated by the amount of mercury in throughflow, stemflow, and litter. Often the rates of dry deposition equal or exceed those of wet deposition.

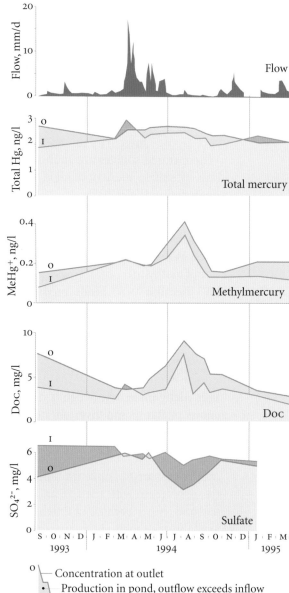

MERCURY FLUXES IN THE PANCAKE HALL CREEK BEAVER POND, 1993–1995

O — Concentration at outlet
• Production in pond, outflow exceeds inflow
— Concentration at inlet
I Storage in pond, inflow exceeds outflow

Redrawn with permission from Driscoll et al., "The chemistry and transport of mercury in a small wetland in the Adirondack region of New York, USA." Copyright 1998 Springer Science and Business Media. One ng/l is one part per trillion. When the blue line is above the brown, the outflow concentration exceeds the inflow and the pond is generating that ion or element. For much of the study period the Pancake Hall Creek beaver pond stored sulfate and released both ionic mercury and methylmercury.

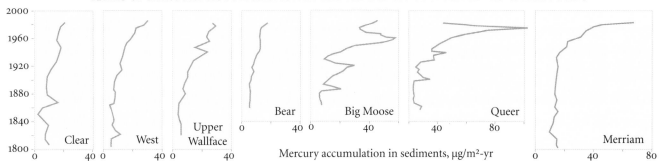

RATES OF MERCURY ACCUMULATION IN THE SEDIMENTS OF SEVEN ADIRONDACK PONDS

In the Sunday Lake watershed the total deposition for 2000–2002 was estimated at 34 µg/m²-yr, of which about 30% was wet deposition and 70% dry deposition.

Accumulation of mercury in soils. Mercury deposited in soils accumulates in the forest floor and other layers that are rich in organic matter, almost entirely in ionic form. Mercury outputs from forest soils are usually less than the inputs, suggesting that mercury is either being stored in the soil or returned to the atmosphere.

Mercury transport. Mercury is exported from the forest floor in groundwater, often in association with dissolved organic carbon. Some of it is immobilized in the mineral soil, some transported to streams and lakes, and some transported to wetlands. At each stage some of it may be stored or lost to the atmosphere. At Sunday Lake, only 7% of the mercury arriving in the watershed each year appeared at the lake output (p. 169).*

Generation of methylmercury. Methylmercury concentrations in precipitation are very low – typically less than 0.5 ppt – and most of the methylmercury reaching lakes seems to be generated locally by the bacterial methylation of ionic mercury. This occurs to some extent in forest canopies and upland soils but is most common in wet anaerobic situations, particularly wetlands and the bottom water and sediments of stratified lakes. In the Sunday Lake watershed small amounts of methylmercury were produced in the forest canopy and larger and ecologically more significant amounts in riparian wetlands.

Much or all of the methylation of mercury in wetlands seems to be done by sulfate-reducing bacteria. These are anaerobic (and apparently very ancient) bacteria that use sulfate as an electron acceptor, in much the same way that many other organisms use oxygen. Their principal metabolic activity is oxidizing carbon and reducing sulfate; their methylation seems to be either a sideline or an accident. They flourish where organic carbon and sulfate are common. Because wetlands affected by acid deposition commonly

From Lorey and Driscoll, "Historical trends of mercury deposition in Adirondack lakes." Copyright 1999 American Chemical Society. Presettlement fluxes of mercury to lake sediments are estimated at 3.4 µg/m²-yr for a lake with a watershed-to-lake surface ratio of 1. Most lakes have watershed-to-surface ratios greater than 1 and the deposition rates are correspondingly larger. On average, current deposition rates are about three times presettlement rates, with most of the increase since 1880. In several of the lakes the accumulation graph is concave, suggesting accelerating trends.

*At Sunday Lake, total mercury inputs to the forest floor ranged from 8 to 189 ng/g. Inputs from deposition were 34 µg/m²-yr and outputs about 5 µg/m²-yr, suggesting that 85% of the incoming mercury is stored or revolatilized.

have lots of stored sulfate and high levels of sulfate reduction, acid-affected waters often have mercury problems as well.

The connection between sulfate reduction and methylmercury generation is shown elegantly in a 1993-1995 study of the mercury budget of a beaver pond on Pancake Hall Creek by Driscoll and his colleagues (p. 170). The beaver pond was a source of both mercury and methylmercury for much of the year. Methylmercury production peaked in summer, when the flow was lowest and the pond least oxygenated, and coincided with peaks in sulfate reduction and DOC production, both indicators of anaerobic decay. Ionic mercury outputs were much less seasonal and not strongly tied to other chemical processes.

Transport and complexing. Methylmercury binds to organic carbon, and dissolved organic carbon concentrations in lakes correlate well with methylmercury concentrations. Because wetlands generate both DOC and methylmercury, this implicates them doubly in the mercury cycle. Grigal, in his recent review of terrestrial mercury fluxes, notes the connection: "Wetlands therefore increase MeHg flux from terrestrial to aquatic systems both because they act as sites of production and because they increase water residence time. … It is ironic that wetlands, sacred landscape elements that both regulation and legislation attempt to protect from disturbance, are the single most identifiable source of MeHg from terrestrial to aquatic systems."

Accumulation of mercury in lake sediments. Lorey and Driscoll took eight Adirondack lake cores gathered by the PIRLA-I project in 1982-1983, divided them into short segments, dated the segments with lead isotopes, and analyzed them for mercury. The resulting mercury accumulation curves (p. 171) look very like the curves for lake acidification. They show slow and relatively constant preindustrial mercury fluxes of 5 to 12 µg/m²-yr, increasing sometime between 1870 and 1990 to contemporary rates of 18 to 64 µg/m²-yr. The flux ratio, the ratio of the modern rate to the presettlement rate, averages 3.5, quite comparable to rates determined in similar studies in the central United States (3.7), Quebec (2.1), and Sweden (3.0).

Accumulation of mercury in watersheds. The rate at which mercury is stored in watersheds cannot be measured directly but can be estimated by the difference between the amount of mercury stored in lake sediments and the total amount of mercury deposited in the watershed. The former can be determined directly from the mercury accumulation curves on page 171; the later by plotting the deposition rate against the watershed area-lake area ratio, as in the graph on page 172. The results suggest that in preindustrial times,

ESTIMATED MERCURY DEPOSITION RATES

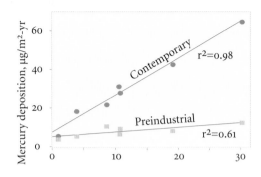

AVERAGE MERCURY RETENTION FOR
SEVEN ADIRONDACK WATERSHEDS

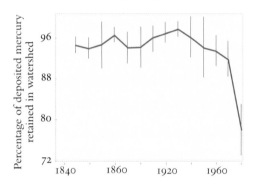

Both graphs redrawn with permission from Lorey and Driscoll, "Historical trends of mercury generation in Adirondack lakes." Copyright 1999 American Chemical Society. Some clever arithmetic is used to get retention rates. The idea is that the rate at which mercury reaches a lake depends on the average rate of deposition in the watershed, the ratio of watershed area to lake area (big watersheds supply more mercury per unit area of lake), and the fraction of the deposited mercury the watershed retains. Average rates of deposition in the lake are calculated for each time interval of each core. Extrapolating a plot of these rates to a watershed-lake ratio of 1 (top graph) gives an estimate of the average rate of deposition for all watersheds in that period. From the observed deposition rate in a particular lake and the watershed-lake ratio for its watershed, the retention rate for that watershed can be calculated.

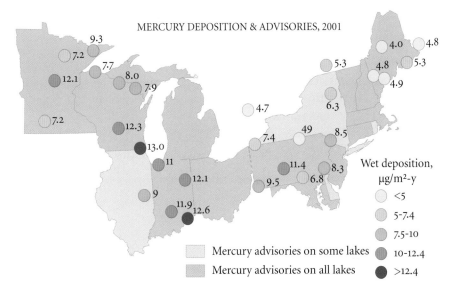

MERCURY DEPOSITION & ADVISORIES, 2001

Wet deposition, μg/m²-y

⊙ <5
⊙ 5-7.4
⊙ 7.5-10
⊙ 10-12.4
● >12.4

☐ Mercury advisories on some lakes
▨ Mercury advisories on all lakes

Data from the website of the National Acid Deposition Program, http://nadp.sws.uiuc.edu/nadpdata/annualReq.asp?site=NY20, based on samples analyzed by the Mercury Deposition Network.

the watersheds exported 5% of the mercury they received to lakes and stored or volatilized the remaining 95%; they are now passing 22% to the lakes and storing or volatilizing 78%.

Bioaccumulation. Because the accumulation of mercury in fish and animals represents a hazard for both wildlife and humans, it has been much studied. A full review is beyond the scope of this chapter. Forty-eight states now have advisories warning against the consumption of fish because of mercury contamination. In the Adirondack region there are advisories for 32 lakes because of high mercury levels. A recent statistical sampling of fish from Vermont and New Hampshire suggests that yellow perch from 40% of the lakes in the two states are likely to have methylmercury concentrations exceeding the proposed EPA criterion of 0.3 parts per million.

In the past ten years researchers have found elevated mercury levels in loons, eagles, ducks, terns, songbirds, otters, mink, and other wildlife species. The literature, which again is beyond what we can review here, suggests that in much of the northeastern United States and eastern Canada, a significant proportion of loons and at least some otters and mink are carrying tissue concentrations of mercury sufficient to alter their reproductive success.

SUMMARY

1 The limited number of studies we have of wetlands indicate that they are *biogeochemically active* and carry out transformations important to the chemistry of acid rain. They fix nitrogen, store nitrates, variously consume and regenerate sulfates and ANC, generate DOC, and methylate mercury. Their activities differ greatly

MERCURY IN ADIRONDACK LOONS, 1998–2000

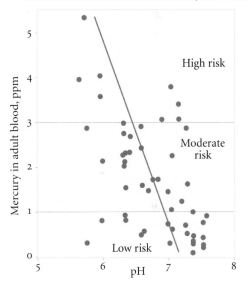

From Schoch and Evers, "Monitoring mercury in common loons: New York field report, 1998-2000," 2002. The data come from 57 adult loons captured on 43 lakes. Nine adult birds (16%) had blood mercury levels of 3 ppm or more, in the range where behavioral effects are visible and reproductive success is likely impaired. Another 51% of adults had blood mercury levels of 1-3 ppm and were at a moderate risk of physiological or behavioral effects. There is a significant correlation between low lake pH and high tissue mercury levels but also much scatter around the correlation.

from season to season and year to year and seem strongly tied to vegetation growth, temperature, and rainfall.

2 The DOC *produced by wetlands* is a keystone substance in aquatic ecosystems, acting as a nutrient, an acid, a buffer, and a complexing agent that alters the solubility of other ions. A recent modeling study suggests that forests generate more total DOC than wetlands, and that DOC from the upper parts of watersheds can reach lakes with surprisingly little loss.

3 Mercury appears to be an *acid-associated* pollutant, sharing sources with acid deposition, being transported and deposited in similar ways, and accumulating in soils in the same way. It is of concern because it is highly toxic and because it bioaccumulates in animal tissue and reaches concentrations 1 million to 10 million times higher than those in the environment.

4 The *cycling* of mercury in remote forests and lakes is currently of great chemical and ecological interest. Significant mercury concentrations were first detected in Adirondack fish around 1970. The concentrations of mercury in lake water were first measured in the early 1990s. The first studies of mercury accumulation in sediments were done in the late 1990s; the first mass-balance studies of Adirondack mercury cycling began in 2000.

5 *Adirondack mercury* seems to originate largely from atmospheric deposition and predominantly (70%) from dry deposition; it is retained in upland soils, transported by DOC, and methylated in wetlands and lake sediments, especially where sulfate is abundant.

6 The *bioaccumulation of methylmercury* is also an active research topic. Methylmercury is affecting sport fisheries throughout the Northeast and is now present in about two-thirds of Adirondack loons in quantities thought to pose a moderate or high risk to their survival.

7 Although there is no direct link between *lake pHs and mercury concentrations*, mercury concentrations in fish tissue are highest in fish from low-pH lakes, probably because of differences in growth rates and the lengths of food chains.

NOTES

p. 153 For a useful review of studies of acid deposition and wetlands, see Gorham, Bailey, and Schindler, "Ecological effects of acid deposition on peatlands: A neglected field in 'acid rain' research," 1984.

p. 161 For the chemistry of DOC, see Driscoll, Fuller, and Schecher, "The role or organic acids in the acidification of surface waters in the eastern U.S.," 1989; Hemond, "Acid-neutralizing capacity, alkalinity, and acid-base status of natural waters containing organic acids," 1990; Munson and Gherini, "Influence of organic acids on the pH and acid-neutralizing capacity of Adirondack lakes," 1993; and Driscoll, Lehtinen, and Sullivan, "Modeling the acid-base chemistry or organic solutes in Adirondack, New York, lakes," 1994.

p. 165 For mercury emissions, see the EPA website http://www.epa.gov/mercury. For mercury cycling, see Driscoll et al., "The mercury cycle and fish in Adirondack lakes", 1994; Driscoll et al., "Chemical and biological control of mercury cycling in upland, wetland, and lake ecosystems in the northeastern U.S.," 2004; and Grigal, "Inputs and outputs of mercury from terrestrial watersheds: A review," 2002.

p. 173 The figures for New Hampshire and Vermont are from Kasmman et al., "Assessment of mercury in waters, sediments, and biota of New Hampshire and Vermont lakes, USA, sampled using a geographically randomized design," 2003. For entrance points to the rapidly growing literature on the effects of mercury on wildlife, see Parker, "Common loon reproduction and chick feeding on acidified lakes in the Adirondack Park, New York," 1988; Evers et al., "Geographic trends in mercury measured in common loon feathers and blood," 1998; and a recent collection of 21 papers on mercury and wildlife edited by Evers and Clair, *Biogeographical patterns of environmental mercury in northeastern North America*, 2005. The Biodiversity Research Institute, *www.briloon.org*, is an excellent online source for recent data on wildlife and mercury.

WETLANDS, DOC AND MERCURY, 1969-2003

1969-1972 The DEC analyzes 3,500 fish from New York waters for mercury and finds fish with high mercury levels in Stillwater Reservoir and Cranberry Lake.

1975-1977 Sloan and Schofield determine mercury levels in fish from 15 small Adirondack lakes and show that mercury levels are higher in drainage lakes with pHs below 5 than in bog and seepage lakes with higher pHs.

1976 The DEC begins the Toxic Substances Monitoring Program, which analyzes fish for mercury, PCBs, and other contaminants.

1978-1980 Bloomfield et al. study mercury at Cranberry Lake. They are able to demonstrate the bioaccumulation of mercury in fish but unable to identify the source of the mercury.

1983-1988 Lazerte studies the mass balance of a conifer swamp in a part of Ontario that receives heavy deposition. He finds that the swamp is exporting hydrogen ions, organic acid anions, and base cations and that it stores sulfate in wet years and exports it in dry ones.

ca. 1985 Clean protocols for the sampling and analysis of nanogram quantities of mercury are developed.

1989 The final report of the Adirondack Biota Project concludes that DOC tends to ameliorate the toxic effects of aluminum and hydrogen ion on biological communities.

1989-1992 Cirmo and Driscoll study the mass balance of an Adirondack beaver pond whose watershed has been limed. Before liming, the beaver pond retained acidity and generated ANC at a low rate. Liming accelerated all its biological transformations: it retained more sulfate, nitrate, and aluminum and released more iron, ammonium, DOC, and base cations.

1990 The Adirondack Lakes Survey finds that the observed pHs of many Adirondack lakes are lower than would be expected if they contained only water and atmospheric carbon dioxide. They attribute the difference to organic acids.

1990-1991 Cirmo and Driscoll study the mass balance of another small beaver pond in the Adirondacks. They find that it retains aluminum, sulfate, and nitrate and exports ammonium, ferrous iron, DOC, and ANC.

1993 Munson and Gherini use the ALS data to evaluate the contribution of organic acids to the observed pHs and ANCs of Adirondack lakes. They find that, contrary

to what has been believed, organic acids can behave as strong acids and produce negative values of ANC.

1994 Driscoll, Lehtinen, and Sullivan use the ALS data to test various models of organic acids. They find that a triprotic acid model fits the data best and, corroborating Munson and Gherini's work, that even at pHs below 4.0, some of the organic acids are ionized.

1994 Simonin et al. find significant levels of mercury in fish from Adirondack lakes.

1995 The National Trends Network begins the monitoring of mercury in wet deposition at 13 stations.

1995 Driscoll et al. find correlations between pH, DOC, and methylmercury in Adirondack lakes.

1995-1996 Mitchell and his collaborators at Huntington Forest begin a series of studies on nitrogen cycling in a forested wetland in the Arbutus watershed.

1998 Driscoll et al. determine the mercury budget for a small beaver pond and determine that the pond is exporting both mercury and methylmercury.

1999 Monitoring of mercury in wet deposition begins at Huntington Forest.

1999 Lorey and Driscoll analyze eight lake cores for mercury. They find that the rates of mercury accumulation have increased in the past 150 years and are now 3.5 times the presettlement rates.

2004 Driscoll et al. describe the mercury cycle of the Sunday Lake watershed.

1998-2004 The Adirondack Park Agency creates the first detailed maps of Adirondack wetlands.

2003 Canham et al. use inverse modeling to determine the amounts of DOC produced by different types of forests and wetlands. They determine that although wetlands produce more DOC per unit area than forests, because watersheds contain more forests than wetlands and because DOC can apparently travel through watersheds with only small losses, forests generate the majority of DOC in many watersheds.

2003 Hrabik and Watras report that decreases in mercury deposition and sulfate concentrations since 1990 have combined to produce a 57% decrease in the mercury concentration of fish in an experimental lake in Wisconsin.

1929-1934 The New York State Conservation Department conducts a statewide biological survey of lakes and rivers.

1976 Schofield surveys 217 Adirondack lakes and reports that 90% of the lakes with pHs of less than 5.0 are fishless.

1977 Schindler et al. begin the experimental acidification of Lake 223 in the Experimental Lakes Area of northwestern Ontario. As they decrease the pH from 6.13 to 5.02, they observe dramatic changes in the abundance of plankton, insects, algae, and fish.

1979 Confer, Kaaret, and Likens sample 20 small lakes in the Adirondacks and White Mountains and find that the more acidic lakes have lower zooplankton diversity and biomass.

1979 Colquhoun et al. find that Adirondack streams with springtime pHs of less than 5.5 tend to be fishless.

1980 Driscoll et al. show that waters with elevated concentrations of inorganic aluminum are toxic to white sucker fry.

1982-1984 As part of the Regionalized Integrated Lake-Watershed Acidification Study, Johnson et al. testcaged fish in the North Branch of the Moose River and show that the high aluminum concentrations during acid episodes can kill adult fish.

1984 The Adirondack Biota Project surveys the water chemistry, plankton, fish, and vegetation of 50 Adirondack lakes and concludes that "Low-pH waters contained simple communities, while the more complex communities were restricted to the higher pH, circumneutral waters. Toxicity related to low pH and, presumably, to high aluminum levels acts to simplify communities."

1984-1987 The Adirondack Lakes Survey conducts biological and chemical surveys of 1,469 Adirondack lakes.

1985 Brezonik et al. divide Little Rock Lake in Wisconsin in half and reduce the pH from 6.1 to pH 5.1 over the next two years. They observe changes in plankton, insects, and algae.

1987-1990 The Lake Acidification and Fisheries Project does an extended laboratory investigation of the physiological responses of brook trout to acidic waters.

1988-90 As part of the Episodic Response Project, which monitors four Adirondack streams during snowmelt and other acid episodes, Simonin, et al. show that the mortality of brook trout and blacknose dace increases during acid episodes.

1990-91 The Adirondack Lakes Survey issues its *Interpretive Analysis,* which finds strong correlations between fish diversity and acidity: because of acidification, sensitive minnows are now absent from at least 19% of the lakes where they once occurred, and brook trout from at least 11% of the lakes in which they once occurred. It examines 346 fishless lakes and, after eliminating other causes of fishlessness, concludes that "the estimated number of surveyed waters for which mineral acids (and acidic deposition) appear to be the primary cause for the lack of fish is 100-113, or about 30% of the fishless lakes surveyed by ALSC."

1990 The National Acid Precipitation Assessment Program's report on the biological effects of surface-water acidification concludes that: "A number of the species that currently occur in surface waters susceptible to acidic deposition cannot survive, reproduce, or compete in acidic waters." They suggest that changes in composition and diversity occur at pHs below 6.0-6.5, and changes in basic ecological processes at pHs below 5.0-5.5.

1991-1994 The Environmental Protection Agency's Environmental Monitoring and Assessment Program, created to "monitor and assess the ecological health of major ecosystems," begins and then ends the biological monitoring of randomly selected Adirondack lakes.

1993 Baker et al. reexamine the ALS fish data. Using estimates of historical acidification from the PIRLA studies (p. 81), they find that the more a lake has acidified, the more fish populations it is likely to have lost.

1994 The U.S. Environmental Protection Agency creates the Adirondack Effects Assessment Program to monitor the biological recovery of 30 acidified lakes.

FISH, ACIDS, AND AQUATIC ECOLOGY

THE BIOLOGICAL EFFECTS OF ACIDIFICATION ARE REVISITED AND DECISIVELY PROVEN

In the 1970s, very little was known about the biology of acidification except that it killed fish and probably other organisms as well. By 1990, as a result of much research here and in Europe, a fairly coherent picture of the effects of acidification had emerged. The picture drew its general outline from a relatively few large, synoptic, multilake studies and its details from a larger number of studies of individual lakes and species. The basic results were that:

> Acidification is biologically harmful both because it increases toxics like aluminum and hydrogen ion and because it decreases the base cations and DOC that can mitigate aluminum and hydrogen ion toxicity.

> Mild acidification acts primarily by reducing or eliminating individual species and thus decreasing diversity.

> Severe acidification acts by eliminating whole taxonomic groups and ecological guilds and thus causing changes in ecological function.

Nothing learned in the 1990s changed this picture, but important details were added. Field experiments proved that acids could kill adult as well as young fish and that transient acid episodes could reduce fish diversity. A reanalysis of records of fish population losses, using data on recent acidification from the PIRLA studies, showed that relatively small changes in average pH had, as long conjectured, been associated with losses in fish diversity. A new generation of large-scale lake surveys quantified several major ecological stresses. And, as described in Chapter 7, the first synoptic surveys of mercury showed that mercury was an acid-related pollutant, and that it was now found in biologically significant quantities in wilderness lakes.

The Biology of Acidification

By 1990, studies in the Adirondacks and elsewhere had established connections between acidification and lake and stream biology. Most aquatic plants and animals, it turned out, could tolerate a fairly broad range of high pHs but were sensitive to low pHs. Below a certain critical pH that was characteristic of the species, organisms experienced stress and often had difficulty growing or reproducing. A few tenths of a pH unit below that and their mortality increased; a few tenths of a pH unit below that and they couldn't live at all.

DIVERSITY OF MACRO-ZOOPLANKTON
IN TEN ADIRONDACK LAKES

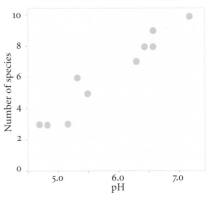

DENSITY OF MACRO-ZOOPLANKTON
IN TEN ADIRONDACK LAKES

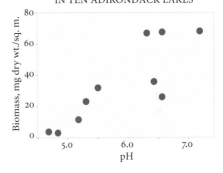

Redrawn with permission from Confer, Kaaret, and Likens, "Zooplankton diversity and biomass in recently acidified lakes." Copyright 1983 National Research Council of Canada. These results are typical of many studies that show that the diversity of many animal and plant groups decreases as pH decreases. For a general review, see Baker and Christensen, "Effects of acidification on biological communities in aquatic ecosystems," 1991.

The critical pHs for a wide variety of organisms lay between 6.0 and 4.0. Above pH 6.0, only the most sensitive species showed pH effects. Below 4.0, only the most acid tolerant could live.

Low pHs affect organisms by creating both physiological and ecological stresses. Physiologically, pH alters respiration, excretion, ionic balance, water retention, and the functioning of ion channels. It also controls the solubility of many other elements and so has important indirect effects. Toxics like aluminum and zinc are typically more abundant in low-pH environments, and necessary nutrients like calcium and magnesium less abundant.

Ecologically, pH changes the reproductive success of many organisms and hence the diversity of the communities in which they live. Through changes in reproductive success it affects population growth and the ability of populations to recover from disturbance; through community changes it affects foraging, competition, and predation. A species whose adults are not strongly acid sensitive in the laboratory may still be reduced or eliminated if its food species are acid sensitive or if its larvae can't survive in low-pH waters.

Some groups of animals and plants are uniformly pH sensitive or insensitive. Many blackflies, midges, dragonflies, and aquatic beetles and bugs are pH tolerant and present even in very low-pH waters. Mayflies, caddis flies, snails, clams, and many crustaceans, on the other hand, are quite pH sensitive. In many waters, amphipods are absent below pH 5.7, mayflies and most crayfish absent below pH 5.5, snails absent below pH 5.2, and most caddis flies absent below pH 5.0. Likewise, chrysophytes, the yellow planktonic algae characteristic of circumneutral softwater lakes, tend to drop out below pH 5.6 and are typically replaced by the more acid-tolerant diatoms and blue-green algae.

Other groups like fish, diatoms, and aquatic vascular plants contain both acid-sensitive and acid-tolerant species. These groups become less diverse at lower pHs, but do not drop out altogether.

Fish are a classic example of a pH-sensitive group. Approximately half of the 53 species and hybrids that occur in the Adirondacks are found only at pHs above 6.0. As would be expected, many of these are rare species. But even some of common northern species that are moderately acid tolerant as adults may be pH sensitive as eggs or immatures. Brook trout, for example, which can tolerate pHs down to 5.2 as adults, show reduced hatching below pH 6.5.

A review of 25 common species of fish by Baker and Christensen found that 3 species became stressed at pHs below 6.2. Another 6 became stressed at pHs between 5.5 and 6.0, and another 11 at pHs between 5.0 and 5.5. All the remaining 5 became stressed somewhere between pH 4.5 and 5.0 As a consequence, Adirondack fish diversity declines strongly with pH (p. 77). Lakes with pHs over

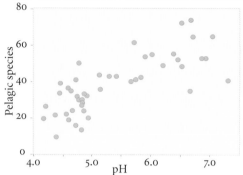

DIVERSITY OF PELAGIC FISH, ZOOPLANKTON, AND PHYTOPLANKTON IN TEN ADIRONDACK LAKES

Redrawn with permission from Havens, "Pelagic food web structure in Adirondack Mountains, USA, lakes of varying acidity." Copyright 1993 National Research Council of Canada. The average number of pelagic species at pH 4.0 is less than a third what it is at pH 7.0. At lower pHs, food chains become shorter and simpler; individual species have fewer food choices, and the effects of losing a species are correspondingly greater.

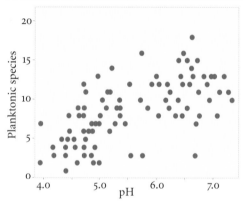

DIVERSITY OF ROTIFERS IN 50 ADIRONDACK LAKES

From Siegfried, Bloomfield, and Sutherland, "Planktonic rotifer community structure in Adirondack lakes: Effects of acidity, trophic status, and related water quality characteristics," 1990. This was part of the Adirondack Biota Project, which examined water chemistry, plankton, fish, and vegetation in 50 Adirondack lakes. The diversity of phytoplankton and planktonic crustaceans decreased with pH in much the same way as the diversity of rotifers. For the complete report of the Biota Project, see Sutherland, ed., *Field Studies of the Biota and Selected Water Chemistry Parameters in 50 Adirondack Mountain Lakes*, 1990.

6.0 average five to six species of fish. Lakes with pHs under 5.0 average less thantwo.

A 1988 study of the vascular plants of Adirondack lakes by Jackson and Charles found a similar relation between diversity and pH. The number of aquatic plants decreased sharply as pH, ANC, and calcium decreased, and only 15 of the 45 species encountered in their study were found in lakes whose pH was less than 6.0.

Ecosystem-Level Effects of Acidification

While no long-term biological studies have followed the progressive acidification of a lake from acid deposition, many field studies have compared lakes of different acidities, and several experimental studies have followed the changes when a lake or stream was experimentally acidified. These studies suggest that there is very a predictable relation between acidification and biodiversity and that major changes in diversity occur between pH 6 and pH 5:

> At about pH 6.0, there are decreases in the most sensitive fish and mayflies.

> Between pH 6.0 and pH 5.5, there are significant decreases in species diversity in all the main ecological groups: phytoplankton, zooplankton, aquatic plants, benthic invertebrates, and fish. Some acid-sensitive or calcium-dependent groups like chrysophytes, mayflies, snails, and amphipods are largely gone. Fish diversity decreases and approximately a third of the common northern fish species experience stress and reduced reproduction.

> Also between pH 6.0 and pH 5.5, acid-tolerant species of algae, cyanobacteria, and midges usually increase. Often the transparency of the water increases, possibly because of changes in the amount of dissolved organic carbon, and surface-living algae proliferate and cause algal blooms.

> Between pH 5.5 and 5.0, diversity decreases further in all groups. The total number of planktonic species drops by 30% to 70%; many benthic invertebrate groups are now gone; and about 80% of the common fish species experience pH stress or reproductive failure.

At pHs between 5 and 6, the effects of acidification on overall ecosystem processes vary considerably. In some experimental lakes there were no trends in primary productivity, nutrients, or

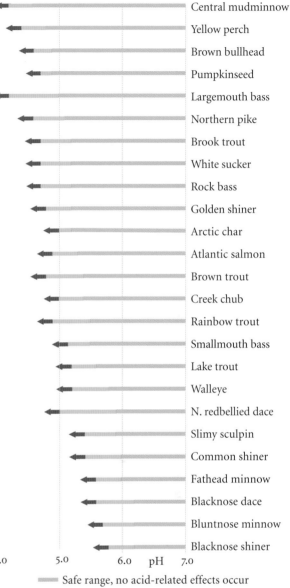

CRITICAL pH RANGES OF FISH

Central mudminnow
Yellow perch
Brown bullhead
Pumpkinseed
Largemouth bass
Northern pike
Brook trout
White sucker
Rock bass
Golden shiner
Arctic char
Atlantic salmon
Brown trout
Creek chub
Rainbow trout
Smallmouth bass
Lake trout
Walleye
N. redbellied dace
Slimy sculpin
Common shiner
Fathead minnow
Blacknose dace
Bluntnose minnow
Blacknose shiner

4.0   5.0   6.0   pH   7.0

Safe range, no acid-related effects occur
Uncertain range, acid-related effects may occur
Critical range, acid-related effects likely

Redrawn with permission from Baker and Christensen, "Effects of acidification on biological communities in aquatic ecosystems." Copyright 1991 Springer Science and Business Media. The critical ranges shown are based on 88 papers from the 1970s and 1980s. Twenty of 25 species suffer at least some acid-related mortality above pH 5.0. All the species except the arctic char and blacknose shiner are found in the Adirondacks.

decomposition rates. In others there were declines in primary productivity, nitrogen mineralization, and phosphorus levels.

The effects of pHs below 5.0 are much less studied. None of the experimental lakes had pHs below 5. In one stream experiment in which the pH was reduced to 4.0, the number of invertebrates was reduced by 75%; simultaneously, the biomass of attached algae increased, likely because the grazing pressure from mayflies and other invertebrate herbivores was reduced.

In summary, both experimental and field studies suggest that pH 6.0 is a critical biological threshold. Above it little happens. Below it, species composition and overall diversity begin to change rapidly. Between pH 6.0 and 5.5 the changes mostly involve individual species. Species that increase replace the ones that decline and, except for the frequent presence of blooms of attached algae, there is little indication of ecosystem-level changes. Below pH 5.5, the diversity changes are severe, often on the order of 50% or more. Whole functional guilds are missing, food chains are altered, and there are indications, though not consistent ones, of ecosystem-level changes. Below pH 5.0, waters enter an ecologically demanding (and insufficiently studied) zone where only a few species seem to prosper. The changes in ecosystem-level functions in this range are still largely uninvestigated.

Do fish die in acid episodes?

By the middle 1980s it was becoming increasingly clear that there were important chemical differences between chronic and episodic acidity (p. 54). Chronic mineral acidity was sulfate controlled, present year-round, and only rarely produced pHs below 5.0. Episodic acidity was nitrate and dilution controlled, relatively short lasting, and often produced pHs below 5.0.

The obvious question was whether there were also biological differences between chronic and episodic acidification. In particular, could the short but intense peaks of acidity and inorganic aluminum that occurred during snowmelt have as much, or even more, effect on fish as the baseline acidity that was present all year?

Several early studies suggested that this might indeed be the case. In 1979, Colquhoun and his collaborators surveyed 42 Adirondack headwaters streams. They found that brook trout, one of the most acid-tolerant fish, were absent from more than half of the streams and that 12 streams had no fish at all. Eight years later Sharpe and his collaborators did a similar study on the Appalachian Plateau in western Pennsylvania and found that 12 of the 61 streams they studied had no trout and 10 had no fish at all.

MORTALITY OF BLACKNOSE DACE IN BIOASSAYS DURING ACID EPISODES

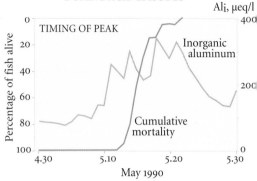

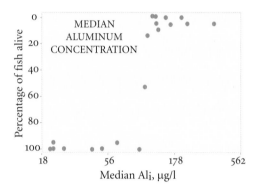

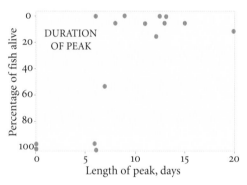

Redrawn from Van Sikle et al., "Episodic acidification of small streams in the northeastern United States: Fish mortality in field bioassays." Copyright 1996 Ecological Society of America via the Copyright Clearance Center. Dace are acid sensitive, and their mortality rose abruptly when a peak lasted more than six days or when the aluminum concentration exceeded 100 µg/l. Brook trout (p. 181, top) are less sensitive but still show a sharp increase in mortality when their critical aluminum concentration of about 200 µg/l is exceeded.

In 1984 and 1985, as part of the RILWAS, Driscoll, Yatsko, and Unangst (p. 51) gave the first detailed description of spring acidity peaks in Adirondack lakes and showed that inorganic aluminum and pH were both at levels believed toxic to fish.

Also in 1984 and 1985 and also as part of the RILWAS, Johnson and his collaborators did the first in-stream bioassays on an Adirondack stream by placing brook trout, lake trout, creek chub, and blacknose dace in cages in the North Branch of the Moose River. They found that acid episodes could kill both young and adult fish of all four species. Blacknose dace were the most sensitive and brook trout the least; pH, aluminum concentration, and duration of exposure were the most important variables.

Thus by the time the Episodic Response Project (ERP, p. 109) began in 1988, there was considerable knowledge of spring acidity peaks and considerable suspicion that these peaks were affecting fish distribution. But there were also doubts. The RILWAS studies had seen mortality in adult fish but only with caged fish and after fairly long exposures. It was possible that free-swimming fish might evade acid peaks by moving to less acid refuges in lakes or to stream pools where neutral groundwater was entering the stream. Furthermore, the RILWAS investigators had sampled chemistry intermittently and so were not really sure how intense the acid peaks had been or how long they had lasted.

The ERP sought to resolve these doubts. The investigators selected 12 streams in New York and Pennsylvania with low baseline ANCs and naturally reproducing brook trout populations, placed both caged and radio-tagged fish in the streams, and then monitored the fish during acid episodes. The mortality studies used brook trout and blacknose dace. The tracking studies and censuses used brook trout.

The results of the bioassays were decisive. As expected, the dace were highly sensitive to low pHs in general and to inorganic aluminum in particular. They could tolerate inorganic aluminum concentrations below 100 µg/l for long periods, but after six days at higher concentrations their mortality increased rapidly and quickly reached 90% to 100%.

Brook trout were less sensitive but still showed significant amounts of mortality in many acid episodes. As with dace, the average aluminum concentration was critical for survival, and above 200 µg/l of inorganic aluminum, mortality rose sharply. The lowest pH reached was also important, especially in conjunction with the calcium and aluminum concentrations. Together the median aluminum and calcium concentrations and the minimum pH explained 72% of the variance in brook trout mortality.

As many biologists had suspected, calcium and DOC (which binds inorganic aluminum) seemed to mitigate the effects of elevated aluminum and low pH. Dissolved organic carbon had the

BROOK-TROUT MORTALITY AND ALUMINUM CONCENTRATION

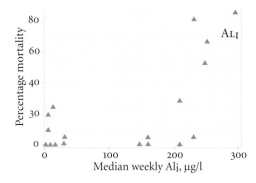

BROOK-TROUT BIOMASS AND STREAM ACIDITY

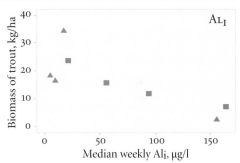

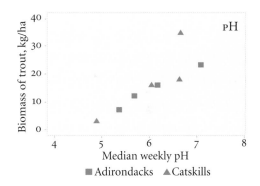

■ Adirondacks ▲ Catskills

Top graph, showing that mortality increases rapidly with the inorganic aluminum concentration, redrawn from Van Sikle et al., "Episodic acidification of small streams in the northeastern United States: Fish mortality in field bioassays." Two lower graphs, showing fish biomass in acid streams, from Baker et al., "Episodic acidification of small streams in the northeastern United States: Effects on fish populations," 1996. All graphs copyright 1996 Ecological Society of America via the Copyright Clearance Center. By using refugia, trout can survive moderate acidity peaks but only in fairly low numbers. Their biomass in the most acidic streams in which they can survive is less than a quarter of that in near-neutral streams.

largest effect: at high aluminum levels, 8 mg/l of dissolved carbon could reduce mortality from 100% to 50%.

The ERP's observations of radio-tagged fish were also interesting. Fish were clearly able to detect acid episodes and often moved downstream or into lakes and tributaries when the pH decreased. In Buck Creek, an inlet stream of the well-buffered Seventh Lake, the majority of the radio-tagged trout in the study area moved into the lake at the start of acid episodes. But refugia and acid-avoiding behavior apparently did not offer complete protection: censuses showed that streams whose median pHs during high flows were less than 5 or whose median aluminum concentrations during high flows were more than 100 μeq/l had half or less the biomass of trout of less acidic streams.

Apparently, acid-avoiding behavior allows the trout to survive in some acidic streams where conditions might otherwise be lethal but does not let them maintain the populations that they have in nonacidic streams. And not all streams have refuges: recall that the ERP studies were limited to streams where brook trout still survived and that half of the streams studied by Colquhoun et al. had no trout and thus very likely no refuges for trout at all.

Historical Losses of Fish Populations

Assessing the historical changes in fish populations is notoriously difficult. The basic problems are that fish populations disappear and reappear for many reasons. Besides the acid-related extinctions of interest to researchers, there may be natural extinctions caused by climate or competition, and human-caused but not acid-related extinctions caused by fishing pressure, lake reclamation, and introduced predators. And besides the natural reintroductions in which, say, fish from a tributary stream recolonize a lake, there are many artificial reintroductions by fishermen and fisheries managers.

Thus the historical record is complex and must be analyzed carefully. A population that appears to have vanished from an acidified lake may have been removed by fishermen or otters, or simply have been missed by the survey team. A population that appears to have persisted may in fact have died out and been restocked.

Although the Adirondack historical record is better than most, there still problems with data quality and sampling bias. Many of the older DEC surveys focused on sport fish and on the larger lakes with good potential for sport fishing. They did not use a uniform sampling protocol and probably overlooked some minnows and smaller forage fish. The Adirondack Lakes Survey was more systematic and sampled far more small ponds and high-elevation lakes than the earlier surveys. But no survey catches all fish with

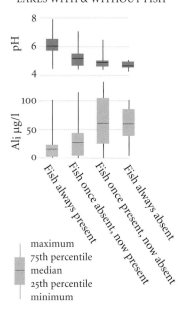

pH AND ALUMINUM RANGES OF ALS LAKES WITH & WITHOUT FISH

Redrawn with permission from Baker et al., "Fish population losses from Adirondack lakes: The role of surface water acidity and acidification." Copyright 1993 American Geophysical Union. Lakes that are fishless or have lost fish populations have consistently lower pHs and higher aluminum concentrations than other lakes.

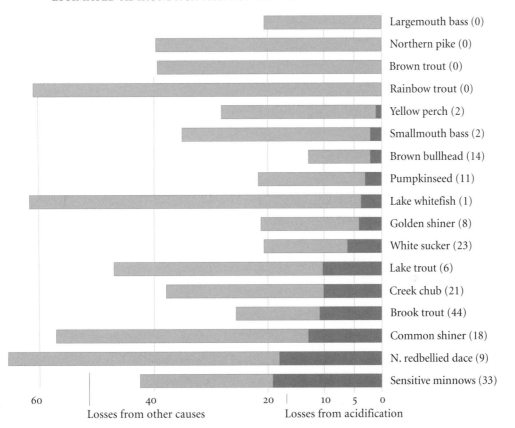

ESTIMATED ADIRONDACK FISH POPULATION LOSSES

Largemouth bass (0)
Northern pike (0)
Brown trout (0)
Rainbow trout (0)
Yellow perch (2)
Smallmouth bass (2)
Brown bullhead (14)
Pumpkinseed (11)
Lake whitefish (1)
Golden shiner (8)
White sucker (23)
Lake trout (6)
Creek chub (21)
Brook trout (44)
Common shiner (18)
N. redbellied dace (9)
Sensitive minnows (33)

60   40   20   10   5   0

Losses from other causes   Losses from acidification

From Baker et al., "Fish population losses from Adirondack lakes: The role of surface water acidity and acidification," 1993. The bars represent the number of Adirondack lakes at which a previously found species was not found during the Adirondack Lakes Survey. The light gray segment of each bar gives the number of lakes at which the population loss may have resulted from stocking, fishing pressure, reclamation, beaver activity, anoxic episodes, etc. The dark gray segment of each bar is the number of unaccounted-for population losses in acidic lakes. These are assumed to be caused by acidification.

equal success, and the ALS may well have missed some species that were found in earlier surveys.

The first comparison of the ALS data with data from earlier surveys was reported by Baker and her colleagues in 1990 (p. 79). The results were mixed. When they examined the set of 295 lakes for which both contemporary and historical data existed they were not able to show a significant change in the percentage of fishless lakes and found only a weak relation between the change in the number of species and the current pH of the lake (p. 79). But they noted that since the early data were biased toward large, deep, high-ANC lakes where extinctions were less likely, there may have been many acid-related extinctions in lakes for which there were no historical records.

When they focused on losses of individual species and examined the set of 988 lakes for which they had both recent and pre-1970 data, the effects of acidification were clearer (graph above). They found 2,824 records of fish populations that had been confirmed by pre-1970 surveys in lakes sampled by the ALS. Of these, 851 (30%) populations had apparently been lost between the original survey and the ALS. They identified possible nonacid-related causes for 659 of these losses and were left with 192 losses that they regarded as probably acid related. This analysis suggested that at least – and their estimates were surely minimums – 6.8% of the populations for which they had historical records had been lost to acidification, and 23% of all fish population losses were acid related.

The losses that they believed to be acid related showed clear ecological patterns. The species that were most often lost were brook trout and several minnows that had previously been identified as acid sensitive. The lakes that had lost any particular species tended to be higher in elevation and to have more acid and more inorganic aluminum than the lakes in which the species still survived. All this suggested that even though they could not quantify the extent of acid-related population losses exactly, there was convincing evidence that such losses had occurred.

The case was made even more convincing a few years later when the results of the PIRLA studies of historical acidification became available. Historical fish data were available for 32 of the PIRLA lakes. When Baker and her colleagues analyzed these lakes in 1993, they found a clear connection between historical pH changes and the loss of fish species. On the graph at right, the lakes that have lost fish species lie below and to the left of the lakes that haven't, showing elegantly that the historical fish and chemical data are in fact consistent: the lakes that have acidified the most or that were the most acid originally are also the ones that have lost fish.

Ecological Monitoring in the 1990s

The heroic period of Adirondack acid rain biology that had begun with Schofield's work in the early 1970s ended with the publication of the results of the Adirondack Biota Project in 1989, the Adirondack Lakes Survey's *Interpretive Analysis* in 1990, and the biological data from the Episodic Response Project in the early 1990s. Nationally, this coincided with the publication of the National Acid Precipitation Assessment Program *State of Science* reports in 1990 and then with a post-

FISH LOSSES IN ADIRONDACK LAKES WHOSE pH HISTORY IS KNOWN

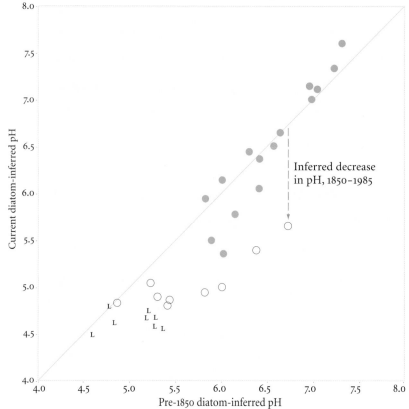

● Fish community that has not lost species to acidification

○ Fish community that has apparently lost one or more species observed in pre-1970 surveys to acidification

L Fish community that has apparently lost stocked species or species reported in the literature that were not observed in pre-1970 surveys

From Baker et al., "Fish population losses from Adirondack lakes: The role of surface water acidity and acidification." Copyright 1993 American Geophysical Union. These are the lakes for which there are both fisheries data and records of historical acidification from sediment cores (p. 85). The graph plots current and historical diatom-estimated pHs; the farther a point is below the line, the more the lake is believed to have acidified. All the lakes that have lost fish species either have current pHs below 5.51 or are estimated to have acidified by 0.5 pH unit or more, or both.

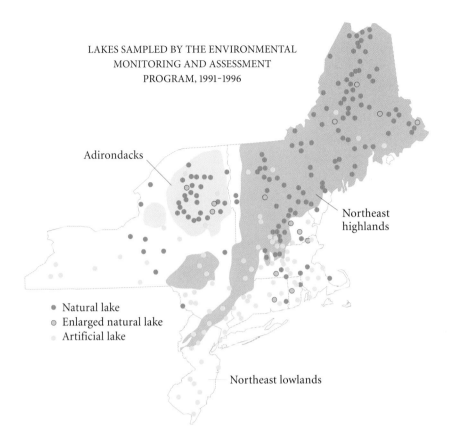

LAKES SAMPLED BY THE ENVIRONMENTAL
MONITORING AND ASSESSMENT
PROGRAM, 1991–1996

Adirondacks

Northeast
highlands

• Natural lake
◎ Enlarged natural lake
• Artificial lake

Northeast lowlands

From Whittier et al., "Indicators of ecological stress and
their extent in the population of northeastern lakes: A
regional-scale assessment," 2002.
Approximately 245 waterbodies
were sampled in the first six
years of the program. The large
number of artificial lakes in the
lowland region occurs because
the lakes are selected randomly,
and in many lowland areas there
are far more artificial lakes than
natural ones.

1990 reduction in federal funding for new biological and chemical
research and a redirection of the remaining funding toward long-
term monitoring.

Unfortunately, relatively little of the Adirondack long-term
monitoring since 1990 has had a biological component. Despite
the importance of the biological surveys of the 1980s, neither the
Adirondack Long-Term Monitoring program nor the Temporally
Integrated Monitoring of Ecosystems project (p. 194) had an integrated biological component. Several one-time studies, including
the Episodic Response Project and the Adirondack mercury studies described Chapter 6, gathered biological information, but relatively few of them did quantitative or statistically based sampling,
and none of them were designed to detect long-term trends.

The lack of new biological data was partially remedied in the
early 1990s when the U.S. Environmental Protection Agency created two biological monitoring programs, the Adirondack Effects
Assessment Program (AEAP) and the Environmental Monitoring
and Assessment Program (EMAP).

The Adirondack Effects Assessment Program is run by
Rensselaer Polytechnic Institute. It is a regional program that collects annual samples from 30 lakes in the southwestern Adirondacks
and focuses on the relations between water chemistry, microbiology, and plankton. It began in 1994 and continues at present.

The Environmental Monitoring and Assessment Program was a national program, run by the EPA with many collaborators, that was intended to monitor trends in ecological resources and appraise ecological health on a community basis. It contains both terrestrial and aquatic programs. Its Aquatic Resources Program began a northeastern lakes survey in 1992, with a complex sampling design using a triangular grid and random sampling around grid points. The program was designed as a long-term, statistically based monitoring program but gathered only three years of data before it was terminated in 1994.

Before it ended, the EMAP produced several regional analyses of lake biology, two of which we describe here. They are interesting both because of the information they provide about Adirondack lakes and because they illustrate the potential, and currently unrealized, value of regional biological monitoring.

Indicators of Ecological Stress

The first analysis of the northeastern EMAP data, by Whittier and his collaborators, compared the levels of ecological stress generated by various human activities. The researchers measured five kinds of biological stress – acidification, nonnative fish, mercury pollution, eutrophication, and shoreline development – and grouped the lakes they studied into three categories they called moderate, high, and severe stress. Thus lakes with summer ANCs between 0 and 50 µeq/l were called moderately stressed, and about 32% of Adirondack lakes fell in this category.

Despite some arbitrariness in the way the different stress levels are defined, the results are fascinating. Acidification, as we would expect, is more important in the Adirondacks than elsewhere in the region. Eutrophication, a major problem in the Northeast lowlands, is less important in the Northeast highlands and rare in the Adirondacks. Severe shoreline development occurs only in the lowlands, but high stress from development occurs on 20% of Adirondack and Northeast highland lakes as well. And mercury in fish is not only a widespread Adirondack problem but, unlike acidification, an important regional problem as well.

Regional Fish Diversity

As the historical analysis by Baker and her collaborators showed (p. 183), many human activities cause fish population losses. An interesting question is whether the effects of these losses are mostly local, or whether they have combined to produce overall changes in the regional diversity of native fish.

Two recent papers based on the 1992-1994 EMAP data by Whittier and his collaborators give an interesting and complex

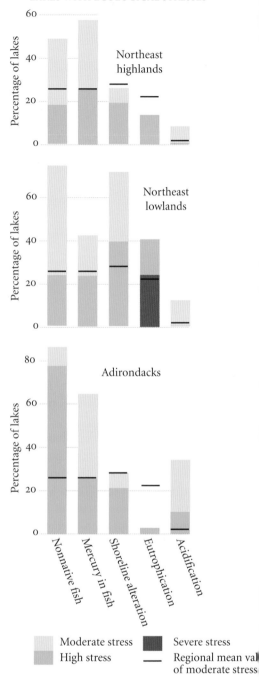

ESTIMATED PERCENTAGES OF EASTERN LAKES WITH ECOLOGICAL STRESSES

From Whittier et al., "Indicators of ecological stress and their extent in the population of northeastern lakes: A regional-scale assessment," 2002. The bars give the estimated percentage of the 11,000 northeastern lakes in which each stress is at or above a given level.

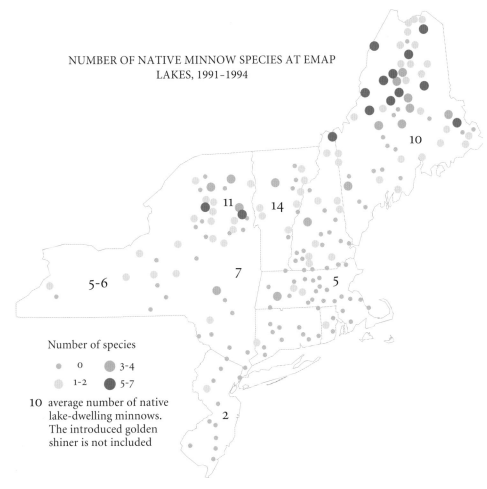

NUMBER OF NATIVE MINNOW SPECIES AT EMAP
LAKES, 1991–1994

10

11   14

5-6   7   5

Number of species

• 0   ● 3-4

• 1-2   ● 5-7

10 average number of native
    lake-dwelling minnows.
    The introduced golden
    shiner is not included

2

From Whittier, Halliwell, and Paulsen:
"Cyprinid distributions in Northeast
U.S.A. lakes: Evidence of regional-
scale minnow biodiversity losses,"
1997. The native minnows are sensitive
to acidification, shoreline development, and introduced predators like
pike and bass. Currently, they are
most diverse in remote lakes where
both acid rain and shoreline development are low and where there are few
introduced species of fish (p. 188).
They are absent from most of the lakes
in developed areas.

answer. Apparently, human activities are both reducing diversity
and converting native-dominated faunas to nonnative faunas, but
the two are not well correlated, and introduced fish do not always
reduce native diversity.

Whittier, Halliwell, and Paulsen used the EMAP survey data
to map cyprinid minnow diversity. The cyprinids are our most
diverse family of freshwater fishes. They are also small, sensitive to
acidification and other chemical changes, and vulnerable to predatory fish and especially to introduced game fish. With the exception of the golden shiner, they are rarely introduced. They are thus
potential indicators of lake integrity and disturbance and should
be most diverse where the lakes have had the least human impact
and least diverse where the impacts have been the greatest.

The map shows that this is in fact the case. Cyprinid diversities
are highest in northern Maine, next highest in the Adirondacks,
still moderately high in northern Vermont and New Hampshire,
and low or absent everywhere else. Ten lakes in northern Maine
had five or more species; only six lakes in all of southern New England had any species at all.

Further analysis by Whittier and his colleagues confirmed that
minnow diversity is closely related to human impact. The number
of minnow species decreased, very predictably, as either the

PERCENTAGE OF NATIVE FISH SPECIES IN
THE EMAP LAKES, 1991–1996

● All native
◐ 75-99% native
◐ < 50-74% native
● < 50% native
○ No fish

From Whittier and Kincaid, "Introduced fish in northeastern USA lakes:
Regional extent, dominance, and
effect on native species richness," 1999.
Extrapolating from their survey to the
full population of northeastern lakes,
they estimate that 74% of the lakes
larger than 1 ha contain introduced
species and that in 32% of the lakes
nonnative fish are more common than
native. The number of nonnative fish
is generally highest in the areas with
the most shoreline development, but it
is also high in the Adirondacks, where
there has been much recreational use
and management of undeveloped lakes.
Interestingly, however, and contrary to
what has been found for stream fish,
the number of native species does not
necessarily decrease as the number of
introduced species increases.

amount of shoreline development or the number of shallow-water
predators like pike, white perch, largemouth bass, and smallmouth
bass increased. Both are measures of human influence. Further,
because many of the shallow-water predators are nonnative sport
fish, development tends to be correlated with exotic fish: almost
every lake with shoreline development has at least one introduced
predator. The Adirondacks, for example, have large numbers of
nonnative fish, which may be one of the reasons that their minnow
diversity is not as high as in Maine.

This being the case for minnows, it might be expected that
overall native fish diversity might decrease as the diversity of
introduced species increased. An analysis of the EMAP data from
the same lakes by Whittier and Kincaid found, rather surprisingly,
that this was not true. What was clearly stressful for native minnows was not necessarily stressful for other native groups. The
percentage of introduced species was, as expected, high in both
the developed areas and areas, like the Adirondacks, with a history of sport fishing and fisheries management. But except along
the New England coast, the total number of native species did
not decrease as the number of nonnatives increased. Possibly, the
authors speculated, "the ecoregional template as characterized by

lake size, elevation, and depth defined a species carrying capacity that was not fully used in presettlement times." In other words, the presettlement Northeast may have had more fish niches than fish. Some introduced fish may have moved into unoccupied niches, and some native fish may have been able to cope with introductions by sharing or changing their niches.

SUMMARY

1 Acidification causes both *species-level and community-level changes* in the biology of lakes and streams. Many common aquatic species have ecological thresholds somewhere between pH 6 and pH 5. When these thresholds are exceeded, even fairly briefly, mortality rises rapidly and species may be decline or vanish altogether. Adirondack biological surveys show this very clearly: in the more acid waters, the diversity of almost all biological groups is reduced.

2 *Fish mortality* from acidification has been demonstrated in both lakes and streams. Acid episodes of the sort that are common on many Adirondack streams kill sensitive minnow species outright, make brook trout move downstream or seek refuges, and cause year-round reductions in the numbers and biomass of the trout that survive. The chronically low pHs and high aluminum concentrations found in many low-ANC Adirondack lakes are associated with increased losses of fish populations, of both relatively sensitive species like the cyprinid minnows and relatively insensitive species like brook trout.

3 Relatively little *new biological work* has been done since 1990, and only one current Adirondack monitoring program, the Adirondack Effects Assessment Program, has a biological component.

4 The EPA's *Northeastern Lakes Program*, which ran from 1992 to 1994, produced interesting regional estimates of ecological stresses and fish diversity. Its stress estimate suggests that there is no region in the Northeast where 50% of the lakes are free from ecological stress. Mercury pollution is a problem throughout the region, acidification is severe in the Adirondacks, and eutrophication and shoreline development are severe in the lowlands. Both cyprinid minnow diversities and the percentage of native species are low in much of the Northeast. If these measures are, as the EMAP researchers suggest, good proxies for naturalness or ecological health, then the only area in which the majority of the lakes sampled were natural or in good health was northern Maine.

NOTES

For general reviews of aquatic biology, see Baker et al., "Biological effects of changes in surface water acid-base chemistry," 1990; Baker and Christensen, "Effects of acidification on biological communities in aquatic ecosystems," 1991; and Ecological Society of America, "Acid deposition: The ecological Response", 1999.

p. 176 Papers in the chronology not cited later in the chapter are Schofield, "Acid precipitation: Effects on fish," 1976; Driscoll et al., "Effect of aluminum speciation on fish in dilute acidified waters," 1980; Schindler et al., "Long-term ecosystem stress: The effects of years of experimental acidification on a small lake," 1985; Brezonik et al., "Experimental acidification of Little Rock Lake, Wisconsin," 1986; Johnson et al., "In situ toxicity tests of fishes in acid waters," 1987; and Sutherland, ed., *Field Studies of the Biota and Selected Water Chemistry Parameters in 50 Adirondack Mountain Lakes*, 1990.

p. 178 For aquatic vascular plants, see Jackson and Charles, "Aquatic macrophytes in Adirondack (New York) lakes: Patterns of species composition in relation to environment," 1988.

p. 180 For fish in acidic streams, see Colquhoun et al., *Preliminary Report of Stream Sampling for Acidification Studies – 1980*, 1981; Driscoll, Yatsko, and Unangst, "Longitudinal and temporal trends in the water chemistry of the North Branch of the Moose River," 1987; and Sharpe et al., "The relation of water quality and fish occurrence to soils and geology in a region of high hydrogen and sulfate ion deposition," 1987. For the RILWAS biological studies see: Johnson et al., "In situ toxicity tests of fishes in acid waters," 1987.

p. 181 For the results of the Episodic Response Project, see the last note on page 127.

p. 185 For the design of the EMAP lake studies, see Whittier and Paulsen, "The surface waters component of the Environmental Monitoring and Assessment Program (EMAP): An overview," 1992.

1963 The Hubbard Brook Experimental Forest in northern New Hampshire begins monitoring precipitation and runoff chemistry.

1976 The U.S. Department of Energy opens the first four precipitation monitoring stations of the Multistate Atmospheric Power Production Pollution Study Network.

1978 A consortium of state and federal agencies and private research organizations opens the first 22 precipitation monitoring stations in the National Trends Network.

1981 Researchers at the DEC begin the monitoring of several Adirondack streams.

1982 The Regionalized Integrated Lake-Watershed Acidification Study begins the monthly monitoring of 20 Adirondack lakes.

1982 Researchers at Huntington Forest begin monitoring the element balances of Arbutus Lake.

1986 The Environmental Protection Agency establishes the National Dry Deposition Network, later the Clean Air Status and Trends Network, with 50 stations.

1987 The DEC opens the first 15 stations in its Atmospheric Deposition Monitoring Network.

1990 The Episodic Response Project (ERP) begins monitoring 13 streams in New York and Pennsylvania.

1991 The Environmental Protection Agency's TIME program begins the annual monitoring of 43 Adirondack lakes, 30 New England lakes, and 30 streams in the mid-Atlantic region.

1992 The Adirondack Long-Term Monitoring program adds 35 lakes and 3 streams, giving it a total of 55 monitored waters.

1992 The first analysis of long-term monitoring data for the eastern United States by Newell finds significant decreases in sulfate at many sites in the Catskills, Adirondacks, and Vermont.

1993 The Mountain Cloud Acid Deposition Program begins to monitor cloudwater chemistry at three sites.

1993 Driscoll and Van Dreason examine eight years of Adirondack LTM data from 17 lakes. They report statistically significant decreases of sulfate in 13 lakes, significant increases of nitrate in 9 lakes, and significant decreases of ANC in 5 lakes. They speculate that the decreases in ANC are being controlled by the increases in nitrate.

1994 The national Mercury Deposition Network begins with 13 precipitation stations, and the Adirondack Effects Assessment Program begins the biological monitoring of 30 Adirondack lakes.

1995 Driscoll et al. extend the analysis of the Adirondack LTM lakes, using data through 1994. They find that the concentration of sulfate in lakes is decreasing more slowly than the concentration of sulfate in precipitation and speculate that this may be caused by the release of sulfates stored in soil. Despite decreases in sulfate, there are no increases in ANC or pH.

1999 Stoddard et al. provide the first comparison of regional trends in Europe and eastern North America. They find widespread decreases in sulfate. ANCs are increasing in Europe, Britain, and Scandinavia but in only a few parts of North America.

2001 Mitchell et al. summarize 16 years of mass-balance data from the Arbutus watershed. The watershed is retaining nitrogen and hydrogen ion and exporting sulfate and base cations.

2002 Driscoll et al. summarize Adirondack LTM data through 2000. They report, for the first time, decreases in nitrate and increases in pH, ANC, and DOC.

2002 Lawrence, Momen, and Roy report on the first 11 years of monitoring the three Adirondack LTM streams. They report a complex relation between ANC and flow, in which ANC increases were observed but were not synchronous between the three streams and were not directly related to trends in deposition.

2003 Stoddard et al. analyze the long-term monitoring data for the eastern United States. They find large decreases in sulfate and base cations, smaller decreases in nitrates, widespread increases in ANC, and almost no changes in hydrogen ion.

MONITORING AND TRENDS

ACID EMISSIONS CHANGE AND SURFACE WATERS BEGIN TO
RESPOND

Because neither atmospheric emissions nor the watersheds they affect are static, the levels of acid deposition and surface water acidification are continuously changing. Any research program that wishes to produce a detailed picture of acid deposition must take these changes into account. And any regulatory program that seeks to control acid rain must compile long-term records to determine whether the regulations have been effective. All this requires monitoring.

The monitoring systems required to do this were first developed in the late 1970s. Since 1980 they have been coordinated by the National Acid Precipitation Assessment Program (NAPAP), a cooperative program involving the Environmental Protection Agency, the Departments of Energy, Agriculture, and the Interior, the National Aeronautics and Space Administration, and the National Oceanic and Atmospheric Administration.

The actual monitoring that NAPAP coordinates is carried out by many institutions: state and federal agencies, universities and colleges, and several private research organizations. The relations between the institutions are complex, and the degree of collaboration involved remarkably high. The National Trends Network (NTN), which is responsible for much of the routine monitoring of deposition, has 143 member institutions: 10 federal agencies, 8 federal research laboratories, 55 colleges and universities, 29 state agencies, 6 local governments, 5 Native American tribes, 14 corporations, and 16 nonprofit research groups. All of these institutions send data to the national network, and many collaborate with each other as well. The Adirondack Lakes Survey, for example, the organization that administers the Adirondack Long-Term Monitoring (ALTM) program (p. vi) , both performs its own research and gathers samples for other researchers; some of these samples, in turn, are sent to yet other researchers or to private laboratories for analysis.

The funding for monitoring is equally various. Many monitoring programs began as research projects with federal funding and then continued with a mix of state and federal funds. Gradually, however, federal support for long-term monitoring has been reduced, and currently states, utilities, and private philanthropies support much of the monitoring effort.

In New York, for example, the major long-term monitoring programs depend largely on public funding. The ALTM program currently receives about 85% of its funding from New York State

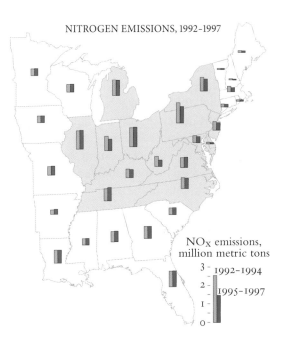

NITROGEN EMISSIONS, 1992-1997

NO$_X$ emissions,
million metric tons
3 -
2 -   1992-1994
-
1 -   1995-1997
-
0 -

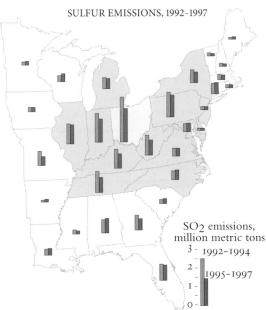

SULFUR EMISSIONS, 1992-1997

SO$_2$ emissions,
million metric tons
3 -   1992-1994
2 -
-   1995-1997
1 -
-
0 -

Maps from Driscoll et al., "Acidic deposition in the northeastern United States," 2001. Emissions from anywhere in the shaded area can reach New York State in less than 24 hours.

Department of Environmental Conservation and the New York State Energy Research and Development Authority. The latter is funded by a state-mandated surcharge (the "systems benefits charge") on electric bills. The New York State Atmospheric Deposition Monitoring Network, which operates precipitation-monitoring stations throughout the state, is wholly state funded.

Monitoring Emissions, Air Chemistry, and Deposition

Emissions of acids and mercury are monitored by the EPA, using data gathered from individual industries by federal and state agencies. Because large numbers of sources are involved, emissions are not measured directly but instead are approximated by a complicated mixture of inventorying, sampling, and modeling. The result is a National Emissions Inventory that estimates the emissions from each 20-kilometer square in the country for each season and each hour of the day.

Air chemistry and dry deposition are monitored by several networks. Air chemistry monitoring is done by the Clean Air Status and Trends Network (CASTNET), operated by the EPA. This is a network of 98 stations that make weekly measurements of the average atmospheric concentrations of sulfate, nitrate, ammonium, sulfur dioxide, and nitric acid, and hourly measurements of the concentration of ozone. There are CASTNET stations at Huntington Forest in the Adirondacks, Claryville in the Catskills, and Connecticut Hill in central New York. There is also a CASTNET station at Lye Book in southern Vermont, and was formerly one at Whiteface Mountain in the Adirondacks.

One major purpose of CASTNET is to estimate dry deposition by a standard method. This is done by measuring pollutant concentrations and basic meteorological data and then using a computer model to estimate the deposition velocities for various pollutants; the velocities determine the rates at which these pollutants would be deposited on a surface of standard characteristics.

More specialized monitoring of aerosols and visibility is done by the Interagency Monitoring of Protected Visual Environments (IMPROVE). IMPROVE, a collaboration between six federal and several state agencies, was created in 1985 to monitor visibility and haze in national parks and other protected areas. It operates 110 stations of its own and receives data from 52 other stations run by collaborating groups. The stations determine the concentrations of aerosols and measure the clarity of the air and the extent to which it scatters light. The nearest IMPROVE stations to the Adirondacks are at Addison Pinnacle on the New York-Pennsylvania border and Lye Brook in southern Vermont.

Another specialized monitoring network, the Atmospheric Integrated Research and Monitoring Network (AIRMON), does

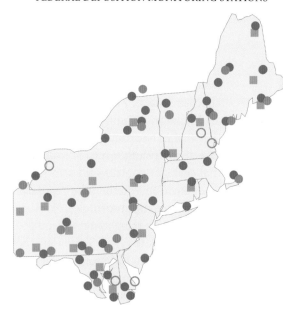

● NTN wet deposition station

■ CASTNET dry deposition station

● MDN mercury deposition station

○ Inactive mercury deposition station

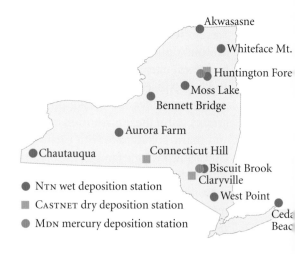

Monitoring stations for wet and dry deposition. National Trends Network (NTN) sites from http://nadp.sws.uiuc.edu/sites/ntnmap.asp?; Clear Air Status and Trends Network (CASTNET) sites from http://www.epa.gov/castnet/site.html; Mercury Deposition Network (MDN) sites from http://nadp.sws.uiuc.edu/mdn/sites.asp.

research on the monitoring process itself. Its goal is evaluate and improve the techniques used by CASTNET and the National Trends Network (see below). AIRMON currently operates 7 wet deposition stations and 13 dry deposition stations. The nearest AIRMON wet deposition stations are in southern Vermont and central New York. The nearest AIRMON dry deposition station is in central Pennsylvania.

Wet deposition is monitored at approximately 245 stations in the National Atmospheric Deposition's National Trends Network. Currently there are three stations in the Adirondacks, at Huntington Forest, Whiteface Mountain, and Moss Lake. There are also 7 stations elsewhere in New York and 15 in New England. Most NTN sites collect weekly samples of wet deposition. Some stations, like the one at Huntington Forest, are parts of other networks and collect dry deposition and mercury data as well.

Wet deposition is also monitored by the New York State Atmospheric Deposition Network, which was authorized by the State Acid Deposition Control Act of 1985 and now has 20 stations, including 5 in the Adirondacks. Its purpose is to provide additional coverage in areas like the Adirondacks and the west of the state where the NTN network is weak.

The first deposition-monitoring station in the Adirondacks was at the Adirondack Ecological Center at Huntington Forest. It began operation in 1978 and now has 26 years of general precipitation chemistry data. The second oldest is the Whiteface Mountain station, run by the State University of New York's Atmospheric Sciences Research Center, which began operation in June 1984 and now has 19 years of chemical data.

Mercury deposition is monitored by the Mercury Deposition Network at a subset of the NTN sites. The network is relatively new and still has somewhat patchy geographic coverage. It began with 13 stations in 1995 and expanded to 50 in 2000 and 84 in 2004. There are two stations in New York: Huntington Forest in the Adirondacks, which began taking data in December 1999, and Biscuit Brook in the Catskills, which began taking data in March 2004.

Cloudwater deposition, which is extremely important in the mountains and may supply 80% or more of the acids received at high elevations, is much less studied than other forms of deposition. It was measured, intermittently, at several mountain sites in the 1980s and then continuously from 1994 to 1999 at Whiteface Mountain in the Adirondacks and two other sites as part of the EPA's Mountain Acid Deposition (MADPRO). The

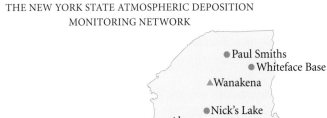

THE NEW YORK STATE ATMOSPHERIC DEPOSITION MONITORING NETWORK

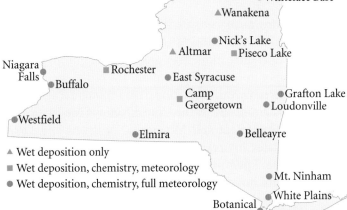

The 20 current stations of the New York State Atmospheric Deposition Network. Fully equipped stations, indicated by the red circles, measure wet deposition, ambient sulfur dioxide and ozone concentrations, temperature, relative humidity, atmospheric pressure, and wind speed. From http://www.dec.state.ny.us/website/dar/baqs/acidrain/network.html.

NEW YORK STATE NITRATE DEPOSITION, 2002

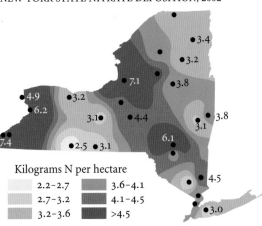

Total wet nitrate deposition for 2002, from the New York State Atmospheric Deposition Network. The 1997-1999 data from the National Trends Network shown on page 10 are generally similar but do not resolve the hotspots and local gradients as well. From http://www.dec.state.ny.us/website/dar/baqs/acidrain/no3do2.html.

EPA ended MADPRO in 1999, but measurements at Whiteface have continued as a cooperative project of the Adirondack Lakes Survey Corporation and the Atmospheric Sciences Research Center of the State University of New York.

Monitoring Surface Waters

Currently, more than 500 waters in Europe and North America are monitored for acidification. The programs are funded and administered by various national environmental agencies and coordinated scientifically by the United Nations International Cooperative on Assessment and Monitoring of Rivers and Lakes. In the United States, five regional monitoring programs are coordinated through the Environmental Protection Agency's Temporally Integrated Monitoring of Ecosystems (TIME) and Long-Term Monitoring (LTM) programs. The EPA provides the overall sampling design and standardizes the methods for sampling and analysis. The organizations running the regional programs do the actual sampling and analysis and are responsible for data handling and quality control.

The TIME program began in 1991. It is statistically based and uses a randomly chosen sample of low-ANC lakes and streams to make predictions about a larger target population that the sample is believed to represent. Currently, the TIME program samples 43 Adirondack lakes, 30 New England lakes, and about 30 streams in the northern Appalachian plateau. These are thought to represent some 2,500 low-ANC lakes and 24,000 kilometers of low-ANC streams. TIME waters are sampled once a year; lakes are sampled in summer, streams in spring.

The LTM program began in the early 1980s and was expanded in the 1990s. Currently, it includes about 100 lakes, over half of them in the Adirondacks, and 80 streams. In the Adirondacks, 3 streams are sampled weekly and 52 lakes are sampled monthly. Elsewhere, lakes are sampled 1 to 4 times a year and the streams 15 times per year. Monitoring of the 17 original Adirondack lakes began in 1982; the others were added in 1992. Monitoring of Adirondack streams began with unpublished work on six streams by Colquhoun and his collaborators in the early 1980s. Several of these streams were studied by the Episodic Response Project in 1988 (p. 109) and then incorporated into the Adirondack Long-Term Monitoring program in 1992.

The effort involved in these monitoring programs is substantial (pp. 200–201). The Adirondack Lakes Survey Corporation has staff of 12, of whom 4 are administrative, 5 involved in sampling and field work, and 3 in laboratory work and quality control. To monitor their 55 waters, every month the ALSC field staff travel 4,400 miles by car, 40 miles by foot and bicycle, and 160 miles or more by helicopter. When the helicopter cannot operate they

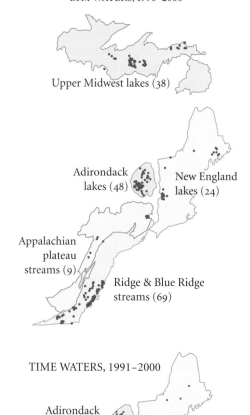

LTM WATERS, 1990–2000

Upper Midwest lakes (38)

Adirondack lakes (48)

New England lakes (24)

Appalachian plateau streams (9)

Ridge & Blue Ridge streams (69)

TIME WATERS, 1991–2000

Adirondack lakes (43)

New England lakes (30)

Appalachian plateau streams (31)

All maps from Stoddard et al., "Response of surface water chemistry to the Clean Air Act Amendments of 1990," 2003. Above, the LTM and TIME waters. The colored areas are the acid-sensitive regions recognized by the EPA. The Adirondack lakes play a special part in the long-term monitoring network because they are the only LTM lakes that are monitored monthly. The monthly monitoring provides more accurate information about annual means and trends than quarterly or annual monitoring and also allows the detection of seasonal acidification patterns like those shown on page 199.

Opposite, deposition maps for the eastern United States. Sulfate deposition has decreased markedly, especially in the most affected areas; nitrate deposition has barely changed.

travel an additional 60 miles by foot. They collect approximately 1,150 samples per year and perform about 15,000 laboratory analyses on them, plus an additional 7,000 quality-control analyses of duplicates, blanks, and samples from other laboratories. The ALTM cumulative database, which extends back to 1989, now contains records of more than a quarter-million measurements on 15,000 samples.

Ecological monitoring is much less extensive than chemical monitoring. From 1991 to 1994 the EPA Northeastern Lakes program did biological sampling at randomly chosen lakes and streams. The Adirondack Effects Assessment Program (AEAP), funded by the EPA and run by the Darrin Freshwater Institute of Rensselaer Polytechnic Institute, has sampled plankton in 30 southwestern Adirondack lakes since 1994. Both are treated briefly in Chapter 8 (p. 185).

TRENDS IN EMISSIONS AND DEPOSITION

Trends in Acid Emissions

Total U.S. nitrogen and sulfur oxide emissions are currently around 33 million metric tons (MT) a year. This is about 2.8 times more than the 12 MT emitted in 1900 and about a third less than the emissions peak of 50 MT in 1973.

Sulfur emissions, which can be calculated from the sulfur content of fuels and come largely from stationary sources, are quite accurately known. They rose for the first 70 years of the 20th century, with declines when industrial output fell during the Depression and after World War II (pp. 2, 13). They peaked at about 29 MT in 1973, began to fall when the 1970 Clean Air Act Amendments took effect, and have fallen ever since. They are expected to be below 13.2 MT in 2010, when the limits required by the 1990 Clean Air Act Amendments are in full effect.

Nitrogen oxide emissions, which come from both stationary and mobile sources and have to be calculated from assumptions about the efficiency of boilers and engines, are less well known. They are believed to have been 2 to 3 MT in 1900, to have climbed steadily to a peak of 25 MT in the early 1980s, and to have declined to about 19 MT in response to decreases in nitrogen oxide emissions since then.

Currently, nitrogen emissions are less regulated than sulfur emissions. The 1990 Clean Air Act Amendments regulate nitrogen oxide emissions per unit of energy driven or per mile driven but place no limits on the total amounts of nitrogen oxides produced. Most of the recent decreases in nitrogen emissions have come from controls on electric utilities (pp. 2, 13). The regulations on vehicles have been offset by increases in the total number of miles

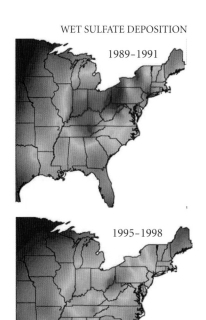

WET SULFATE DEPOSITION

Average wet sulfate deposition, kg/ha-yr

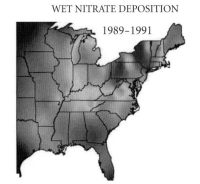

WET NITRATE DEPOSITION

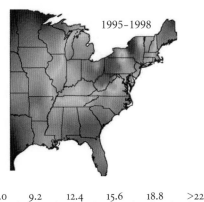

Average wet nitrate deposition, kg/ha-yr

traveled, and currently 56% of all nitrogen oxide emissions come from vehicles.*

As a result, the relative significance of nitrogen and sulfur emissions has changed greatly in the past 25 years. In 1970, when acid rain was newly discovered and the Clean Air Act Amendments were being debated, nitrogen oxides made up a third of the total atmospheric acids and were considered a minor part of acid rain. Today nitrogen oxides are estimated to make up 57% by weight of all atmospheric acids and are considered to have a critical role in lake acidification (Chapter 5).

Trends in Wet Deposition

In the past 25 years Adirondack precipitation has become less acid but also poorer in calcium and other bases.

The major change has been a decrease in sulfuric acid. Sulfate concentrations in deposition are about half what they were in 1980, and pHs have climbed by 0.2–0.3 units, corresponding to a 40% to 50% decrease in hydrogen ion concentration. These decreases are the result of the decreases in sulfur emissions required by the Clean Air Act Amendments of 1970 and 1990.

In this period, the average rate of decrease of sulfate in precipitation has been about 1 microequivalent per liter per year at both Huntington Forest and Whiteface Mountain. This is an encouraging and significant decline, but since U.S. sulfur emissions have already been reduced to near the level mandated by the 1990 Clean Air Act Amendments, the trends may not continue that far into the future.

The changes in other ions are smaller and their causes less clear. Adirondack base cation concentrations have decreased, somewhat erratically, by about a third, possibly because of changes in the amount of airborne particulates from industry and agriculture. This parallels a trend observed elsewhere in the Northeast and is of concern because many acidified soils currently have depleted base cation pools, and the decrease in cation inputs may further reduce their ability to support plant growth and neutralize acid deposition (Chapter 7).

Nitrogen concentrations in precipitation have also declined throughout much of the Northeast but more slowly than sulfate concentrations and mostly after 1995. The declines probably reflect recent declines in NO_x emissions but may also involve climate-driven changes in nitrogen transport or deposition, or other factors that we do not understand. See Butler et al. (2003) for a recent review.

The uncertainty about the cause of the decreases in nitrogen concentrations is compounded by the considerable variability in the trends at different stations. Sulfate concentrations are decreas-

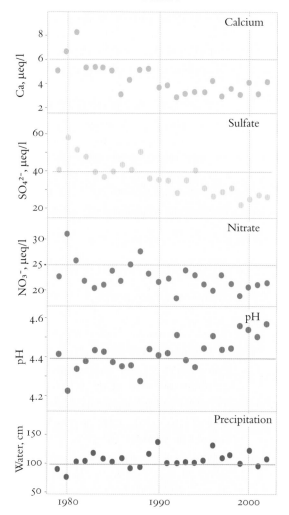

TRENDS IN WET DEPOSITION AT HUNTINGTON FOREST

Wet deposition data from the National Trends Network station at Huntington Forest; the points give the annual volume-weighted averages of weekly observations. From the National Trends Network website, http://nadp.sws.uiuc.edu/sites/siteinfo.asp?id=NY20&net=NTN. Sulfate has declined steadily and pH risen steadily. Calcium decreased in the 1980s and since then has been mostly constant; nitrate has perhaps declined, but the variability in the record makes it difficult to be sure.

*For recent changes in NO_x emissions estimates, see the graphs on page 13. For a recent study of eastern NO_x emissions, see Butler et al., "The relation between NO_x emissions and precipitation NO_3^- in the eastern USA," 2003.

ing almost everywhere. Nitrogen concentrations are much more erratic. In the Adirondacks they seem to be decreasing at Huntington Forest and Piseco Lake and varying without a clear trend at Whiteface Mountain and Wanakena.

TRENDS IN ADIRONDACK LAKES AND STREAMS

What should recovery look like?

Lake acidification is, by definition, the decrease in ANC and pH that occurs when mineral acids are deposited on a watershed and some of the hydrogen ions and acid anions are transmitted to the lake. Lake recovery will be, again by definition, the increase in ANC and pH that occurs as deposition declines.

If watersheds were impervious or inactive – if, that is, they transmitted all the acid they received directly to surface waters – recovery would be instantaneous: as soon as the ANC and pH of deposition increased, there would be parallel increases in the ANCs and pHs of surface waters.

But acidified watersheds, as we know from much research (pp. 92–93, 132–138), are anything but inactive. They accumulate acids that can be subsequently released and export the bases that they require to neutralize mineral acids. Both of these processes can delay recovery. The mobilization of stored acids can increase the supply of acid anions to surface water; the loss of bases can decrease the supply of base cations to surface waters. Both processes reduce ANC.

The diagrams to the right illustrate this. In the lake that is recovering (upper graph), the sulfate concentrations are decreasing rapidly, paralleling a decrease in sulfate deposition. Base cation concentrations are also decreasing (because less acid is getting neutralized) but, because the watershed has base cation reserves, less rapidly than sulfate. The ANC, which is proportional to the difference between base cations and sulfate (the blue band), is rising.

In the lake that is not recovering, the sulfate concentrations are decreasing less rapidly than sulfate deposition, indicating that stored sulfates are being released. The base cation concentrations are falling at the same rate as sulfate concentrations, indicating that the base cation reserves have been depleted. The ANC, again proportional to the difference between base cations and sulfate, remains constant and there is no recovery.

Trends at Big Moose Lake

Big Moose Lake was one of the original RILWAS lakes and the first Adirondack lake at which recent acidification was shown by sediment cores (pp. 52, 59). It is believed to have acidified by about 1

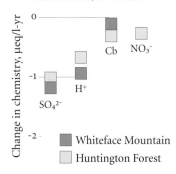

TRENDS IN ADIRONDACK PRECIPITATION CHEMISTRY, 1978–2000

Trends in Adirondack wet deposition, from Driscoll et al., "Chemical responses of lakes in the Adirondack region of New York to declines in acidic deposition," 2003. Only trends that are significant at the p=0.05 level are shown.

A LAKE WHOSE ANC IS RECOVERING

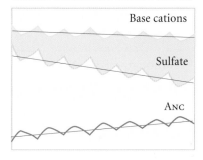

A LAKE WHOSE ANC IS NOT RECOVERING

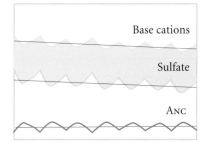

Two hypothetical lakes with declining sulfate concentrations. The blue bands show the difference between base cations and sulfate, which is proportional to the ANC. The lake in the upper graph still has substantial pools of base cations in the watershed; base cations are declining more slowly than sulfate, and the ANC is increasing. The base cation pools of the watershed of the lake in the lower graph have been largely depleted; base cations are decreasing as fast as sulfate, and the ANC is not increasing.

ADIRONDACK LAKES SURVEY LONG-TERM MONITORING WATERS

Squash · Big Moose Lake · Constable

West

Dart · Windfall

Moss · Cascade

Bubb

Rondaxe

1 km · THE BIG MOOSE GROUP

Little Clear
Grass (3)

Little Hope
Big Hope

Black

Middle · Sochia · Sunday · Owen
East Copperas
Little Echo

Heart
Marcy Dam

Little Simon

Avalanche
Lake Colden

Arbutus · Clear

Loon Hollow · Willys · Nate

Woods

Big Moose · Queer · Long
group · Raquette Lake Reservoir
Fly Pond Outlet · Sagamore
Bald Mountain Brook · Buck Creek
Middle Branch · Grass (4) · Limekiln
Middle Settlement · Carry
Squaw · Lost
Indian · Brooktrout

Barnes

North
South

G · Willis

Jockeybush

Otter

● Lake monitored since 1982   ☐ Limed lake

● Lake monitored since 1992   ● Stream monitored since 1992

The Adirondack Long-Term Monitoring program currently monitors 52 lakes and three streams. The initial 17 lakes, shown in red, were part of the Regionalized Integrated Lake-Watershed Acidification Study and have been monitored monthly since 1982. The remaining 35 lakes were added in 1992. One of the original lakes and three of the remaining ALTM lakes (in boxes) were artificially limed and are not used for regional trend analysis. The three streams were originally studied from 1988 to 1990 as part of the Episodic Response Project and have been monitored by the Adirondack Lakes Survey Corporation since 1992.

pH unit between 1900 and 1980. Its chemistry since then suggests a moderate recovery, possibly delayed by watershed processes and by the continued input of atmospheric nitrates. Sulfate concentrations have declined steadily and are now about a third less than they were in 1982. Their decline has paralleled, but not kept pace with, declines in sulfate concentrations in precipitation, which are now less than half what they were in 1982. The ANC has risen but only at about a third of the rate that sulfate concentrations are falling and only in the past few years; neither ANCs nor pHs rose much at all in the 1980s. Nitrate concentrations showed a slight increase in the 1980s followed by a slight decrease in the 1990s. Neither the increase nor the decrease was clearly related to changes in emissions, and neither seems to indicate a long-term trend. Inorganic aluminum concentrations have fallen, but spring aluminum peaks are still high, suggesting that the nitrate-driven acidity peaks (Chapter 6) are still displacing significant amounts of aluminum from soils.

Trends in the ALTM Lakes

The trends in the Big Moose data are generally similar to those of the other ALTM lakes. In the first analysis of trends in the original 17 ALTM lakes in 1993, Driscoll and Van Dreason noted that although almost all the ALTM lakes had strongly declining trends in sulfate between 1982 and 1991, about half had weakly increasing trends in nitrate and about a third had weakly decreasing trends in ANC. Trends in hydrogen ion and aluminum were weak and mostly nonsignificant. Trends in base cations were strongly increasing in two lakes and nonsignificant in the rest.

This pattern gradually changed in the 1990s. In their 1995 analysis Driscoll et al. found that decreases in sulfates were being offset by nearly equal decreases in base cations, and thus ANCs and pHs were not recovering. They noted that nitrate concentrations were now decreasing, and that the rate at which sulfate was decreasing was less than might have been expected from the decreases in sulfate deposition. This last finding paralleled results from Arbutus Lake (p. 97) and suggested that "previously deposited SO4 is released from soil in the ALTM watersheds, thereby delaying the recovery of lakes to decreases in atmospheric SO4."

A third analysis of the ALTM data in 1998, again by Driscoll and his collaborators, found a similar pattern. Sulfate was decreasing

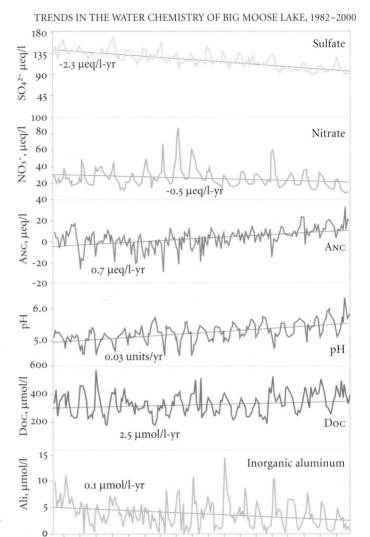

TRENDS IN THE WATER CHEMISTRY OF BIG MOOSE LAKE, 1982–2000

From Driscoll et al., "Chemical response of lakes in the Adirondack region of New York to declines in acidic deposition." Copyright 2003 American Chemical Society.

There have, thus far, been four analyses of the Adirondack long-term lake data: Driscoll and van Dreason, "Seasonal and long-term temporal patterns in the chemistry of Adirondack lakes," 1993; Driscoll et al., "Long-term trends in the chemistry of precipitation and lake water in the Adirondack region of New York, USA," 1995; Driscoll et al., "The response of lake water in the Adirondack region of New York to changes in acidic deposition," 1998; and Driscoll et al., "Chemical response of lakes in the Adirondack region of New York to declines in acidic deposition," 2003.

MONITORING THE ADIRONDACK LONG-TERM LAKES

The lake monitoring program carried out by the Adirondack Lakes Survey Corporation samples 52 ALTM lakes monthly and 43 TIME lakes annually. The lakes are by visited by two-person crews who travel by foot, truck, boat, and helicopter. The crew measures the lake height and temperature, notes whether there has been recent precipitation, and collects two bottles of water, either by hand or with a Kemmerer sampler. The samples are sealed, labeled, iced, and transported to the ALSC laboratory in Ray Brook.

In the laboratory, the samples are divided into seven aliquots that are variously filtered, stabilized with acid, and analyzed for 20 parameters using eight instruments. Between field samples, blanks, duplicates, and various quality-control samples the laboratory analyzes about 90 samples and makes about 1,500 determinations each month.

The Adirondack lake-monitoring program is noteworthy both for the number of lakes involved and for the level of temporal and chemical detail it produces. Its extensive coverage – a total of 89 lakes in a 7,000-square-mile area – provides a unique picture of the lake chemistry of the entire Adirondack Park. Its technical detail – the ALTM takes monthly samples, separates organic and inorganic aluminum, and determines 17 other laboratory parameters – allows investigators to determine trends with great accuracy and to detect features like snowmelt acidity and peaks in inorganic aluminum that could not be seen in simpler studies.

THE ADIRONDACK LONG-TERM MONITORING LAKES

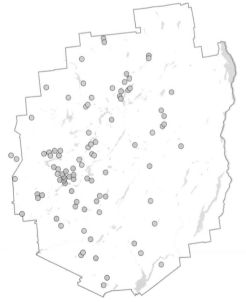

○ Sampled by ALTM (46) ○ Sampled by TIME (37) ○ Sampled by both (6)

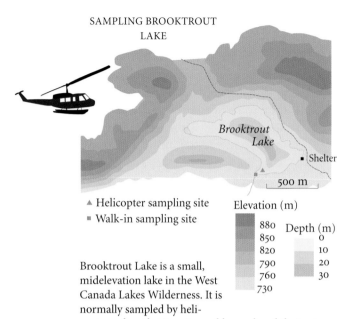

SAMPLING BROOKTROUT LAKE

▲ Helicopter sampling site
■ Walk-in sampling site

Elevation (m)
880
850
820
790
760
730

Depth (m)
0
10
20
30

Brooktrout Lake is a small, midelevation lake in the West Canada Lakes Wilderness. It is normally sampled by helicopter; when that is not possible, workers hike in six miles from the Moose River Plains Road. Samples are taken at the outlet. Hand samples are taken by filling bottles at the surface. Helicopter samples are taken from below the surface with a Kemmerer sampler.

THE KEMMERER SAMPLER

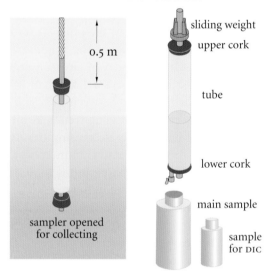

0.5 m

sliding weight
upper cork

tube

lower cork

main sample

sample for DIC

sampler opened for collecting

The Kemmerer sampler is used to gather water from below the surface at lakes that are sampled by boat or helicopter. It is lowered to the desired depth and then a weight is dropped down the rope, pushing the tube and top cork downward and closing the sampler. The sampler and bottles are rinsed in the lake before filling and are handled with vinyl gloves. The samples are cooled and kept in the dark until they are analyzed.

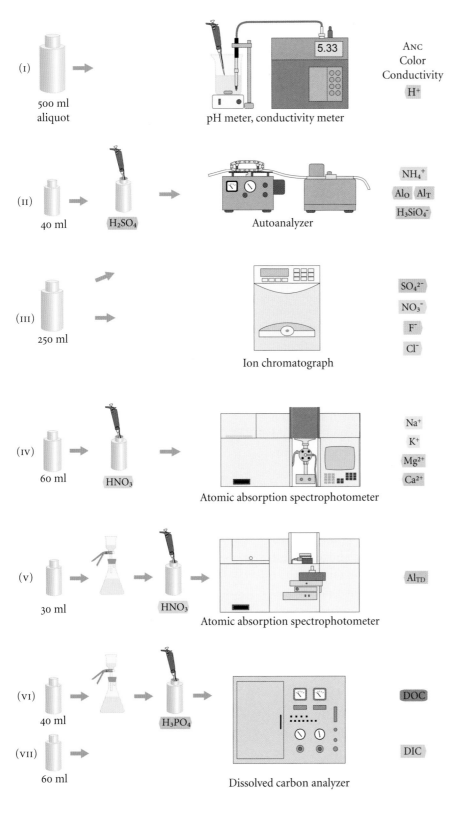

(I)

500 ml
aliquot

pH meter, conductivity meter

ANC
Color
Conductivity

H^+

(II)

40 ml

H_2SO_4

Autoanalyzer

NH_4^+

Al_O Al_T

$H_3SiO_4^-$

(III)

250 ml

Ion chromatograph

SO_4^{2-}

NO_3^-

F^-

Cl^-

(IV)

60 ml

HNO_3

Atomic absorption spectrophotometer

Na^+

K^+

Mg^{2+}

Ca^{2+}

(V)

30 ml

HNO_3

Atomic absorption spectrophotometer

Al_{TD}

(VI)

40 ml

H_3PO_4

DOC

(VII)

60 ml

Dissolved carbon analyzer

DIC

When the samples arrive in the laboratory, they are subdivided, filtered or acidified if necessary, stored, and then analyzed. Five basic analytical techniques are used.

Conductivity, pH, and ANC are determined electrometrically (I), using Orion and YSI meters with glass electrodes. Conductivity and pH are read directly; ANC is calculated from a Gran titration: the sample is acidified to about pH 3.9 with hydrochloric acid, and then the pH changes are recorded as small amounts of acid are added.

Ammonium, monomeric aluminum, and reactive silica are determined by colorimetric methods using a Technicon Autoanalyzer (II). These are wet-chemical methods in which color-generating reagents are added to the sample and the resulting colors measured photometrically.

The major anions (sulfate, nitrate, fluoride, chloride) are determined chromatographically in a Dionex ion chromatograph (III). The ions are separated with an ion exchange column and then measured by a conductivity meter.

The base cations (sodium, potassium, magnesium, calcium) and total dissolved aluminum (Al_{TD}) are measured by atomic absorption spectrometry. The samples are ionized in a flame and generate characteristic absorption lines (dark bands in the emission spectrum) that can be read in a spectrophotometer. The base cations are determined in a conventional flame spectrophotometer (IV). Aluminum, which occurs in a variety of inorganic and organic complexes, is determined in a spectrophotometer fitted with a high-temperature graphite furnace that volatilizes the complexes (V).

Dissolved carbon is read in a Dohrmann carbon analyzer, which converts the carbon to carbon dioxide and then detects the carbon dioxide with an infrared spectrometer. Dissolved inorganic carbon, which is volatile and easily lost to the atmosphere, is determined on a 60 ml sample, which is collected separately and kept sealed until it is analyzed (VII). Dissolved organic carbon is determined on a 40 ml aliquot of the main sample that has been preserved with phosphoric acid (VI).

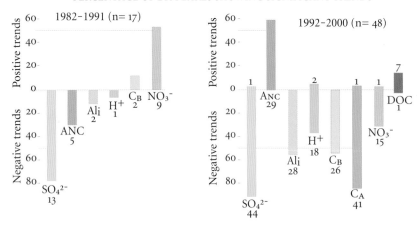

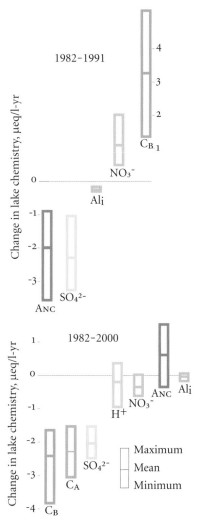

in all lakes but at rates considerably less than the rate at which it was declining in deposition. Mass-balance calculations suggested that the majority of the drainage lakes were releasing more sulfur than they received in wet deposition (p. 217). The source of the additional sulfur was not known; it may have been from dry deposition, weathering, or the release of previously deposited sulfur that was stored in the watershed. Nitrogen-balance calculations showed that rates of nitrogen retention were highly variable. Some lakes were retaining as much as 95% of the nitrogen deposited every year, and others as little as 42%. Nitrogen modeling with a new watershed model that accounted for forest growth suggested that if the present nitrogen inputs remained unchanged, it would take about a hundred years for the forests to reach nitrogen saturation.

In the 1998 analysis, most of the 16 unlimed lakes that had been monitored since 1982 showed only slight trends in ANC. One lake, Little Echo, showed a moderately rapid rate of increase of ANC of 1.02 µeq/l-yr. Two others, Big Moose and Squash Pond, showed somewhat slower increases of 0.42 and 0.65 µeq/l-yr, and one, West Pond, was decreasing at the rate of 0.88 µeq/l-yr. The remaining 12 showed little change. The authors noted a "close correspondence" between base cation and acid ion concentrations and suggested, for the first time in an ALTM analysis, that base cation depletion might be delaying recovery. They also noted that other contributing factors – buffering by DOC and aluminum, release of nitrates and sulfates from watersheds – might be involved as well.

The most recent analysis of the Adirondack LTM lakes, using data through 2000 and including the 35 lakes added to the monitoring program in 1992, showed clear signs of chemical recovery. Significant decreases in sulfate were observed in 44 of the 48 unlimed ALTM lakes. Inorganic aluminum and base cations, both indicators of the rate of soil acidification, were decreasing in more than half the lakes; ANC was increasing in 60%, and pH in 37%.

From 1982–1991 data in Driscoll and van Dreason, "Seasonal and long-term temporal patterns in the chemistry of Adirondack lakes," 1993; and 1982–2000 data in Driscoll et al., "Chemical response of lakes in the Adirondack region of New York to declines in acidic deposition," 2003. Above left, the number of Adirondack LTM lakes showing significant trends in the first and second decades of monitoring. The bars give percentages; the numbers below the columns are the number of lakes. In the first decade relatively few lakes showed significant trends for any ions other than sulfate and nitrate; in the second decade more than half the lakes showed significant trends in sulfate, ANC, aluminum, base cations, and acid anions.

Above, a box plot of trends for the 17 original Adirondack LTM lakes. Sulfate showed significant declines throughout the period; ANC, which decreased in the 1980s, shows an increase for the whole period; and nitrate, which increased slightly in the 1980s, now shows a slight decrease for the whole period.

Nitrates, as ever the wildcard of the acidification deck, had shown slight and rather puzzling decreases in 15 lakes but no significant changes in the other 33. Dissolved organic carbon, which is believed to be a bellwether element that can mark the switch from inorganic to organic acidity, had increased significantly in seven lakes and decreased in one. All of this suggested definite signs of chemical recovery, but the changes were not large and were not occurring in all lakes. After 30 years of emissions reductions, the recovery of Adirondack lakes had finally begun, but only in some lakes and only slowly in those.

Recovery Times

In 2003, Driscoll and his collaborators used the individual ANC trends for the 28 Adirondack LTM lakes whose ANCs are currently increasing to calculate the time it will take for these lakes to reach mean ANCs of 50 µeq/l. This is an ANC value commonly used in modeling recovery and represents an ANC at which a lake is assumed to be moderately safe from damaging acid episodes.

The results suggest that most lakes will take another 20 to 50 years to recover. About a quarter of the lakes will recover in the next 15 years, another half between 15 and 40 years, and the remaining quarter in 40 to 80 years. No estimate is possible for the 20 lakes whose ANCs have not thus far shown increases.

Because ANC trends change frequently, and because there is no way of predicting how nutrient cycling will change as climate and deposition change, the details of the predictions may not be very accurate. But they are still generally important because they give an empirical measure of the time lag between changes in emissions and ecologically meaningful recovery. By 1993, 20 years after sulfur emissions began declining, recoveries of ANC and pH were just starting to be observed. In 2003, 30 years after the first reductions in deposition, the most optimistic prediction was that 20 to 50 more years – a total of 50 to 80 years in all – would be the minimum required for the most responsive of the acid-sensitive lakes to recover from acidification.

Trends in Adirondack Streams, 1991-2001

Long-term monitoring data are available for only three Adirondack streams, and the interpretation of the data is complicated because their flows are not directly measured and have to be inferred from other gauges some distance away.

The issue of flow is important because stream chemistry varies strongly with flow. At high flows streams are dilute and acid: dilute because they contain much surface water, and acid because the acids in the precipitation have not been neutralized by bases in

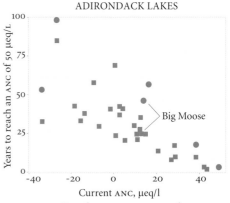

ESTIMATED RECOVERY TIMES OF LOW-ANC ADIRONDACK LAKES

• Based on 1982-2000 trend
■ Based on 1992-2000 trend

Redrawn with permission from Driscoll et al., "Chemical response of lakes in the Adirondack region of New York to declines in acidic deposition." Copyright 2003 American Chemical Society. The squares give the estimated time it will take the lake to reach an ANC of 50 µeq/l at the average rate of ANC increase for 1992-2000. The circles give a second estimate, based on the 1982-2000 trend, for the six lakes with 18 years of data.

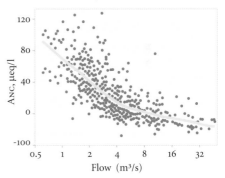

ANC VS. FLOW, BALD MOUNTAIN BROOK

Redrawn from Lawrence, Momen, and Roy, "Use of stream chemistry for monitoring acidic deposition effects in the Adirondack region of New York." Copyright 2004 American Society of Agronomy Inc. via the Copyright Clearance Center. The line is a LOWESS fit. The ANC decreases as the flow increases, probably because of a combination of dilution effects and snowmelt acids that were mobilized at high flows. The residuals from the LOWESS fit were used to produce the flow-corrected graph on the next page. The other two ALTM streams, Buck Creek and Fly Pond Outlet, showed similar patterns.

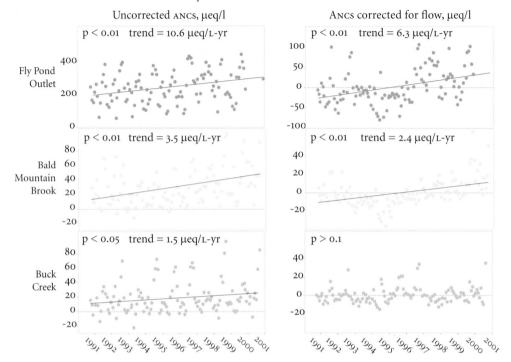

The monthly ANCs of the three Adirondack LTM streams, before and after correcting for the dependence of ANC on flow. Redrawn from Lawrence, Momen, and Roy, "Use of stream chemistry for monitoring acidic deposition effects in the Adirondack region of New York." This and the illustration below, copyright 2004 American Society of Agronomy Inc. via the Copyright Clearance Center. The probability values are obtained from the seasonal Kendall Tau test by fitting an ANC-flow relationship for each stream and subtracting it from the data.

the soil (p. 112). At lower flows, when they contain deeper ground-water that has been concentrated by evaporation and contact with mineral soil, they are more concentrated and less acid.

The result is that streamflow and water chemistry interact: increases in the amount of rainfall, which dilute basic ions, are chemically similar to increases in the acidity of rainfall, which increase the supply of acids. Thus any analysis that attempts to detect the results of a change in the acidity of precipitation must also account for the effects of flows.

Lawrence, Momen, and Roy have recently analyzed the monitoring data for the three Adirondack LTM streams. The three left-hand panels at the top of the page show the raw data; the right-hand panels are the same data after subtracting the changes caused by flow.

The raw data for all three streams showed significant increases in ANC. Buck Creek, the most acidic and least buffered of the streams, had the lowest rate of increase; Bald Mountain Brook, with moderate buffering, had a higher rate; and Fly Pond Outlet, with the most buffering, had the highest rate of increase. The rates of increase for Bald Mountain Brook and Fly Pond Outlet were 3.5 and 10 μeq/l-yr, higher than most of those observed in the ALTM lakes. The rate of increase for Buck Creek was 1.5 μeq/l-yr, comparable to those observed in several lakes.

When the effects of flow are removed, the trends change considerably. Fly Pond Outlet, whose ANC appeared to increase uni-

TRENDS IN THE ANC AND pH OF THREE ADIRONDACK STREAMS, 1981-2001

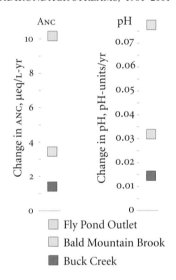

From Lawrence, Momen, and Roy, "Use of stream chemistry for monitoring acidic deposition effects in the Adirondack region of New York," 2004. These are the uncorrected trends in ANC and pH from regressions of concentrations against time.

formly in the uncorrected data, now seems to increase its ANC abruptly about 1997. Bald Mountain Brook, which showed a slight non-linearity in the uncorrected data, now decreases for four years and increases for six. And Buck Creek, which had a weak but significant trend in the uncorrected data, now has no trend at all.

There is no way to say which of the trends, the corrected or the uncorrected, is more meaningful, or which (if any) better predicts the future changes in the stream. The uncorrected values are real values: all three streams have in fact increased their ANC. But the corrected values suggest that these increases are not as simple as they look, and that if the streams are responding to the overall declines in acid deposition at all, they are responding individually and in complex ways.

REGIONAL TRENDS

A basic question for researchers studying trends is whether the trends in the Adirondacks are comparable to those elsewhere in the Northeast. If they are, then changes in precipitation chemistry, which are fairly uniform, are controlling the recovery of acidified waters, and it should be possible to make some general predictions about recovery. If they are not, then the details of watershed processes are controlling recovery, and each region may recover in its own way and on its own timetable.

Three analyses have thus far examined chemical trends on a regional basis. The first, in 1993, included 91 lakes in the northeastern United States. The second, in 1999, included a large set of nearly 200 lakes and streams in both Europe and North America. The third, in 2003, included an enlarged set of U.S. waters containing both the original lakes of the LTM network and the statistically selected lakes of the TIME network as well.

Acidification vs. Dilution

The first regional analysis of trends, done by Avis Newell of the EPA in 1990, used eight years of data from 91 LTM waters in Maine, Vermont, New York, and the upper Midwest (graph at right). It is of interest both because it provided the first regional view of trends in lake chemistry and because it was the first (and, somewhat oddly, is still the only) study to try to identify dilution-related trends in lake chemistry.

Newell found significant decreases in sulfate at a majority of the sites in the high-deposition areas of the Adirondacks, Catskills, and Vermont but only at a few of the lower-deposition sites in Maine and the upper Midwest. Significant nitrate increases were found at a majority of the Adirondack and Catskill sites but not in the other

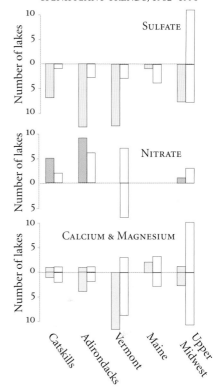

MONITORED LAKES WITH
SIGNIFICANT TRENDS, 1982–1990

— Nonsignificant positive trend
— Nonsignificant negative trend
— Significant negative trend

From Newell, "Inter-regional comparison of patterns and trends in surface water acidification across the United States," 1993. Trends were considered significant if the seasonal Kendall Tau test gave a p < 0.1.

regions. Base cation trends were highly variable in most areas; only in Vermont was there a consistent pattern of decrease.

The possibility of dilution effects arises because the changes in ions at individual sites tend to be strongly correlated. In particular, decreases in sulfate, nitrate, and base cations are often correlated with increases in precipitation. This suggests that some apparent decreases in ANC are dilution effects and do not represent long-term trends.

Newell used a cluster analysis to identify sites with similar trends and found that the sites divided, fairly cleanly, into three groups. The first group, shown in dark blue on the map, were those at which sulfate was decreasing and ANC and base cations were increasing. These she considered to show decreasing acidification. The second group, those in which sulfate, ANC, and base cations were all decreasing, she considered to be showing dilution effects but no clear trends. The third group, in which sulfate and base cations were increasing and ANC was decreasing, she considered as showing increases in acidity.

Because the analysis was based on only eight years of data and many of the trends that she was correlating were statistically weak, Newell's detailed results are probably not important here. What is important is the suggestion that hydrological and chemical trends can be closely intertwined and require a careful analysis to separate them. This was also true in the analysis of the Adirondack LTM streams (p. 202) and may prove increasingly true for lakes in the climate-change century we are entering.

Stoddard 1999: ANCs Begin to Recover in Europe

The second regional analysis was done by Stoddard and his collaborators in 1999. They examined 196 LTM sites in North America and Europe for responses to recent declines in acid deposition. Because many trends changed about 1990, they analyzed trends for the 1980s and 1990s separately.

By the mid-1990s, Europe, Britain, and North America had all reduced their sulfur emissions substantially. The European cuts took effect somewhat earlier than the British and North American ones. In 1996 sulfur emissions in Europe were down 63% from their 1970s peak. In Britain sulfur emissions were down 32%, and in North America, 29%.

The regional trends in lake chemistry reflected the differences in emissions. In the 1980s, there were strong declines in sulfate and increases in ANC in western Europe but not in Scandinavia, Britain, or North America. By the 1990s strong sulfate declines were observed in most monitored waters in all regions.

As was the case in the Adirondack lakes discussed on page 199, reductions in sulfate did not automatically translate into increases in ANC. In Europe there were major increases in ANC. In Scandi-

ANC TRENDS IN NEW YORK & NEW ENGLAND, 1982–1990

○ Diluted at high flows, no long-term trend
● ANC increasing   ● ANC decreasing
5 Number of waters being monitored

From Newell, "Inter-regional comparison of patterns and trends in surface water acidification across the United States," 1993. Streams were considered to be showing dilution effects if sulfate, ANC, and base cations were all decreasing. This pattern is also consistent with the effects of base cation depletion, which had not been recognized in 1993.

LONG-TERM MONITORING SITES IN BRITAIN, EUROPE, & EASTERN NORTH AMERICA

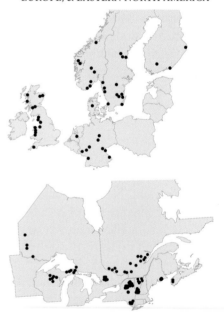

From Stoddard et al., "Regional trends in aquatic recovery from acidification in North America and Europe," 1999. The dots are the 168 LTM sites used in their analysis.

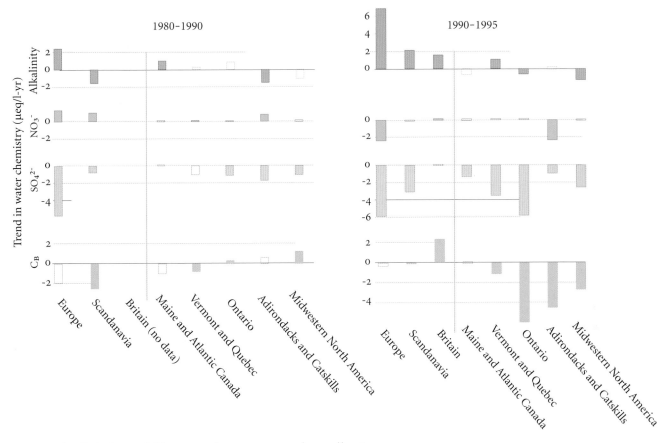

REGIONAL TRENDS IN SURFACE WATER CHEMISTRY, EUROPE & NORTH AMERICA, 1980-1995

navia, Britain, and Vermont there were much smaller increases. In Maine and New York there were no significant changes, and in Ontario and the midwestern United States there were slight decreases.

To no one's surprise, the problem in the last three regions was the base cation supply. In Ontario, New York, and the Midwest, base cation concentrations were falling as fast as or faster than sulfate and nitrate concentrations. Thus whatever waters were gaining from reductions in acid anions they were losing to reductions in base cations; as a result the ANC, which reflects the balance of acids and bases, was not increasing.

Stoddard 2003: ANCs Improve in the United States

A few years later, with a few more years of data, much had changed. When Stoddard and his collaborators analyzed data from 188 LTM sites in the eastern United States, focusing on the period from 1990 to 2000, they found clear evidence of ANC increases of about 1 µeq/l per year in Adirondack and upper Midwest lakes and northern Appalachian streams. They found very small increases in ANC in New England lakes and very small decreases in streams in

Based on Stoddard et al., "Regional trends in aquatic recovery from acidification in North America and Europe," 1999. The 1980s trends are based on data from 168 LTM sites, the 1990s trends on data from 196 sites. The open boxes are trends that the authors considered questionable, either because they were not statistically significant at the p<0.1 level or because the data on which they were based were exceptionally heterogeneous.

the central Appalachians. These increases in ANC were the first evidence of a widespread decrease in acidity since research began.

Accompanying the ANC increases were small decreases in hydrogen ion, averaging 0.2 μeq/l per year for the Adirondacks. These are equivalent to small but biologically significant increases in pH, like the 0.03 pH unit per year increase in Big Moose shown on page 199.

Stoddard and his collaborators also found significant increases in DOC (about 60 μg/l per year in the Adirondacks). DOC is believed to have decreased during acidification as natural organic acids were replaced with mineral acids (p. 161). The recent increases in DOC, which have been observed widely in Europe and North America, may either be a sign of recovery or a consequence of the increased decay associated with climate warming.

As in Stoddard's 1999 survey (p. 204), decreases in base cations in most regions are clearly delaying or preventing recovery. Only the upper Midwest seems to be showing an orthodox recovery pattern in which base cations are decreasing more slowly than sulfate. In the Adirondacks, New England, and the northern Appalachians base cations are decreasing nearly as fast as or faster than sulfate. As a result, in New England the ANCs are nearly constant; in the Adirondacks and northern Appalachians the ANCs are showing definite increases, but the increases are dependent on decreases in nitrates as well as decreases in sulfates. This is somewhat surprising because, as noted on page 197, the changes in nitrate deposition are small and erratic.

All this should make us very cautious about how we interpret the trend data. Very clearly, the data show what appears to be the beginnings of a significant recovery. But equally clearly, the recovery is neither universal nor certain. Four of the five regions are showing signs of recovery, but in one the recovery is small, and in two others it depends on nitrate changes that are unexplained and may not continue. Forty years after the first clean air legislation and 30 years after the peak in sulfur emissions, the effects of acid deposition on waters and watersheds are proving very tenacious.

But Recovery Is Delayed

The graphs on page 208, from Stoddard's 2003 summary, give several measures of that tenacity. The first compares the rates at which the sulfate concentrations of lake water and deposition have been changing. For a very few waters, which lie in the region where the blue and brown lines approach one another in the upper graph on the right page, the rates are similar. For most other waters, the brown line lies above the blue, showing that

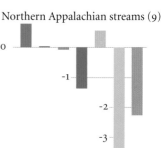

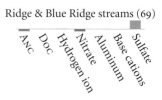

Based on data from Stoddard et al., "Response of surface water chemistry to the Clean Air Act Amendments of 1990," 2003. In the above figure the trends for aluminum are in μg/l-yr and those for DOC are in mg/l-yr. All others are in μeq/l-yr. The increase in sulfate in the Blue Ridge is believed to result from the release of sulfates from soils, which are unglaciated and have stored large amounts of sulfate from atmospheric deposition.

the amount of sulfate in deposition is decreasing faster than the amount of sulfate in surface water. The most likely explanation of this is that some sulfates thatwere stored in soils are now being freed.

The next graph compares spring and summer acidities. Almost every low-ANC Adirondack lake still experiences spring acidity peaks in which the ANC drops below the summer baseline. Almost every lake with a summer ANC of 30 µeq/l or less has a springtime ANC of 0 µeq/l or less. Depending on the water, these acidity peaks may be the result of low base cation supplies or atmospheric and nitrogen-cycle acids that have accumulated in the winter (pp. 109-113). In either case, they are an indicator of persistent acidification of the watershed.

The bottom graph is one of several from the Stoddard report that compare the results from the TIME and LTM networks (p. 194). The TIME network contains 103 statistically chosen lakes and streams that are sampled annually; the LTM network contains 188 nonrandomly chosen lakes and streams that are sampled 3 to 15 times a year. The LTM network is larger and older and has the most detailed information about seasonal patterns and trends. The TIME network, smaller and more recent, is statistically representative of a large target population of lakes and can be used to make predictions about that population.

Satisfyingly, the trends displayed by the two networks are in fact very similar, both in the Adirondacks and elsewhere. In the bottom graph at right, the two networks differ on the number of Adirondack lakes with small positive trends. wwith the TIME network (light-blue line) showing more recovering lakes than he LTM. Significantly, both networks agree agree at the ends of the distribution where the lakes with strong positive and negative trends lie. This is an important result, suggesting both that the nonrandom LTM lakes are still in many ways representative of the region and that the less frequently sampled TIME lakes still capture the significant long-term trends accurately.

Because the TIME lakes are statistically chosen, they can be used to estimate the total number of lakes at different levels of acid-

Graphs from Stoddard et al., "Response of Surface Water Chemistry to the Clean Air Act Amendments of 1990," 2003. The top and bottom figures are *cumulative distribution graphs,* where the y-value gives the percentage of lakes with rates of change equal to or more negative than the x-value. Thus the point marked by the black dot in the upper graph indicates that in about 48% of the deposition records sulfate is decreasing by 4% per year or more. The top graph shows that sulfate concentrations are decreasing at a slower percentage rate than those in precipitation; the second graph shows that spring ANCs are still lower than those in summer, indicating that snowmelt acidification is still a problem. The third indicates the general agreement between estimates from the Adirondack TIME and LTM lakes.

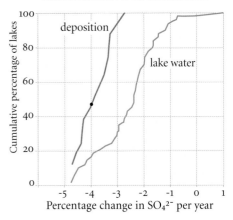

DELAYED RECOVERY OF ADIRONDACK LAKE WATER RELATIVE TO DEPOSITION

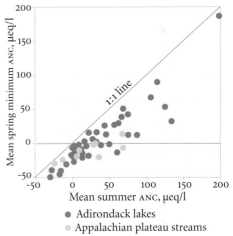

SPRING AND SUMMER ANCS

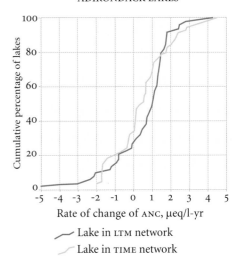

ANC TRENDS IN TIME AND LTM ADIRONDACK LAKES

ity. The TIME analysis of the early 1990s (which did not take into account springtime acidity peaks) estimated there were 238 lakes in the Adirondacks and 386 lakes in New England with summer ANCs of less than 0 µeq/l. Stoddard et al. apply the median rates of ANC increase (0.8 µeq/l-yr in the Adirondacks, 0.3 µeq/l in New England) to these groups of lakes and estimate that 89 of the Adirondack lakes but only 12 of the New England lakes have improved sufficiently that their summer ANCs are now above zero.

This analysis shows that lake ANCs are gradually improving. But note that it says nothing about the springtime ANCs, which we know can be 50 µeq/l or more below the summer ones. A more practical measure of recovery might be the number of lakes whose summer ANCs are now above 50 µeq/l, the level at which their spring ANCs will likely remain above zero.

WATERSHED MONITORING AT ARBUTUS LAKE

The monitoring we have been considering thus far describes the chemical conditions in lakes and streams but not the fluxes through them. It can tell you, for example, that Big Moose Lake contained 100 microequivalents of sulfate per liter on a certain day but not how much sulfate is supplied to the lake every year or how much of this the lake stores and how much it sends downstream.

To understand how watersheds work – and in particular, to understand how acids and nutrients cycle within them – we must measure fluxes as well as concentrations. This requires frequent measurements of precipitation, streamflow, and chemistry. It is not difficult in theory, but it is demanding in practice and so is not included in most monitoring programs. It has frequently been done on a short-term basis in individual studies but has only rarely been done on a long-term basis.

The most famous American flux studies have been done at the Hubbard Brook Experimental Forest in the White Mountain National Forest since 1963. Results from Hubbard Brook have been mentioned several times in this book, particularly in the chapters on element cycling.

The Arbutus Lake watershed at the Huntington Forest in the central Adirondacks, which is monitored by Adirondack Ecological Center (a part of the State University of New York's College of Environmental Science and Forestry) is the Adirondack's Hubbard Brook. The watershed has an area of 309 ha; the lake itself is 50 ha. Monitoring began in 1983 and is currently supervised by Myron Mitchell and his collaborators, many of whom work at Hubbard Brook as well. Like Hubbard Brook, precipitation chemistry, streamflow and water chemistry are monitored on a weekly basis, allowing ion budgets (the net fluxes of ions in and out) to be calculated for both the watershed and the lake.

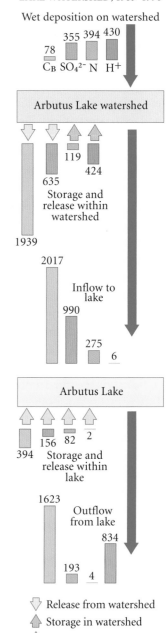

AVERAGE ANNUAL FLUXES AT ARBUTUS LAKE WATERSHED, 1985-1998

Wet deposition on watershed

78 355 394 430
C_B SO_4^{2-} N H^+

Arbutus Lake watershed

119 424 635 1939
Storage and release within watershed

2017
Inflow to lake
990 275 6

Arbutus Lake

394 156 82 2
Storage and release within lake

1623
Outflow from lake
193 4 834

▽ Release from watershed
△ Storage in watershed
△ Storage in lake
82 µeq/ha-yr

Based on data from Mitchell et al., "Role of within-lake processes and hydrobiogeochemical changes over 16 years in a watershed in the Adirondack Mountains of New York State, USA," 2001.

Individual results from the Arbutus project have already been described in the sections on nitrogen, sulfur, and calcium. Here we give a brief description of the overall pattern of storage and release.

The diagram to the left gives the average yearly budgets for sulfate, nitrate, hydrogen ion, and base cations for 1985–1998. Each ion has a different pattern of storage and release.

Hydrogen is the most abundant ion in precipitation but one of the least abundant in stream water. The watershed is base-rich, and all but about 1.5% of the hydrogen ion is neutralized in the watershed. Only a small amount enters the lake, and an even smaller amount is discharged downstream.

Nitrogen is currently the second most abundant solute in precipitation, about 10% more abundant than sulfur and 10% less abundant than hydrogen ion. The watershed and the lake together, somewhat surprisingly, retain a little less than half of the incoming nitrogen. About 30% is taken up by the watershed, another 21% is stored in the lake, and the remainder is discharged downstream.

Sulfate is the third most abundant ion in precipitation. Substantial amounts are also generated in the watershed, probably by the release of previously stored sulfur, and the amount released to the lake each year is more than twice what arrives from precipitation. About 20% of the sulfate that enters the lake is stored there, probably by sulfur-reducing bacteria, and the rest is exported downstream.

Base cations are scarce in precipitation but abundant in the watershed soils, and so base cation concentrations in groundwater are high. The watershed supplies some 30 times as much calcium and magnesium to the lake as it receives in rainfall. This is four times as much as is required to neutralize the acid in the rain and shows that, unlike many Adirondack watersheds, the Arbutus watershed has an abundance of bases, and most of their release is a natural process and not driven by acid rain. About a fifth of the base cations released by the watershed every year are retained in the lake; the rest are discharged downstream.

Seasonal Uptake and Release

The fluxes of ions into and out of the Arbutus watershed have strong seasonal patterns. Much of the outflow – some 78% of the

AVERAGE ION FLUXES AT ARBUTUS LAKE WATERSHED, 1995–1998

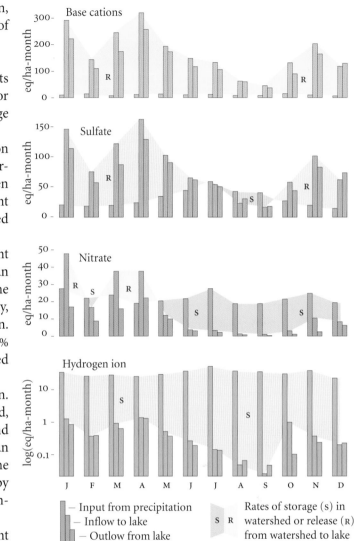

From Mitchell et al., "Role of within-lake processes and hydrobiogeochemical changes over 16 years in a watershed in the Adirondack Mountains of New York State, USA," 2001. The groups of bars show the average fluxes in precipitation from watershed to lake and from lake downstream for 1995–1998. The shaded polygons equal the difference between the flux in precipitation and the flux from the watershed to the lake (first and second bars in each group) and give the amount of that ion stored in or released by the watershed.

total flux of solutes and 84% of the total flux of water – from the watershed occurs in the six months when the vegetation is dormant. Releases of sulfate and base cations, the elements being supplied by the watershed, are low during the growing season, climb to a peak in late fall just before freeze-up, drop during the coldest part of winter, and then climb to a second major peak in spring. Hydrogen ion, which is stored in the watershed throughout the year, shows a similar pattern: the highest rates of storage are during the growing season, the lowest rates of storage (and so the greatest fluxes) during late fall and early spring.

Nitrogen, the element whose cycles are most tied to biological activity, has the most complex pattern. Nitrate is stored for the entire growing season, though at decreasing rates in the late summer and fall. It is released in early winter, then apparently stored again (the numbers are close and there is uncertainty in the data) in deep winter, and finally released again in early spring.

Even though Arbutus is far from a typical Adirondack watershed, the magnitude of these fluxes and the complexity of the seasonal patterns are very instructive. The watershed neutralizes 98% of the hydrogen ion from wet deposition but exports almost three times as much sulfur as it receives. More than twice as much hydrogen is neutralized in August as in February, and roughly as much nitrogen is released from the watershed in April as is stored in it in June. All these patterns, as we have discussed in previous chapters, have important ecological consequences.

SUMMARY

1 *Monitoring networks* are of critical importance to our efforts to understand and control acid deposition. They allow us to track emissions and deposition, measure the response of watersheds and surface waters, and assess the effects of regulatory changes on chemistry and biology.

2 The current U.S. *acid deposition monitoring network* consists of at least 550 air and deposition monitoring stations and 300 waterbodies that are measured regularly. It developed gradually over the past 25 years and involves extensive collaborations among government agencies, educational institutions, and private research organizations. Initially, it was funded through a mix of federal, state, and private money. More recently, the federal contribution has decreased, and the state and private funders are paying more of the cost. This is notably true in New York, where the state runs its own network of deposition monitoring stations and where the state and the electric power companies provide 85% of the funds for the Adirondack Long-Term Monitoring program.

3 In the Adirondacks, *acid-deposition monitoring* is done at three federal deposition monitoring stations and four New York State stations. Fifty-two lakes are sampled monthly by the Adirondack Lakes Survey as ALTM waters and another 43 lakes sampled yearly as TIME waters. In addition, three ALTM streams are sampled weekly, and 30 lakes are sampled annually as AEAP waters.

4 Over the past 30 years U.S. *sulfur emissions* have decreased by about 50%. Nitrogen oxide emissions have decreased about 25% in the same period. The wet deposition of sulfur has decreased with the decreases in emissions; nitrate deposition was constant or increasing in the 1980s and early 1990s and seems to have declined in the late 1990s.

5 The first three analyses of the *Adirondack Long-Term Monitoring data*, in 1993, 1995, and 1998, showed clear decreases in sulfate concentrations but no general increase in pH or ANC. The fourth analysis, using data through 2000 from the full set of 48 unlimed lakes, showed sulfate decreases in 92% of the lakes, ANC increases and inorganic aluminum decreases in 60%, pH increases in 38%, and nitrate increases in 31%.

6 The *trends in Adirondack streams* are more difficult to analyze because only a few streams are monitored and because stream chemistry varies strongly with streamflow. Raw data from the three streams showed ANC increases. When the data were corrected for flow changes, the ANC trends disappeared in one stream but persisted in two others.

7 *Regional trends* in the United States and Europe are generally similar to those in the Adirondacks. Decreases in sulfates were widely noted by the early 1990s. Increases in ANC were first noted in the early 1990s in Europe and the late 1990s in much of the eastern United States.

8 The *improvements in pH and ANC* thus far noted in the United States are important indicators of the local recovery of surface waters but differ from region to region and must be examined carefully. In New England and the Blue Ridge, there has been little improvement. In the Adirondacks and northern Appalachians, the improvements that have occurred depend on decreases in nitrates that are not associated with changes in nitrate deposition and may not be sustainable.

9 Many *chemical indicators* – the small changes in stream sulfates relative to deposition, the large decreases in stream base cations, and the persistence of springtime acidity peaks – all suggest that surface water recovery is being slowed, or perhaps in some cases prevented, by cation depletion and the release of acids that have been stored in watersheds.

CONCLUSIONS

WHAT WE KNOW AND WHAT WE NEED TO DO

10

The research we have reviewed in this book – some 200 papers, illustrated by 400 graphs, maps, and diagrams – was designed to answer practical questions about the origins, effects, and regulation of acid rain. One measure of the success of this research – and it has been, in our opinion, very successful – is that we can now answer many of these questions. In this chapter we do just that, posing and answering nine questions that summarize our current knowledge of acid rain and then, by way of a conclusion, offering our opinions on five further questions related to scientific needs and future research.

1 When did acid deposition begin, and when did it reach its peak?

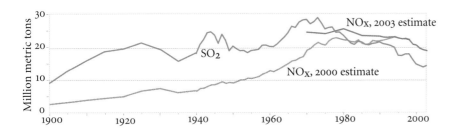

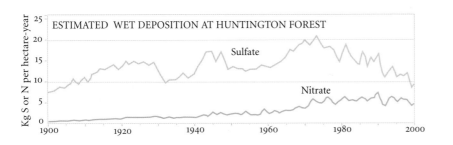

Acid deposition began sometime after 1850, when the use of sulfur-containing coals became widespread. Levels of sulfate deposition were significant in 1900, fell in the Depression, rose sharply during World War II, fell equally sharply after the war, rose in the 1960s to a peak in 1973, and have now declined to near the 1900 level again. Nitrate deposition grew more slowly but has been less regulated. Current estimates are that it peaked around 1980 and has declined slightly since then; if a cap on nitrate emissions is eventually enacted, deposition will likely continue to decline.

The upper graph combines pre-1940 data from Irving et al., *Acidic Deposition, State of Science and Technology,* Vol. 1, *Emissions, Atmospheric Processes, and Deposition,* 1990; estimates for 1940-1998 from U.S. Environmental Protection Agency, *National Air Pollutant Emission Trends, 1900-1998,* 2000; and current estimates through 2003 from EPA website, http://www.epa.gov/airtrends. Methods for estimating NOx emissions have changed recently; the upper line, marked "NOx, 2003," is the most recent estimate. See the figures on page 13 for more information.

Lower graph redrawn with permission from Chen and Driscoll, "Modeling the response of soil and surface waters in the Adirondack and Catskill regions of New York to changes in atmospheric deposition and historical land disturbance." Copyright 2004 Elsevier. The rates of deposition are estimated from empirical relations between historical emissions, precipitation, and deposition. The 2000 deposition rates correspond to about 560 equivalents of sulfate and 350 equivalents of nitrate per hectare per year.

For direct evidence of historical deposition, see the graphs of pH and mercury accumulation from lake cores on pages 82 and 171.

2 How does acid deposition in the Adirondacks compare with acid deposition elsewhere in the country?

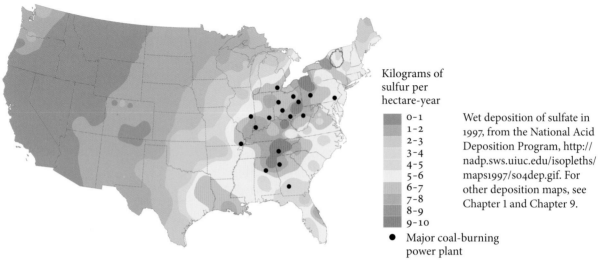

Kilograms of
sulfur per
hectare-year

0–1
1–2
2–3
3–4
4–5
5–6
6–7
7–8
8–9
9–10

● Major coal-burning
power plant

Wet deposition of sulfate in 1997, from the National Acid Deposition Program, http://nadp.sws.uiuc.edu/isopleths/maps1997/so4dep.gif. For other deposition maps, see Chapter 1 and Chapter 9.

It is very high. Their wet deposition rates of sulfur and nitrogen in the western Adirondacks are among the highest currently recorded in the nation, and the average pH of the wet deposition is near the U.S. minimum. The eastern Adirondacks are less affected but still receive significant amounts of deposition.

3 Have Adirondack surface waters been acidified by acid deposition?

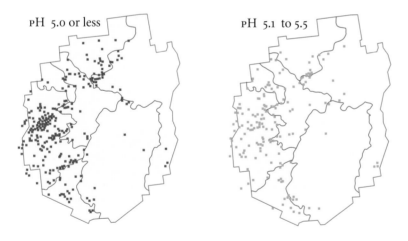

pH 5.0 or less   pH 5.1 to 5.5

Low-pH lakes found by the Adirondack Lakes Survey, 1984–1987. From Gallagher and Baker, "Current status of fish communities in Adirondack lakes," in Baker et al., *Adirondack Lakes Survey: An Interpretive Analysis of Fish Communities and Water Chemistry, 1984–1987,* 1990. These maps include both naturally acid and atmospherically acidified waters. In at least 36% of them the dominant acids are sulfuric and nitric acids and the acidity is mostly the result of acid deposition. The remaining lakes contain mixtures of both kinds of acid and are, to a greater or lesser degree, naturally acidic lakes that have been further acidified by acid deposition.

Yes. The Adirondacks are particularly sensitive to acid deposition because of their high precipitation, shallow acidic soils, and low-calcium bedrock. The Adirondack Lakes Survey found that 26% of the lakes they sampled had summer ANCs of less than 0 µeq/l and so were chronically acid, and another 20% had ANCs between 0 and 50 µeq/l and were considered vulnerable to episodic acidification. The first comprehensive stream survey has only recently been undertaken, but previous research strongly suggests that many streams in the western Adirondacks (and most streams in the Catskills) are subject to acid episodes during snowmelt.

For the base content of Adirondack bedrock, see page 42; for other graphics showing the extent of acidification, see Chapter 3, especially pages 66-67, 74-75, and 80-81.

4 How much have Adirondack lakes acidified?

HISTORICAL pH CHANGES INFERRED FROM SEDIMENT CORES

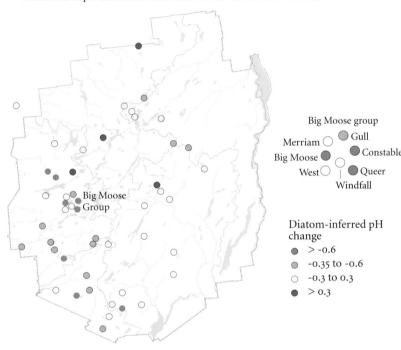

Based on Sullivan et al., "Quantification of changes in lakewater chemistry in response to acidic deposition." Copyright 1990 Nature Publishing Group via the Copyright Clearance Center. Additional data from Sullivan et al., *NAPAP Report 11: Historical Changes in Surface Water Acid-Base Chemistry in Response to Acidic Deposition*, 1990, Section 4.2.1.2. The inferred pH change is the difference between the contemporary pH inferred from the diatom assemblages at the top of the core and the pre-1850 pH inferred from those at the bottom of the core. For more results from the PIRLA studies, see Chapter 4, pages 81-86.

Based on the PIRLA reconstructions, almost all lakes whose original pH was less than 6.0 have acidified, typically between 0.3 and 1.0 pH units. Only a few lakes whose original pHs were above 6.0 have acidified by more than a few tenths of a pH unit.

Taken together, the PIRLA results showing recent acidification and the Adirondack Lakes Survey results showing mineral acidity in most of the PIRLA drainage lakes are our clearest demonstration that acid deposition has caused significant acidification over the past 150 years.

5 Has the acidification of Adirondack waters had biological effects?

Yes. Acidification reduces general biological diversity and, below pH 5.5, changes ecosystem functioning as well. Both chronic and episodic acidity and, in particular, the high aluminum concentra-

Lakes with fish   Lakes without fish

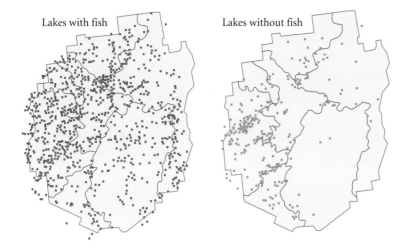

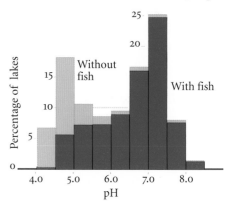

tions associated with them have been shown to kill fish. In the Adirondacks fish diversity decreases and the number of fishless lakes increases as pH decreases. Extinctions of fish populations are more common in lakes with recent pH decreases, and a least a third of the fishless lakes are believed to be fishless because of acid deposition.

Maps from Baker and Gallagher, "Fish communities in Adirondack lakes," in Baker et al., *Adirondack Lakes Survey: An Interpretive Analysis of Fish Communities and Water Chemistry, 1984-1987,* 1990. Bar graph from Figure 3-16 in Kretser, Gallagher, and Nicolette, *Adirondack Lakes Survey: 1984-1987,* 1989. For other results connecting pH and aquatic diversity, see Chapter 3, pages 77–78, and Chapter 8, pages 177–179, 184.

6 Has acid deposition had cumulative effects on watersheds?

DELAYED RECOVERY OF LAKE WATER
COMPARED WITH DEPOSITION

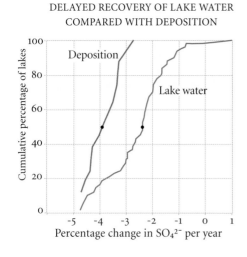

NITROGEN DEPOSITION AND
NITROGEN RETENTION

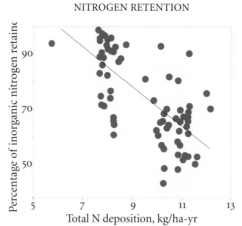

Left figure redrawn from Stoddard et al., "Response of surface water chemistry to the Clean Air Act Amendments of 1990," 2003. The median rate of decrease of sulfate in deposition is 1.6 times that of sulfate in the Adirondack LTM lakes (black dots), suggesting that sulfate retained in the watersheds is slowing recovery. Right figure redrawn from Aber et al., "Is nitrogen deposition altering the nitrogen status of northeastern forests?" Copyright 2003 American Institute of Biological Sciences via the Copyright Clearance Center. Adirondack watersheds receiving more than 8 kg of deposition export 10% to 50% of the nitrogen they receive, suggesting that their capacity to store nitrogen is becoming saturated.

Yes. Acid deposition has altered the cycling of sulfur, nitrogen, and base cations in lakes and forests. It has increased the pools of sulfur and nitrogen in the soil, depleted the pools of base cations, mobilized aluminum, and increased the rate of nitrification and the production of nitrogen-cycle acids.

The discovery of the cumulative effects of acid rain on watersheds is one of the major scientific advances in acid rain research in the past 20 years. In essence, almost every recently acidified drainage lake is surrounded by an acidified watershed, and before the lake can recover completely, the watershed must recover as well.

The existence of cumulative changes in watersheds is now corroborated by five lines of evidence:

Historical comparisons, showing changes in soils.

Elevated aluminum concentrations in streams, which indicate low base saturation in the watershed.

Long-term monitoring studies, which show delayed surface water recovery because of depleted bases and stored acids.

Mass-balance studies, showing base cation depletion, reduced nitrogen retention, and sulfur export.

Historical reconstructions, showing sulfur storage and cation depletion in watershed soils.

We show evidence for delayed recovery, low nitrogen retention, and sulfur export here. For mass-balance studies see pages 132-135; for delayed recovery see page 206; for historical changes in soils see page 135; for high aluminum concentrations in streams see pages 55 and 110; and for reconstructions of calcium depletion see page 139.

7 How much has acid deposition been reduced?

Sulfate concentrations in wet deposition at Huntington Forest and Whiteface Mountain decreased at an average rate of about 1 μeq/l-yr between 1978 and 2000, making a total decrease of about 40%. The pH at Huntington Forest has increased 0.3 units in this time, or 0.014 unit per year. Nitrate deposition has shown a slight overall decrease, but unlike sulfate deposition, the variations in nitrate deposition are not correlated with variations in emissions and may have other causes.

SULFUR EXPORTS FROM ADIRONDACK WATERSHEDS

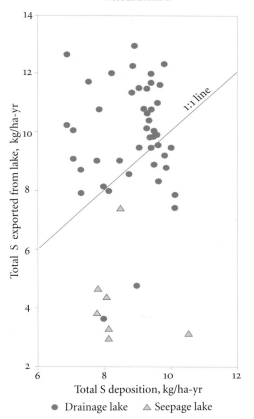

From Driscoll et al., "The response of lake water in the Adirondack region of New York to changes in acidic deposition." Copyright 1998 Elsevier. Except for the seepage lakes, which are less influenced by watershed processes and tend to be associated with sulfur-retaining wetlands, most Adirondack LTM lakes have been exporting more sulfur than they receive from deposition, suggesting either that sulfur inputs from dry deposition have been underestimated or that these lakes are currently releasing sulfur that was stored in soil organic matter when sulfur deposition was higher.

Wet deposition data from the National Trends Network station at Huntington Forest http://nadp.sws.uiuc.edu/sites/sit-einfo.asp?id=NY20 net=NTN. For more data from this station, see page 196; other deposition data is on pages 8-10 and 195.

TRENDS IN SULFATE, NITRATE, AND pH IN WET DEPOSITION

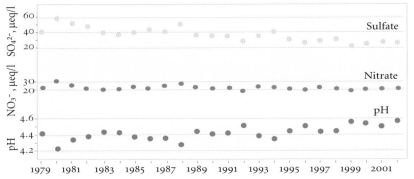

8 Have the reductions been reflected in changes in surface water chemistry?

TRENDS IN THE CHEMISTRY OF DART LAKE, 1982-2001

TRENDS IN LTM WATERS, 1990-2000

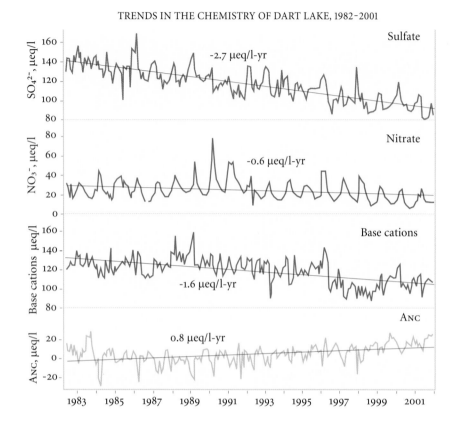

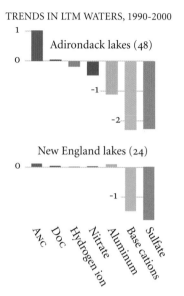

Both figures based on Stoddard et al., "Response of surface water chemistry to the Clean Air Act Amendments of 1990," 2003. In the above figure the trends for aluminum are in µg/l-yr and those for DOC are in mg/l-yr. All others are in µeq/l-yr. In Dart Lake base cations are declining more slowly than sulfate and so there has been a definite increase in ANC, especially since 1993. In other Adirondack lakes the base cations are declining as fast as sulfate and the ANCs are not increasing. For more data showing trends and recovery, see pages 199–207.

Yes. Sulfate concentrations have decreased since the early 1980s, though, as shown in the graphs on pages. 133 and 218, at slower rates than the concentrations in deposition. Base cation concentrations have also decreased and for a long time offset the beneficial effects of the decreases in sulfate. Until 1997 there was no clear evidence that the decreases in sulfate were associated with increases in lake ANCs. Since then, positive trends in ANC, averaging 1 µeq/l-yr over the past ten years, have been detected in about 60% of the Adirondack LTM lakes.

The relative size of the trends in deposition, lake sulfate, and lake ANC should be noted. The sulfate in deposition is decreasing faster than the sulfate in lakes, and the sulfate in lakes is decreasing faster than lake ANC is increasing. This is an indication of the current slowness of the recovery and of the extent to which watershed processes are intervening between reductions in deposition and increases in the ANCs of lakes.

THE RECOVERY OF CONSTABLE POND UNDER THREE SCENARIOS

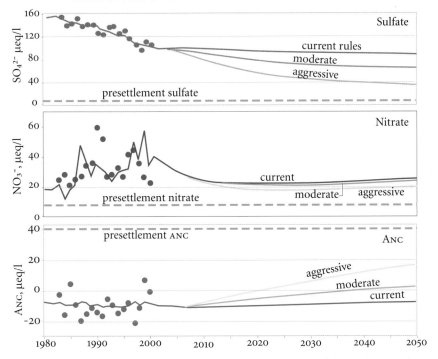

— Predicted values with current Clean Air Act regulations fully implemented

— Moderate further controls: predicted values with 20% reduction in NO_X and 35% reduction in SO_2 beyond current regulations, implemented in 2010

— Aggressive further controls: predicted values with 30% reduction in NO_X and 50% reduction in SO_2 beyond current regulations, implemented in 2010

● Measured values

SPRING AND SUMMER ANCS

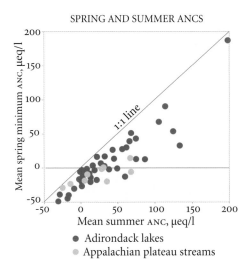

● Adirondack lakes
● Appalachian plateau streams

Above, springtime depression of ANCs of lakes and streams, from Stoddard et al., "Response of surface water chemistry to the Clean Air Act Amendments of 1990," 2003. The springtime decreases in ANC, which in low-ANC lakes and streams are controlled by nitrates, are an index of the extent to which recovery is being delayed by nitrogen stored in watersheds.

Left, a simulation of the recovery of Constable Pond under three deposition scenarios, redrawn with permission from Chen and Driscoll, "Modeling the response of soil and surface waters in the Adirondack and Catskill regions of New York to changes in atmospheric deposition and historical land disturbance." Copyright 2004 Elsevier.

It appears that they will be. Currently, most of the emissions reductions required by the 1990 Clean Air Act Amendments have already been achieved, and so there will be relatively little further reduction in sulfate or nitrogen deposition under the current rules. The simulations of lake and watershed responses to the current reductions by Chen and Driscoll suggest that for chronically acidified watersheds like Constable Pond – whose presettlement ANC is estimated to have been around 40 µeq/l and whose current ANC is about -10 µeq/l – the current regulations will produce only a slight recovery. Based on these simulations, and assuming the regulations don't change, in 2050 Constable Pond will still have an ANC below zero and sulfate and nitrate levels much higher than presettlement levels.

With increased controls on emissions there are predicted to be further improvements. With "aggressive" controls that reduce sulfate emissions 50% beyond present levels and nitrate emissions 30% beyond present levels, by 2050 the pool of adsorbed sulfur is

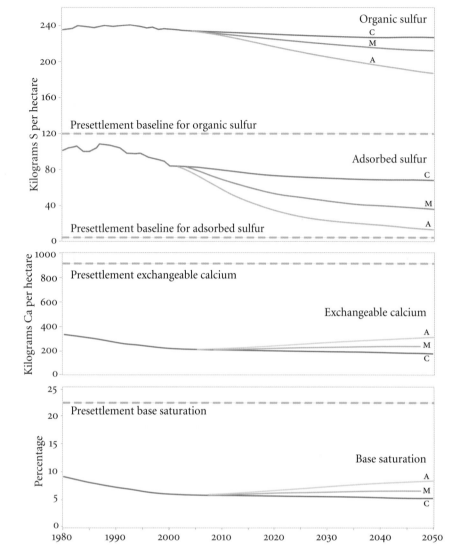

A simulation of the recovery of the soils of the Constable Pond watershed under three emissions-control scenarios, redrawn with permission from Chen and Driscoll, "Modeling the response of soil and surface waters in the Adirondack and Catskill regions of New York to changes in atmospheric deposition and historical land disturbance." Copyright 2004 Elsevier. In 50 years, under an "aggressive" emissions-control scenario, the pool of adsorbed sulfur almost vanishes and the pool of organic sulfur is reduced by a quarter. But, because of the low inputs of base cations to this watershed (and many others in the western Adirondacks), the base saturation and the pool of exchangeable calcium increase only slightly and remain well below presettlement levels.

C Predicted values with current Clean Air Act regulations fully implemented in 2010

M Moderate further controls: predicted values with 20% reduction in NO_X and 30% reduction in SO_4 beyond current regulations, implemented in 2010

A Aggressive further controls: predicted values with 30% reduction in NO_X and 50% reduction in SO_4 beyond current regulations, implemented in 2010

predicted to decrease to near zero, the sulfur concentrations in the lake to decrease to near their presettlement levels, and the ANC to rise to between 15 µeq/l and 20 µeq/l, a little less than half of its presettlement level.

While reductions can protect the remaining base cations, they can't make up for the cations that have already been lost. Only weathering and deposition, both slow processes, can replenish the cation pools of depleted soils. If the simulations are correct, the recovery of exchangeable calcium pools and base cation saturation will also be slow. The graphs above suggest that even with aggressive regulations, in 2050 the pool of exchangeable calcium will be a third of the presettlement calcium and the base saturationstill well below the critical level of 20%. Because adequate calcium pools and base saturation levels are essential both for forest growth and to protect surface waters from acid episodes, this suggests that the biological effects of acid rain in the most acidified watersheds will continue for at least the next 50 years, if not beyond.

10 What were the most important scientific results of the 1990s?

In our opinion, they were that:

A large number of lakes are responding to decreases in sulfate deposition with increases in ANC and pH (pp. 200-201, 204-206).

Both mercury and its toxic derivative methylmercury are widespread in the Adirondacks in physiologically significant quantities. Their distribution is linked, also significantly, to acidity, DOC production, and sulfate reduction (p. 170-172).

Cumulative, acid-related changes in watershed soils, including the storage of sulfur and nitrogen and the depletion of base cations, are also widespread and will delay the rate at which lakes and streams recover from acidification by acid rain (Chapters 5, 6).

The dynamics of nitrogen cycling are tied in a particularly complex way to forest biology and climate as well as to deposition. As a result, the trends in the nitrate levels of surface waters cannot be accurately predicted by any current model (Chapter 5).

11 What are the main scientific tasks of the next decade?

Our best answer to this comes from a study of research needs and priorities conducted by the New York State Energy Research and Development Authority (NYSERDA) in 2002.* The results of this assessment, in which two of the authors of this book participated and with which we all concur, suggest that they will involve:

Monitoring the chemical and biological responses of lakes and streams to decreases in atmospheric deposition, and determining whether the chemical improvements observed at the end of the 1990s continue through the next decade.

*The NYSERDA recommendations were prepared by a working group of about 50 researchers and administrators and are contained in *Environmental Research and Monitoring in New York State: A Multi-Year Research Plan for the New York Energy research and Development Authority's Environmental Monitoring, Evaluation, and Protection Program,* 2002.

Further assessing the sources and extent of mercury pollution and the extent to which mercury is being concentrated by biological food chains.

Assessing the effects of acid deposition on forest soils and forest health.

Assessing the extent of the episodic acidification of streams and its links to nitrogen saturation and cation depletion.

Understanding the links between climate, forest biology, and nitrogen-cycle acidification.

Improving the measurement and modeling of dry deposition.

Several things are noteworthy about this list. First, it addresses an interrelated mixture of new and old problems. Mercury pollution, lake acidification, and changes in lake biology, first detected 30 years ago, are still central concerns today. Nitrogen saturation, cation depletion, and forest health issues are much more recent problems, barely glimpsed 15 years ago and now becoming increasingly important.

And second, much of the research it proposes is old-fashioned monitoring and sampling. As a result of much effort in the 1980s and 1990s, much basic research has already been done. We know that mercury and cation losses and nitrogen acids are problems. What we don't know is how widespread these problems are, where they are having the most biological effect, and whether they are getting better or worse.

In many ways our situation is similar to that of the acid rain scientists of the middle 1980s. They had identified serious chemical and ecological problems and needed monitoring networks and synoptic studies to determine their extent. Likewise, we have now identified a new set of chemical and ecological problems and will need expanded monitoring networks and new synoptic studies to determine their extent. We need to know, for example, just how many watersheds have elevated mercury levels or depleted calcium levels, and we need to track mercury in animals and calcium in plants to establish baselines and determine whether recovery is occurring.

12 How important are the current Adirondack long-term monitoring programs?

If we accept that the control of acid emissions and the recovery of acidified forests and waters are national priorities, they are very important. They are both our only way of assessing whether the our current acid-related problems are improving and our best way for detecting new acid-related problems as they emerge.

13 Are current programs adequate to monitor acidification and recovery?

Given the priorities listed by the NYSERDA study, they are not adequate. The current deposition and lake monitoring programs – 52 ALTM lakes monitored monthly, 43 TIME lakes monitored annually – gives us an excellent picture of lake chemistry. But unfortunately, we have no comparably detailed pictures of stream chemistry or of the chemistry of the watersheds from which the water in the lakes and streams comes. And with the exception of the southwestern Adirondacks where there is on-going biological monitoring, our knowledge of surface water biology is now 15 to 20 years out of date.

14 What might an expanded monitoring system include?

Again using the NYSERDA recommendations, it might involve:

> More long-term monitoring streams, with gauging stations and some provision for "event-driven" monitoring of high-water episodes.

> Long-term monitoring of mercury levels in surface waters and animal tissue.

> An extension of the current biological monitoring program for southwestern Adirondack lakes (scheduled to end in 2006) and its expansion to lakes and streams elsewhere in the park.

> A reference database of Adirondack soil chemistry and monitoring of soil and foliar chemistry in a set of ALTM watersheds.

Approximately 18 of the studies we discuss in this book were large projects involving multiple host institutions and funders. For readers who would like a chronology of these studies, or who want to find where a particular program is discussed, we offer the following synopsis.

The *Integrated Lake-Watershed Acidification Study,* 1977-1981 (ILWAS). Sponsor: Electric Power Research Institute (EPRI). Researchers: Peters, April, Gherini, Chen, Galloway, Schofield, Newton, Johannes, Clesceri, and Hendrey. (pp. 45-47)

The *Regionalized Integrated Lake-Watershed Acidification Study,* 1982-1984 (RILWAS). Sponsors: EPRI, Empire State Electric Energy Research Corporation (ESEERCO). Researchers: Driscoll, Newton, Schofield, April, Peters, and Gherini. (pp. 48-54)

The first *Paleoecological Investigation of Recent Lake Acidification Study,* 1983-1986 (PIRLA-1). Sponsors: EPRI, U.S. Environmental Protection Agency (EPA). Researchers: Charles, Mitchell, Whitehead, Smol, and Norton. (pp. 81-83)

The second *Paleoecological Investigation of Recent Lake Acidification Study,* 1988 (PIRLA-II). Sponsor: EPA. Researchers: Charles, Smol, Cumming, and Sullivan. (pp. 84-85)

The first *Eastern Lake Survey,* 1984 (ELS-1). Sponsor: EPA. Researchers: Linthurst, Landers, and Eilers. (pp. 65-67, 88-89)

The second *Eastern Lake Survey,* 1986 (ELS-II). Sponsor: EPA. Researchers: Herlihy, Whittier, and Sullivan. (p. 68)

The *Adirondack Lakes Survey,* 1984-1987 (ALS). Sponsors: ESEERCO, New York State Department of Environmental Conservation (DEC). Researchers: Baker, Beauchamp, Christensen, Coe, Driscoll, Gallagher, Gherini, Kretser, Munson, Newton, Nicolette, Reckhow, Shaakir-Ali, Schofield, Smith, Warren-Hicks. (pp. 69-81)

The *Direct Delayed Response Project,* 1984 (DDRP). Sponsor: EPA. Researchers: Church, Schnoor, Cosby, and Gherini. (p. 96)

The *Episodic Response Project,* 1988-1990 (ERP). Sponsor: EPA. Researchers: Wigington, Baker, Van Sickle, Simonin, and Murdoch. (pp. 109-110, 180-181)

The *Integrated Forest Study,* 1985-1989 (IFS). Sponsors: EPRI, ESEERCO. Researchers: Johnson, Lindberg, Mitchell, and Friedland.

The *Adirondack Long-Term Monitoring program,* 1982 to present (ALTM/LTM). Sponsors: ESEERCO, New York State Energy Research and Development Authority (NYSERDA), DEC, EPA. Researchers: Driscoll, Kretser, and Roy. (pp. 197-205)

The *Lake Acidification Mitigation Project,* 1983-1986 (LAMP). Sponsors: EPRI, ESEERCO. Researchers: Schofield, Gloss, Driscoll, DePinto, and Young. (pp. 144-147)

The *Adirondack Manipulation and Modeling Project,* 1990-1995 (AMMP). Sponsors: NYSERDA, ESEERCO, National Council of the Paper Industry for Air and Stream Improvement, Inc. Researchers: Mitchell, Driscoll, and Raynal.

The *Experimental Watershed Liming Study,* 1989-1992 (EWLS). Sponsors: Living Lakes Inc., ESEERCO, U.S. Fish and Wildlife Service. Researchers: Driscoll, Fahey, Raynal, Leopold, Burns, and Newton. (pp. 148-150)

The *Lake Mercury Study,* 1991-1993. Sponsors: ESEERCO, NYSERDA, DEC. Researchers: Driscoll, Munson, Schofield, and Newton. (p. 167)

The *Environmental Monitoring and Assessment Program,* 1991-1994 (EMAP). Sponsor: EPA. Researchers: Larsen, Paulsen, Thorton, and Urquart. (p. 185)

The *Temporally Integrated Monitoring of Ecosystems program,* 1991 to present (TIME). Sponsor: EPA, NYSERDA, DEC. Researchers: Stoddard, Paulsen, Driscoll. (pp. 193-194.)

The *Adirondack Effects Assessment Program,* 1994 to present (AEAP). Sponsor: EPA. Researchers: Lawrence, Momen, Boylen, Sutherland, Nierzwicki-Bauer, and Zehr. (pp. 184-185)

In 2001, as a part of its public outreach program, the Adirondack Lakes Survey Corporation created a website, www.adirondacklakessurvey.org. The website contains historical information about the ALSC and data from the Adirondack Lakes Survey and Adirondack Long-Term Monitoring program.

Three sorts of data are available on the website: the complete 1984–1987 data set for lakes and ponds examined by the Adirondack Lakes Survey, the 1992–2004 data from Big Moose Lake, and the complete 1992–2004 set of monthly observations and annual averages for the 52 ALTM lakes.

The Adirondack Lakes Survey data are available as a series of on-line tables that describe the morphometry, landscape features, chemistry, and fish populations of each pond visited during the survey.

The Big Moose Lake data are presented graphically: there are graphs showing the trends in chemical parameters from 1992 to the present and GIS maps showing the topography and chemistry of the watershed.

The ALTM data, which are the official scientific record of the monitoring program, are available for download as an Excel™ spreadsheet. The spreadsheet currently contains the monthly observations for 21 parameters at 52 lakes. A separate spreadsheet of annual averages is also available.

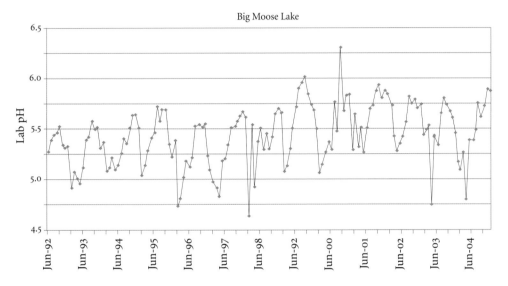

Big Moose Lake

Laboratory pHs of Big Moose Lake, 1992-2004, redrawn from the ALSC website. The annual pH cycle consists of a spring minimum and a summer peak. The average pH increased in the 1990s as the Clean Air Act Amendments began to take effect (p. 2), but low snowmelt pHs still occur.

DATE	POND	SO4 (mg/L)	NO3 (mg/L)	Cl (mg/L)	F (mg/L)	ANC (ueq/L)	DIC (mg/L)	DOC (mg/L)	SiO2 (mg/L)
1/Jun/92	020058	4.24	0.072	0.45	0.090	27.90	0.86	12.695	1.81
1/Jun/92	020059	4.04	0.026	1.32	0.078	31.90	0.21	9.740	1.17

A portion of the ALSC database, showing the first long-term monitoring data, from June 1992, for Little Hope (020058) and Big Hope (020059) ponds. The complete spreadsheet currently contains about 5,500 records, each giving the values for 21 measurements from a particular lake on a particular date.

Links to other acid deposition websites can be found on the menu bar of the ALSC website, www.adirondacklakessurvey. org. Descriptions and locations of other intensive research programs can be found on the NYSERDA website, at www.nyserda.org/programs/environment/EMEP/home.asp.

The bibliography contains the print works cited in the text and the web pages for on-line sources. Works whose results are illustrated in this book are preceded by an asterisk; the page on which the illustration occurs is given in parentheses after the citation.

Aber, J.D., Nadelhoffer, K.J., Steudler, P., and Melillo, J.M. 1989. "Nitrogen saturation in northern forest ecosystems: Hypotheses and implications." *BioScience* 39: 378-386.

*Aber, J.D., Goodale, C.L., Ollinger, S.V., Smith, M., Magill, A.H., Martin, M.E., Hallett, R.A., and Stoddard, J.L. 2003. "Is nitrogen deposition altering the nitrogen status of northeastern forests?" *BioScience* 53: 375-389. (119, 120, 218)

April, R.H. 1983. *Mineralogy of the ILWAS Lake-Watersheds.* Electric Power Research Institute. EPRI EA-2827.

*Asbury, C.E., Vertucci, F.A., Mattson, M.D., and Likens, G.E. 1989. "Acidification of Adirondack lakes." *Environmental Science & Technology* 23: 362-365. (56, 57)

Bailey, S.W., Hornbeck, J.W., Driscoll, C.T., and Gaudette, H.E. 1996. "Calcium inputs and transport in a base-poor forest ecosystem as interpreted by Sr isotopes." *Water Resources Research* 32: 707-719.

Baker, J.P. and Schofield, C.L. 1982. "Aluminum toxicity to fish in acidic waters." *Water, Air, & Soil Pollution* 18: 289-309.

*Baker, J.P., Bernard, D.P., Christensen, S.W., Sale, M.J., Freda, J., Heltcher, K., Rowe, L., Scanlon, P., Stokes, P., Suter, G., and Warren-Hicks, W. 1990. *Biological Effects of Changes in Surface Water Acid-Base Chemistry.* U.S. National Acid Precipitation Assessment Program. SOS/T 13.

Baker, J.P. and Gallagher, J. 1990. "Fish communities in Adirondack lakes." In Baker, J.P. et al., *Adirondack Lakes Survey: An Interpretive Analysis of Fish Communities and Water Chemistry, 1984-1987.* Adirondack Lakes Survey Corporation. Ray Brook, NY. pp. 3-1-3-10. (216)

*Baker, J.P., Gherini, S.A., Christensen, S.W., Munson, R.K., Driscoll, C.T., Newton, R.M., Gallagher, J., Reckhow, K.H., and Schofield, C.L. 1990. *Adirondack Lakes Survey: An Interpretive Analysis of Fish Communities and Water Chemistry, 1984-87.* Adirondack Lakes Survey Corporation. Ray Brook, NY. (69)

*Baker, J.P., Warren-Hicks, W., Gallagher, J., and Christensen, S. 1990. "Historical changes in fish communities in Adirondack lakes." In Baker, J.P. et al., *Adirondack Lakes Survey: An Interpretive Analysis of Fish Communities and Water Chemistry, 1984-1987.* Adirondack Lakes Survey Corporation. Ray Brook, NY. pp. 3-105-3-150. (79)

*Baker, J.P. and Christensen, S.W. 1991. "Effects of acidification on biological communities in aquatic ecosystems." In Charles, D.F., ed., *Acidic Deposition and Aquatic Ecosystems, Regional Case Studies.* Springer-Verlag. New York. pp. 83-106. (177, 179)

*Baker, J.P., Warren-Hicks, W.J., Gallagher, J., and Christensen, S.W. 1993. "Fish population losses from Adirondack lakes: The role of surface water acidity and acidification." *Water Resources Research* 29: 861-874. (182, 183, 184)

*Baker, J.P., Van Sickle, J., Gagen, C.J., DeWalle, D.R., Sharpe, W.E., Carline, R.F., Baldigo, B.P., Murdoch, P.S., Bath, D.W., Kretser, W.A., Simonin, H.A., and Wigington, P.J. Jr. 1996. "Episodic acidification of small streams in the northeastern United States: Effects on fish populations." *Ecological Applications* 6: 422-437. (181)

*Baker, L.A., Kaufmann, P.R., Herlihy, A.T., and Eilers, J.M. 1990. *Current Status of Surface Water Acid-Base Chemistry.* U.S. National Acid Precipitation Assessment Program. SOS/T 9. (66)

Battles, J.J., Johnson, A.H., Siccama, T.G., Friedland, A.J., and Miller, E.K. 1992. "Red spruce death: Effects on forest composition and structure on Whiteface Mountain, NY." *Bulletin of the Torrey Botanical Club* 119: 418-430.

Biodiversity Research Institute. 2005. http://www.briloon.org/

*Bischoff, J.M., Bukaveckas, P., Mitchell, M.J., and Hurd, T. 2001. "N storage and cycling in vegetation of a forested wetland: Implications for watershed N processing." *Water, Air, & Soil Pollution* 128: 97-114. (153)

Blette, V.L. and Newton, R.M. 1996. "Effects of watershed liming on the soils of Woods Lake. New York." *Biogeochemistry* 32: 175-194.

*Bloomfield, J.A., Quinn, S.O., Scrudato, R.J., Long, D., Richards, A., and Ryan, F. 1980. "Atmospheric and watershed inputs of mercury to Cranberry Lake, St. Lawrence County, New York." In Toribara, T.Y., Miller,

M.W., and Morrow, P.E., eds., *Polluted Rain*. Plenum Press. New York. pp. 175-210. (165)

Bormann, F.H. and Likens, G.E. 1979. *Pattern and Process in a Forested Ecosystem*. Springer-Verlag. New York.

Brezonik, P.L., Baker, L.A., Eaton, J., Frost, T., Garrison, P., Kratz, T., Magnuson, J., Perry, J., Rose, W., Shepard, B., Swenson, W., Watras, C., and Webster, K. 1986. "Experimental acidification of Little Rock Lake, Wisconsin." *Water, Air, and Soil Pollution* 30: 115-122.

Bukaveckas, P.A. 1988. "Effects of calcite treatment on primary producers in acidified Adirondack lakes. I. Response of macrophyte communities." *Lake and Reservoir Management* 4: 107-113.

Burgess, N.M. 1998. "Mercury and reproductive success of common loons breeding in the Maritimes." In *Mercury in Atlantic Canada: A Progress Report*. Environment Canada. Sackville, New Brunswick. pp. 104-109.

Burns, D.A. 1996. "Effects of CaCO3 application to an Adirondack lake watershed on outlet stream chemistry." *Biogeochemistry* 32: 339-362.

*Camburn, K.E. and Charles, D.F. 2000. *Diatoms of Low-Alkalinity Lakes in the Northeastern United States*. The Academy of Natural Sciences of Philadelphia. Philadelphia. (28)

*Canham, C.D., Pace, M.L., Papaik, M.J., Primack, A.G.B., Roy, K.M., Maranger, R.J., Curran, R.P., and Spada, D.M. 2004. "A spatially explicit watershed-scale analysis of dissolved organic carbon in Adirondack lakes." *Ecological Applications* 14: 839-854. (162, 163)

*Charles, D.F. 1984. "Recent pH history of Big Moose Lake (Adirondack Mountains. New York, U.S.A.) inferred from sediment diatom assemblages." *Verh. Internat. Verein. Limnol.* 22: 559-566. (59)

*—— 1985. "Relationships between surface sediment diatom assemblages and lakewater characteristics in Adirondack lakes." *Ecology* 66: 994-1011. (57)

*—— 1990. "Effects of acidic deposition on North American lakes: Palæolimnological evidence from diatoms and chrysophytes." *Philosophical Transactions of the Royal Society of London* B327: 403-412. (84)

—— , ed., 1991. *Acidic Deposition and Aquatic Ecosystems: Regional Case Studies*. Springer-Verlag. New York.

Charles, D.F. and Whitehead, D.R. 1986. "The PIRLA Project: Paleoecological investigations of recent lake acidification." *Hydrobiologia* 143: 13-20.

*Charles, D.F., Whitehead, D.R., Engstrom, D.R., Fry, B.D., Hites, R.A., Norton, S.A., Owen, J.S., Roll, L.A., Schindler, S.C., Smol, J.P., Uutala, A.J., White, J.R., and Wise, R.J. 1987. "Paleolimological evidence for recent acidification of Big Moose Lake, Adirondack Mountains, N.Y. (USA)." *Biogeochemistry* 3: 267-296. (59)

*Charles, D.F. and Smol, J.P. 1988. "New methods for using diatoms and chrysophytes to infer past pH of low-alkalinity lakes." *Limnological Oceanography* 33: 1451-1462. (82)

Charles, D.F. and Smol, J.P. 1990. "The PIRLA II Project: Regional assessment of lake acidification trends." *Verh.Internat.Verein.Limnol.* 24: 474-480.

*Chen, C.W., Gherini, S.A., Peters, N.E., Murdoch, P.S., Newton, R.M., and Goldstein, R.A. 1984. "Hydrologic analyses of acidic and alkaline lakes." *Water Resources Research* 20: 1875-1882. (46, 47)

*Chen, L. and Driscoll, C.T. 2004. "Modeling the response of soil and surface waters in the Adirondack and Catskill regions of New York to changes in atmospheric deposition and historical land disturbance." *Atmospheric Environment* 38: 4099-4109. (13, 122, 139, 215, 221, 222)

Church, M.R., Thornton, K.W., Shaffer, P.W., Stevens, D.L., Rochelle, B.P., Holdren, G.R., Johnson, M.G., Lee, J.J., Turner, R.S., Cassell, D.L., Lammers, D.A., Campbell, W.G., Liff, C.I., Brandt, C.C., Liegel, L.H., Bishop, G.D., Mortenson, D.C., Pierson, S.M., and Schmoyer, D.D. 1989. *Future Effects of Long-Term Sulfur Deposition on Surface Water Chemistry in the Northeast and Southern Blue Ridge Province*. U.S. Environmental Protection Agency. EPA/600/3-89/061. (96)

*Cirmo, C.P. and Driscoll, C.T. 1993. "Beaver pond biogeochemistry: Acid-neutralizing capacity generation in a headwater wetland." *Wetlands* 13: 277-292. (154, 155, 156)

*—— 1996. "The impacts of a watershed CaCO3 treatment on stream and wetland biogeochemistry in the Adirondack Mountains." *Biogeochemistry* 32: 265-297. (159, 160, 161)

Cogbill, C.V. and Likens, G.E. 1974. "Acid precipitation in the northeastern U.S." *Water Resources Research* 10: 1133-1137.

Colquhoun, J.R., Symula, J., and Karcher, R.W. 1982. *Report of Adirondack Sampling for Stream Acidification Studies 1981 Supplement*. New York State Department of Environmental Conservation. SAN-P29 (10/82).

*Colquhoun, J.R., Symula, J., Pfeiffer, M.H., and Feurer, J. 1981. *Preliminary Report of Stream Sampling for Acidification Studies–1980*. New York State Department of Environmental Conservation. FW-P182 (9/81). (41)

Colquhoun, J.R., Dean, H.J., Symula, J., Skea, J.C., and Jackling, S.J. 1983. *Non-Target Effects of the Adirondack Black-fly (Simuliidae) Treatment Program*. New York State Department of Environmental Conservation. FW P-229 (4/83).

Colquhoun, J.R., Kretser, W.A., and Pfeiffer, M.H. 1984. *Acidity Status Update of Lakes and Streams in New York State*. New York State Department of Environmental Conservation. WM P-83 (6/84).

Committee on Air Quality Management in the United States, National Research Council. 2004. *Air Quality Management in the United States*. The National Academies Press. Washington. DC.

*Confer, J.L., Kaaret, T., and Likens, G.E. 1983. "Zooplankton diversity and biomass in recently acidified lakes." *Canadian Journal of Fisheries and Aquatic Sciences* 40: 36-42. (177)

Cronan, C.S. and Schofield, C.L. 1979. "Aluminum leaching response to acid precipitation: Effects on high-elevation watersheds in the Northeast." *Science* 204: 304-306.

Cronan, C.S., Conlan, J.C., and Skibinski, S. 1987. "Forest vegetation in relation to surface water chemistry in the North Branch of the Moose River, Adirondack Park, N.Y." *Biogeochemistry* 3: 121-128.

Cronan, C.S. and Grigal, D.F. 1995. "Use of calcium/aluminum ratios as indicators of stress in forest ecosystems." *Journal of Environmental Quality* 24: 209-226.

*Cumming, B.F., Smol, J.P., Kingston, J.C., Charles, D.F., Birks, H.J.B., Camburn, K.E., Dixit, S.S., Uutala, J., and Selle, A.R. 1992. "How much acidification has occurred in Adirondack region lakes (New York, USA) since preindustrial times?" *Canadian Journal of Fisheries and Aquatic Sciences* 49: 128-141. (89)

*Cumming, B.F., Davey, K.A., Smol, J.P., and Birks, H.J.B. 1994. "When did acid-sensitive Adirondack lakes (New York, USA) begin to acidify and are they still acidifying?" *Canadian Journal of Fisheries and Aquatic Sciences* 51: 1550-1568. (88)

*David, M.B., Mitchell, M.J., and Scott, T.J. 1987. "Importance of biological processes in the sulfur budget of a northern hardwood ecosystem." *Biology and Fertility of Soils* 5: 258-264. (93, 94, 95)

*Davis, R.B., Anderson, D.S., Charles, D.F., and Galloway, J.N. 1988. "Two-hundred-year pH history of Woods, Sagamore, and Panther lakes in the Adirondack Mountains, New York State." *Aquatic Toxicology and Hazard Assessment* 10: 89-111. (46, 60)

*Dise, N.B. and Wright, R.F. 1995. "Nitrogen leaching from European forests in relation to nitrogen deposition." *Forest Ecology and Management* 71: 153-161. (117)

*Dixit, S.S., Smol, J.P., Charles, D.F., Hughes, R.M., Paulsen, S.G., and Collins, G.B. 1999. "Assessing water quality changes in the lakes of the northeastern United States using sediment diatoms." *Canadian Journal of Fisheries and Aquatic Sciences* 56: 131-152. (28)

*Driscoll, C.T., Baker, J.P., Bisogni, J.J. Jr., and Schofield, C.L. 1980. "Effect of aluminum speciation on fish in dilute acidified waters." *Nature* 284: 161-164. (43)

*Driscoll, C.T. and Schafran, G.C. 1984. "Short-term changes in the base-neutralizing capacity of an acid Adirondack lake, New York." *Nature* 310: 308-310. (99)

*Driscoll, C.T. and Newton, R.M. 1985. "Chemical characteristics of Adirondack lakes." *Environmental Science & Technology* 19: 1018-1024. (47, 48, 49, 51)

*Driscoll, C.T., Yatsko, C.P., and Unangst, F.J. 1987. "Longitudinal and temporal trends in the water chemistry of the North Branch of the Moose River." *Biogeochemistry* 3: 37-61. (23, 51, 53, 55)

*Driscoll, C.T., Ayling, W.A., Fordham, G.F., and Oliver, L.M. 1989. "Chemical response of lakes treated with CaCO3 to reacidification." *Canadian Journal of Fisheries and Aquatic Sciences* 46: 258-267. (145, 146, 147)

Driscoll, C.T., Fordham, G.F., Ayling, W.A., and Oliver, L.M. 1989. "Short-term changes in the chemistry of trace metals following calcium carbonate treatment of acidic lakes." *Canadian Journal of Fisheries and Aquatic Sciences* 46: 249-257.

Driscoll, C.T., Fuller, R.D., and Schecher, W.D. 1989. "The role of organic acids in the acidification of surface waters in the eastern U.S." *Water, Air, and Soil Pollution* 43: 21-40.

*Driscoll, C.T., Newton, R.M., Gubala, C.P., Baker, J.P., and Christensen, S.W. 1991. Adirondack Mountains. In Charles, D.F., ed., *Acidic Deposition and Aquatic Ecosystems: Regional Case Studies*. Springer-Verlag. New York. pp. 133-211. (65, 66, 67, 80, 81, 89)

*Driscoll, C.T. and Schaefer, D.A. 1991. *The Nitrogen Cycle and Its Role in Soil and Drainage Water Acidifica-*

tion. Final Report to the Empire State Electric Energy Research Corporation. (98)

*Driscoll, C.T. and Van Dreason, R. 1993. "Seasonal and long-term temporal patterns in the chemistry of Adirondack lakes." *Water, Air, and Soil Pollution* 67: 319-344. (202)

Driscoll, C.T., Lehtinen, M.D., and Sullivan, T.J. 1994. "Modeling the acid-base chemistry of organic solutes in Adirondack, New York, lakes." *Water Resources Research* 30: 297-306.

*Driscoll, C.T., Yan, C., Schofield, C.L., Munson, R., and Holsapple, J. 1994. "The mercury cycle and fish in the Adirondack lakes." *Environmental Science & Technology* 28: 136A-143A. (166, 168)

*Driscoll, C.T., Blette, V., Yan, C., Schofield, C.L., Munson, R., and Holsapple, J. 1995. "The role of dissolved organic carbon in the chemistry and bioavailability of mercury in remote Adirondack lakes." *Water, Air, and Soil Pollution* 80: 499-508. (166, 167)

Driscoll, C.T., Postek, K.M., Kretser, W.A., and Raynal, D.J. 1995. "Long-term trends in the chemistry of precipitation and lake water in the Adirondack region of New York, USA." *Water, Air, and Soil Pollution* 85: 583-588.

*Driscoll, C.T., Cirmo, C.P., Fahey, T.J., Blette, V.L., Bukaveckas, P.A., Burns, D.A., Gubala, C.P., Leopold, D.J., Newton, R.M., Raynal, D.J., Schofield, C.L., Yavitt, J.B., and Porcella, D.B. 1996. "The Experimental Watershed Liming Study: Comparison of lake and watershed neutralization strategies." *Biogeochemistry* 32: 143-174. (144, 148, 149)

*Driscoll, C.T., Holsapple, J., Schofield, C.L., and Munson, R. 1998. "The chemistry and transport of mercury in a small wetland in the Adirondack region of New York, USA." *Biogeochemistry* 40: 137-146. (170)

*Driscoll, C.T., Postek, K.M., Mateti, D., Sequeira, K., Aber, J.D., Kretser, W.A., Mitchell, M.J., and Raynal, D.J. 1998. "The response of lake water in the Adirondack region of New York to changes in acidic deposition." *Environmental Science & Policy* 1: 185-198. (123, 219)

*Driscoll, C.T., Lawrence, G.B., Bulger, A.J., Butler, T.J., Cronan, C.S., Eagar, C., Lambert, K.F., Likens, G.E., Stoddard, J.L., and Weathers, K.C. 2001. "Acidic deposition in the northeastern United States: Sources and inputs, ecosystem effects, and management strategies." *BioScience* 51: 180-198. (191)

*Driscoll, C.T., Driscoll, K.M., Roy, K.M., and Mitchell, M.J. 2003. "Chemical response of lakes in the Adirondack region of New York to declines in acidic deposition." *Environmental Science & Technology* 37: 2036-2042. (197, 199, 202, 203)

Driscoll, C.T., Whitall, D., Aber, J., Boyer, E., Castro, M., Cronan, C.S., Goodale, C.L., Groffman, P.M., Hopkinson, C., Lambert, K.F., Lawrence, G.B., and Ollinger, S. 2003. "Nitrogen pollution in the northeastern United States: Sources, effects, and management options." *BioScience* 53: 357-374.

*Driscoll, C.T., Yavitt, J., Newton, R., and Munson, R. 2004. *Chemical and Biological Control of Mercury Cycling in Upland, Wetland, and Lake Ecosystems in the Northeastern U.S.* Final Report to Eenvironmental protection Agency, 99-NCERQA-J1. (169)

Eagar, C. and Adams, M.B. 1992. *Ecology and Decline of Red Spruce in the Eastern United States.* Springer-Verlag. New York.

Ecological Society of America 1999. *Acid Deposition: The Ecological Response.* The Ecological Society of America. Washington, DC.

Evers, D.C. 1998. "Geographic trends in mercury measured in common loon feathers and blood." *Toxicological Chemistry* 17: 173-183.

Evers, D.C., Kaplan, J.D., Meyer, W.M., Reaman, P.S., Major, A., Burgess, N.M., and Braselton, W.E. 1998. "Geographic trends in mercury measured in common loon feathers and blood." *Environmental Toxicology and Chemistry* 17(2): 173-183.

Evers, D.C. and Clair, T.A., eds. 2005. "Biogeographical patterns of environmental mercury in northeastern North America." *Ecotoxicology* 14(1-2).

*Federer, C.A., Hornbeck, J.W., Tritton, L.M., Martin, C.W., Pierce, R.S., and Smith, C.T. 1989. "Long-term depletion of calcium and other nutrients in eastern U.S. forests." *Environmental Management* 13: 593-601. (133)

*Fordham, G.F. and Driscoll, C.T. 1989. "Short-term changes in the acid/base chemistry of two acidic lakes following calcium carbonate treatment." *Canadian Journal of Fisheries and Aquatic Sciences* 46: 306-314. (146)

*Friedland, A.J., Miller, E.K., Battles, J.J., and Thorne, J.F. 1991. "Nitrogen deposition, distribution and cycling in a subalpine spruce-fir forest in the Adirondacks, New York, USA." *Biogeochemistry* 14: 31-55. (101, 102, 104)

*Gallagher, J. and Baker, J. 1990. Current status of fish communities in Adirondack lakes. In Baker, J.P. et al., *Adirondack Lakes Survey: An Interpretive Analysis of Fish Communities and Water Chemistry, 1984-1987.* Adirondack Lakes Survey Corporation. Ray Brook, NY. pp. 3-11 – 3-44. (71, 76, 77, 78, 216)

Galloway, J.N., Aber, J.D., Erisman, J.W., Seitzinger, S.P., Howarth, R.W., Cowling, E.B., and Cosby, B.J. 2003. "The nitrogen cascade." *BioScience* 53: 341-356.

Gbondo-Tugbawa, S.S. and Driscoll, C.T. 2003. "Factors controlling long-term changes in soil pools of exchangeable basic cations and stream acid-neutralizing capacity in a northern hardwood forest ecosystem." *Biogeochemistry* 63: 161-185.

Geary, R. and Driscoll, C.T. 1996. "Forest soil solutions: Acid/base chemistry and response to calcite treatment." *Biogeochemistry* 32: 195-220.

Gherini, S.A., Munson, R.K., Altwicker, E.R., April, R.H., Chen, C.W., Clesceri, N., Cronan, C.S., Driscoll, C.T., Johannes, A.H., Newton, R.M., Peters, N.E., and Schofield, C.L. 1989. *Regional Integrated Lake-Watershed Acidification Study : Summary of Major Findings.* Electric Power Research Institute. Palo Alto, CA.

Goldstein, R.A., Gherini, S.A., Chen, C.W., Mok, L., and Hudson, R.J.M. 1984. "Integrated Lake-Watershed Acidification Study (ILWAS): A mechanistic ecosystem analysis." *Philosophical Transactions of the Royal Society of London* B305: 409-425.

Goldstein, R.A., Gherini, S.A., Driscoll, C.T., April, R., Schofield, C.L., and Chen, C.W. 1987. "Lake-watershed acidification in the North Branch of the Moose River: Introduction." *Biogeochemistry* 3: 5-20.

Gorham, E., Bayley, S.E., and Schindler, D.W. 1984. "Ecological effects of acid deposition upon peatlands: A neglected field in acid rain research." *Canadian Journal of Fisheries and Aquatic Sciences* 41: 1256-1268.

Gorham, E. 1998. "Acid deposition and its ecological effects: A brief history of research." *Environmental Science & Policy* 1: 153-166.

Grigal, D.F. 2002. "Inputs and outputs of mercury from terrestrial watersheds: A review." *Environmental Review* 10: 1-39.

Gubala, C.P. and Driscoll, C.T. 1991. "The chemical responses of acidic Woods Lake, NY, to two different treatments with calcium carbonate." *Water, Air, and Soil Pollution* 59: 7-22.

*Havens, K.E. 1993. "Pelagic food web structure in Adirondack Mountain, USA, lakes of varying acidity." *Canadian Journal of Fisheries and Aquatic Sciences* 50: 149-155. (178)

Hedin, L.O., Granat, L., Likens, G.E., Buishand, T.A., and Galloway, J.N. 1994. "Steep declines in atmospheric base cations in regions of Europe and North America." *Nature* 367: 351-354.

Hemond, H.F. 1990. "Acid-neutralizing capacity, alkalinity, and acid-base status of natural waters containing organic acids." *Environmental Science & Technology* 24: 1486-1489.

*Herlihy, A.T., Landers, D.H., Cusimano, R.F., Overton, W.S., Wigington, P.J. Jr., Pollack, A.K., and Mitchell-Hall, T.E. 1990. T*emporal Variability in Lakewater Chemistry in the Northeastern United States: Results of Phase II of the Eastern Lake Survey.* U.S. Environmental Protection Agency. EPA/600/3-91/012. (68)

Hrabik,T.R. and Watras,C.J. 2002. "Recent declines in mercury concentration in a freshwater fishery: isolating the effects of de-acidification and decreased atmospheric mercury deposition in Little Rock Lake." *Science of the Total Environment* 297(1-3): 229-37.

Hunsaker, C.T., Christensen, S.W., Beauchamp, J.J., Olson, R.J., Turner, R.S., and Malanchuk, J.L. 1986. *Empirical Relationships between Watershed Attributes and Headwater Lake Chemistry in the Adirondack Region.* Oak Ridge National Laboratory. ORNL/TM-9838.

Hurd, T.M., Raynal, D.J., and Schwintzer, C.R. 2001. "Symbiotic N2 fixation of *Alnus incana* spp. *rugosa* in shrub wetlands of the Adirondack Mountains, New York," USA. *Œcologia* 126: 94-103.

Irving, P.M., ed., 1990. *Acidic Deposition: State of Science and Technology, Volume I: Emissions, Atmospheric Processes, and Deposition* U.S. National Acid Precipitation Assessment Program. Washington, DC.

—— 1990. *Acidic Deposition: State of Science and Technology, Volume II: Aquatic Processes and Effects.* U.S. National Acid Precipitation Assessment Program. Washington, DC.

—— 1990. *Acidic Deposition: State of Science and Technology, Volume III: Terrestrial, Materials, Health and Visibility Effects.* U.S. National Acid Precipitation Assessment Program. Washington, DC.

*Ito, M., Mitchell, M.J., and Driscoll, C.T. 2002. "Spatial patterns of precipitation quantity and chemistry and air temperature in the Adirondack region of New York." Atmospheric *Environment* 36: 1051-1062. (1)

Jackson, S.T. and Charles, D.F. 1988. "Aquatic macrophytes in Adirondack (New York) lakes: patterns of species composition in relation to environment." *Canadian Journal of Botany* 66: 1449-1460.

*Jenkins, J. 2004. *The Adirondack Atlas: A Geographic Portrait of the Adirondack Park*. Syracuse University Press. Syracuse, NY. (42, 140, 168)

Johannes, A.H. and Altwicker, E.R. 1980. "Atmospheric inputs to three Adirondack lake watersheds." In Drablos, D., and Tollan, A. eds., *Ecological Impact of Acid Precipitation: Procedings of International Conference.* Oslo, Norway. pp. 230-231.

*Johannes, A.H., Galloway, J.N., and Troutman, D.E. 1981. "Snow pack storage and ion release." In *The Integrated Lake-Watershed Acidification Study (ILWAS),* Electric Power Research Institute, EA-1825 . Palo Alto, CA. (42)

Johnson, A.H., Andersen, S.B., and Siccama, T.G. 1994. "Acid rain and soils of the Adirondacks. I. Changes in pH and available calcium, 1930-1984." *Canadian Journal of Forest Research* 24: 39-45.

Johnson, A.H., Friedland, A.J., Miller, E.K., and Siccama, T.G. 1994. "Acid rain and soils of the Adirondacks, III: Rates of soil acidification in a montane spruce-fir forest at Whiteface Mountain, NY." *Canadian Journal of Forest Research* 24: 663-669.

Johnson, A.H., Schwartzman, T.N., Battles, J.J., Miller, R., Miller, E.K., Friedland, A.J., and Vann, D.R. 1994. "Acid rain and the soils of the Adirondacks, II: Evaluation of calcium and aluminum as causes of red spruce decline on Whiteface Mt., New York." *Canadian Journal of Forest Research* 24: 654-662.

Johnson, D.W., Simonin, H.A., Colquhoun, J.R., and Flack, F.M. 1987. "In situ toxicity tests of fishes in acid waters." *Biogeochemistry* 3: 181-208.

Kamman, N.C., Lorey, P.M., Driscoll, C.T., Estabrook, R., Major, A., Pientka, B., and Glassford, E. 2003. "Assessment of mercury in waters, sediments, and biota of New Hampshire and Vermont lakes, USA, sampled using a geographically randomized design." *Environmental Toxicology and Chemistry* 23: 1172-1186.

*Kirchner, J.W. and Lydersen, E. 1995. "Base cation depletion and potential long-term acidification of Norwegian catchments." *Environmental Science & Technology* 29: 1953-1960. (134)

*Kretser, W.A., Gallagher, J., and Nicolette, J. 1989. *Adirondack lakes Study 1984-1987: An Evaluation of Fish Communities and Water Chemistry.* Adirondack Lakes Survey Corporation. Ray Brook, NY. (69, 73, 74, 77, 78, 89, 218)

*Lawrence, G.B. 2002. "Persistent episodic acidification of streams linked to acid rain effects on soil." *Atmospheric Environment* 36: 1589-1598. (91, 137, 138)

Lawrence, G.B., David, M.B., and Shortle, W.C. 1995. "A new mechanism for calcium loss in forest-floor soils." *Nature* 378: 162-165.

*Lawrence, G.B., David, M.B., Bailey, S.W., and Shortle, W.C. 1997. "Assessment of soil calcium status in red spruce forests in the northeastern United States." *Biogeochemistry* 38: 19-39. (135)

*Lawrence, G.B., David, M.B., Lovett, G.M., Murdoch, P.S., Burns, D.A., Stoddard, J.L., Baldigo, B.P., Porter, J.H., and Thompson, A.W. 1999. "Soil calcium status and the response of stream chemistry to changing acidic deposition rates." *Ecological Applications* 9: 1059-1072. (136, 137)

Lawrence, G.B. and Huntington, T.G. 1999. *Soil-Calcium Depletion Linked to Acid Rain and Forest Growth in the Eastern United States.* U.S. Geological Survey. WRIR 98-4267.

*Lawrence, G.B., Momen, B., and Roy, K.M. 2004. "Use of stream chemistry for monitoring acidic deposition effects in the Adirondack region of New York." *Journal of Environmental Quality* 33: 1002-1009. (203, 204)

*Lazerte, B.D. 1993. "The impact of drought and acidification on the chemical exports from a minerotrophic conifer swamp." *Biogeochemistry* 18: 153-175. (157, 158)

Likens, G.E., Bormann, F.H., and Johnson, N.M. 1972. "Acid rain." *Environment* 14: 33-40.

Likens, G.E. and Bormann, F.H. 1974. "Acid rain: A serious regional environmental problem." *Science* 184: 1176-1179.

*Likens, G.E., Driscoll, C.T., and Buso, D.C. 1996. "Long-term effects of acid rain: Response and recovery of a forest ecosystem." *Science* 272: 244-246. (133)

*Likens, G.E., Driscoll, C.T., Buso, D.C., Siccama, T.G., Johnson, C.E., Lovett, G.M., Fahey, T.J., Reiners, W.A., Ryan, D.F., Martin, C.W., and Bailey, S.W. 1998. "The biogeochemistry of calcium at Hubbard Brook." *Biogeochemistry* 41: 89-173. (130, 131, 132, 135)

*Likens, G.E., Driscoll, C.T., Buso, D.C., Mitchell, M.J., Lovett, G.M., Bailey, S.W., Siccama, T.G., Reiners, W.A., and Alewell, C. 2002. "The biogeochemistry of sulfur at Hubbard Brook." *Biogeochemistry* 60: 235-316. (97)

Linthurst, R.A., Landers, D.H., Eilers, J.M., Brakke, D.F., Overton, W.S., Meier, E.P., and Crowe, R.E. 1986. *Characteristics of Lakes in the Eastern United States, Volume I: Population Descriptions and Physico-Chemical Relationships.* U.S. Environmental Protection Agency. EPA/600/4-86/007a.

*Lorey, P. and Driscoll, C.T. 1999. "Historical trends of mercury deposition in Adirondack lakes." *Environmental Science & Technology* 33: 718-722. (171, 172)

Mackun, I.R., Leopold, D.J., and Raynal, D.J. 1994. "Short-term responses of wetland vegetation after liming of an Adirondack watershed." *Ecological Applications* 4: 535-543.

Martin, C.W., Hornbeck, J.W., Likens, G.E., and Buso, D.C. 2000. "Impacts of intensive harvesting on hydrology and nutrient dynamics of northern hardwood forests." *Canadian Journal of Forest Research* 57: 19-29.

McHale, M.R., Mitchell, M.J., McDonnell, J.J., and Cirmo, C.P. 2000. "Nitrogen solutes in an Adirondack forested watershed: Importance of dissolved organic nitrogen." *Biogeochemistry* 48: 165-184.

McHale, M.R., McDonnell, J.J., Mitchell, M.J., and Cirmo, C.P. 2002. "A field-based study of soil water and groundwater nitrate release in an Adirondack forested watershed." *Water Resources Research* 38: 2-1 - 2-17.

McHale, M.R., Cirmo, C.P., Mitchell, M.J., and McDonnell, J.J. 2004. "Wetland nitrogen dynamics in an Adirondack forested watershed." *Hydrological Processes* 18: 1853-1870.

McIntyre, J.W. 1993. In Morse, L., Stockwell, S., and Pokras M., eds., *The Loon and Its Ecosystem: Status, Management, and Environmental Concerns.* U.S. Fish and Wildlife Service. Concord, NH. pp. 73-79.

*McNulty, S.G., Aber, J.D., McLellan, T.M., and Katt, S.M. 1990. "Nitrogen cycling in high elevation forests of the northeastern US in relation to nitrogen deposition." *Ambio* 19: 38-40. (116)

Miller, E.K., Blum, J.D., and Friedland, A.J. 1993. "Determination of soil exchangeable-cation loss and weathering rates using Sr isotopes." *Nature* 362: 438-441.

*Mitchell, M.J., Driscoll, C.T., Kahl, J.S., Likens, G.E., Murdoch, P.S., and Pardo, L.H. 1996. "Climatic control of nitrate loss from forested watersheds in the Northeast United States." *Environmental Science & Technology* 30: 2609-2612. (124)

*Mitchell, M.J., Raynal, D.J., and Driscoll, C.T. 1996. "Biogeochemistry of a forested watershed in the central Adirondack Mountains: Temporal changes and mass balances." *Water, Air, and Soil Pollution* 88: 355-369. (105, 113)

*Mitchell, M.J., Driscoll, C.T., Owen, J.S., Schaefer, D., Michener, R., and Raynal, D.J. 2001. "Nitrogen biogeochemistry of three hardwood ecosystems in the Adirondack region of New York." *Biogeochemistry* 56: 93-133. (103, 104)

*Mitchell, M.J., McHale, P.J., Inamdar, S., and Raynal, D.J. 2001. "Role of within-lake processes and hydrobiogeochemical changes over 16 years in a watershed in the Adirondack Mountains of New York State, USA." *Hydrological Processes* 15: 1951-1965. (97, 103, 104, 129, 208, 211)

Momen, B., Zehr, J.P., Boylen, C.W., and Sutherland, J.W. 1999. "Determinants of summer nitrate concentration in a set of Adirondack lakes, New York." *Water, Air, & Soil Pollution* 111: 19-28.

*Munson, R.K., Driscoll, C.T., and Gherini, S.A. 1990. "Phenomenological analysis of ALSC chemistry data." In Baker, J.P. et al., *Adirondack Lakes Survey: An Interpretive Analysis of Fish Communities and Water Chemistry, 1984-1987.* Adirondack Lakes Survey Corporation. Ray Brook, NY. pp. 2-27 - 2-69. (19, 20, 70, 162)

*Munson, R.K., Gherini, S.A., Reckhow, K.H., and Driscoll, C.T. 1990. "Integrated analysis." In Baker, J.P. et al., *Adirondack Lakes Survey: An Interpretive Analysis of Fish Communities and Water Chemistry, 1984-1987.* Adirondack Lakes Survey Corporation. Ray Brook, NY. pp. 2-92 - 2-116. (75)

Munson, R.K. and Gherini, S.A. 1993. "Influence of organic acids on the pH and acid-neutralizing capacity of Adirondack lakes." *Water Resources Research* 29: 891-899.

National Acid Precipitation Assessment Program 1998. *NAPAP Biennial Report to Congress: An Integrated Assessment.* U.S. National Acid Precipitation Assessment Program. Washington, DC.

*National Atmospheric Deposition Program. n.d. "Annual data for site: NY20 (Huntington Wildlife)."

http://nadp.sws.uiuc.edu/nadpdata/annualReq. asp?site=NY20 (196)

*—— n.d. "Estimated sulfate ion deposition." http:// nadp.sws.uiuc.edu/isopleths/maps1997/so4dep.gif (2, 215)

*—— n.d. "Hydrogen ion concentration as pH from measurements made at Central Analytical Laboratory, 1999." http://nadp.sws.uiuc.edu/isopleths/maps1999/ phlab.gif (6)

*—— n.d. "NADP/NTN monitoring locations." NY20. http://nadp.sws.uiuc.edu/sites/siteinfo. asp?net=NTN&id=NY20 (192)

*—— n.d. National Atmospheric Deposition Program/ NTN seasonal precipitation-weighted mean concentrations. http://nadp.sws.uiuc.edu/nadpdata

*—— n.d. "NTN sites." http://nadp.sws.uiuc.edu/sites/ ntnmap.asp (192)

*—— n.d. "Sites in the NADP/MDN network." http:// nadp.sws.uiuc.edu/nadpdata/mdnsites.asp (192)

*—— n.d. "Total mercury wet deposition, 2001." http:// nadp.sws.uiuc.edu/mdn/maps/map.asp?imgFile=2001/ 01MDNdepo.gif (173)

*—— n.d. "Total mercury wet deposition, 2003." http:// nadp.sws.uiuc.edu/mdn/maps/map.asp?imgFile=2003/ 03MDNdepo.gif (12)

*New York State Department of Environmental Conservation. n.d. "NYSDEC- nitrate ion deposition, 2002." http://www.dec.state.ny.us/website/dar/baqs/acidrain/ no3d02.html (193)

*—— n.d. "New York State DEC acid deposition monitoring locations". http://www.dec.state.ny.us/website/ dar/baqs/acidrain/network.html (193)

New York State Energy Research and Development Authority. 2002. *Environmental Research and Monitoring Needs in New York State: A Multi-Year Research Plan for the New York Energy Research and Development Authority's Environmental Monitoring, Evaluation, and Protection Program.* New York State Energy Research and Development Authority. Albany, NY.

*Newell, A.D. 1993. "Inter-regional comparison of patterns and trends in surface water acidification across the United States." *Water, Air, and Soil Pollution* 67: 257-280. (205, 206)

Newton, R.A. 1983. *Distribution and Characteristics of the Surficial Geologic Materials in the ILWAS Watersheds.* Electric Power Research Institute. Palo Alto, CA. EPRI-2827.

*Newton, R.M., Weintraub, J., and April, R. 1987. "The relationship between surface water chemistry and geology in the North Branch of the Moose River." *Biogeochemistry* 3: 21-35. (53, 54)

*Newton, R.M. and Driscoll, C.T. 1990. "Classification of ALSC lakes. In Baker, J.P. et al., *Adirondack Lakes Survey: An Interpretive Analysis of Fish Communities and Water Chemistry, 1984-1987.* Adirondack Lakes Survey Corporation. Ray Brook, NY. pp. 2-70 - 2-91. (72, 73, 74, 80, 81)

Newton, R.M., Burns, D.A., Blette, V.L., and Driscoll, C.T. 1996. "Effect of whole catchment liming on the episodic acidification of two Adirondack streams." *Biogeochemistry* 32: 299-322.

Overton, W.S., Kanciruk, P., Hook, L.A., Eilers, J.M., Landers, D.H., Brakke, D.F., Blick, D.J.Jr., Linthurst, R.A., DeHaan, M.D., and Omernik, J.M. 1986. *Characteristics of Lakes in the Eastern United States, Volume II: Lakes Sampled and Descriptive Statistics for Physical and Chemical Variables.* U.S. Environmental Protection Agency. EPA/600/4-86/007b.

Park, J., Mitchell, M.J., McHale, P.J., Christopher, S.F., and Meyers, T.P. 2003. "Impacts of changing climate and atmospheric deposition on N and S drainage losses from a forested watershed of the Adirondack Mountains, New York State." *Global Change Biology* 9: 1602-1619.

Parker, K.E. 1988. "Common loon reproduction and chick feeding on acidified lakes in the Adirondack Park, New York." *Canadian Journal of Zoology* 66: 804-810.

Peters, N.E. and Driscoll, C.T. 1987. "Hydrogeologic controls of surface-water chemistry in the Adirondack region of New York State." *Biogeochemistry* 3: 163-180.

Pfeiffer, M.H. and Festa, P.J. 1980. *Acidity Status of Lakes in the Adirondack Region of New York in Relation to Fish Resources.* New York State Department of Environmental Conservation. FW-P168 (10/80).

*Rascher, C.M., Driscoll, C.T., and Peters, N.E. 1987. "Concentration and flux of solutes from snow and forest floor during snowmelt in the west-central Adirondack region of New York." *Biogeochemistry* 3: 209-224. (107)

Rodhe, H., Grennfelt, P., Wisniewski, J., Agren, C., Bengtsson, G., Johansson, K., Kauppi, P., Kucera, V., Rasmussen, L., Rosseland, B., Schotte, L., and Selden,

G., 1995. "Acid reign '95– Conference summary statement." *Water, Air, and Soil Pollution* 85: 1-14.

Rossell, I.M., Leopold, D.J., and Raynal, D.J. 1995. "Competition among shoreline plants: Responses to watershed liming." *Environmental and Experimental Botany* 35: 507-518.

*Roy, K.M., Allen, E.B., Barge, J.W., Ross, J.A., Curran, R.P., Bogucki, D.J., Franzi, D.A., Kretser, W.A., Frank, M.M., Spada, D.M., and Banta, J.S. 1997. "Wetlands." In *Influences on Wetlands and Lakes in the Adirondack Park of New York State: A Catalog of Existing and New GIS Data Layers for the 400,000-Hectare Oswegatchie/ Black River Watershed*. Adirondack Park Agency. Ray Brook, NY. (157)

*Schaefer, D.A., Driscoll, C.T.Jr., Van Dreason, R., and Yatsko, C.P. 1990. "The episodic acidification of Adirondack lakes during snowmelt." *Water Resources Research* 26: 1639-1647. (105, 106)

*Schaefer, D.A. and Driscoll, C.T. 1993. "Identifying sources of snowmelt acidification with a watershed mixing model." *Water, Air, and Soil Pollution* 67: 345-365. (108)

Schindler, D.W., Mills, K.H., Malley, D.F., Findlay, D.L., Shearer, J.A., Davies, U., Turner, M.A., Linsey, G.A., and Cruikshank, D.R. 1985. "Long-term ecosystem stress: The effects of years of experimental acidification on a small lake." *Science* 228: 1395-1401.

Schlessinger, W.H. 1991. *Biogeochemistry: An Analysis of Global Change*. Academic Press. New York.

*Schoch, N., and Evers, D.C. 2002. *Monitoring Mercury in Common Loons: New York Field Report, 1998-2000*. Biodiversity Research Institute. Falmouth, ME. http://www.adkscience.org/loons/BRI%20NY%2098-2000%20Report-2002.pdf (173)

*Schofield, C.L. 1976. "Acid precipitation: Effects on fish." *Ambio* 5: 228-230. (41, 57)

*Schofield, C.L. and Driscoll, C.T. 1987. "Fish species distribution in relation to water quality gradients in the North Branch of the Moose River basin." *Biogeochemistry* 3: 63-85. (52)

Schofield, C.L. and Keleher, C. 1996. "Comparison of brook trout reproductive success and recruitment in an acidic Adirondack lake following whole lake liming and watershed liming." *Biogeochemistry* 32: 323-338.

Scott, T.J., Siccama, T.G., Johnson, A.H., and Breisch, A.R. 1984. "Decline of red spruce in the Adirondacks, New York." *Bulletin of the Torrey Botanical Club* 111: 438-444.

*Seigneur, C., Lohman, K., Vijayaraghavan, K., and Shia, R.L. 2003. "Contributions of global and regional sources to mercury deposition in New York State." *Environmental Pollution* 123: 365-373. (164)

Sharpe, W. E., Leibfried, V.G., Kimmel, W.G., and DeWalle, D.R. 1987. "The relation of water quality and fish occurrence to soils and geology in a region of high hydrogen and sulfate ion deposition." *Water Resources Bulletin* 23: 37-46.

Shepard, J.P., Mitchell, M.J., Scott, T.J., Zhang, Y.M., and Raynal, D.J. 1989. "Measurements of wet and dry deposition in a northern hardwood forest." *Water, Air, and Soil Pollution* 48: 225-238.

*Shortle, W.C. and Bondietti, E.A. 1992. "Timing, magnitude, and impact of acidic deposition on sensitive forest sites." *Water, Air, and Soil Pollution* 61: 253-267. (134)

*Siegfried, C.A., Bloomfield, J.A., and Sutherland, J.W. 1989. "Planktonic rotifer community structure in Adirondack lakes: Effects of acidity, trophic status, and related water quality characteristics." In Sutherland, J.W., ed., *Field Studies of the Biota and Selected Water Chemistry Parameters in 50 Adirondack Mountain Lakes*. New York State Department of Environmental Conservation. Albany, NY. pp. 5-1 - 5-29. (178)

Simmons, J.A., Yavitt, J.B., and Fahey, T.J. 1996. Response of forest floor nitrogen dynamics to liming.' *Biogeochemistry* 32: 221-244.

Simonin, H.A. 1990. *Final Generic Environmental Impact Statement on the New York State Department of Environmental Conservation Program of Liming Selected Acidified Waters*. New York State Department of Environmental Conservation. Albany, NY.

Simonin, H.A., Kretser, W.A., Bath, D.W., Olson, M., and Gallagher, J. 1993. "In situ bioassays of brook trout (*Salvelinus fontinalis*) and blacknose dace (*Rhinichthys atratulus*) in Adirondack streams affected by episodic acidification." *Canadian Journal of Fisheries and Aquatic Sciences* 50: 902-912.

*Simonin, H.A. and Kretser, W.A. 1997. 'Nitrate deposition and impact on Adirondack streams.' *Proceedings of Acid Rain and Electric Utilities II Conference*. Scottsdale, AZ. pp. 1-11. (111)

*Sloan, R. and Schofield, C.L. 1983. 'Mercury levels in brook trout (*Salvelinus fontinalis*) from selected acid and limed Adirondack lakes." *Northeastern Environmental Science* 2: 165-170. (165)

*Stoddard, J.L. 1994. "Long-term changes in watershed retention of nitrogen: Its causes and aquatic consequences." In L.A.Baker, ed., *Environmental Chemistry of Lakes and Reservoirs*. American Chemical Society. Washington, DC. pp. 224-284. (114, 115, 116, 117, 118)

*Stoddard, J.L., Jeffries, D.S., Lükewille, A., Clair, T.A., Dillon, P.J., Driscoll, C.T., Forsius, M., Johannessen, M., Kahl, J.S., Kellogg, J.H., Kemp, A., Mannio, J., Monteith, D.T., Murdoch, P.S., Patrick, S., Rebsdorf, A., Skjelkvåle, B.L., Stainton, M.P., Traaen, T., van Dam, H., Webster, K.E., Wieting, J., and Wilander, A. 1999. "Regional trends in aquatic recovery from acidification in North America and Europe." *Nature* 401: 575-578. (206, 207)

*Stoddard, J.L., Traaen, T.S., and Skjelkvåle, B.L. 2001. "Assessment of nitrogen leaching at ICP-Waters sites (Europe and North America)." *Water, Air, and Soil Pollution* 130: 781-786. (118)

*Stoddard, J.L., Kahl, J.S., Deviney, F.A., DeWalle, D.R., Driscoll, C.T., Herlihy, A.T., Kellogg, J.H., Murdoch, P.S., Webb, J.R., and Webster, K.E. 2003. *Response of Surface Water Chemistry to the Clean Air Act Amendments of 1990*. U.S. Environmental Protection Agency. EPA 620/R-03/001. (194, 195, 208, 209, 218, 220, 221)

Stumm, W. and Morgan, J.J. 1996. *Aquatic Chemistry: Chemical Equilibria and Rates in Natural Waters*. John Wiley & Sons. New York.

*Sullivan, T.J., Charles, D.F., Smol, J.P., Cumming, B.F., Selle, A.R., Thomas, D.R., Bernert, J.A., and Dixit, S.S. 1990. "Quantification of changes in lakewater chemistry in response to acidic deposition." *Nature* 345: 54-58. (85, 87, 217)

*Sullivan, T.J., Small, M.J., Kingston, J.C., Cumming, B.F., Dixit, S.S., Smol, J.P., Bernert, J.A., Thomas, D.R., and Uutala, A.J. 1990. *Historical Changes in Surface Water Acid-Base Chemistry in Response to Acidic Deposition*. U.S. National Acid Precipitation Assessment Program. SOS/T 11. (82, 83, 85, 86, 217)

*Sullivan, T.J., Kugler, D.L., Small, M.J., Johnson, C.B., Landers, D.H., Rosenbaum, B.J., Overton, W.S., Kretser, W.A., and Gallagher, J. 1990. "Variation in Adirondack,New York, lakewater chemistry as function of surface area." *Water Resources Bulletin* 26: 167-176. (80)

*Sullivan, T.J., Eilers, J.M., Cosby, B.J., and Vaché, K.B. 1997. "Increasing role of nitrogen in the acidification of surface waters in the Adirondack Mountains, New York." *Water, Air, and Soil Pollution* 95: 313-336. (112, 121)

*Sullivan, T.J., Charles, D.F., Bernert, J.A., McMartin, B., Vaché, K.B., and Zehr, J. 1999. "Relationship between landscape characteristics, history, and lakewater acidification in the Adirondack Mountains, New York." *Water, Air, and Soil Pollution* 112: 407-427. (141, 142)

Sutherland, J.W., ed., 1989. *Field Studies of the Biota and Selected Water Chemistry Parameters in 50 Adirondack Mountain Lakes: Final Report*. New York State Department of Environmental Conservation. Albany, NY.

U.S. Environmental Protection Agency 1995. *Acid Deposition Standard Feasibility Study: Report to Congress*. EPA 430-R-95-001a.

*—— 2000. *National Air Pollutant Emission Trends 1900-1998*. U.S. Government Printing Office. EPA-454-R-00-002. (13, 215)

*—— 2003. *Clean Air Status and Trends Network (CASTNET) 2002 Annual Report*. http://www.epa.gov/castnet/library/annual02.html (7)

—— 2003. *National Air Quality and Emission Trends Report: 2003 Special Studies Edition*. EPA 454-R-03-005.

*—— n.d. "Affected sources under the Acid Rain Program." http://www.epa.gov/airmarkets/cmap/mapgallery/mg_affected_sources.html (3)

*—— n.d. "Comparison of ambient sulfur dioxide concentrations in the eastern United States from CASTNET monitoring data (1989-1991 vs. 1997-1999)." http://www.epa.gov/airmarkets/cmap/mapgallery/mg_so2.html (4)

*—— n.d. "Trends in wet nitrate deposition following implementation of Phase I of the Acid Rain Program 1989-1991 vs. 1997-1999 (CASTNET and NADP/NTN data)." http://www.epa.gov/airmarkets/cmap/mapgallery/mg_wetnitratephase1.html (10)

*—— n.d. "Annual mean HNO3 concentrations (μg/m3) for 2002." http://www.epa.gov/castnet/library/annual02/2002ar-2.pdf (5)

*—— n.d. "NO2 air quality, 1983-2002 based on annual arithmetic average." http://www.epa.gov/airtrends/nitrogen.html (6)

*—— n.d. "Trends in wet sulfate deposition following implementation of Phase I of the Acid Rain Program 1989-1991 vs. 1997-1999 (CASTNET and NADP/NTN

data).” http://www.epa.gov/airmarkets/cmap/mapgallery/mg_wetsulfatephase1.html (9)

*—— n.d. “Total N deposition CTH 110.” http://www.epa.gov/castnet/charts/cth110tn.gif (8)

*—— n.d. “CASTNET sampling stations.” http://www.epa.gov/castnet/site.html (192)

*—— n.d. “Composition of N deposition for 1999-2001 CTH 110”. http://www.epa.gov/castnet/charts/cth110pn.gif (7)

*—— n.d. “Composition of S deposition for 1999-2001 CTH 110.” http://www.epa.gov/castnet/charts/cth110ps.gif (7)

*—— n.d. “SO2 emissions, 1983-2002.” http://www.epa.gov/airtrends/sulfur.html (2)

*—— n.d. “NOx emissions, 1983-2002.” http://www.epa.gov/airtrends/nitrogen.html (2)

*—— n.d. 2005. “Trend in annual mean NO2 concentrations by type of location, 1982-2001.” http://www.epa.gov/airtrends/nitrogen2.html (6)

*—— n.d. 2005. “Annual mean SO2 concentrations (µg/m3) for 2002.” http://www.epa.gov/castnet/library/annual02/2002ar-2.pdf (3)

*—— n.d. “Data and publications about mercury.” http://www.epa.gov/mercury/data.html (164)

*—— n.d. “SO2 air quality, 1983-2002, based on annual arithmetic average.” http://www.epa.gov/airtrends/sulfur2.html (5)

*—— n.d. “Total S deposition CTH 110.” http://www.epa.gov/castnet/charts/cth110ts.gif (8)

*Van Sickle, J., Baker, J.P., Simonin, H.A., Baldigo, B.P., Kretser, W.A., and Sharpe, W.E. 1996. “Episodic acidification of small streams in the northeastern United States: Fish mortality in field bioassays.” *Ecological Applications* 6: 408-421. (180)

Wesselink, L.G., Meiwes, K.J., Matzner, E., and Stein, A. 1995. “Long-term changes in water and soil chemistry in spruce and beech forests, Solling, Germany.” *Environmental Science & Technology* 29: 51-58.

*Whitehead, D.R., Charles, D.F., Jackson, S.T., Smol, J.P., and Engstrom, D.R. 1989. “The developmental history of Adirondack (N.Y.) lakes.” *Journal of Paleolimnology* 2: 185-206. (58, 59)

Whittier, T.R. and Paulsen, S.G. 1992. “The surface waters component of the Environmental Monitoring and Assessment Program (EMAP): An overview.” *Journal of Aquatic Ecosystem Health* 1: 119-126.

*Whittier, T.R., Halliwell, D.B., and Paulsen, S.G. 1997. “Cyprinid distributions in Northeast U.S.A. lakes: Evidence of regional-scale minnow biodiversity losses.” *Canadian Journal of Fisheries and Aquatic Sciences* 54: 1593-1607. (187)

*Whittier, T.R. and Kincaid, T.M. 1999. “Introduced fish in northeastern USA lakes: Regional extent, dominance, and effect on native species richness.” *Transactions of the American Fisheries Society* 128: 769-783. (188)

*Whittier, T.R., Paulsen, S.G., Larsen, D.P., Peterson, S.A., Herlihy, A.T., and Kaufmann, P.R. 2002. “Indicators of ecological stress and their extent in the population of northeastern lakes: A regional-scale assessment.” *BioScience* 52: 235-247. (185, 186)

*Wigington, P.J. Jr., DeWalle, D.R., Murdoch, P.S., Kretser, W.A., Simonin, H.A., Van Sickle, J., and Baker, J.P. 1996. “Episodic acidification of small streams in the northeastern United States: Ionic controls of episodes.” *Ecological Applications* 6: 389-407. (109, 110, 111)

Wigington, P.J. Jr., Baker, J.P., DeWalle, D.R., Kretser, W.A., Murdoch, P.S., Simonin, H.A., Van Sickle, J., McDowell, M.K., Peck, D.V., and Barchet, W.R. 1996. “Episodic acidification of small streams in the northeastern United States: Episodic Response Project.” *Ecological Applications* 6: 374-388.

Wright, R.F., Dale, T., Gjessing, E.T., Hendrey, G.R., Henriksen, A., Johannessen, M., and Muniz, J.P. 1976. “Impact of acid precipitation on freshwater ecosystems in Norway.” *Water, Air, and Soil Pollution* 6: 483-499.

Yanai, R.D., Siccama, T.G., and Arthur, M.A. 1993. “Changes in forest floor mass and nutrient content over 17 years in a northern hardwood forest.” *Bulletin of the Ecological Society of America* 74: 496.

Yavitt, J.B. and Fahey, T.J. 1996. “Peatland porewater chemical responses to CaCO3 applications in wetlands next to Woods Lake. New York.” *Biogeochemistry* 32: 245-263.